The Elementary
Principal's Handbook

Fourth Edition

The Elementary Principal's Handbook

A Guide to Effective Action

Larry W. Hughes
The University of Houston

Gerald C. Ubben
The University of Tennessee

Allyn and Bacon
Boston • London • Toronto • Sydney • Tokyo • Singapore

Series Editor: Ray Short
Editorial Assistant: Christine Shaw
Cover Administrator: Linda Dickinson
Manufacturing Buyer: Megan Cochran
Editorial-Production Service: Walsh Associates
Cover Designer: Suzanne Harbison

Copyright © 1994, 1989 by Allyn and Bacon
A Division of Simon & Schuster, Inc.
160 Gould Street
Needham Heights, Massachusetts 02194

Library of Congress Cataloging-in-Publication Data

Hughes, Larry W., 1931–
    The elementary principal's handbook : a guide to effective action /
    by Larry W. Hughes and Gerald C. Ubben. — 4th ed.
        p.   cm.
    Includes bibliographical references and index.
    ISBN 0-205-15368-2
    1. Elementary school administration—United States—Handbooks,
manuals, etc.   2. Elementary school principals—United States—
Handbooks, manuals, etc.   I. Ubben, Gerald C.   II. Title.
LB2822.5.H83   1993
372.12'01—dc20   93-25696
                                                            CIP

BK
$24.00

Printed in the United States of America

10 9 8 7 6 5 4 3 2 1   98 97 96 95 94 93

Contents

Preface   **xi**

PART 1   **The Role: Organizational Realities and Societal Impingements**   **1**

    1   **The Effective Principal: Leader and Manager**   **3**
Introduction   *3*
Functional Aspects of the Job   *4*
Leaders and Effective Schools   *4*
What Do Effective Managers Do?   *6*
Leadership: Historical Underpinnings; Current Practice   *7*
Vision   *11*
Political Acumen and Creative Insubordination   *12*
Total Quality Management   *12*
Summary   *14*
Endnotes   *15*
Selected Readings   *17*

    2   **School Organization and Culture**   **19**
Introduction   *19*
The Two-Dimensional Organization   *20*
Social Systems Theory   *21*
Conditions Affecting Individual Behavior in the Organization   *25*
The Developing Organization: New Perspectives   *26*
Summary   *29*
Endnotes   *29*
Selected Readings   *30*

    3   **A Legal Framework**   **31**
Introduction   *31*
Legal Bases for the Schools   *33*

Issues of Equity   35
Rules and Regulations in the Effective Elementary School   43
Balancing Rights and Privileges, Constitutional and Otherwise   44
Due Process   48
Common Tort Liability Settings   50
Child Abuse   59
Summary   60
Endnotes   60
Selected Readings   63

4   Understanding the Community   65
Introduction   65
The Community in Perspective   66
Community Influence Systems   68
Need for Well-Developed Policies   76
Working with Other Community Agencies and Organizations   77
Summary   78
Endnotes   78
Selected Readings   79

PART 2   Leadership and Management Tasks and Functions   81

5   Guidelines and Goals for Planning School Programs   83
Introduction   83
Beliefs, Goals, and Objectives   83
Framework for Establishing Beliefs or Philosophy Statements   86
Beliefs Development   87
Developing Goals for Improvement   88
Program Improvement   95
Summary   96
Endnotes   96
Selected Readings   96

6   School Improvement through Systematic Planning   99
Introduction   99
Needs Assessment/Problem Identification/Campus Planning   99
Action Planning/Project Management   101
Getting Started with a New Staff   109
What the Principal Needs to Know about Managing Major Projects   111
Summary   114
Endnotes   115
Selected Readings   115

7 Individual Differences and Student Placement   117
Introduction   117
Differences in Learning Style   118
Learning Interests   119
Student Growth and Maturity   120
Grouping Students   123
Summary   131
Endnotes   132
Selected Readings   132

8 Developing an Orderly and Positive Learning Climate   135
Introduction   135
Maintaining Positive Student Control   136
Helping Children   142
The School as a Coordinating Social Agency   151
Summary   152
Endnotes   153
Selected Readings   154

9 Special Students; Special Services   155
Introduction   155
Special Education and Related Services   156
Disciplining Students with Disabilities   161
Dealing with Parents of Special Children   161
Special Education and the Regular Classroom Teacher   164
Outside Public Agencies   165
Summary   169
Endnotes   169
Selected Readings   170

10 Restructuring the Curriculum   171
Introduction   171
Curriculum Structure   172
Curriculum Alignment   175
Curriculum Density   179
Considerations for Curriculum Redesign   179
A Curriculum Model   181
Offering Curriculum Breadth   185
Summary   187
Endnotes   188
Selected Readings   188

11 Restructuring Learning   191
Introduction   191
Instructional Processes   192

Research about Instructional Practice   193
Cooperative Learning   199
Computer-Assisted Instruction   201
Mastery Learning   201
Summary   201
Endnotes   202
Selected Readings   203

12 Restructuring the Deployment of Instructional Personnel   205
Introduction   205
Participation by Staff   206
Staffing Patterns   208
Team Planning   214
Paraprofessionals   217
Summary   220
Endnotes   220
Selected Readings   221

13 Restructuring Time: Scheduling Staff and Students   223
Introduction   223
Schedule Attributes   224
Scheduling Techniques   225
Sample Schedule   227
Team Planning Time   230
Middle School Schedules   231
Summary   233
Selected Readings   235

**14 Staffing the School: Recruitment, Selection, and
Termination Processes   237**
Introduction   237
Recruitment   237
The Selection Process   242
Employee Probationary Status   245
Teacher Tenure   245
Involuntary Termination   245
Voluntary Termination   247
Summary   249
Endnotes   249
Selected Readings   250

15 Human Resource Development   251
Introduction   251
A Human Resource Development Model   252

Implementing a Staff Development Program   254
HRD at the Building Level   255
Teacher Appraisal   258
The Staff Evaluation Cycle   259
Mentoring   271
Organizational Development   273
Implications for Leaders   275
Summary   277
Endnotes   277
Selected Readings   278

16   The Principal's Role in Collective Bargaining Agreements   281
Introduction   281
How to Handle Grievances   282
The Principal's Role in Negotiation   285
Contract Administration   285
Summary   288
Endnotes   288
Selected Readings   288

17   Creative Budgeting and Sound Fiscal Accounting   291
Introduction   291
The School Budget   292
Fiscal Management   300
Summary   308
Endnotes   309
Selected Readings   309

18   Building and Facilities Management   311
Introduction   311
Making the Most of the Facility   311
Care of the School Plant   315
The School Site   316
Maintenance of the Building   318
Supplies and Equipment Management   319
Summary   324
Endnotes   325
Selected Readings   325

19   Public Relations Processes and Techniques   327
Introduction   327
The "Public" is Plural   328
One-Way Public Relations Efforts   328

Two-Way Public Relations Efforts   333
Summary   341
Endnotes   342
Selected Readings   342

PART 3   Leadership Processes   343

20   Decision Making at the School Site   345
Introduction   345
Executive Decision Making: A Perspective   346
Decision Making as Problem Solving   348
Decision Settings   350
Decision Processing   353
The Work Group as a Problem Solving Unit   362
Summary   366
Endnotes   367
Selected Readings   367

Index   369

Preface

This is the fourth edition of our book about the elementary school principalship. Has anything changed? A lot. The role of the elementary school principal has become far more complex in the past sixteen years. It was always an important and challenging role and properly executed always has resulted in children well educated and able to make their way successfully in life. But, new responsibilities, new ways of looking at schooling, changing community dynamics, and a more demanding, more skeptical society have placed even more demands on the person who becomes a principal.

Has our book changed? Of course. Not in focus, not in intent, not in the effort to make better bridges from research and theory to effective practice, but in response rather to new demands, as well as continuing demands made in different ways, on the principal.

Clearly, to establish a productive and humane society, we need responsive schools. Even more clearly, we need leadership at the school site to establish these responsive schools. New terms, sometimes simply old wine in new bottles, sometimes not; old terms used in different ways; and truly new concepts and understandings about the school organization require new response patterns and new knowledge.

This book, as the three editions that came before, is organized into three parts: "Organizational Realities and Societal Impingements;" "Leadership and Management Tasks and Functions;" and "Leadership Processes." But the composition of the parts and the substance of the chapters reflect the new demands on the principal.

In Part 1 we focus on both the inside and outside roles of the principal and the inside and outside demands that are made. The complexities of leadership in these days of greater decentralization and so called "site-based" management are explored. Issues of "teacher empowerment," "organizational culture building," "total quality management," "school-business partnerships;" increasingly specific state mandates "to insure quality," among others, are discussed, and jargon aside, the implications of these concepts to the administration of the truly effective school are provided. As before, guidelines for action as well as understanding are provided. Legal principles to guide action in the humane school are presented. The effect of external social and political forces on administrative practice and guidelines for responding to these are the subject of the concluding chapter in Part 1.

Many have called Part 2 "nuts and bolts." These respondents were not using that phrase in a pejorative sense. Going about leading and managing the productive school—

the responsive school—requires specific skills and understanding about what it takes to carry out the five functions of the principalship.

The second part of the book comprises fifteen chapters. How to help a staff set and implement goals begins this part. These leadership tasks seem fundamental. Subsequent chapters focus on students, including the needs of special students. Achieving a positive learning climate is also a subject that receives attention. Three chapters address the subject of staffing the school. Two chapters focus on budget development and accounting and building management. The final chapter in Part 2 describes the need for the elementary principal to be a public relations specialist. Practices that help maintain good relationships with the "publics" are presented.

Part 3 is composed of only one chapter, but the subject is pervasive and of relevance to all of the chapters that have come before. The subject is getting the job done: executive decision-making at the school site. The need for well-honed decision processing/decision making skills is clear. There are processes for analyzing problems and issues that will result in the maximum feasible decision—that decision that will solve the problem and that staff, students, and community will work hard to implement. This final chapter presents frameworks for problem resolution and guidelines for action.

We hope that this book will continue to be of use to the reader long after graduate studies have been completed and an administrative career is well underway. We wrote this book initially as "a practical guide and daily reference for elementary school principals and those in training for the elementary school principalship." In the first preface we wrote, "It is a comprehensive and straightforward treatment of the role and functions of the elementary principal." We have tried to keep this edition consistent with the original intent.

It is not a brand new world, but it is a world fraught with change and increasing expectations for school productivity, whatever "productivity" might conjure in the mind of the particular individual. Our system of schooling at the elementary level carries an immense responsibility. We hope this book will help those persons charged with leading the endeavor, and their professors and mentors, meet that responsibility.

LARRY W. HUGHES
GERALD C. UBBEN

The Role: Organizational Realities and Societal Impingements

Part 1 comprises four chapters. The focus is intra- and extra-organizational demands of the principalship.

In Chapter 1 we describe the complexities of leadership and management from both research and practice perspectives. The chapter concludes with an examination of the implications of "total quality management" to the effective school.

In Chapter 2 there is an examination of certain organizational realities and the impact of the organizational structure on productive schooling. Organizational "culture building" is presented as an important leadership function.

Chapter 3 contains an extensive review of the legal principles and practices that undergird the humane school.

We move outside the school building for the subject of Chapter 4. The concluding chapter in the first part focuses on the community and the effect of changing community dynamics on the operation of the elementary school.

The Effective Principal:
Leader and Manager

> *As often as any important business has to be done in the monastery, let the abbot call together the whole community and himself set forth the matter. And, having heard the counsel of the brethren, let him take counsel with himself and then do what he shall judge to be most expedient. Now the reason why we have said that all should be called to council is that God often reveals what is better to the younger. Let the brethren give their advice with all deferences and humility, nor venture to defend their opinions obstinately, but let the decision depend rather on the abbot's judgment, so that when he has decided what is the better course, all may obey. ... But if the business to be done in the interests of the monastery be of lesser importance, let him use the advice of seniors only.*[1]

Introduction

The effective demonstration of leadership and management at the operational site has been the subject of many works produced over a long span of time. The quotation above is from the Benedictine Rule, promulgated by St. Benedict in 529 A.D. Disregarding some of the sectarian language, it is as good a description of prescribed modern administrative practice as can be found in any current textbook. All the elements are there—participation and counsel by the staff, assigned responsibility, recognition of the value of new ideas as these might be generated by new staff members, using the wisdom of veterans to help with the routine stuff.

Oh, the references to deference and humility and divine inspiration and obedience may strike an unharmonious note to those who are literal-minded, but nevertheless, St. Benedict has provided us with a good conceptual model of certain elements—not all elements—that make a difference in the effective leadership of an organization. And, we intend to build on those elements in this chapter, and throughout the book.

There are two purposes to this opening chapter. One is to provide a historical grounding of sorts to the study of leadership and management as that relates to the operation of the elementary school. We believe the principal to be the fundamental element in whether or not a school is productive, and we believe the role of the principal is leadership coupled with well-developed managerial skills. Both leadership and management will be discussed.

The second purpose of this chapter is to examine the current scene in schooling and address the implications of this on leading and managing elementary schools. Site-based management and staff empowerment might be things that were considered also in 529 A.D., but a lot has happened since the sixth century that makes the Benedictine Rule an insufficient guideline to the day-to-day operation of the good school. How does one marshal the collective wisdom of a faculty and staff to develop a curriculum and school organization that is at once responsive to the needs of a highly diverse society? This chapter will open the subject. Subsequent chapters will provide additional insights.

Functional Aspects of the Job

Schools vary in size and complexity. Similarly, the role of the principal will vary from place to place, as a result of organizational and community expectations. Nevertheless, the functions that must be managed by the principal are similar, irrespective of where the position is located or how many pupils there are.

Five functional aspects comprise the principalship. Four of these take place inside the school; the other occurs in interaction with the outside world. The "inside" functions include staffing and instructional improvement, curriculum development, pupil services, and resource procurement and building utilization, including budgeting and maintenance. The "outside" function is public relations.

It is important to distinguish between the principal as a person and the principalship as a collection of important tasks and responsibilities that must be carried out in order for the goals of the school to be achieved efficiently. It is, in a phrase, essential to distinguish between managing and doing. Careful delegation, matching the skills and interests of staff members with functional aspects, and providing for a coordinated effort are elements of good management.

There are two dimensions to these five functions: leadership and managerial acumen. Leadership is the way principals use themselves to create a school climate characterized by staff productivity, pupil productivity, and creative thought. Managerial acumen is the systematic application of an array of skills that provide an orderly, efficient, and effective school environment. Figure 1-1 depicts the relationship of the five functions and the two dimensions.

Leaders and Effective Schools

The importance of good leadership at the school building level and the effect of certain managerial and leadership behaviors of the principal are both explicit and implicit in the professional literature and research.

The early work of Halpin and Croft[2] on elementary school climates, Trump's[3] research in the 1950s and 1960s, Goldhammer's[4] study of the elementary school princi-

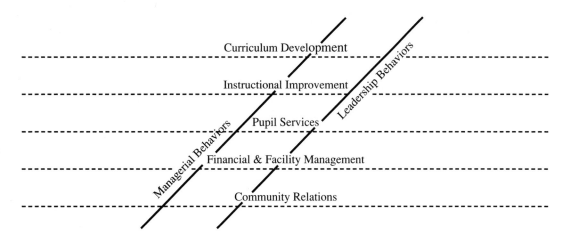

FIGURE 1–1.   The Five Functions and Two Dimensions of the Principalship

pal for the NAESP in the 1960s, and the Peterfreund[5] studies of about the same time, among others, all established the critical nature of principal behavior in the effective school. More recently the work of Lezotte,[6] Achilles,[7] Reitzug and Reeves,[8] and Mitchell[9] among others, have singled out the principal as the most significant individual in the creation of an effective school.

A recent research synthesis from the Northwest Regional Educational Laboratory provides specificity. Among other findings, the Laboratory reported the following characteristics of leaders in effective schools:

- Leaders portray learning as the most important reason for being in school; public speeches and writings emphasize the importance and value of high achievement.
- The leader has a clear understanding of the school's mission and is able to state it in direct, concrete terms; instructional focus is established that unifies staff; the principal believes that all students can learn and that the school makes a difference between success and failure.
- Building leaders know and can apply teaching and learning principles; they know research, legitimize it and foster its use in problem solving; effective teaching practices are modeled for staff as appropriate.
- Leaders set expectations for curriculum quality through the use of standards and guidelines; alignment is checked and improved; priorities are established within the curriculum; implementation is monitored.
- Principals protect learning time from disruption; administrative matters are handled with time conserving routines that don't disrupt instructional activities; time use priorities are established, communicated widely and enforced.
- A safe, orderly school environment is established and maintained.
- Leaders set up systems of incentives and rewards to encourage excellence in student and teacher performance; they act as figureheads in delivering awards and highlighting the importance of excellence.

- There is frequent, two-way communication with parents; principals highlight the accomplishments of students, staff, and the school as a whole.
- Instructional leaders expect all staff to meet high instructional standards; agreement is obtained on a schoolwide instructional model; classroom visits for the purpose of observing instruction are frequent; teacher supervision focuses on instructional improvement; staff development opportunities are secured and monitored.
- Leaders involve staff and others in planning implementation strategies; they set and enforce expectations for participation; commitments are made and followed through with determination and consistency; leaders rally support from different constituencies in the school community.[10]

Note the nature of these leadership characteristics and the relationship to the five functional aspects of the principalship.

Thus, the leadership role of the principal in the effective school can be examined from four perspectives: (1) An assertive, achievement-oriented leadership that includes both what the principal does and what the principal allows to happen. The principal sets the direction for the school and holds staff accountable for that direction. (2) An orderly, purposeful, and peaceful school climate in which there are rules, regulations, and guidelines, and teachers and pupils are expected to know and observe these. (3) High expectations for staff and pupils. (4) Well-designed and well-understood instructional objectives and evaluation systems.

Good leaders are also good managers. Essential managerial skills also have been the subject of considerable research effort.

What Do Effective Managers Do?

Much of what is known about the skills comprising good management practices is a result of developments in assessment center technology. Research dating from 1954 and the initial studies to identify skills necessary for success as a first-line supervisor at American Telegraph and Telephone Company[11] to the more recent and continuing research and development efforts of such professional organizations as the National Association of Secondary School Principals[12] has uncovered discrete skills, the presence of which determine effectiveness.

NASSP's research reveals six abilities that are important to successful school administration:[13]

- The ability to plan and organize work
- The ability to work with and lead others
- The ability to analyze problems and make decisions
- The ability to communicate orally and in writing
- The ability to perceive the needs and concerns of others
- The ability to perform under pressure

These are the result of extensive and intensive job and task analyses of what it is that principals have to do and be good at in order to manage the enterprise effectively.

In their analysis, DeMont and Hughes discovered marked similarities between the skills identified for private and public sector mid-managers. They did conclude that even with the similarities in labels and definitions among the several systems, there would be differences in the relative need to use the skill and differences in the level of acceptable performance between different kinds of organizations and depending on at what hierarchical level the person was performing.[14]

Many school systems across the nation are employing assessment centers as a means to identify who should become a principal in the district; other systems are using the process for targeted professional development purposes. Some states require successful scores in the NASSP Assessment Center as a requirement for certification to practice.[15]

Leadership: Historical Underpinnings; Current Practice

While there has been interest in the subject of leadership for a great part of human history, truly systematic study about leadership is of relatively recent vintage, St. Benedict notwithstanding. We will not detail here the rich body of research and theoretical constructs that have been conducted about organizational management and leadership during the first half of the twentieth century. Many standard works provide an excellent grounding in the historical foundations of what is now known about leadership in complex organizations. (Hunt,[16] Bass,[17] Vroom and Jago,[18] Boyan,[19] and Wexley and Yukl[20] offer a good start.)

For our purposes, we start with concepts that have been refined within the past 50 years, St. Benedict notwithstanding to the contrary.

The Ohio State Leadership Studies

An array of leadership studies was conducted at The Ohio State University in the early 1950s. Persons in various kinds of organizations were asked to describe their leaders. Two major behavior categories ultimately were uncovered. These were labeled "consideration" and "initiating structure."[21]

Consideration was defined as the degree to which a leader acts in a warm supporting way and shows concern for subordinates. Being approachable, accepting suggestions, looking out for the welfare of subordinates, consulting with subordinates before making decisions and other similar qualities comprised this category.

Initiating structure was defined as the degree to which leaders define and structure their own roles and the roles of subordinates toward the attainment of the organization's formal goals. Examples of specific behaviors in this category included criticizing unsatisfactory work, letting subordinates know what is expected of them, maintaining definite standards of performance, offering new approaches to problems, and other similar qualities.

The Michigan Studies

Additional leadership studies were conducted at the University of Michigan, also in the 1950s, largely under the direction of Rensis Likert and the Institute of Social Research.[22,23] Behavioral comparisons of ineffective and effective managers revealed that effective managers had a task orientation that generally focused on such administrative functions as planning, coordinating, and facilitating work. This did not occur at the expense of good interpersonal relations, however. Effective managers were more likely to treat subordinates considerately and to allow them some degree of autonomy in deciding how to conduct their work and at what pace. Importantly, though, effective managers set high performance goals for subordinates and used group methods of supervision. Also discovered was that high morale (defined as the total satisfaction a worker gets from a work situation), does <u>not</u> necessarily result in high productivity. However, the kind of managerial practice that results in high productivity also tends to result in high morale.[24] High morale may only describe what Blake and Mouton (to follow) call a 1,9 management style orientation characterized by great concern for people but with no evident thrust toward productivity.

Blake and Mouton

Conceptually related to, but independent from, both The Ohio State leadership studies and the Michigan leadership studies is the work of Robert Blake and Jane Mouton. Their concept results in the Managerial Grid®. The Grid is based on two dimensions (attitudes) about the workplace: "concern for people" and "concern for production." *Concern for people* closely parallels the concept of "consideration," and *concern for production* is comparable to "initiating structure."

The concept is useful for analyzing what managerial attitudes might get in the way of achieving the best job. Is there balance, or is one or the other of the dimensions being emphasized to the exclusion or near exclusion of the other? Or, are either emphasized enough? The answers to these questions permit the development of managerial training programs that are skill focused and developmental so that a managerial deficiency that will deter the effectiveness of the organizations can be, if not totally corrected, at least positively addressed.[25]

From Traditional Leadership Theory to Contingency Theory

As seemingly historically supportive of the effective school research findings as are the leadership studies at Ohio State and Michigan and the research applications of Blake and Mouton, none of these take into account the difference in situations demanding leadership or the expectations and normative behavior of subordinates and superordinates.

The dominant trend in leadership theory over the past several years has been toward the development of a situational or "contingency" theory of leadership. Fiedler's work is basic to this trend.[26]

Fiedler's Contingency Model

The reason why it is difficult to describe the ideal leader may be best clarified by the seminal work of Fred Fiedler. His model suggests that there is a situational nature to effective leader behavior. It helps explain why some studies have shown that a highly directive, task-oriented leadership style promoted effective work group performance while other studies have revealed that a non-directive, "human relations" orientation worked best, and still others found some sort of balance to result in high performance.[27]

From a large number of studies, Fiedler concluded that interaction of three factors will determine leader effectiveness:

1. *Leader-Member Relations.* This refers to the leader's feeling of being accepted by subordinates. A leader's authority depends at least partly on the acceptance of the group to be led. A person who is respected and inspires loyalty in the work group needs few of the vestments of rank to get the group to perform the task at hand in a willing and competent manner.

2. *Task Structure.* This is the degree to which the subordinates' jobs are routine and precisely defined as opposed to being relatively unstructured and loosely defined. On a continuum of "tight" to "loose," one could posit that teaching would tend toward the loose end.

3. *Power Position.* This refers to the power inherent in the leadership position and includes the means available to the leader from those at higher administrative levels and authority. This is the extent to which the leader possesses reward, coercive, and legitimate power. The ability to hire, discipline, transfer, provide salary increases, among other less direct rewards and punishments affect the power position.

In measuring the style of the leader Fiedler returned to the product of The Ohio State University studies. He used two styles as his points of measurement: task-oriented (initiating structure) and relationship-oriented (consideration). Fiedler's research indicates that the behavior of effective leaders varies according to the nature of three contingency variables: leader-group relations, the degree of structure in the task, and the position power of the leader.

Fiedler hypothesized that the nature of group productivity resulted from a match between leader orientation ("task" or "relationship" orientation) and the favorableness of the particular work situation (a mix of personal traits, group beliefs, and situational variables). He concluded that one could not simply speak of effective and ineffective leadership practices, only of effective and ineffective practices in one situation or another.[28]

While his methodologies and conclusions have been criticized by some, a great contribution of Fiedler's work is in his questioning that there is one best way to lead. Fiedler has established the usefulness of the contingency approach to the study of leadership.

But while Fiedler's provides an expanded way of thinking about the need for varying leader behavior and introduces the notion that successful leaders will manifest more *or* less in the way of "relationship" and "task" oriented behavior given certain situations and certain kind of work groups, the theory really doesn't have very much to say about how a leader ought to go about successfully managing a work group. A contingency concept advanced by Hersey and Blanchard does examine the specific behavior that is most likely to result in successful problem solving and group productivity."[29]

Hersey and Blanchard and Situational Leadership
Four distinct leadership styles are posited by Hersey and Blanchard: "telling," "selling," "participating," and "delegating." Each is viewed as an appropriate style depending on

the particulars in the situation. The key variable in the situation is what Hersey and Blanchard call the "maturity" of the work group; *maturity* is defined as the "readiness to tackle the task facing the group." Readiness might include attitude as well as ability.

Groups that are highly mature respond best to delegation; immature groups to a high degree of direction (telling). As the group grows in maturity, the leader is most effective next by selling the group, then, as greater maturity occurs, by engaging in practices that call for group participation. Hersey and Blanchard's guiding principle is that as subordinates acquire greater experience, ability, and commitment to the tasks that confront them, better productivity will be attained through greater sharing of decision-making.

This seems reasonable and is consistent with other theories, in that power-sharing through delegation and participation should result in greater productivity in groups that have demonstrated mature attitudes and high skills.

The Hersey-Blanchard model suffers from an inadequate research base. Neither the model itself nor any of its components has been validated. Perhaps the best researched contingency model has been that of House's Path-Goal theory of leadership.[30]

Path-Goal Theory of Leadership

This theory was expounded by R. J. House in 1971, then refined and extended by a number of others in subsequent years in an effort to explain how a leader's behavior makes a difference in the motivation and the satisfaction of his or her subordinates. House wrote:

> . . . *the motivational function of the leader consists of increasing personal payoffs to subordinates for work-goal attainment, and making the path to those payoffs easier to travel by clarifying it, reducing roadblocks and pitfalls, and increasing the opportunities for personal satisfaction en route.*[31]

The effect of leader behavior on satisfaction and motivation to work toward organizationally productive ends depends on the situation. Characteristics of subordinates, such as ability and personality, and characteristics of the organizational environment, such as the type of task and importance of the work, are the key determinates. Situational variables also determine the kind of leadership behavior preferred by the work group.

House identified four categories of leader behavior.[32] *Supportive leadership* is leadership that includes giving consideration to the needs of subordinates, displaying concern for their welfare, and creating a friendly climate in the work unit. *Directive leadership* lets subordinates know what they are expected to do, gives specific guidance, asks subordinates to follow rules and procedures, schedules, and coordinates the work. *Participative leadership* is consultative and takes subordinates opinions and suggestions into account when making decisions. *Achievement-oriented leadership* sets challenging goals, seeks performance improvements—emphasizes excellence in performance, and shows confidence that subordinates will attain high standards. It is more than interesting to note how closely this combination of categories relates to certain correlates of leadership in effective schools: climate, clear expectations, emphasis on excellence, and decision-making practices.

Leader behavior has an impact on subordinate performance in several ways. In situations where there is role ambiguity and/or task ambiguity, directive leadership that clarifies the roles and tasks will increase motivation and performance because it will increase the expectancy of subordinates that their efforts will lead to higher performance.

In situations where the tasks to be accomplished are tedious, boring, or stressful, supportive leadership behaviors are most likely to increase satisfaction and performance. By being considerate, offering kind words and moral and physical support, by trying to minimize the negative aspects of the work that needs to get done, the leader makes the situation more tolerable.

Achievement-oriented leadership results in subordinates who have more confidence in their ability to attain high goals and thus increases the likelihood that there will be a serious and sustained effort. House describes two conditions that make participative leadership appropriate: 1) when subordinates are assigned a challenging task that is also ambiguous; 2) in other tasks when subordinates have a high need for independence or are "anti-authoritarian" in their personalities.

Contingency theory rests on a rich research base and not a little of that research came from studies that undergird non-contingency theory. Systematic inquiries continue to uncover even more about the complexities of leadership. The important thing is that students and practitioners of school administration are provided with great insights about leadership variables that will determine the effectiveness of schools. Much of the effective school research, not surprisingly, simply reaffirms historical studies of leadership in organizations. And, the study of leader behavior in schools has itself been the subject of much inquiry for over forty years, particularly as that leader behavior was manifest at the school building level.

Implications of Contingency Theory to Site-based School Management
Contingency theory certainly has many implications for the degree to which successful implementation of wide-latitude site-based school management is expected to occur, not to mention the degree to which the issues of teacher and client empowerment are addressed. Expectations of the work group, "maturity" of the work group, positional power, other conditions in the environment, and personality variables and skill of the ascribed leader himself/herself make predictions about organizational effectiveness complex indeed.

And the "beat goes on." Enough is known to influence the direction of thinking and training positively, but not enough to stop the study of the phenomenon.[33]

Two things that have been pondered frequently recently are the qualities of "vision" and "political acumen" as these seem to relate to effective leadership behavior. The sections following focus on what has been pondered, puzzled about, and seen. We turn now to the issue of vision.

Vision

It is vision that seems to distinguish leaders from those who are simply good managers. Vision may be thought of as "the capacity to create and communicate a view of the desired state of affairs that induces commitment among those working in the organization."[34]

"Create," "communicate," and "commitment" are the focus words. Organizational study after study, whether that organization was in the public sector or the private sector, a school or a business, reveal that leaders have "vision." Bennis[35] found that the key ingredient among executives of highly successful organizations was "compelling vision." Others both before and after the Bennis inquiry have found much the same thing.

Norris,[36] for example, labels it "creative leadership" and writes, "Leadership is creative to the extent that the leader:

- has a wide knowledge of educational theory and principles;
- possesses the ability to analyze current situations in light of what should be;
- can identify problems;
- can conceptualize new avenues for change."

She continues, "Creative leadership requires that the leader make full use of the analytical as well as the intuitive mind." Visionary leaders ask such questions as "who are the human beings that inhabit the school setting; what are the needs of these individuals; what unique problems face them as they seek to bring meaning to their lives?"[37] And, we add, what is it going to take to get the answers to these questions?

Vision, then, is asking questions about what might be, standing for something, making certain others know what that is, and determining courses of action for getting to expressed goals.

Political Acumen and Creative Insubordination

Good principals know how to get the right things done, on time, and within budget. They have the skills to *work in* the system and they know *how to work* the system. Sometimes, this means getting things done in an irregular manner. Achilles and his colleagues use the word "political" to represent how the principal gets things that need to be done in an unpredictable, uncertain world.[38] These are situations where principals use all of the resources at hand—students, teachers, parents, other school system administrators—to build support for a desirable outcome or to overcome opposition to such an outcome.

It's difficult to express this ability in words. We're not even sure it can be taught, or if it can, how it can be taught. It seems, to use Norris' terminology, to be "intuitive." But, it's there—a *je ne sais quoi*, an indescribable something. It is knowing when to break the rules; when to short circuit the system. Prescribing when to do this is impossible. Good leaders seem to know when it's more important to risk having to "beg forgiveness" instead of "asking permission."

We label that behavior creative insubordination and submit that such behavior is characteristic of leaders.

Total Quality Management

The current guidewords are "total quality management." The term comes from the work of W. Edwards Deming.[39,40] Deming is credited with rebuilding the Japanese economy after World War II. He has only recently become a prophet in his own land. His "14 Points" buttress much of the research about effective schools and what it takes to become effective. They also have much to say about the kind of leadership necessary to achieve excellence in schooling. Figure 1-2 summarizes the 14 points and applies these to the school organization. Note the consistency of the dictums and their relationship to what have long been known, if not practiced, to be characteristics of productive organizations.

Fundamental is a clear and well-understood sense of purpose at all levels of the organization, teamwork and empowerment of all workers, and a prevailing drive to serve the "customer." The customer is anyone inside or outside the organization to whom members of the organization provide services and products. The customers of the third grade teacher are, for example, students, parents, community, *and the fourth grade teacher* for whom the third grade teacher is preparing students.

Total quality management is an integrated, strategic system to achieve client satisfaction which involves all administrators, teachers, and other staff members to improve the school's services and products continuously. *Quality* means providing clients with services that meet their expectations and needs, *the first time and every time*. We will return to the concept of total quality management consistently throughout the remainder of this book.

Total Quality Management: Deming's Fourteen Essentials Applied to the School Organization

Point 1:   *Create a constancy of purpose for improvement of products and services.* This means that the focus must be on helping students reach their maximum potential by providing a basis for students and teachers to work together continuously to improve.

Point 2:   *Adopt a new philosophy.* Continuous improvement will occur through greater empowerment of teacher-student teams. Instructional decisions and decisions regarding scoping and sequencing of learning events are to be joint efforts involving all the stakeholders.

Point 3:   *Cease dependence on mass inspection to achieve quality.* Using test scores as the primary way to assess student achievement and progress is wasteful and frequently unreliable. The end of a unit or a term is too late to assess student progress. Tests should be diagnostic and help to prescribe new learning events rather than as summative evidence of the achievement of short-term goals. Too, students must be taught to assess their own work and progress.

Point 4:   *Stop awarding business on the basis of price tag alone.* Use high quality instructional materials—the best available. Free or cheap materials are too often that way because they do not serve learners well.

Point 5:   *Improve constantly the system of production and service.* The litany of the school organization should be "why are we doing what we are doing?" (a goals question) "What are we doing?" (an examination of the way we are trying to do "it") and "Can it be done a better way?" (an evaluation question) All in the organization need to be empowered to both ask and answer these questions.

Point 6:   *Institute training on the job.* In-house programs for both new and old staff members should characterize the work environment. Educators must show students and community what being a good learner is all about. Skills improvement for all in the school organization should be the goal and mechanisms to insure this must be in place.

Continued

FIGURE 1–2.

FIGURE 1-2. *(Continued)*

Point 7:   *Institute leadership.* Leadership acts should be encouraged irrespective of title or position. Leadership consists of working with all members of the school organization and the community as coach and mentor. Leading is helping others achieve worthwhile goals.

Point 8:   *Drive out fear.* Fear is counterproductive. In a free society and in a productive school no one is motivated by fear. Positive institutional changes result from shared responsibilities, shared power, and shared rewards.

Point 9:   *Break down barriers between departments [and grade levels].* Synergy is required, not just collective energy. Competition between departments dissipates energy that should be directed toward common ends. Create cross department and multi-level teams devoted to quality. Implement link-pin task forces to break down role and status barriers.

Point 10:   *Eliminate slogans, exhortations, and targets.* Educators, students, community members may collectively arrive at slogans and symbols that harness energy and cause them to pursue common goals and celebrate success, but these will develop out of their working together. Externally imposed sloganeering is hollow, however, and to little result.

Point 11:   *Eliminate numerical quotas.* It is not possible to summarize all of the ways a person can grow and learn in the barest symbol of language—a number or a letter. So, stop trying to do this. When a grade or a score becomes the basic symbol of success, short-term gains replace long-term learning and development.

Point 12:   *Remove barriers to pride of workmanship.* Humans generally want to do good work, and when they do, feel pride in it. They should be helped to do so. Self-fulfillment is a strong motivator. Realistic and cooperatively established goals result in satisfaction and pride.

Point 13:   *Institute a vigorous program of education and self improvement.* Educators and students require continuous learning programs. Self renewal must be goal oriented, systematic and regular, and the effective organization provides the mechanisms for this to take place within the workplace.

Point 14:   *Put everybody in the [organization] to work to accomplish the transformation.* Teachers, administrators, staff, students and community are stakeholders and should contribute to the realization of the new philosophy. Top level commitment and community commitment are required. Teachers and students cannot do it alone. Nor can an administrator.

Summary

In this chapter we have examined a number of characteristics of effective leaders and effective managers. Addressing the five functions of the principalship requires excellence in leadership and in identified managerial skills.

It is clearly evident from early research efforts that where principals are good, schools are good. Good management practices contribute mightily to a well-run school; certain leadership causes an effective school. Setting and maintaining high standards and helping others to do likewise are characteristic of principals in productive elementary schools.

Endnotes

1. St. Benedict, *The Rule of St. Benedict*, translated by Abbot J. McCann. Westminster, MD: Newman Press, 1952. Originally promulgated by St. Benedict in 529 A.D.

2. Andrew W. Halpin and Don B. Croft, *The Organizational Climate of Schools*. Chicago: Midwest Administration Center, the University of Chicago, 1963. For updated and re-normed versions of the O.C.D.Q. see Wayne Hoy *et al.*, *Open Schools; Healthy Schools*. Newbury Park, CA: Corwin Press, 1991.

3. J. Lloyd Trump, *Images of the Future*. Washington, DC: NASSP, 1959.

4. Keith Goldhammer *et al.*, *Elementary School Principals and Their Schools*. Eugene, OR: Center for the Advanced Study of Educational Administration, University of Oregon, 1971.

5. Stanley Peterfreund Associates, *Innovation and Change in Public School Systems*. Englewood Cliffs, NJ: The Associates, 1970.

6. Larry W. Lezotte and B.A. Bancroft, "Growing Use of Effective Schools Model for School Improvement." *Educational Leadership*, 42:6 (March, 1985), 23-27.

7. Charles M. Achilles, John Keedy, and Reginald High, "The Political World of the Principal: How Principals Get Things Done," Chapter 2 in Larry W. Hughes, *The Principal as Leader*. Columbus, OH: Merrill, 1994.

8. Ulrich C. Reitzug and Jennifer E. Reeves, "Miss Lincoln Doesn't Teach Here: A Descriptive Narrative of a Principal's Symbolic Leadership Behavior." *Educational Administrative Quarterly*, 28:2 (May, 1992), 185-219.

9. Douglas Mitchell, "Principal Leadership: A Theoretical Framework for Research." Urbana, IL: National Center for School Leadership, 1992.

10. Northwest Regional Educational Laboratory, *Effective Schooling Practices: A Research Synthesis*. Portland, OR: The Laboratory, 1984, 7-8.

11. Douglas W. Bray *et al.*, *Formative Years in Business: A Long-Term AT&T Study of Managerial Lives*. New York: Wiley-Interscience, 1974. See also Douglas W. Bray and D.L. Grant, "The Assessment Center in the Measurement of Potential for Business Management." *Psychological Monographs*, 80, 1966.

12. NASSP has available a variety of descriptive materials and research reports, including validation studies. Write Paul W. Hersey, NASSP, 1904 Association Drive, Reston, Virginia 22091. The NASSP process is designed for the K-12 spectrum; the skills identified are generic and applicable for elementary as well as secondary school principals.

13. In the NASSP system there are actually twelve discrete skills and attributes: Problem Analysis, Judgment, Organizational Ability, Decisiveness, Leadership, Sensitivity, Stress Tolerance, Oral and Written Communication, Personal Motivation, Educational Values, and Range of Interests. What is described here are the more general categories of skills.

14. Roger A. DeMont and Larry W. Hughes, "Assessment Center Technology: Implications for Administrator Training Programs." *Planning and Changing*, 15:4 (Winter 1984), 219-225.

15. Kentucky, South Carolina, Georgia, and Missouri are among those states.

16. Hunt, J. G., *Leadership, A New Synthesis*. Newbury Park, CA: Sage, 1991.

17. Bass, B.M., *Bass and Stodgill's Handbook of Leadership* (3rd edition). New York: Free Press, 1990.

18. Vroom, V.H. and Jago, A.G., *The New Leadership: Managing Participation in Organizations*. Englewood Cliffs, NJ: Prentice-Hall, 1988.

19. Boyan, N.J. (ed.), *Handbook of Research on Educational Administration*. New York: Longman, 1988.

20. Wexley, K.N. and Yukl, G.A., *Organizational Behavior and Personnel Psychology*. Homewood, IL: Richard D. Irwin, 1984. (especially chapters 7, 9 and 10)

21. Andrew W. Halpin and B.J. Winer, "A Factorial Study of the Leader Behavior Descriptions" in R.M. Stogdill and A.E. Coons (eds.), *Leader Behavior in Description and Measurement*. Columbus, OH: Bureau of Business Research, The Ohio State University, 1957.

22. Rensis Likert, *New Patterns of Management*. New York: McGraw-Hill, 1961.

23. Rensis Likert, *The Human Organization: Its Management and Value*. New York: McGraw-Hill, 1967.

24. Rensis Likert, *Motivation: The Core of Management*. New York: American Management Association, Personnel Series #155, 1953. For a high-

ly specific application of Likert to school administration, the reader is directed to Thomas Sergiovanni and R.J. Starratt, *Emerging Patterns of Supervision: Human Perspectives* (third edition). New York: McGraw-Hill, 1988.

25. Robert R. Blake and Jane S. Mouton, *The Managerial Grid III: The Key to Leadership Excellence*. Houston, TX: Gulf Publishing Company, 1985. See also Blake and Mouton, *The Managerial Grid*. Houston, TX: Gulf Publishing Company, 1964; Blake and Mouton, *Corporate Excellence Through Grid Organization Development*. Houston, TX: Gulf Publishing Company, 1968.

26. Fred Fiedler, *A Theory of Leadership Effectiveness*. New York: McGraw-Hill, 1967.

27. Fred Fiedler, *Leadership*. New York: General Learning Press, University Program Module Series, 1971. Readers interested in pursuing this further may find the work of Hersey and Blanchard helpful. Paul Hersey and Kenneth H. Blanchard, *Management of Organizational Behavior* (3rd edition). New York: McGraw-Hill, 1977.

28. F.E. Fiedler, *Leadership*. New York: General Learning Press, 1971. See also F.E. Fiedler and M.M. Chemers, *Leadership and Effective Management*. Glencoe, IL: Scott-Foresman, 1974.

29. Paul Hersey and Kenneth Blanchard, *Management of Organizational Behavior: Utilizing Human Resources* (4th edition). Englewood Cliffs, NJ: Prentice-Hall, 1982.

30. Robert J. House, "A Path-Goal Theory of Leader Effectiveness." *Administrative Science Quarterly*, 16 (1971), 321-338.

31. *Ibid.*, p. 324.

32. R.J. House and T.R. Mitchell, "Path-Goal Theory of Leadership." *Contemporary Business*, 3 (Fall, 1974), 81-91.

33. "Site-based management" and "empowerment" have become almost fad words—little understood and even less defined. Good insights about the problems confronting the leader regarding these can be found in the following references. G.I. Maeroff, "A Blueprint for Empowering Teachers." *Phi Delta Kappan*, 69:7 (July, 1988), 481-491; C.R. Harrison, *et al.*, "Site-based Management: The Realities of Implementation." *Educational Leadership*, 46:8 (August, 1989), 55-58; and V.I. Karant, "Supervision in the Age of Teacher Empowerment." *Educational Leadership*, 46:8 (August, 1989), 27-29; Larry W. Hughes, "School-Based Management, Decentralization, and Citizen Control—A Perspective." *Journal of School Leadership*, 3:1 (January, 1993), 40-44.

34. Thomas J. Sergiovanni, *The Principalship: A Reflective Practice Perspective*. Boston, MA: Allyn and Bacon, 1987, p. 57.

35. Warren Bennis, "Transformation Power and Leadership," in T.J. Sergiovanni and J.E. Corbally (eds.), *Leadership and Organizational Culture*. Champaign-Urbana, IL: University of Illinois Press, 1984.

36. Cynthia Norris, "Developing Visionary Leaders for Tomorrow's Schools." *NASSP Bulletin*, 74:526 (May, 1990), 6-10.

37. *Ibid.*

38. Charles M. Achilles, John Keedy, and Reginald High, *loc. cit.*

39. M. Walton, *Deming Management at Work*. New York: Putnam, 1987.

40. W. Edwards Deming, "Transformation of Today's Management." *Executive Excellence*, 4:12 (December, 1987), 8.

Selected Readings

AASA, *Introduction to Total Quality for Schools*. Washington, DC: The Association, 1991.

Achilles, Charles M.; Keedy, John; and High, Reginald, "The Political World of the Principal." Chapter 2 in Hughes, Larry W., *The Principal as Leader*. Columbus, OH: Merrill, 1994.

Bass, B.M., *Bass and Stodgill's Handbook of Leadership* (3rd edition). New York: Free Press, 1990.

Blase, Joseph and Kirby, Peggy C., *Bringing Out the Best in Teachers*. Newbury Park, CA: Corwin Press, 1992.

Deming, W. Edwards, "Transformation of Today's Management." *Executive Excellence*, 4:12 (December, 1987), 8.

Hughes, Larry W., *The Principal as Leader*. Columbus, OH: Merrill, 1994. Chapters 1, 2, and 3 especially.

Hughes, Larry W., "School-Based Management, Decentralization, and Citizen Control—A Perspective." *Journal of School Leadership*, 3:1 (January, 1993), 40-44.

Hughes, Larry W., "Site-Based Management and Restructured Schools." *Texas Educational Policy Research Report*. Houston, TX: University of Houston, 1:2 (1992), 5-9.

Hunt, J.G., *Leadership, a New Synthesis*. Newbury Park, CA: Sage, 1991.

Norris, Cynthia J., "Cultivating Creative Cultures." Chapter 3 in Hughes, Larry W., *The Principal as Leader*. Columbus, OH: Merrill, 1994.

Reitzug, Ulrich C. and Reeves, Jennifer E., "Miss Lincoln Doesn't Teach Here: A Descriptive Narrative and Conceptual Analysis of a Principal's Symbolic Behavior." *Educational Administration Quarterly*, 28:2 (May, 1992), 185-219.

Walton, M., *Deming Management at Work*. New York: Putnam, 1987.

$$C \quad h \quad a \quad p \quad t \quad e \quad r \quad 2$$

School Organization and Culture

A school's culture is a representation of what its members collectively believe themselves to be: it is their "self concept." It reflects what they value and what they express to others as being "important around here." . . .

Culture is a shared reality . . . Since it is constructed over time, it includes both past as well as present perceptions and its perceived reality is reflected in its symbols, rituals, and purpose. Cultures may be cohesive or fragmented, strong or weak, and functional or dysfunctional dependent upon the degree to which the same "reality" is shared by its members.[1]

Introduction

Effectively managing and leading any organization requires daily interaction with a large number of groups and a wide variety of individuals that make up these groups. Teachers, parents, children, administrators, classified personnel, tradespersons, merchants, and a host of other "outsiders" and "insiders" all become important reference points. Moreover, persons within these groups, although often sharing common goals, rarely behave similarly or see the same things similarly. People have varying perceptions of the nature of schooling and their own role in the schooling process. They are influenced and motivated in different ways and by different means.

For the administrator intent on getting maximum results, it is useful to think of the school as a social system. Social systems theory provides a sound basis for understanding the behavior of people in organizations. The implications of social systems theory to the elementary school principal are many. It explains why even well-thought-out plans sometimes turn out badly. It explains why different motivational strategies must be employed for individual staff members. And it helps explain why much attention needs to be directed to the informal interactions of people in the organization.

All of us have experienced the puzzlement that accompanies the outright refusal of another person to respond to some simple (to us) request. Why did the person behave that way? Doesn't she know it's her job? Doesn't he know it's best for the children? Doesn't she know it's in the best interests of the school? Maybe, maybe not, to some or all of these questions. And, perhaps more to the point, how can you get the person to do what it is that must be done? What is an administrator to do, anyway?

The school organization as a social system will be examined in this chapter. The intent is to explain the puzzle described above and provide a firm basis for diagnosis and productive action.

The Two-Dimensional Organization

Two dimensions of an organization can be identified: the institutional dimension and the personal, or individual, dimension. The institutional dimension of an organization is made up of the official roles occupied by individuals. These roles define the official behavior of people holding particular positions, offices, or statuses. Positions have certain normative obligations and responsibilities. Thus, the principal has certain responsibilities and should behave in certain ways. Similarly, a teacher, a student, and a night custodian all have certain responsibilities.

The institutional dimension of an organization can be discerned rather readily from the formal organization chart and the job descriptions. From a formal organizational point of view the responsibilities are clear, and so the organization would appear to have no difficulty in responding directly and authoritatively to problem situations. The formal organization chart suggests that each role incumbent, each position holder is devoid of individual personality. A principal is to do these things and react in certain ways; a teacher is to do these things and react in certain ways. This situation would result in a certain predictability of behaviors and reactions, provided, of course, that the individuals in the organization have the same perceptions or nearly the same perceptions about role definitions and what behaviors are appropriate for what roles.

If that were all there was to it, organizational management would be very easy. Each person would understand what was to be done, would do it, and move on to the next task with a minimum of misunderstanding and false starts. However, official roles in a school are not filled with automatons. Roles are filled with people with individual personalities, and no two are the same.

Personal Dimension of the School Organization

It is not enough to understand the organizational chart and the job descriptions. There must be some understanding of the nature of the individuals inhabiting the various roles or positions in an organization. The individual style each person brings to a particular role differs from the style of other individuals performing that same role.

The worker has needs and ambitions, and any effort to derive the greatest productivity from the individual worker must take these into consideration. Social psychologists call these traits needs-dispositions. In large part, an individual's *needs-dispositions* comprise the personality and determine how the person acts and reacts to other people and situations. They help determine what information will be accepted and what information will be rejected, how closely the person is "in tune" with the school operation, or for that matter, how closely the person is in tune with his or her own assignment within the organization. The greater the degree of congruency between person and job, and person and organization, the more effective the person will be and the more effective the organization will be.

How a person behaves, where the person thinks he or she stands in relation to others and the organization in general, and how much he or she understands is dependent upon his or her own perceptual framework. People see and understand what their individual background permits them to see and understand.

Schools are complex, unpredictable social organizations that are extremely vulnerable to a host of powerful external and internal forces. They exist in a vortex of government mandates, social and economic pressures, and conflicting ideologies associated with school administrators, teachers, students, and parents.[2]

Moreover,

Consciously motivated actions may be intended, calculated, strategic, or purposive. Unconsciously motivated actions may refer to routine action, nondecisionmaking, negligence, nonaction, habitual actions resulting from socialization, and actions that prevent others from exercising influence.[3]

Social Systems Theory

Social systems theory helps explain these phenomena. The work of Jacob Getzels and Egon Guba is fundamental to the application of social systems theory to schools.[4] Essentially, Getzels and Guba posit two dimensions to the organization: the nomothetic (institutional) dimension and the idiographic (personal) dimension. It is the interaction of these two dimensions that results in the observed behavior of individuals in the organization. It is the principal's responsibility to serve as the agent for productive interaction. Figure 2-1 is a depiction of social systems theory.

If the principal is to be able to understand the nature of the observed behavior and thus have the opportunity to predict and control it, the elements of the theory and the interrelationships need definition.

Institution simply refers to the fact that all organizations have certain necessary functions that must be carried out, no matter what. The necessary function of the school is to provide an articulated program of studies and insist that all eligible children participate in this program.

Roles are the official positions and offices that have been established to carry out the functions of the organization. The behaviors that are to comprise a role are called *role expectations*. Every role has certain normative responsibilities and these will differ by role. The role expectations for a learning resource specialist, an assistant principal, and a

Nomothetic (Institutional) Dimension

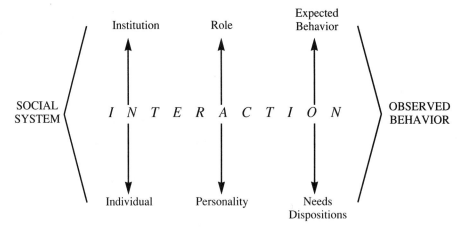

FIGURE 2–1. **Depiction of a Social Systems Theory**

first-grade teacher are very different. Job descriptions are an attempt to differentiate the official organizational expectations of each role incumbent.

Thus, there is established at least some gross understandings and predictability of *behavior*. But it's not easy, because roles are occupied with real people who stamp each role with their own individuality. The principal must therefore consider the idiographic or personal aspects of social behavior. These too require definition and, as the model in Figure 2-1 indicates, these aspects may be analyzed in parallel fashion to the nomothetic dimension.

Personality in the context of the social systems model may be defined as the dynamic interactions within an individual of those *needs-dispositions* that govern personally unique reactions to the environment. In other words, every one of us is a complex of previous experiences that have provided us with differing orientations to life, to organizations, and to other people. These affect our sense of what is pleasurable, important, and real. Personality is to needs-disposition as role is to role expectation.

In order for the principal to understand and reasonably predict the behavior of a teacher or other staff members, it is essential that the principal know both the role expectation of the particular job and the needs-disposition of the individual. In the productive organization, much attention is directed to helping all workers understand what the organizational expectations are.

The challenge to the principal, given competence on the part of the job incumbent, is to try to address both individual and organizational needs to achieve as much congruence as possible. The greater the congruence, the more satisfied and productive the worker and the more effective the organization.

Addressing this issue, Hughes developed a competency statement as follows:

Concept 1: The school organization is multi-functional and some of the functions are a product of the personal needs and wants of individual organizational members.

Performance statement: The principal recognizes that the private goals of organizational members affect the achievement of the public goals of the school.

Indicators: The principal—

1. Recognizes and supports differing teaching styles.
2. Flexibly schedules institutional demands on employee time.
3. Is able to identify personal needs of individual colleagues and provides intra-organizational ways in which these needs may be satisfied, consistent with organizational goals.
4. Matches teaching skills with teaching arrangements.[5]

This particular performance statement simply recognizes the uniqueness of individual teachers and suggests that in order to get the best out of teachers, administrators should arrange the teaching environment in a manner consistent with the style, attitude, and orientation of the teacher. This does not mean team teaching for all, or open spaces for all, or committees for all. If anything, research about human beings tells us that there is no one consistently productive pattern, and this knowledge may be the key to the way administrative behavior can positively affect teacher and learner behavior.

The Organizational Iceberg

A different way of thinking about the two dimensions is to picture an iceberg with the visible part of the iceberg representing the formal or institutional dimension of the organization. This is the public part of the organization and is manifest in the stated goals and objectives, the organization chart, the job descriptions—all of those things that are official.

Not readily apparent is that part of the organization that lies below the surface—the personal or informal dimension. Manifest in this dimension are the perceptions of organization members about the organization, the differing influence and power patterns that exist irrespective of formal title, the informal reward and sanctioning systems, feelings of trust and confidence, and incipient individual or group paranoia. The below-the-surface organization affects mightily the degree to which the above-the-surface organization is really as it appears and whether or not, or the degree to which, the organization reaches its stated and legitimate goals. The "iceberg" is depicted in Figure 2-2.

Informal Groups

Many informal groupings of people not found on the organizational chart function within the formal framework of any school organization. These nonofficial groupings are characterized by a feeling of general agreement, not necessarily spoken but tacitly understood, about certain values and goals. These are groupings of people who tend to see things somewhat similarly, who meet over a cup of coffee during work and perhaps

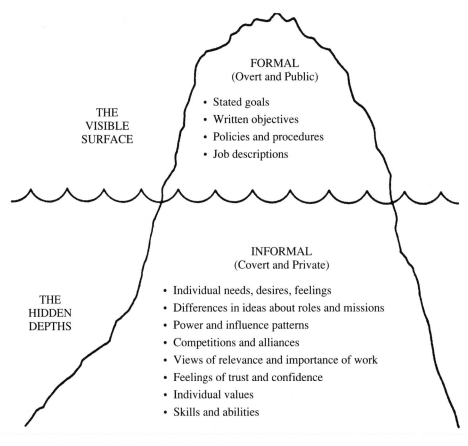

FIGURE 2–2.   The Organizational Iceberg

socialize afterward. This highly personalized system of interaction operates to modify the effect of the formal organization on individuals. The groups may or may not tend to agree with the institutional goals or the expectations of the formal organization, although overtly they may behave as if they did. Leadership within the informal organization is earned through power, personality, or prestige rather than ascribed, as in the formal organization.

Commonly, one thinks of the professional teaching staff as being the most important locus of informal groups, but informal groupings also are found among administrators, noncertificated employees, and students. In some cases there may be a mixing of role incumbents—as in the "boiler room gang," which might include a custodian or two.

There are, then, loosely organized, but potentially influential, groups of people operating outside the formal organization of the institution. These groups have their own norms, values, and needs, and individual members may perceive their functions as being somewhat different than the official organization would define them. In the negative extreme, these groups may actually operate in such a way as to inhibit the school as it moves toward its goals. The more congruence in terms of values and goals that the informal and formal organizations can develop, the more successful the school will become.

One function of administrative leadership is to maintain the institution while moving it toward its goals. The principal must be aware of the functioning of the informal dimension and its various needs and must seek to achieve a congruence between the two. Further, a rich source of information and leadership exists in the informal dimension, a source that the perceptive principal will tap in the problem-resolution process.

Because of their nature, informal groupings are not intensely stable. There are shifts in leadership as members leave the system or the building, or as other leaders emerge. The principal must be aware of these shifts and the implication that they may have to the informal communication channels that have been set up. Informal groups are a natural part of any organization and provide for a sense of personal significance within what may be a very impersonal structure. Also, there is not only one group operating within the informal structure but a number of groups. Thus, different ways of relating and dealing with these groups must be developed, depending on the situation and the group.

Loose Coupling

It is especially pertinent to our discussion here to think of the educational enterprise as a combination of loosely coupled systems. Weick[6] suggests that, rather than being composed of tightly interrelated subsystems, the elements of an educational organization (for example) are frequently only loosely tied together. By using the term loose coupling to describe an organization, Weick connotes that its subsystems (elements) are responsive to each other but that each still preserves its own identity and its own physical and logical separateness.

> . . . Elements may consist of events like yesterday and tomorrow (what happened yesterday may be tightly or loosely coupled to what happens tomorrow) or hierarchical positions like top and bottom, line and staff, or administrators and teachers. Another interesting set of elements that lends itself to loose coupling imagery is means and ends. Frequently, several different means lead to the same outcome. When this happens, it can be argued that any one means is loosely coupled to the end in the sense that there are alternative pathways to achieve the same end. Other elements that might be found in loosely coupled educational systems are teachers-materials, voters-school board, administrators-classroom process-outcome, teacher-teacher, parent-teacher, and teacher-pupil.[7]

If the system is only loosely coupled, or if particular elements within the system are only loosely coupled, then the possibility of much miscommunication and distortion exists.

Conditions Affecting Individual Behavior in the Organization

Several conditions affect individual behavior in organizations:

1. People work in organizations, and organizational expectations, real or perceived, affect individual behavior and beliefs.

2. At least part of an individual's energy is devoted to trying to adapt to organizational realities and expectations of superordinates, peers, and subordinates.

3. Although individuals rarely have total control over their work life, they do materially affect what happens in organizations.

4. People are different: They are variously motivated and they do not always perceive the same set of circumstances similarly.

5. People are most affected by the expectations and conditions in their immediate work group.

These conditions may be either encouraging or discouraging when one considers the need for and nature of information exchanges in order to keep the organization moving. They are encouraging because they reveal the influence the formal organization, especially that part of it that exists at the school building level—the immediate work group—has on individual behavior. This manifests itself in general conformity to the official goals of the school as these are revealed in policy statements, rules and regulations, tradition, and existing curricula. Most people try to do what is expected of them insofar as they can and still maintain an integrated personality.

The conditions may be discouraging because they also reveal that individuals have a great impact on what the organization does and determine in great part whether or not goals are reached. The wise principal recognizes the staff's need for accurate information and organizes accordingly. He or she is also aware of staff and organizational idiosyncrasies that sometimes inhibit or distort information flow. Responding to problems in an effective way requires reliable information. Fact gathering, information seeking, perception testing, all initial steps in the decision-making process, require a smooth lateral and vertical flow of information throughout an organization. Two responsibilities comprise the task of administrative leadership. One is the task of moving the organization, in this case the individual school, toward its ultimate goals. At the same time, a school principal has the responsibility of maintaining the organization so it is both efficient and effective.

The Developing Organization: New Perspectives

In the first chapter we wrote about "transformational leadership" and the importance of building an organization that was at once responsive to client and member needs, an adaptive organization that reflected unswerving commitment to excellence.

Organizational Culture

Three phases in school development now seem apparent. The "custodial school" with its traditional, top-down manner of structuring control and decision-making clearly lacks promise for the future. The "effective school" movement, much researched and in many places at least partially if not fully implemented, is seen by many to be an interim step in the evolution from custodial to a totally restructured schooling system, highly decentralized and characterized by individually strong organizational cultures of accomplishment.[8]

Sergiovanni[9] compares effective schools to schools with strong organizational cultures:

Effective Schools	*Schools with Strong Organizational Cultures*
• agreed on goals	• shared values
• principal as leader; teacher as role model	• principal as hero-maker; teacher as hero
• strong believes about teaching and learning	• widely spread beliefs and supporting rituals
• staff training	• cultural renewal
• participation by others decision making	• widespread participation in cultural rituals

The model is a "value-added" model. Dimensions of the effective school are not given up; rather these are enhanced by the addition of dimensions in the strong culture model. The emphasis in the new school reform model is on rituals, ceremony, shared values, and widespread common beliefs. A "bonding" occurs and school effectiveness increases.

Getting There

Effective organizations are characterized by committed and energetic people who sit down together, examine problems confronting the organization and figure out ways to overcome these problems. The principal's job is to facilitate this. The questions to be answered, as stated before in this chapter, are:

- Why are we doing what we are doing? (Goals)
- What are we doing? (Processes)
- Can it be done a better way? (Evaluation)

In Chapter 6 we recommend that this process begin with the statement asked of all: "This is a good school but it could be better if . . . ", and provide guidance about how to conduct the process. A school community confronted by such a question will quickly uncover problems that need to be a focus for campus improvement.

Why Involve Others in Goal Setting and Action Planning?

The question is rhetorical, of course. Principals engage staff, students, and community in goal-setting and problem-solving (the result of action planning) because all are stakeholders and each, to one degree or another, has a contribution to make and a responsibility to assume for why things are the way they are.

Four assumptions guide the school executive who expands problem-solving to include all of the stakeholders:

1. People at the working level tend to know the problems best.
2. The face-to-face work group is the best unit for diagnosis and change.

   3. People will work hard to achieve objectives they have helped develop.
   4. Initiative and creativity are widely distributed in the population.

These assumptions undergird the implementation of strategic independence for individual schools and supply the reason for decentralized decision-making. But, positive results are not achieved necessarily from philosophic pronouncements. How can a sound philosophic base be translated into action?

Cooperative Goal-Setting Facilities Good Decentralized Decision-Making

It is axiomatic that any effective organization must have a clear sense of direction—a sense of where it is desirably headed and what it will take to get there. These goals and objectives should be the result of the collective thinking of all of the stakeholders.

   Once developed, the goals need to be explicated by specific objectives and subjected at regular intervals to a review in light of 1) the degree to which they are being achieved, and 2) whether they continue to be appropriate. A focus is thus provided for particular endeavors at the school and a means provided to evaluate the efficacy of these endeavors.[10]

High Expectations, Praise, and Hoopla: The Motivating Work Environment

High standards of accomplishment are characteristic of productive schools. Research about productive educational settings has shown that invariably present was a leader who had high expectations, advertised these expectations, facilitated efforts to achieve the expectations, and monitored progress. This has been so whether the leader was a teacher in a single classroom working with children, a principal with a staff to manage, or a superintendent of a school system.

   High expectations result in high performance. Even where excellence is not obtained, the result is far higher than what might ever have been predicted. Moreover, staff and principal have a benchmark from which to move to the next higher level, and a diagnostic basis to determine how to get there.

Hoopla.   Effective organizations celebrate success! Good leaders use every device at their disposal to call attention to excellent work and great accomplishments (so do good teachers). Recognition lunches, awards banquets, T-shirts emblazoned with "We're Number 1," gold stars, trophies, public announcements, acknowledged favors and special privileges, "Teacher of the Week," "Student of the Day," "Custodian of the Month," "Cafeteria Worker of the Hour," school-created important sounding titles, whatever and whenever, when well-intended and well-merited, enhance school productivity. In writing about such activities in highly successful private sector organizations, Peters and Waterman call this "unabashed hoopla and people respond to it."

> When we first looked at this phenomenon, we thought large doses of hoopla and celebration might be limited to companies like Tupperware, where the president and his senior managers are said to participate for thirty days a year in Jubilees, aimed at feting the success of their top *15,000* salespersons and managers. But

we found hoopla going on in high tech companies as well. . . . And at Caterpillar we were told of an event to introduce new equipment where huge pieces of earth-moving machinery were dressed in costume.

. . .The people orientation also has its tough side. The excellent companies are measurement-happy and performance oriented, but this toughness is born of mutually high expectations and peer review rather than emanating from table-pounding managers and complicated control systems.[11]

Summary

In this chapter we have examined the organizational milieu within which leadership acts occur. The importance of well-understood and agreed-on goals has been well established. Also well established is the very "humanness" of organizations and the importance of leadership structures, patterns of interaction, and belief systems in the informal dimension of organizations. "Culture building" may be the most important task of the principal in the developing organizations. Effective organizations are inhabited by committed, caring, and energetic people who engage in joint problem solving. The principal's role is to facilitate this and to participate in setting high standards of accomplishment.

Endnotes

1. Cynthia J. Norris, "Cultivating Creative Culture." Chapter 3 in Larry W. Hughes (ed.), *The Principal as Leader*. Columbus, OH: Merrill, 1994.

2. Joseph Blase, "The Micropolitical Perspective." Chapter One in Blase, *The Politics of Life in Schools*. Newbury Park, CA: Sage, 1991, p. 1.

3. *Ibid*, pp. 11-12.

4. Jacob W. Getzels and Egon G. Guba, "Social Behavior and the Administrative Process." *School Review*, 65 (Winter, 1957), 423-441.

5. Larry W. Hughes, "Achieving Effective Human Relations and Morale." Chapter 5 in Jack Culbertson *et al.* (eds.), *Performance Objectives for School Principals: Concepts and Instruments*. Berkeley, CA: 1974, pp. 141-142.

6. Karl E. Weick, "Educational Organizations as Loosely Coupled Systems." *Administrative Science Quarterly*, 21 (March, 1976), 1-19.

7. *Ibid.* p. 4.

8. Roland S. Barth, *Improving Schools from Within*. San Francisco, CA: Jossey-Bass, 1990; Thomas J. Sergiovanni, *Value-Added Leadership: How to Get Extraordinary Performance in Schools*. Orlando, FL: Harcourt Brace Jovanovich, 1990. Among others.

9. *Ibid*.

10. Processes and procedures for the development and implementation of the strategic goals that comprise campus improvement plans are discussed at length in Chapters 5, 6, and 20.

11. Thomas J. Peters and Robert H. Waterman, *In Search of Excellence*. New York: Harper and Row, 1982, p. 240.

Selected Readings

Blase, Joseph (ed.), *The Politics of Life in Schools.* Newbury Park, CA: Sage, 1991.

Bolman, L.G. and Deal, Terrence E., *Reframing Organizations: Artistry, Choice, and Leadership.* San Francisco, CA: Jossey-Bass, 1991.

Greer, John T. and Short, Paula M., "Restructuring Schools." Chapter Six in Hughes, Larry W. (ed.), *The Principal as Leader.* Columbus, OH: Merrill, 1994.

Hughes, Larry W., *The Principal as Leader.* Columbus, OH: Merrill, 1994.

Hunt, James G., *Leadership: A New Synthesis.* Newbury Park, CA: Sage, 1991. (Chapters 2, 9, and 10 especially.)

Norris, Cynthia J., "Cultivating Creative Cultures." Chapter Three in Hughes, Larry W. (ed.), *The Principal as Leader.* Columbus, OH: Merrill, 1994.

Schein, Edgar H., *Organizational Culture and Leadership.* San Francisco, CA: Jossey-Bass, 1985.

Ubben, Gerald C. and Hughes, Larry W., *The Principal: Creative Leadership for Effective Schools*, (2nd edition). Boston, MA: Allyn and Bacon, 1992.

$$C\ h\ a\ p\ t\ e\ r\quad 3$$

A Legal Framework

Ignorance of the laws excuses no man, not that all men know the law, but because 'tis an excuse every man will plead, and no man can tell how to refute him.[1]

Introduction

Principals do not have to have law degrees to be successful in this litigious society, but they had better know the laws that frame American education, and more particularly the laws that frame schooling in the states in which they practice. The state laws may differ somewhat although none may be at variance with United States Constitutional Law.

Constitutional Bases

Most of the individual rights enjoyed in this country derive from the Constitution of the United States, and are largely located in the first ten amendments of the Constitution, the Bill of Rights, and in some subsequent amendments, notably the Fourteenth Amendment. Those amendments of especial relevance to the operation of the schools are:

> *Amendment One* deals with freedom of religion and expression and rights to peaceful assembly and petition. It grants the rights of all citizens to peacefully assemble and to petition the government for redress of grievances. Amendment One has often been cited in civil rights cases involving students.

> *Amendment Four* focuses on the rights of persons and states that the people and property shall be protected against "unreasonable searches and seizures," meaning that appropriate warrants must precede such police action. The educational implications here affect the confidentiality of records, interrogation of pupils, and the proceedings of juvenile court.

> *Amendment Five* guarantees the due process of law. It says that certain rights to life, liberty, and property are inviolate and people cannot be deprived of them without due process of law.

Amendment Six provides for judicial procedure and guarantees a speedy public trial, an impartial jury, information about the nature of the charge, confrontation by witnesses against the party, the right of the accused to obtain witnesses in his or her own behalf, and the right to have counsel.

Amendment Eight prohibits cruel and unusual punishment and excessive bail. The educational implications are clear, especially with regard to the question of corporal punishment, although undue mental anguish has also been cited as a "cruel and unusual" punishment.

Amendment Nine guarantees the "rights of the people" and states that the enumeration in the Constitution of certain rights shall not be construed to deny or discourage other rights retained by the people. This simply means that even if the Constitution is explicitly silent, it does not mean that other rights are not enjoyed.

Amendment Ten indicates that the powers that are not delegated to the United States by the Constitution nor prohibited by it to the states are reserved to the states respectively or to the people.

Later, the Fourteenth Amendment extended federal rights to the citizens of the states:

All persons born or naturalized in the United States . . . are citizens of the United States and of the State wherein they reside. No State shall make or enforce any law which shall abridge the privileges or immunities of citizens of the United States; nor shall any State deprive any person of life, liberty, or property, without due process of law, nor deny to any person within its jurisdiction the equal protection of the laws. . . .

Is this of relevance to the school administrator? Much in the way of civil rights legislation, including school desegregation, has occurred as a result of the Fourteenth Amendment.

This amendment has also been used to restrict the authority of school boards in other ways. At times the Court has engaged in admonishments that reflect very perceptive pedagogy. Consider the language of the 1943 case *West Virginia* v. *Barnett*:

The Fourteenth Amendment . . . is now applied to the State itself and all of its creatures—boards of education not excepted. These (i.e., boards of education) have, of course, important, delicate and highly discretionary functions, but none that they may perform except within the limits of the Bill of Rights.

Further, this same court said:

That they are educating the young for citizenship is reason for scrupulous protection of the constitutional freedom of the individual *if we are not to strangle the free mind at its source and teach youth to discount important principles of our government as mere platitudes.*[2] [Emphasis supplied.]

Nevertheless, even though pupils do have rights at school, these rights must be balanced against the responsibilities of administrators and teachers to maintain order and a good learning climate. Courts have been particularly careful to ensure that school personnel are enabled to carry out effectively the mission of schooling.

The focus of this chapter is on recurring and developing legal issues that affect the productive operation of the school. Fundamental principles are presented and applied to the elementary school setting.

The reader is cautioned, however. Some rules of law are not universally accepted. Different courts often hand down conflicting decisions in seemingly similar cases—even within the same state. The opinions of attorneys general will vary over the years at both federal and state levels and between states. At the federal level, a change in the party controlling the executive branch will often affect the vigor with which an attorney general or Justice Department enforces law. Legislative acts at both state and federal levels vary from term to term as this or that current concern becomes law or is countermanded by new law, or reaches a "sunset" provision. Also, the interpretation and the application of laws sometimes change over the years.

It is important for the principal to keep continually abreast of new developments on the legal front. This chapter will help, but laws are constantly evolving. Subscribing to a legal update service provided by many of the professional associations, as well as attention to the day-to-day occurrences in one's community and state is good advice to any educator.

This chapter begins with an examination of the legal environment in the United States as that influences schooling. Subsequent sections focus on the legal rights of staff and students and the responsibilities of administrators. Attention is directed to issues of educational equity, due process, and tort liability.

Legal Bases for the Schools

Even though historically the schools are creatures of the states, in practice the support and control of schools has been a partnership between local, state, and federal governments. Even private and parochial schools and school systems do not exist as autonomous entities because these too must meet certain state curricular, and teacher certification standards. Also, certain federal regulations impinge when these schools accept available federal funds.

The legal framework within which school systems operate is manifest in the acts passed by federal, state, and local legislative bodies, court decisions, constitutional law, and rules and regulations enacted by regulatory and administrative bodies such as the state departments of education or health departments. A further source of legal guidelines are general opinions of various attorneys general that stand until tested in a court of law or modified by subsequent legislative acts. Within this legal framework local administrators have latitude in the development of policies, rules, regulations, and procedures. The authority for local school board and administrative action is depicted in Figure 3–1. One extralegal impingement exists: community sanctions, attitudes, and belief structures that modify, often very directly, the development and implementation of local policies.

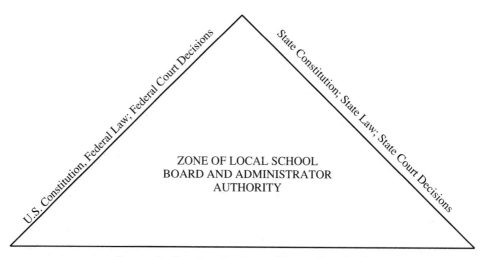

FIGURE 3–1. Circumscribed Local Authority for School Operation

Source: Adapted from Larry W. Hughes and Robert J. Simpson, *Education and the Law in Tennessee* (Cincinnati, Ohio: W. H. Anderson Co., 1971), p. 5.

Limitations on local authority depend also on prevailing court philosophy in any state. In some states, the prevailing philosophy is that boards of education may adopt any reasonable policy not specifically prohibited by statute. In other states courts insist that there be specific statutory permission before a particular policy can be adopted. Generally speaking, courts have tended to uphold the rule of reason—that boards of education may adopt any reasonable policy within the law. Courts in all states do insist on strict adherence to laws concerning management of public funds, however. School boards and administrators must find clear statutory authority for the expenditure of funds derived from public revenues.

It is at the school building level that the policies of the school board and the laws governing education are most often implemented. It is also at the school building level that most of the litigation involving the school system occurs. Laws and policies injudiciously applied, or incorrectly interpreted, at this level may result in children and personnel inhumanely or illegally treated. More and more frequently the result is a lawsuit listing principals and teachers as defendants. The law insures the fairest "shake" for everyone.

People have no more rights today than they have ever had, but the according of these rights is under increasing review by the courts. Unfortunately, school administrators have sometimes trapped themselves into acting simultaneously as judge, jury, and prosecuting attorney, in many instances overstepping their authority and jurisdiction. Sometimes teachers, administrators, and other school employees have behaved *in loco deo* rather than *in loco parentis* and have placed themselves in untenable legal positions.[3]

More recently, the United States Supreme Court has raised questions about the universal application of *in loco parentis*. In *New Jersey* v. *T.L.O.*[4] the Court held that *in loco parentis* is in conflict with the Fourth Amendment when school authorities, acting as agents of the state, carry out searches and other disciplinary functions. In its judgment in this case the Court also said, "the concept of parental delegation [as a source of school authority] is not entirely consonant with compulsory education laws."

In general, the courts have made it clear that constitutional protections apply to students both in and out of school. Freedom of expression and other basic rights, if not always clearly defined in the schools, are well-established in the law. Courts require specified procedures to safeguard those rights against the abuse of institutional authority. The matter of procedural due process, which will be discussed more completely later in this chapter, guarantees certain rights by the fair application of rules and regulations. As pointed out in *Tinker* v. *Des Moines School District*, "Students do not surrender their rights at the school house door."[5]

There is balance, however. *Tinker*, for example, would not allow a pupil to carry out First Amendment rights to the detriment of the schooling function. Another example of the concept of "balance of rights" would be in the just previously cited *T.L.O.* case where the Supreme Court balanced the need to search students against the degree of invasion of privacy that such a search requires.

Issues of Equity

There has been increasing attention placed on the need to assure that all persons have equal access to the fruits of education irrespective of their sex, race, ethnicity, or any handicapping condition. A host of laws, often federally generated, have been promulgated and much litigation has occurred in an effort to ensure equity. Of special relevance to the elementary school principal are the laws, court decisions, and educational guidelines with respect to sex discrimination, racial desegregation, and the provision of the least restrictive educational environment for handicapped children.

Moreover, as principals and their staffs assume more direct control over personnel selection and assignment—a product of the site-based management movement—much attention must be given to issues of equity with regard to who it is that is selected and how that person will be accommodated in the workplace. There is an extensive body of law that applies to the latter two issues and the local school staff needs to be aware of this body of law. This section describes the legal framework surrounding both equity in student programming and for staffing.

Sex Discrimination

In both academic matters and cocurricular matters, the issue of sex discrimination has arisen. Although the issue of sex discrimination in academic matters has not been a specific problem at the elementary school level, it is something about which elementary principals need be aware. More frequently in recent years, issues of sex discrimination have been located in the cocurricular realm.

In the matter of academic assignments, sex discrimination has been found to occur most often in class assignment and admission to programs or schools. Gender has been determined to be an illegal criterion for assignment and admission. It has been held also, for example, to be a violation of the equal protection clause of the Fourteenth Amendment to use higher admission standards for females than for males for admission to an academic school. The circuit court, in *Berkleman* v. *San Francisco Unified School District*[6] said that merit is the only sound basis for admission, not such "unsupported" needs suggested by the school district officials' position that "an equal number of male and female students is an essential element in a good high school education."[7]

Nevertheless, the "separate but equal" concept with regard to schools for boys and girls is still viable where a school district (or any educational unit) can show that genuinely equal educational opportunities are provided students in these schools, when these schools are compared to all other schools or units in the system.[8] The burden of proof is, however, on the school system.

In some schools, too, females have been excluded from certain specialized vocational and prevocational courses. This practice has been challenged, and in most such cases the women were admitted to the courses before the cases came to trial. Clearly, even though there is little in the way of case law, such exclusion practices are contrary to the current thrust of the law. Unless the school administrator or the school board can show some rational basis for excluding one sex or the other from a course or program, there should be no policy that would differentiate the enrollment. It is doubtful that such a basis can be developed; few human activities are physiologically determined.

Most of the litigation focusing on sex discrimination has had to do with participation in cocurricular activities, specifically participation in athletic competition. Title IX of the 1972 Education Act amendment is a buttress against sex discrimination in the cocurricular realm. Title IX established, among other things, that participation in organized athletic programs in the public schools must be accessible irrespective of sex.

There are two situations in which claims have arisen. The first is the failure of a school district to fund and provide a team for a specific sport for its female students, and then, while not providing a team, also prohibiting females from participating on the team it does have. The issue in these cases is not whether a girl has a constitutional right to participate in a particular sport but whether the state, having provided an athletic program, can deny an opportunity for equal participation to members of one sex. The asserted protective purpose in maintaining separate teams is frequently stated this way: Girls cannot compete effectively with boys in sports because of the inherent physical differences between the sexes: thus, it is argued frequently, separate teams are reasonable and indeed even necessary. *Several courts have accepted this conclusion but have held that they could not sanction a failure to provide a separate athletic program for girls.*[9] Separate but equal athletic programs are also statutory law in section 86.41 of Title IX(B), "Administration of Athletics." Moreover, there is a provision included that states if a school district does not fund and offer separate athletic programs, it must allow members of the excluded sex to try out for the team it does have, unless the "sport involved is a contact sport."

When a school policy states safety as the rationale for forbidding co-educational teams, the school must show that there is a sufficient relationship between the announced goal of safety and a rule that would automatically exclude one sex.[10] Accordingly, girls must be given an opportunity to demonstrate that any presumption that they are more prone to injury is invalid. "They must be given the opportunity to compete with boys in interscholastic contact sports if they are physically qualified."[11]

Handicapped Children

Public schools historically have been involved in the education of handicapped young-sters, but over the last few years such activities have taken on a more precise and legally defined basis. Legislation culminating with the Education of All Handicapped Children Act of 1975 (Public Law 94-142) has mandated the provision of the "least restrictive learning environment" for handicapped children. Public Law (PL) 94-142 provides for ready access to appropriate public education for handicapped children between ages three and twenty-one and mandates the integration of these children into settings that may have been formerly limited to nonhandicapped children. The term *mainstreaming* has been applied to this practice.

PL94-142 is buttressed by other federal laws, PL 94-143 and the earlier PL 93-112, which have established certain rights to education and fair treatment for handicapped children.[12] These rights include:

- Right to free appropriate education at public expense, without regard to severity of handicap.
- Right to service in the least restrictive setting when the handicap requires service in something other than the normal school setting.
- Right to prior notice before any decision is made to change services given to a child.
- Right of parents to give consent before their child is evaluated, placed in a special program, or changed in placement.
- Right to full due process, including representation by legal counsel, right to confront and cross-examine school personnel, right to a verbatim transcript, right to appeal, and right to be heard by an impartial hearing officer (not a school employee).
- Right to assignment without discrimination on the basis of sex, race, or culture.
- Right to program placement without discrimination on the basis of sex, race, or culture, and to placement in a facility that is comparable to that offered to non-handicapped clients of the system.
- Right to be served in accordance with an individual program plan that states annual goals, measurable intermediate steps, the names of persons who will provide services and their qualifications, a timetable for beginning each step in the service and its anticipated duration, a schedule for evaluating the success of the program, and the right to be transferred if the program is failing.
- Right to be protected from harm through use of unregulated experimental approaches, untrained staff, inclusion in a program with others who are physically assaultive, freedom from unreasonable corporal punishment, and freedom from work assignments without compensation.
- Right to see all records and to contest them in a hearing, with the right to place in the record information that the client feels presents a balanced picture.

Thus, "separate but equal" as a concept appropriate to the education of handicapped children has been found to be generally unacceptable.

The passage of PL 94-142 was the culmination of many years of litigation and legislation to protect the civil rights of children who are handicapped. The legislative act insures specified substantive and procedural provisions for handicapped children as well as an escalating funding formula to insure a free and appropriate public education for all handicapped students.

Of specific importance to school principals is that the law insists on:

1. A zero reject policy
2. Specific due process procedures
3. Nondiscriminatory testing
4. A written and promulgated individual educational plan (with specific evaluation procedures about its effectiveness) for every handicapped child. This plan is to be developed jointly with parents and reviewed at least annually.
5. Provision of a least-restrictive environment

There are several ways to meet the objectives of the act, and, although they are not mutually exclusive, each requires careful planning. Among the ways to accomplish the purposes of the act are:

- Employ paraprofessionals to assist those regular teachers who have handicapped students.
- Schedule special education teachers in the regular classroom to work directly with handicapped students.
- Arrange for diagnostic-prescriptive teachers to work with regular teachers to plan instructional strategies for those handicapped children in a class. (The diagnostic-prescriptive teacher would provide no direct assistance to the student.)
- Purchase individualized sequential materials for use by regular teachers to work with handicapped students.
- Schedule handicapped students as needed, and arrange for a special-education teacher to be in the classroom for part of the school day.

The Individualized Education Plan

For each child who will be placed in a program for handicapped learners, there must be a formally developed Individualized Education Plan (IEP). The plan is developed by a team of professional educators working with the child's parents. Parents must give consent before a child can be placed in a program. The IEP must contain:

1. The child's current level of performance
2. A statement of goals and objectives
3. The nature of the educational services to be provided
4. The place(s) and time(s) the services will be provided
5. The person(s) who will be working with the child

The litmus test is whether the IEP is "reasonably calculated" to enable the child to advance from grade to grade.[13] Even removing a handicapped child to a disciplinary setting may be considered a change in placement and thus require agreement on a new plan.[14] And, if the school district cannot meet the needs of the handicapped child in the usual 180-day academic year, the Act requires that the program extend beyond the academic year.[15]

The Supreme Court has also held that schools may be required to reimburse parents for expenditures incurred as a result of placement in a private school, if it is ultimately determined that such a placement is proper and the school district proposed IEP is not proper under the act.[16]

Admission, Review, and Dismissal (ARD) Committees

Decisions regarding the educational program and placement of a student referred for special education are made by an ARD committee. This is a clinical team composed of appropriate professional educators including an administrator and the child's parent, guardian, or their representative. The ARD committee develops and revises the IEP. All decisions are by majority vote, although much effort is made to achieve consensus, if not unanimity.

The committees are usually scheduled to meet at least annually to review pupil progress but may meet more often. A parent may request an ARD meeting at any time.

The Desegregated School Environment

In 1954, the historic declaration was made that, with regard to race, separate schools were not equal schools.[17] As executive officer of the operational desegregative unit, the principal has a critical role to play in the provision of an unrestricted educational environment—and this is true whether one is discussing equity issues with regard to sex or handicap or, as in the present case, race and ethnicity. Although a principal may not have participated in the preparation of pupil assignment policies or in the development of the attendance zones, there are certain activities in which he or she should engage in order to meet the spirit and intent of the law and to manage the school effectively.

Distinguishing Between Desegregation and Integration

The terms *integration* and *desegregation* are not synonymous, although there is a certain relationship. Desegregation refers only to the deliberate physical mixing of children from different racial and ethnic groups. Integration refers to a process that results in the mutual acceptance of, and respect for, other races and ethnic groups, and includes some level of cultural assimilation. Most social scientists argue that integration cannot occur without desegregation, however.

> In *Brown* v. *Board of Education* some of the compelling arguments centered on multi-racial interaction in desegregated situations, but the Court only spoke within its jurisdiction to break down any and all governmental barriers that deprived citizens of their Fourteenth Amendment rights. Thus, the Court ordered that public schools be desegregated, that is, to proceed in the "physical mixing of races without regard to the relative status of the two groups."[18]

Thus, desegregation is the law of the land and the courts can only require that there be compliance with the law. Integration, a far more difficult process, can only result because of extralegal efforts by school and lay leaders—principals, teachers, parents, and community members.

Grouping Children

Nothing in the law prohibits grouping children by ability, but great caution is required. The courts have said:

> It goes without saying that there is no constitutional prohibition against an assignment of individual students to particular schools on a basis of intelligence, achievement, or other attributes upon a *uniformly administered program, but race must not be a factor in making the assignments.*[19] [Emphasis supplied.]

Although it may appear that wide latitude exists in grouping practice, attention is called to the italicized statement in the quotation—uniformity in administration and the absence of race as a motivation. The burden of proof for these conditions is on the school. Moreover, subsequent court cases have also served to restrict grouping or tracking of students and these too have been racially motivated. The most celebrated of these cases is *Hobson* v. *Hansen*.[20]

In *Hobson*, the plaintiffs claimed that the District of Columbia school system deprived them of equal educational opportunity because of the "tracking" system which was then a part of the district's curricular structure. The district placed students into honors, college preparatory, general, or basic classes on the basis of their performance on scholastic aptitude and standardized achievement tests. It was revealed that a disproportionate number of poor white and black children were in the lowest tracks and, significantly, once relegated to those tracks, they rarely if ever moved out of them. The court found that the system violated the equal protection clause of the Fourteenth Amendment because:

> These tests are standardized primarily on and are relevant to a white middle class group [producing] inaccurate and misleading test scores when given to lower class and Negro students.[21]

In *Larry* v. *Riles*[22] black students alleged similar discrimination and they provided statistical evidence of a disproportionate number of blacks in educable mentally retarded classes in a California district. The court said that where such an imbalance occurs, the school district must assume the burden of demonstrating that the testing procedures are rationally related to the separation of pupils on the basis of their abilities.

Regardless of the manner or the degree to which a school is desegregated, its primary mission is realized through educational programming. The focus must be on accommodating each child in a learning setting that addresses the needs of that child. If academic and social integrity are to be realized, the school program must not be influenced by predetermined attitudes about the learning, social, emotional, and physical abilities of different racial and ethnic groups.

Sensitive planning can provide an equitable learning environment. In *A Handbook for Integrated Schooling*,[23] Forehand and Ragosta establish that a well-integrated school will exhibit four features:

1. *Salience.* Successful integration is a highly salient goal for most people in effective schools, and for the most influential people in a school. Salience has both motivational and perceptual components. Motivationally, successful integration needs to be an important goal, internalized by both staff and students. It must take a high position among the myriad goals that a school must have. Perceptually, there must be a high degree of attentiveness to progress in integration and alertness to indications of success and failure.

Salience implies absence of racially prejudiced behavior. The association of lack of prejudice on the part of students is one of the most pervasive findings in our study. Absence of racial prejudice on the part of the school staff is an important goal. Even if attitude change is not achieved for every staff member, a professional attitude that minimizes prejudiced behavior can be demanded. Salience also implies intention to act positively to achieve good race relations. Such intention may be motivated by a professional attitude and dedication to duty. It need not imply any particular political or ideological position.

2. *Intercultural Sensitivity.* People in effective schools are sensitive to the cultural backgrounds of the students, to the effect of backgrounds on behavior, self-concept, and aspirations, and to the need to design and carry out educational programs responsively.

3. *Interdependence.* Many respondents in effective schools often used the term "school family." It implies shared objectives, mutual concern, and mutual sensitivity. Members of a successful school family include the administration, faculty, and students. In successful schools, family feeling is regarded as desirable and rewarding.

4. *Equity.* In successful schools, the races and individual members of races are treated equitably. The term equity implies fairness and justice. It is neither synonymous with nor antithetical to equality. A school may provide equal opportunity to participate in its activities—in the sense that the activities are open to all—yet without establishing equity. If geographic location, cultural tradition, or minority status are barriers to equal participation, the mere absence of school-imposed barriers does not constitute equity. If minority students must work harder because of a heavier burden of transportation, or need to overcome negative expectations, or informal discrimination, the effect is inequity. The establishment of equity in a school requires positive action. Passively administered policies of equality are not enough.[24]

Other Programs That Provide Educational Equity

There are a number of federally funded programs designed to help provide educational equity for special groups. For example, funds to provide remedial education programs for the children of migrant workers are available through the Education Consolidation and Improvement Act of 1981. Under this program, as well, children of migrant farm workers are entitled to have the opportunity to make up work and earn credits for the fall semester.[25]

Otherwise educationally disadvantaged children may be helped by projects using funds from the Education Consolidation Act (ECA), Chapter I. The funds acquired for such projects must be used as a supplement to state and local expenditures for the program.

Employment Issues

School administrators have the responsibility to employ fair employment practices and provide equal opportunity for job aspirants. Increasingly, in these days of greater authority for employment decisions to be made at the school site level, there is a need for the principal and the school staff to be aware of the federal and state laws and court decisions that regulate decision-making about personnel selection and termination.

At the federal level the Equal Employment Opportunity Commission (E.E.O.C.) is specifically charged with the enforcement of Title VII of the Civil Rights Act of 1964 (race, color, religion, sex, and national origin); the Equal Pay Act of 1963; the Age Discrimination in Employment Act of 1967; the Rehabilitation Act of 1973; the Americans with Disabilities Act of 1990; and the Federal Civil Rights Act of 1991. The E.E.O.C. actively prosecutes complaints to obtain full compensation and benefits for employees who have been discriminated against in an unlawful manner.

Frels[26] points out:

> Site-based management gives the principal and others who share decision making a greater say in who joins the school as teachers or in other staff positions. The rationale for school-based staff selection is based on the premise that the principal should not be held responsible for what teachers do when the principal has little or no voice in the selection of staff. . . . [But] With the right of the principal and others at the campus level to make more staffing decisions comes greater legal risks that discrimination in hiring will occur.

Frels[27] also identifies five important steps that should be taken to lessen the legal exposure of principals in personnel matters:

1. Non-discrimination criteria for selection must be mandated.
2. Those who are involved in staff selection should receive adequate training.
3. Pools of qualified candidates can be screened centrally, with ultimate selection by the campus process.
4. The termination process should afford the necessary due process and have enough *system-wide uniformity* to guard against claims of unequal treatment individually and on a class basis. [Emphasis supplied]
5. Some centralized authority should retain oversight and control of the employment and termination process to ensure non-discriminatory treatment.

Americans with Disabilities Act

This 1990 piece of federal legislation specifically protects the rights of the physically handicapped. The law is sweeping in its protection for disabled persons in employment and in state and local government services. Organizations in both the public and private sectors come under the act, whether or not the particular entity receives any federal funds. Students and employees are covered and certain accommodations are required.

Generally speaking, the following guidelines apply to employment practices:

1. All positions are open to qualified applicants with disabilities.
2. Position openings must be posted in places that can be reached by disabled persons.

3. Applicants may not be asked if they have a disability or how it was caused. Only those questions that have to do with the ability to perform essential job functions should be asked.

4. Medical information on an employee's disabilities must be kept in separate file.

5. Employers must accommodate disabled employees unless the changes would impose an "undue hardship."

6. Readers, interpreters, and attendants should be provided unless that would be a "hardship."

7. Pre-employment testing cannot discriminate against persons with sight, hearing, or speaking limitations.

The implications of the Act to the school administration seem clear. Essential job skills will need to be even more carefully established and demonstratively related to the tasks that need to be performed before an otherwise qualified disabled person is denied employment because of a presumed inability to carry out job responsibilities. The burden for showing this will rest with the school district and the school administrator.

Rules and Regulations in the Effective Elementary School

The efficient routine operation of any complex organization requires a well-developed, well-understood, and consistent set of rules and regulations. It is axiomatic that if staff and students are to be held accountable for certain standards, these expectations must be established and promulgated *ahead of their application* in a manner that makes them easily disseminated, learned, and understood.

What is "reasonable"? A rule of thumb applied most frequently by the courts is, "Does the regulation enhance the education of the children, promote their interest and welfare, and is it for the common good of education?" Implicit is that the regulations be within the legal authority of the school district. Regulations beyond the province of the school board are not enforceable. A long-standing decision has held that "boards are not at liberty to adopt according to their humor regulations which have no relevance to the schools' purposes."[28] It follows that this would be no less true in the matter of rules and regulations prescribed by the principal.

Moreover, while it is sound management practice to develop procedures and guidelines that provide for consistency of school operation, we think the rule of parsimony should be followed. Developing long lists of do's and don'ts in an attempt to cover every contingency can create a school climate in which the name of the game becomes beating the system, a climate in which staff and students derive a perverse joy from testing the limits. Rules and regulations that attempt to define every type of situation and recourse are not necessary. In fact, the enumeration of prohibited actions may foreclose any discretion on actions not so listed. It is better to have some general guidelines and a few specific dictums to cover the hazardous situations and common management problems than to go overboard.

Establishing Good Rules

Three guidelines provide good rules and regulations:

- The principal's own common sense will provide some insights into the kinds of rules and regulations routinely needed to guide the school. The orderly development of a school program does require certain specified times when activities are to begin, when the school lunch period will be, common standards of good conduct, and teacher responsibilities. These rules and regulations should be appropriate to the age and maturity of the children under the school's charge.
- Rules and regulations developed for a particular elementary school, of course, should be consistent with the general policies of the school district.
- A faculty/student advisory committee should be constituted to help identify areas needing more specific regulations and to serve as a review board for existing rules and regulations.

Neither the extreme of rules for every occasion nor its opposite, no rules at all, is sensible. Principals within the school and teachers within the classroom have the right *and the obligation* to determine reasonable policies governing the conduct of their charges, not only to maintain a proper educational climate, but also for safety. Courts have spoken to the need for rules to keep pupils from injuring themselves and have held that the absence of such rules is grounds for negligence. The failure to enforce an already existing rule also incurs a liability. When challenged in the courts, particular rules and regulations will in all probability be upheld, provided, of course, the rule is a reasonable application of an educational function and not contrary to a higher enactment by the school board or federal and state bodies.

The principal is the person most often responsible for the promulgation and enforcement of rules and regulations. The state and district will hold the principal responsible for ensuring an orderly learning climate and principals cannot relieve themselves of this legal responsibility.

Balancing Rights and Privileges, Constitutional and Otherwise

The school's power to control students is not broad enough to proscribe protected speech. In *Tinker*,[29] three students wore black armbands to protest the Vietnam conflict and were subsequently suspended from school. The Supreme Court held that wearing armbands was protected because it was closely related to protected political speech.

Student Publications

Scholastic newspapers and the like fall within the ambit of the First Amendment prohibition on censorship. A court would require a strong showing on the part of the school in order for it to uphold any censorship. It would have to be shown that the publication of the forbidden articles would materially and substantially interfere with the requirements of discipline in the orderly operation of the school. Pupils are not free to publish without supervision, however. Administrative review of material to be published has been held to be appropriate. For example:

> Writers on school newspapers do not have an unfettered constitutional right to be free from pre-publication review. The special characteristics of the school environment . . . call for supervision and review by faculty and administration. The administrative review of a small number of sensitive articles for accuracy rather than for possible censorship or official imprimatur does not implicate First Amendment rights.[30]

The same court also held that school personnel possess a substantial educational interest in teaching student writers journalistic skills that stress the tenets of accuracy and fairness.

Instructional Material

The courts have held that although school boards (and by implication administrators) have broad discretionary authority to add books and other materials to the classroom and school library, they may not remove books in order to "prescribe what shall be orthodox in politics, nationalism, religion, or other matters of opinion."[31] The question of whether or not the removal of books is an unconstitutional abridgement of a student's First Amendment rights is decided on by an analysis of the board's intention. Books may not be removed in order to prevent access to ideas of which the board disapproves or when those ideas fall under the protection of the First Amendment. The circumstances that permit an exception to this principle are narrow. Nevertheless, it is not impermissible to remove books that are "pervasively vulgar" or educationally unsuitable.[32,33] "Pervasive vulgarity" is one of those phrases that defy definition, of course, and result in even more lawsuits. (No one ever said it was easy to be a school administrator.)

These are times of great controversy. Conservative and liberal groups alike are placing great pressure on school boards, administrators, and teachers about a wide variety of instructional materials including classroom textbooks as well as books in the library. In some communities the search for "prurient" materials has taken on a Salem-like quality.

Members of the rest of the publics, which consider themselves neither conservative nor liberal, are simply confused. Some state courts and some federal district courts are handing down frequent opinions that seem contrary to the concept of free access to ideas. On appeal, it is most likely that First Amendment rights will be upheld. It seems clear, however, that it will be very important that the principal and the professional staff be prepared to justify on educational grounds why any specific piece of instructional material appears on a required or supplemental list or on the shelves of the library.

Wise principals will work with the staff to develop criteria to determine "educational suitability." Help is available from the National Council for the Teaching of English and the American Library Association.

In *Grove* v. *Mead School District No. 354*,[34] a student and her parents argued that the use of a particular book which was a part of the English curriculum violated the First

Amendment prohibition of state establishment of religion. The court held that the factors that must be considered were whether (1) there was a heavy burden upon the individual's exercise of religion; (2) there was a compelling state interest in justifying that burden; and (3) there could be some accommodation that would not impede the school's objective. The court decided that the burden on the student's exercise of religion was minimal because she *was allowed to read an alternative book and avoid classroom discussions of the other book.*

And that's probably the way it is going to go in many other cases. Educational justification and "alternative works" may keep the pressure groups at least at legal bay. When there is no coercion and the school is pursuing a valid end of education, such an accommodation does not violate a student's rights.

Dress and Personal Appearance Codes

Students have the right to dress as they please—within limits—and students have the right to groom themselves as they please—within limits. And school districts have the right to impose those limits. But what are the limits? Modesty, presumed disruption, and safety seem to be basic criteria. All three criteria are subject to interpretation. Case and constitutional law offer guidance for policy development covering all three.

A *carefully developed* and *well-advertised* dress and personal appearance policy will save a lot of administrator headaches. "Carefully developed?" Parents, teachers and administrators should work jointly to frame the policy. Minor and Minor[35] in their book on risk management suggest the following as important dimensions of such a policy:

1. Realize that case law advocates that there is no connection between hair length and educational functions.
2. Impose restrictions on appearance that are based on safety (e.g., hair net for long hair in shop class.)
3. Prohibit acts of immodesty or violations of common decency (e.g., low-cut blouses).
4. When policies that impose restrictions on symbolic expressions are long-standing, based on preventing disruption, and not arbitrarily applied, they are permissible.

The key concern should be whether or not the learning process is disrupted by a particular mode of dress or appearance. And, it is up to the school authorities to demonstrate that is so.

"Well-advertised" simply means the policies should appear in student, teacher, and parent handbooks and that on the first day of each school year teachers should discuss the policy with their students.

The courts from state to state have been inconsistent in decisions in cases that had to do with issues of dress or grooming. As a general rule, though, courts have upheld policies prohibiting immodest or suggestive clothing, clothing that would be distracting, or clothing that would be unsafe or create a safety hazard.

Messages displayed on clothing such as tee shirts have been the source of many problems. Some schools, for example prohibit clothing that advertises alcohol and tobacco products. Rarely are these challenged.

In *Gano* v. *School District No. 411 of Tivin Falls* (1987)[36] students produced shirts that satirically portrayed school administrators as drunk and holding up several kinds of alcoholic beverages. These were prohibited by the school and the court granted no injunctive relief to plaintiffs. The court upheld the disciplinary action against the students because the message conveyed "interfered with proper administrative role models."

Where there has been school disruption because of student gang activity and where the gangs adopt a distinctive manner of dress or wear specific insignia, the courts have also upheld school rules prohibiting the use of these by students.[37]

But when a school sets standards for dress and appearance, it is important to remember the previously cited Tinker case as well as the words of warning in *Westley* v. *Rossi*:[38]

> The standards of appearance and dress of last year are not those of today nor will they be those of tomorrow. Regulations of conduct by school authorities must bear a reasonable basis to the ordinary conduct of the school curriculum or to carrying out the responsibility of the schools.

This is why we recommend the involvement of parents and teachers in the establishment of codes. Such involvement could quite easily occur as an activity of community advisory councils. Strahan has written: "Basic conflict often develops from policy that has become anachronistic because of a change in social mores."[39] Community involvement in policy analysis and policy development can be of great assistance in keeping policies current and the school responsive to changing attitudes.

Fourth Amendment Rights of Students

Another particularly difficult legal issue falls under the Fourth Amendment. The issue is that of conducting searches of students and their property. Freedom from unreasonable searches and seizures of property is a Fourth Amendment right.

The Amendment prohibition applies to searches conducted by public school authorities. When carrying out searches and other disciplinary policies pursuant to school policies, administrators and teachers act as representatives of the state, *not merely as surrogates for parents* and therefore they cannot claim the parents' immunity from the strictures of the Fourth Amendment.

School officials may search student lockers without a search warrant because the lockers are the exclusive property of the school. Law officers may *not* search student lockers without a search warrant, nor should school officials themselves conduct searches at the request of law officers.

Administrators and teachers may search students, or their possessions, when it is "reasonable" to do so, but the courts have not given many specific examples of what is reasonable. Whether or not a search is reasonable depends on the factual context of the search. The search of a child's person or property is a violation of the expectation of privacy of the student; however, this expectation of privacy must be balanced against the interest of teachers and administrators in maintaining discipline and security.

The test of legality is the answer to the question: Was the search reasonable under *all* of the circumstances of the search? Specifically, (1) was the search justified at its inception, and (2) was the search related in scope to the circumstances that justified the interference in the first place?

Under ordinary circumstances a search by a school official will be justified at its inception when there are reasonable grounds for suspecting that the search will show that the student has violated, or is violating, the law or the rules of the school. The severity of the violation is a factor, however. Students should not be searched for minor violation.

Due Process

The general issue addressed by due process considerations is that of the constitutional rights of personnel and students balanced against the duty of the school board to control and protect the school system and protect the rights of students to obtain an education. There are two kinds of due process: substantive and procedural.

Substantive Due Process

Substantive due process is concerned with the basic legality of a legislative enactment. School policies, rules, and regulations must stand the test of substantive due process. A person punished or denied the right to behave in some way by an existing law, rule, or regulation when that law, rule, or regulation is itself contrary to certain constitutional guarantees has legal recourse to set aside the punishment or denial and make the rule invalid. Moreover, substantive due process requires that there must be sufficient evidence or documentation of violation to warrant action by school officials or sufficient reason to believe that, if the rule is not invoked, current or subsequent acts by the parties involved will result in disruption of the educational process. The burden of proof rests with the school officials, not the transgressor.

The *Tinker* case is often cited in reference to presumed disruption.[40] Rules are invoked because the school principal says, in effect, "If this rule is not enforced and obeyed, the process of education in the school will be impeded." In the *Tinker* case, students were suspended for wearing black armbands to school in mourning for American military personnel who had died in Vietnam, as well as to protest continued American involvement in that country. The school promulgated a rule prohibiting this subsequent to which some students continued to wear the armbands in open defiance. Two important legal principles of a substantive nature were applied by the Supreme Court in holding for the students: (1) there was no disruption, so therefore the presumption of the rule was false and students had the constitutional right to defy the rule; and (2) the wearing of the armbands was analogous to free speech (a First Amendment guarantee), and the students had the right to express themselves.

The two rules of thumb that must be applied are: (1) will the behavior cause substantial disorder to the education process or normal operation of the school? (2) will the behavior be an invasion of the rights of others? If the school principal believes the answer is yes, it must be remembered that the burden of proof rests on the principal. Courts are critical of administrator action predicated on presumption. The collection of sufficient evidence to show reason for administrative action is essential.

Guidelines to Ensure Substantive Due Process

School policies, rules, and regulations, and the administrative actions enforcing these should be subjected to the following guidelines:

- *Legality*. Is there a basis in state and federal constitutional and legislative law for the policy, rule, or regulation? Are the constitutional rights of those for whom it was written protected?
- *Sufficient Specificity*. Are the conditions under which the policy, rule, or regulation will be invoked detailed? Are the terms and phraseology used definitive? Vague and unclear statements are sufficient to cause the courts to abrogate.
- *Reason and Sensibleness*. Does the rule or regulation really enhance the educational climate; that is, is it really necessary? Is there sufficient reason to believe that without the rule, the rights of others will be unprotected or the school will be disrupted? A rule may be declared unreasonable in and of itself or in its particular application.
- *Adequate Dissemination*. Has information about the rule been distributed in such a way that persons affected can be expected to know about it, what it means, and what the penalties are?
- *Appropriate Penalties*. Are the punishments appropriate to the nature of the infraction? Severe penalties for minor transgressions must be avoided.[41]

Procedural Due Process

Procedural due process is an orderly established process for arriving at an impartial and just settlement of a conflict between parties.[42] It has the elements of fair warning and fair hearing.

Fair Warning

Fair warning simply means that a person must be made cognizant of the rules to follow or behavior that must be exhibited and the potential penalties for violation. The age of the person and the length of experience must be taken into consideration as well. Moreover, there must be a correlation between the penalty and the rule that has been broken.

Fair Hearing

A fair hearing is composed of the following specific aspects:

1. *The individual must be given a written statement of the charges and the nature of evidence.* This is often called "A Bill of Particulars." Clarity is very important. The accused, and in the instance of pupils, the accused's parents, must comprehend the contents of the written statement. The background and educational level of the individuals involved and the complexity of the statement should be taken into account. A personally delivered statement to the parent would provide an opportunity for clarifying charges and might be appropriate at times. The precise nature of the charges and the evidence must be incorporated in the statement. Vague rules and imprecise charges have resulted in the reversal of more school board and administrative decisions than any other defect.[43]

2. *The individual must be informed of his or her procedural rights.* Having rights but being kept unaware of them is the same as not having rights. Individuals must be provided information specifying the appeal and defense processes available. Information such as to whom the appeal should be made, the time limit under which the appeal can be advanced, and other elements of procedural due process is necessary.

3. *Adequate time must be provided to prepare a defense.* In serious issues ordinarily a minimum of five days should be provided for an individual to prepare a defense; ten days almost certainly will sustain a court inquiry.[44]

4. *The opportunity for formal hearing must be accorded.*[45] There are five components in the proper conduct of a formal hearing:

a. The case must be presented to an impartial hearer. The school official bringing the charge may not also serve as hearer. The same person may not serve at once as judge, jury, and prosecuting attorney.
b. The individual must have the opportunity to present evidence.
c. The individual has the right to know and confront whoever brought the charges and to question that person or those persons.
d. The individual has the right to produce witnesses and to cross-examine witnesses. The individual must have the opportunity to disprove the accusations of a hostile witness and include testimony of those who can explain the defendant's side of the issue.
e. The individual has the right to counsel. This does not necessarily mean an attorney. It may be simply a friend, parent, or citizen on whose advice the defendant wishes to rely. It would be a foolish board of education or administrator, however, who would try to prohibit an individual from having an attorney present even though at this writing there has been no court decision mandating legal counsel at hearings such as these.

Common Tort Liability Settings

A tort is defined as *an act or an omitted act*, including breach of contract, that results in damage, injury, or loss to the injured person(s), who then may seek relief by legal action. Torts may be intentional, may result from negligence, or be caused by careless acts. School employees are liable for their individual acts of negligence[46] and for their failure to carry out prescribed duties, or the failure to carry out these duties correctly. School employees are expected to behave in a reasonable manner in the discharge of their duties, avoiding acts that are capricious, arbitrary, or negligent.

Familiarization with the elements of tort liability is a must for all school employees. Tort liability suits usually demand adequate evidence of the following:

- A prescribed or implicit duty on the part of the defendant for the care of the plaintiff,
- An error of commission or omission by the defendant,
- Damage, loss, or injury sustained by the plaintiff,

- Indication of a cause-and-effect relationship between the error and the circumstance at issue,
- Absence of contributory negligence on the part of the plaintiff.[47]

The principal who devotes some inservice training time with staff to legal aspects of the school operation will be performing an important service. The best defense against lawsuits is proper precaution. Principals and teachers cannot be expected to be prescient, but they should anticipate possible dangers. The discussion that follows will examine common liability settings and describe certain aspects of the legal environment.

Hazardous Settings

A school is not usually a hazardous place, but children frequently do sustain injuries in and about the school. Most of these injuries are accidental and minor, the result of normal behavior. Nevertheless, teachers and administrators do have a responsibility to provide reasonable and prudent protection for their charges and they are legally liable in tort for injuries arising from their negligence.[48] The main test of negligence is "foreseeability." That is, the behavior of an individual would be called negligent if an ordinarily prudent person would have foreseen that certain actions, or a failure to act, would lead to injury to another.

The principal is responsible for taking all steps to promote the well-being of the children within the school and to guard the welfare of the staff. Therefore, to both staff and students, the principal has a particular duty to plan and supervise to minimize the possibility of injury. At the very least, this involves supplying information to staff members about their legal responsibilities and cooperatively developing a set of rules and regulations that, if carefully followed, would result in protection for students and the elimination of negligent behavior. Pupil injuries are most likely to occur in certain settings, discussed below.

Physical Education and Extracurricular Programs

Field trips, other extracurricular programs, as well as the physical education curriculum itself, are inherently more hazardous than the regular academic program. They require greater supervision to avoid liability as a result of negligence, and carefully developed and well-understood written rules and regulations for their governance are important.

Adequate regulations should cover such categories as pupil conduct while a participant or spectator, medical examination for participants, medical care for sick and injured participants, transportation to and from the activity, duties of teachers and other supervisors, notification and approval in advance by parent or guardian.[49] Figures 3-2 and 3-3 depict teacher field trip request and parent permission forms.

The Classroom

Teachers are normally in charge in the classroom and thus are most frequently held responsible for the safety of the children there. However, the principal has some responsibilities that, if not met, may result in a charge of negligent behavior. The primary responsibility of the principal with regard to classroom activities is to ensure that there is

OFF-CAMPUS TRIP REQUEST

Please fill out this form and send it and its duplicates to the Director of Instruction one week prior to the date of the trip. Upon approval of the trip, the white copy will be returned to the principal to be filed, the yellow copy will be given to the supervisor, and the pink copy will be kept by the principal.

Date Submitted _____ School _____

Grade, Subject, or Organization _____

No. of students making the trip _____ Date of trip_____

Method of transportation _____ When bonded carriers are

used, give the per pupil cost _____ How will these costs be

defrayed?_____ Time of departure_____ of return _____

Destination _____

Purpose of trip (state the relationship to current study) _____

_____

What are your plans to follow up and evaluate the trip? _____

_____

Will parent permission slips be filed with the principal prior to the trip?_____

List staff members and other adults who will make the trip. _____

_____

_____

Requested by:

_____
    Teacher

_____
    Teacher

Approved:

_____
    Principal

FIGURE 3–2.

a teacher or a responsible adult present at all times. Therefore, the principal should always be aware of a teacher's absence from the classroom. Failure to have a plan to provide for pupil supervision when a teacher becomes ill or is tardy to class could cause the principal to be charged with negligence if an injury resulted while the children were unsupervised. For example, a common practice is to have a check-in sheet for teachers in the morning so that the principal can know immediately of any unanticipated absence or tardiness of personnel who have responsibility for the supervision of children.

HUGHES MIDDLE SCHOOL

Parent Permission Slip

Date _____

Dear Parents:
In order for your child to be allowed to go on an off-campus trip, we must have the following agreement signed by a parent/guardian giving permission.

Sincerely,

_____
James Cain, Principal

Please allow _____ to go with his or her group to _____
on the date set for the trip. By signing this statement I give my full permission for my child to go on this off-campus trip.

_____   _____
Date   Parent/Guardian

FIGURE 3–3.

Generally speaking, however, the temporary short-term absence from the classroom by a teacher would not, in and of itself, be considered a negligent act of general supervision. If, for example, a child misbehaves and in so doing injures another child during a teacher's brief absence from the room, a court would not ordinarily find negligence, because the teacher's absence was not the proximate cause of the accident. However, in all cases, the age, maturity, and intelligence of the student will bear on the question of teacher negligence in such absences. The best rule is not to leave children unattended.

Laboratories and Shops
These two instructional areas present more hazards than any other in the school. Elementary school general science classes more and more frequently engage in experiments within the classroom, often involving chemicals as well as common electric- or gas-powered laboratory equipment. Moreover, good educational practice in teaching science involves such outside classroom events as off-campus field trips and on-campus land laboratory activities.

Similarly, greater emphasis on career education and career exploration means that more elementary schools are developing prevocational shops with at least rudimentary power equipment as well as common hand tools. In addition, classes in home arts such as cooking and sewing continue in popularity and require power- and hand-operated equipment.

Constant and immediate supervision is expected of teachers functioning in these activities. Teachers must adequately instruct children in the care and use of equipment they will be operating. If there is evidence that a child has been permitted to use a particular tool, or perform an experiment, before being trained and told the consequences of improper usage, negligence will be difficult to disprove. Greater care is expected of teachers supervising children who are exposed to dangerous equipment. Teacher absence from a room where a class is engaged in hazardous activities, no matter how temporary, is very risky.

Playgrounds

Where supervision is regular, planned, reasonable, and proper, a negligence charge in case of pupil injury on the playground is less likely. Considerations in determining the suitability of playground supervision include the kind of playground equipment in use, the size of the playground, and the number and age of the pupils to be supervised.

The courts generally appreciate the fact that a teacher is unable to keep every child within view and out of hazard at all times. Nor do they expect the teacher to be prescient. Nevertheless, negligent supervision is often held to be the proximate cause of injury. If, for example, a teacher permits a child to leave a supervised group and the child is injured in a known existing hazardous condition, then the teacher may be liable. If a teacher assigned to playground duty leaves a post for no good cause and a child is injured in a known or foreseeable dangerous condition, there may be tort liability because of negligence. Also, while teachers would not be expected to repair playground equipment, permitting pupils to use equipment known to be faulty, or beyond the maturity level of the child, could result in negligence.

The principal must organize and administer playground use and has responsibility for three major aspects. First, proper rules of behavior, consistent with good safety practices, must be developed and implemented. Second, the management system should always provide adequate adult supervision on the playground when children are present. Third, the principal must provide for frequent and regular inspection of the playground and playground equipment, reporting any hazardous conditions, apprising staff and students of these, and take action to have the condition corrected.

Regulating Pupil Conduct

In even the best-run schools students misbehave. There is agreement that principals and teachers may prescribe reasonable controls against the misconduct of children and many kinds of disciplinary action are available to school administrators and teachers when pupils violate school policies and rules. These include such minor punishments as short-term removal from the classroom, withholding certain privileges, detention after school, isolation from the rest of the class, being sent to the principal's office, and so on. The courts have generally upheld the right of school administrators and teachers to impose such minor punishment. Other forms of disciplinary action, however, such as suspension[50] and expulsion from school, or the use of corporal punishment are more often tested in the courts, and school administrators and teachers must take great care in the prescription of these punishments. Figure 3-4 depicts a basic information form about disciplinary action.

In any case, the question of both substantive and procedural due process is extremely important.[51] The reasonableness and legality of the rule or regulation violated must be examined with care, and the legal issue of whether or not the student has a right to a prior hearing is important.

Clearly, administrators should take care in imposing minor as well as major punishments to ensure that pupils or personnel are treated fairly and not victimized by capricious or arbitrary action.

Corporal Punishment

Corporal punishment is defined as disciplinary action by the application of physical force. As a means of modifying behavior, it is probably the oldest disciplinary tool. It also may be one of the most inefficacious. More recently, acts of corporal punishment are probably the cause of more court cases than anything else.[52] However, under the legal concept *in loco parentis,* the courts continue to uphold the right of teachers and principals to use "reasonable" force to ensure proper conduct, or to correct improper conduct.[53]

REPORT ON DISCIPLINARY ACTION
HUGHES MIDDLE SCHOOL

DATE _____

STUDENT'S NAME _____ HOMEROOM _____ GRADE _____

TIME _____   SEX _____

PERSON REPORTING _____

TITLE OF PERSON REPORTING _____

NATURE OF OFFENSE:

STUDENT'S ACCOUNT:

ACTION TAKEN:

I have had a chance to tell my side _____
(student signature)

DATE OF HEARING _____ PERSON CONDUCTING HEARING _____

TIME _____ OTHER PERSON(S) PRESENT _____

INFRACTION: STATE LAW _____ SCHOOL POLICY _____

BOARD OF EDUCATION POLICY _____

CENTRAL OFFICE POLICY _____

TEACHER RULE _____ COMMON SENSE _____

FIGURE 3–4.

Important guidelines, however, must be followed if the use of corporal punishment is to be adjudicated as prudent and reasonable. Corporal punishment is generally held to be prudent providing:

- The state law and the local policy permit it.
- The punishment takes into consideration the age, size, sex, and health of the pupil and is not excessive.
- There is no malice; the punishment is given for corrective purposes only and is not immoderate.
- The pupil understands why punishment is required.
- An appropriate instrument is used.

Sometimes courts consider other attendant circumstances such as whether there was permanent injury suffered as a result of the punishment.

To avoid legal suit and to ensure the fairest treatment possible for the student, is is important for the principal and the teacher to establish reasonable rules and to make sure that the punishment for breaking these rules is suitable. It is also important to administer the rules reasonably and apply them equally to all students. It is possible to administer a reasonable rule so improperly that it becomes unreasonable. Any vindictiveness or viciousness in administering corporal punishment must be avoided. If the teacher or the principal knows that he or she is uncontrollably angry, then it is not the time to punish the child corporally, or any other way for that matter. In all cases, the purpose of punishment is for the child's benefit, not for the vindication of the school's posture.

Suspension/Expulsion

Suspension from school has been defined as a dismissal, most often by the principal, from the school for a specific, but relatively short, length of time. Expulsion means permanent or long-term dismissal from school and in most states can only be accomplished by the board of education, permanent exclusion usually being outside the authority of any school administrator. Attendance at a public school is generally viewed as a right rather than a privilege, but the enjoyment of this right is conditioned by the student's willingness to comply with reasonable regulations and requirements of the school. Violations of these may be punished by suspension or in extreme cases by permanent exclusion. Under a suspension a pupil is usually required to meet some set of conditions established by the administrator before being readmitted.

The dividing line between a short- and a long-term exclusion from school is not clearly defined, but as a result of *Goss* v. *Lopez* has probably been established as ten days.[54] Longer exclusions, irrespective of what they are called, will require greater attention to all the vestments of due process because they clearly bear more heavily on a student's right to an education.

In *Goss*, the court clearly established the right of school administrators to suspend students to maintain order in the school system. However, the court did find that school officials had violated the students' constitutional right to procedural due process. In this instance, nine students were temporarily suspended from school *without a hearing*, and thus were held to be denied due process. The school board had contended that due process was not applicable to suspensions because there was not a "constitutional right" to public education. The court disagreed with this:

> Although Ohio may not be constitutionally obligated to establish and maintain the public school system, it has nevertheless done so and has required its children to attend. Those young people do not "shed their constitutional rights at the school house door. . . ." The authority possessed by the State to prescribe and enforce standards of conduct in its schools, although concededly very broad, must be exercised consistently with the constitutional safeguards.[55]

Second, the school board argued that even if public education was a right that was protected by due process, in this instance the due process clause should not apply because the suspensions were limited to ten days and this was not a severe nor grievous infringement on the students' right to an education. The court disagreed here also and faced the question of what kind of process is due in the instance of short-term student suspensions. The court held that only rudimentary process was required to balance student interests against the educator's need to take quick disciplinary action. The court said:

> [T]he student [must] be given a written notice of the charges against him, if he denies them, an explanation of the evidence the authorities have and an opportunity to present his side of the story. . . . There need be no delay between the time "notice" is given and the time of the hearing. In the great majority of cases the disciplinarian may informally discuss the alleged misconduct with the student minutes after it has occurred. We hold only that, in being given an opportunity to explain his version of the facts at this discussion, the student first be told what he is accused of doing and what the basis of the accusation is.[56]

This is important because it implies that while due process provisions must always be present, even in less than major punishment, the nature of the punishment and the infraction will determine the degree to which one must engage in elaborate vestments of due process. In minor infractions it would be necessary only to provide rudimentary forms of hearing. Even here, however, the important lesson is that the child to be punished must in all instances be treated fairly and that there must be clear indication of the absence of capricious action. Expulsions are a different matter. In the case of an expulsion it would seem clear that all of the vestments of due process need to be applied.

Opposition to the use of suspensions and expulsions as punishment for misconduct is growing. The authors like the following statement detailing four counterproductive effects of the exclusion of children from school:

> While precise measurement of the psychological and educational harm done by suspension is impossible, it is clear that any exclusion from school interrupts the child's educational process. . . . It is not clear what good such punishment does. In fact, it may work against the child's improvement in at least four ways. First, it forbids the

child from participating in academic work. If children with discipline problems are also weak in their studies, their missed classes, assignments and exams may doom them to fail completely. Second, suspensions merely remove troubling children. They do not set in motion diagnostic or supportive services that might uncover and remediate causes of a child's misbehavior. Thus, suspensions deny help to children. Third, suspension is a powerful label that not only stigmatizes a child while in school (or out of it), but follows the child beyond school to later academic or employments pursuits and fourth, suspensions are highly correlated with juvenile delinquency. Putting children out of school, leaving them idle with no supervision, especially when they are demonstrating they have problems, leaves children alone to cope with their future.[57]

Many schools have developed in-school suspension as a means of avoiding the negative effects cited above. In-school suspension usually involves taking the student out of the regular classroom for a period of time, and placing the student in another learning situation within the school building, either in an independent learning situation with supervision or in a designated special class. When this procedure is coupled with counseling by the principal, the guidance counselor, or some other clinician to diagnose and treat the problem, it is a sound practice.

Detention
Principals and teachers do have the authority to detain students temporarily from participating in extracurricular activities and even to keep children after school as a punishment, providing, of course, that the student has a way of getting home. As in other punishments, the detention must be reasonable. False imprisonment may be claimed if the principal or a teacher either wrongfully detains a student or detains a student for an unreasonable amount of time as a punishment.

In this, as in all other punishments, the main test is one of fairness. If school officials act fairly and in good faith in dealing with students, their actions will probably be upheld by the courts.

Privacy and the Confidentiality of Student Records

The question of the confidentiality and accuracy of student records is important and since the passage Public Law 93-380, The Family Educational Rights and Privacy Act (FERPA), the issue has been legally clarified.[58] This act states that students and parents are permitted to inspect and review records and must be given a copy of any part or all of the educational record on request. Further, it requires that in any dispute concerning the contents of a student's educational record, due process must be provided. Where a record is found to be inaccurate, the inaccuracies must be expunged.

In essence, to protect the privacy of individuals, the act requires that the schools and other agencies permit an individual to: determine what relevant records are maintained in the system of records; gain access to relevant records in such a system of records and to have copies made; and to correct or amend any relevant record.

Further, the records about an individual may not be disclosed to outsiders except by the consent of the individual in question. The consent must be in writing and must be specific in stating to whom the record may be disclosed, which records may be disclosed, and, where applicable, the timeframe during which the records may be disclosed.

In some instances disclosures may be made without the consent of the pupil or the pupil's parents. Information may be disclosed within the school to teachers or guidance counselors who have a need to know, where there is a court order, where there is required disclosure under the Freedom of Information Act, and for routine usage such as the publication of names of students who made an honor roll or information for a directory such as class lists or sports brochures, which might include such information as the student's name, address, sex, or birthplace. Even in this latter instance, however, it would be best to get prior permission through some sort of routine process.

Guidelines to assist principals to develop defensible policies about student records include:

- There should be explicit procedures to ensure that all parents and pupils know what kinds of information are contained in the school records at any given time and are informed of their rights concerning information collection, recording, and dissemination. Principals should be diligent in their efforts to provide parents this information.
- Parents and mature pupils should be encouraged to inspect their records. The rights of parents to do this are well established but many are unaware of these rights. Increased communication and trust might be the result. Another important result might be a more accurate record.
- Systematic procedures should be in place to obtain explicit and informed parent or pupil consent before information is released to outsiders. This should be so regardless of the reasons for such release or the nature of the third party. Even the release of such information as honor roll students or other such apparently innocuous or honorific announcements would best be released only after a blanket announcement to the home that this is school practice, but any individual name will be withheld if there is a written objection.

Child Abuse

It is an ugly subject, but some of the children who arrive at school may have been both physically and emotionally abused. The former is more easily recognized than the latter but either requires the immediate attention of principals and teachers. Neglect is also a form of child abuse. Abuse is both a moral and legal issue, of course, but here we will discuss only the legal ramifications. Those ramifications are easy to understand.

If child abuse is suspected it *must* be reported. To not do so may subject any school official to prosecution. Report to whom? To the Child Protective Services or whatever label this public agency may be identified by—all states have departments that are charged with social and rehabilitation services.[59] Teachers need to be advised to report at once any indications of abuse to the principal. And follow-up should be automatic.[60]

Summary

Knowledge about the laws and policies governing schooling is important so that orderly, productive, and humane learning environments obtain. Principals should not be expected to have law degrees, but common sense and fundamental moral principles suggest that a good working knowledge of the legal framework within which institutions in this society must operate is essential to school effectiveness.

The increasing complexity of school programming, the extended and extensive responsibility for the care and learning of children, and the many and varied aspects of the growth, development, and protection of "everyman's child" has many legal implications for school personnel. Too, schools and school personnel have been greatly affected by a seemingly exponential expansion of lawsuits and threats of lawsuits charging non-, mis-, and malfeasance. It is a litigious society in which we live.

The implications of constitutional law, case law, and legislative enactments that guarantee the rights and demarcate the responsibilities of students, teachers, administrators—indeed all who work or are affected by schools and schooling—have been the subject of this chapter.

Endnotes

1. John Seldon (1584-1654), *Table Talk: Law.* Seldon was an English jurist and was active in the assertion of Parliament's rights against the Crown. He is best known in the U.S. for his 1689 published *Table Talk*, a record of his conversations made by his secretary.

2. *West Virginia* v. *Barnett*, 319 U.S. 624 (1943).

3. *In loco parentis* is a common-law legal principle about the rights and duties of school authorities with regard to students. It holds that school authorities stand in place of the parent when the child is at school. Basic is that school authorities may establish rules and require obedience for the general welfare of students. Moreover, the principle establishes that punishment may be inflicted if the rules are disobeyed. The legal test is whether or not a reasonably prudent parent would so act.

It is a presumption of the law that those having authority under *in loco parentis* will exercise that authority properly. In claims of improper application, the burden of proof falls on the person making the claim. This, for example, a parent objecting to a rule or to a punishment usually must prove "unreasonableness."

4. *New Jersey* v. *T.L.O.*, 53 U.S.L.W. 4083 (January, 1985).

5. *Tinker* v. *Des Moines Independent Community School District*, 393 U.S. 503; 89 S. Ct. 733 (1969).

6. 501 F. 2d. 1264 (9th Cir., 1974). See also *Bray* v. *Lee*, 337 F. Supp. 034 (D.C. Mass., 1972).

7. *Ibid.* at 1269.

8. For example, *William* v. *McNair*, 316 F. Supp. 134 (D.C.S.C., 1970 aff'd mem.), 401 U.S. 951 (1971).

9. See, for example, *Brenden* v. *Independent School District*, 342 F. Supp. 1224 (D. Minn., 1972); *Herver* v. *Meiklejon* 430 F. Supp. 164 (D. Col. 1977).

10. *Force by Force* v. *Pierce City School District*, 570, F. Supp. 1020 (W.D. Mo. 1983).

11. *Yellow Springs School District Board of Education* v. *Ohio School Athletic Association*, 433 F. Supp. 753 (S.D. Ohio 1978).

12. P.L. 94-143 is entitled "The Developmentally Disabled Assistance and Bill of Rights Act;" P.L. 93-112 is the "Rehabilitation Act" and was enacted in 1973.

13. See *Board of Education of Hendrick Hudson Central School District* v. *Rowley*, 458 U.S. 176 (1982).

14. See *Adams Central School District* v. *Deist*, 334 N.W. 2nd 775 (Neb. 1983).

15. See *Board of Education for the City of Savannah* v. *Georgia Association of Retarded Citizens*, 52 U.S.L.W. 3932 (June 26, 1984).

16. *School Committee of the Town of Burlington, Massachusetts* v. *Massachusetts Department of Education*, 53 U.S.L.W. (April 30, 1985).

17. *Brown* v. *Board of Education of Topeka, Kansas*, 347 U.S. 483 (1954).

18. Larry W. Hughes *et al.*, *Desegregating America's Schools*. New York: Longman, Inc., 1980, p. 12.

19. *Stell* v. *Savannah-Chatham County Board of Education*, 333 F. 2nd. 55 at 61-62 (1964).

20. 269 F. Supp. 401 (1967).

21. *Ibid.* at 514.

22. 343 F. Supp. 1306 (1972) aff'd 502 F. 2nd. 963 (9th Cir. 1974). See also *Georgia NAACP* v. *Georgia*, 570 F.S. 314 (S.D. Ga., 1983).

23. Garlie A. Forehand and Marjorie Ragosta, *A Handbook for Integrated Schooling*. Princeton, NJ: Educational Testing Service, 1976.

24. *Ibid.*, pp. 10-11.

25. *Zavela* v. *Contreras*, 581 F. Supp. 701 (D.C. Tex., 1984).

26. Kelly Frels, "Legal Aspects of Site-Based Management." *School Law in Review 1992*. Washington: National School Boards Association, 1992, p. 5.

27. *Ibid.*

28. *State* v. *Fond du Lac Board of Education*, 63 Wis. 234; 23 N.W. 102; 53 Am Rep 262 (1885).

29. *Tinker* v. *Des Moines Independent Community School*, 393 U.S. 503; 89 S. Ct. 733 (1969).

30. *Nicholson* v. *Board of Education, Torrance Unified School District*, 682 F. 2nd. 858 (9th Cir. 1982).

31. *Board of Education Island Trees Free Union School District No. 26* v. *Pico*, 457 U.S. 853 (1982).

32. *Ibid.* Standards of "educational suitability" are best established before book selection, however, and these are best established by subject matter authorities.

33. The reader is referred to Chapter 4, wherein we discuss a policy for the selection of potentially controversial instructional material.

34. 735 F. 2nd. 1528 (1985).

35. Jacqueline K. Minor and Vern B. Minor, *Risk Management in Schools: A Guide to Minimizing Liability*. Newbury Park, CA: Corwin Press, 1991, p. 38.

36. 674 F. Supp. 796 (D. Idaho, 1987).

37. *Hill* v. *Lewis*, 323 F. Supp. 55 (E.D. N.C. 1971). See also *Milton* v. *Young*, 465 F. 2nd 1332 (6th Cir. 1972).

38. 305 F. Supp. 714 (1969).

39. Richard D. Strahan, "Building Leadership and Legal Strategies." Chapter 11 in Larry W. Hughes, *The Principal as Leader*. Columbus: Charles E. Merrill, 1994.

40. *Tinker* v. *Des Moines Independent Community School*.

41. Procedures and punishment must be appropriate to both the offender and the offense.

42. The seriousness of transgressions may vary widely, from a minor behavior problem to a major infraction, the result of which could inflict bodily harm. The seriousness of the infraction will determine the degree to which due process procedures are formally and publically accorded. Nevertheless, even in the instance of minor infractions, the guarantees of this process should at least be mentally gone over by the teacher or administrator, if for no other reason than to be sure the right miscreant is being punished and that the punishment is fair.

43. This includes a full explanation of the evidence the school officials have about the infraction. See *Goss* v. *Lopez*, 419 U.S. 565 (1975) and *Board of Curators of University of Missouri* v. *Horowitz*, 435 U.S. 78 (1978).

44. Procedural due process does vary from state to state and often depends on the issue. The question of a timeline for various appeals varies and is specifically established in many state laws. This is especially so with personnel termination proceedings.

45. Although this process takes on some of the vestments of a court of law, it is not a court of law. It is a provision for fair and impartial treatment. If, after going through such a process, the individual still may take the case to a court of law if he or she feels that the act for which the punishment occurred was not a punishable one, or that the punishment was unreasonable. Nevertheless, providing procedural due process will be influential with courts; it avoids the charge of capricious action.

46. Negligence is usually defined as the failure to do something that any reasonably prudent person would have done in a similar situation.

47. Contributory negligence is determined by whether or not the party who was injured exercised the same degree of caution others of the same age, sex, maturation level, and experience would have exercised under the same conditions. More supervision would be expected of those in charge of young children; teachers and administrators in the elementary school have less chance of avoiding a lawsuit by claiming contributory negligence than those who are charged with the supervision of older children. Nevertheless, a pupil who disregarded or acted in direct defiance of an admonishment of a school official probably would be held guilty of contributory negligence if the result was a injury.

48. Not all injuries are actionable; some are unavoidable, the result of pure accident. Only those injuries resulting from negligence provide the injured the right to recover damages.

49. Approval in advance by a parent of guardian *does not waive* the right of the child to sue for damages in the instance that the child is injured. But an advance approval policy does serve an important purpose. It informs the parent, and the fact that such an approval was required is some evidence that care was exercised by the school.

50. *Suspension* generally is defined as dismissal from school for a specific and short period of time, usually no more than ten days and more frequently for a week or less. In most states and districts the principal has the authority to suspend a student. *Expulsion* is defined as a permanent dismissal and normally is an action that legally can be taken only by the school board. There is a question about whether or not a pupil, otherwise within the legal school age, can be permanently excluded from a public school. It has been established that for good cause a student can be permanently removed from a regular public school provided that the student is placed in an appropriate special school at public expense. Acts of suspension and expulsion involving the handicapped require especial care.

51. In the instance of suspension, one of the most favorable due process cases is *Mills* v. *Board of Education*, 348 F. Supp. 866 (1972) in which the court ordered that there must be a hearing prior to a suspension invoked for any period in excess of two days.

52. If a teacher or principal uses excessive force or causes injury, he or she may be held liable for battery. *Battery* is the actual unlawful infliction of physical violence on another person. (*Assault* is a threat to commit battery. There can be assault without battery.)

53. The Supreme Court has affirmed the right of school personnel to use corporal punishment. See *Baker* v. *Owen*, 385 F. Supp. 294 (1975) and *Ingraham* v. *Wright*, 430 U.S. 651 (1977).

54. *Goss* v. *Lopez*, 95 S. Ct. 729 (1975).

55. *Ibid.* at 736.

56. *Ibid.* at 740.

57. Children's Defense Fund. *Children Out of School in America*. Boston: The Fund, 1974, p. 135.

58. FERPA is commonly known as the Buckley Amendment.

59. See *Mattingly* v. *Casey*, 509 N.E. 2nd 1220 (Mass. App. 1987), p. 71.

60. The National Center for Prevention and Treatment of Child Abuse and Neglect, 1215 Oneida Street, Denver, Colorado 80220 is a good source for further information about how to handle suspected child abuse.

Selected Readings

Frels, Kelly, "Legal Aspects of Site-Based Management." *School Law in Review 1992.* Washington: National School Boards Association, 1992.

Minor, Jacqueline K. and Minor, Vern B., *Risk Management in Schools: A Guide to Minimizing Liability.* Newbury Park, CA: Corwin Press, 1991.

Shoop, R.J. and Dunklee, D.R., *School Law for the Intuitive Principal.* Boston: Allyn and Bacon, 1991.

Strahan, Richard D., "Building Leadership and Legal Strategies." Chapter 11 in Larry W. Hughes, *The Principal as Leader.* Columbus: Charles E. Merrill, 1994.

Strahan, Richard D. and Turner, Charles L., *The Courts and the Schools: The School Administrator and Legal Risk Management Today.* White Plains, NY: Longman, 1987.

West's Education Law Reporter. St. Paul: West Publishing Company, current and previous years. (This is a biweekly legal update service.)

Yearbook on School Law. Topeka: National Organization on Legal Problems in Education, current and previous years.

Zirkel, Perry A. and Richardson, S.N., *A Digest of Supreme Court Decisions Affecting Education.* Bloomington, IN: Phi Delta Kappa Educational Foundation, 1988.

Chapter 4

Understanding the Community

"You gotta know the territory!" [1]

Introduction

Schools do not exist apart from the community that is served. The principal's role as both communicator to the community and facilitator of various community members' and groups' involvement in schools is well established. This role assumes even greater importance as issues of site-based management and school restructuring are addressed. The school organization must be seen in the context of the surrounding environment. There are many power bases in the community, as well as a decisional infrastructure, that the principal must understand and work with if the resources of the local community are to be utilized effectively for improved schooling.

In many school communities, cultural diversity is the predominant characteristic. Even those schools and school districts where ideological unity and cultural sameness prevail are not unaffected by pluralistic cultural patterns. There is a growing awareness on the part of educators about the complexities of operating a responsive school in such an atmosphere of diversity. The implications to the elementary school principal are many.

It is the principal who will have the most direct contact with parents, and much contact with other local groups and individuals who have a vested interest in the operation of the school. And, all taxpayers, willingly or not, have a vested interest in the school.

Moreover, the elementary school is "just around the corner," closer than the fire station and much nearer than city hall or the central administrative offices of the school district. The principal's role is crucial in interpreting school policies, programmatic thrusts, financial needs, among other sometimes difficult to understand things.

The "territory" to be known shifts rapidly as neighborhoods change, as new school-attendance zones are created, as urban renewal creates a different kind of clientele or no immediate clientele at all, as schools are closed and populations combined, as ethnic and racial composition changes markedly, and as English is discovered not to be the language of a student's home.

The Community in Perspective

Ideological unity is not characteristic of very many cities and towns, and there may be distrust, disenchantment, misconception, and a general depth of concern by many in society about school effectiveness and cost. This age is characterized generally by criticism and skepticism about public agencies and their efficiency.

The concept of ideological unity needs some consideration. Ideological unity in a community context refers to a community that is inherently in tune with itself, with well-understood belief structures and mores, where the eternal verities are indeed eternal and true for all. This type of community has been described by sociologists as *sacred* in orientation. It doesn't describe very many places in this country today.[2]

What does describe much of American life today is the term *secular*. A secular community struggles with a conflict in values, with old virtues viewed as hypocritical or evidence of blind conformity. People are unified largely by civil units rather than by any kinship ties. There is a great division of labor and proliferation of organizations, each with special membership and interests. Formalized social controls are set by law and enforced by various civil agencies. Finally, secular communities have a basic anonymity to the extent that people live *in* the community without being *of* the community.

Where a community lies on the sacred-secular continuum does influence the nature of the decision process.

School districts that tend toward the sacred end of the sacred-secular continuum are likely to emphasize public consensus politics that continue to characterize rural school districts in the United States. Conflict is kept from the public by working out disagreements in private. This is the natural and functional way of managing affairs because of the shared values and commitments of those in power. And, although policies, facilities, personnel, and programs change over time, they occur in such a way as to produce relatively little occasion for conflict, that is, through death, retirement, and routine updating.

In a pure sacred school district, change of any type—for example, board membership, administrators, programs, school practices—is very slow to come barring highly unusual circumstances. Successful changes in the schools are minor indeed and/or are presented as logical extensions or variance of existing programs and practices.

Secular communities, on the other hand, are more likely to have mechanisms that permit, even encourage conflict over major educational issues. The school board is, in part, a public forum for the discussion of major policies and decisions confronting schools. Conflict is seen as inevitable and functional in the decision-making process and, thus, does not have to occur only in private.[3]

Speaking to this same point earlier, Hughes wrote:

The problem in an urbanized society such as we live in, with its evident cultural pluralism, is that various groups and individuals will reflect differing points on the sacred-secular continuum, and thus will hold different perceptions of what the institutions serving that community ought to look like. The politics of confrontation and conflict within which the school and other social institutions are caught is simply a manifestation of this.[4]

Role of the School

The mass public education system of this country is generally considered to have two primary roles: (1) to provide, effectively and efficiently, the important knowledge and skills needed to be a productive human being, and (2) to provide for a fluid social structure.

Attending to the demands of the first role produces about as much conflict as the second, although the conflict is often of a more specialized nature. Most citizens would agree that this is indeed the *raison d'être* for the public school system, but there is much controversy about the processes that should be used to achieve mastery of the important knowledge and skills. Further, responses to the question of what knowledge is most useful vary widely and cause misunderstanding and conflict.

The second role of the school, that of providing for a fluid social structure, is more honored in the breach than in the observance. It is generally accepted that the United States and Canada do not have the rigid class lines of many countries and that it is important to facilitate mobility up the social scale. Class lines in America do tend to be blurred. However, members of a minority group will point out that this has been primarily true only if one happened to be an "Anglo." Moreover, the many impinging negative variables mean that even if one had the appropriate ethnic characteristics, the American Dream—If one tries hard, one can succeed—becomes an impossibility for many members of the poverty-ridden social understructure.

The idea that the school's role is to provide for a fluid social structure therefore continues to be under fire and will continue to be so in the foreseeable future. But aggressive efforts on the part of school leaders to implement the concept with magnet schools, breakfast programs, compensatory education programs, the reorganizing of school district boundaries, multilingual instruction, among a host of policies, procedures, and processes ongoing in many schools, are met with resentment, misunderstanding, and downright hostility by many in the majority culture. Similarly, perceived or actual non-attention to inequities in school programming, organization, and instruction receive hostile reaction and frequent precipitative action by members of groups outside the mainstream.

The public school system has been viewed as an instrument of social reform for a century or more, but only in the last few decades has it overtly engaged in reform activities and these have occurred mostly as a result of outside forces such as federal and state legislation, acts of the courts, or community pressures.

Schools often are caught in a crossfire, as first one group or individual and then another attempts to make the school reflect his or her beliefs about the world. Because of the nature of the public educational enterprise, the school must derive its support from the outside world. People who influence policies in the community that affect the school reside in that outside world and inevitably seek ways to develop policies for the schools in conformity with their own desires and values.

Progress in education today depends in large part on the consent of parents and other citizens in the community as well as upon relationships that the school maintains with other community agencies and the government. In an economy of rising costs and an expanding sense of cultural pluralism and multiethnicity, the acquisition of additional support for the educational program, or at least the development of a firm understanding about the nature and role of education, assumes increasing importance. The problem, however, of securing adequate psychological as well as fiscal support for the schools goes well beyond the understanding of fiscal need alone.

Establishing community advisory councils, identifying and working with "key influentials," and developing partnerships with private and other public sector organizations will help cultivate a necessary base of support and community understanding. We return to this subject and offer guidelines in Chapter 19.

Community Influence Systems

Schools and any agency or organization, public or private, are influenced mightily by attitudes and beliefs prevalent in the community. But there is not single "public" and therefore no such thing as a public opinion. There are "publics" and there are opinions.[5]

There are opinion leaders, however, and the influence of opinion leaders is not uniformly distributed throughout any complex community. Power and influence are unequally apportioned; sometimes it depends on the issue, sometimes on the personality of a person, sometimes on the temper of the times.

In all communities, however, there is an informal system of influence that affects daily life. The nature of the system may vary from community to community but there will be a way in which community leaders will exert influence, which affects the community, on the direction of those decisions to be made. The school administrator needs to be aware of this influence system, understand how it works in his or her community, and be able to communicate with it.

> What kinds of people have the greatest influence on decisions? Are different kinds of decisions all made by the same people? From what strata of the community are the most influential people, the leaders, drawn?
>
> Do leaders tend to cohere in their policies and form a sort of ruling group, or do they tend to divide, conflict, and bargain? Is the pattern of leadership, in short, oligarchical or pluralistic?
>
> What is the relative importance of the most widely distributed political resource—the right to vote? Do leaders respond generally to the interests of a few citizens with the greatest wealth and highest status—or do they respond to the many with the largest number of votes? Are there important differences that in turn result in difference in influence?[6]

Community Power Structures

Sociologists, political scientists, and educational researchers have all examined the phenomenon of power in a community. It is not necessary here to review and synthesize this research. The bibliography at the end of this chapter contains entries to assist in an examination of the concepts and constructs of community power. It does seem important, however, to examine briefly the nature of community power structure and to discuss some contrasting views about it.

Power is distributed in unequal degrees throughout communities. Informal power often refers to the power of relatively few people at the top of their respective social and occupational hierarchies who have decision-making capabilities. These are often the people to see if one is interested in promoting some program in the community, for without their help any large-scale undertaking would be in some jeopardy.

Informal power must be distinguished from formal power. Formal power is manifested by the elected and appointed officers of a community—the mayor, city council, superintendent, board of education, for example. Often, members of the informal power structure neither seek nor serve in formal power positions, but they do influence in many ways the decisions of the formally constituted bodies.

Research supports the view that there are two kinds of informal community leaders: the generalist and the specialist. The influence of an informal leader designated as specialist depends upon a specific situation. The generalist, on the other hand, is a community leader who demonstrates leadership and influence in a wide variety of situations.

Two Views of Community Influence Systems

Floyd Hunder, C. Wright Mills, and the writings of many other sociologists have led to a theory of community power structure that may be depicted by a pyramid (Figure 4–1).[7] That is to say, they posit a small group of key influentials at the top who interact among each other and who exert influence on an interactive second stratum composed of a larger number of individuals who, in their turn, exert influence on several other strata below them. The base of the pyramid is composed of the people in the community. Essentially, the theory is that there develops within a community and within the society a core of individuals who are all-powerful and of the generalist type. These are the individuals who make decisions of importance in all areas of the community or nation that impinge upon them or their group or affect in any way the operational sphere of their control.

A contrasting view of the nature of power structure is illustrated in the writings of Robert Dahl and other political scientists who dissent from the notion that any one person or group of persons is so powerful as to be able to exert such generalized influence on all community matters all of the time. Instead, power distribution is viewed as *pluralistic* in nature with the influence of any individual or group being particularized to issues. The crowd interested in the schools, for example, is not composed of the same people who are influential in some other aspect of the community.[8]

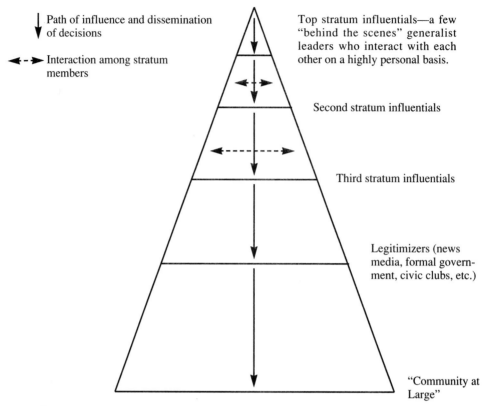

FIGURE 4–1.   One Type of Community Influence System: The Power Pyramid

Further, some theorists say the term "ruling elite" or "top influential" is a confused one and misleads since it is conferred upon a group with only a *high potential for control.* For example, a set of individuals in a community control certain resources. This can lead to a high probability that they will agree on key political alternatives. And, if they choose to act in some specified way, those alternatives will be chosen. This group could be said to have a high potential for control.

But, while a group may have a high potential for control, it may not have a *high potential for unity.* Political effectiveness, or power, can be considered a product of the group's potential for control *plus* its potential for unity. Moreover, a group with a low potential for control but a very high potential for unity might, in the end, on any particular issue be more effective politically than the reverse. It is this latter point that may be of greatest importance to school leaders seeking to develop programs necessary to the total community but without support from an existing power elite.

Some members of what might be called the community understructure have shown a remarkable ability to exert influence by unifying their fellows on any given issue. Some testimony that this indeed occurs may be provided by such diverse examples as the unionization and the development of political clout of migrant workers in the west; the wresting away of formal political control from whites by blacks in some areas of the country; and any number of instances where groups, not in control of any significant amount of dollar resources or the equivalent, have organized around a basic principle or cause and through adroit political maneuvering have been able to exert sufficient pressure to bring about a change.

In none of these examples could the groups exerting influence be said to have much potential for control by any standard measure. Yet, often because of a developing leadership structure, they do exhibit a potential for unity and thus represent forces for change well outside any traditionally posited oligarchic power structure. It is also important that community power structure not be viewed as static, but rather subject to great change over time. Thus, typing a power structure is analogous to taking a photograph; it is a picture of a moment in history. Movement can be expected and the direction this movement takes might even be predictable as situations such as a changing population or changing social conditions are studied.

No one event in a community can possibly capsule the kind of organization of power that exists; few communities reflect that kind of stability. Yet, power relationships are also not totally random. Patterns of influence, while not static, are nevertheless marked with some stability, allowing a degree of predictability over a span of time.

In a pluralistic community the schools must serve many publics, each with its values and orientations. In such a setting, the role of the school administrator often becomes that of mediating conflicts between various competing pressure groups. This simply means that educational administrators must be able to work successfully with many groups often pulling in conflicting directions. Among several implications the nature of power in a community may have for principals, the importance of identifying key community or neighborhood influentials and the development of informal working relations with these people cannot be overemphasized, not because these people or groups are always right, but because they usually represent the best thinking of the community and are, many times, most influenced by a rational approach to problem solving.

The Pluralistic School Community

Confounding the problem of communicating with school patrons in a pluralistic community is that, more and more frequently, districts are reorganizing school attendance zones to achieve desegregated student bodies or to provide special educational opportunities. Thus, the neighborhood served by a school may be quite dispersed. Conventional parent and patron groups, such as booster clubs and PTOs, may be difficult to maintain because of time and distance problems. Such groups are worth the energy it takes to maintain them, however. A considerable effort will be required to work with existing community groups in the various neighborhoods from which students come, as well as to develop schoolwide advisory groups with cross-sectional representation.

Neighborhood Influence Systems

Neighborhoods also have influence systems and these may be especially important in the principal's sphere of interaction. As was noted earlier, the individual school building remains, in most communities, the closest public agency, certainly in terms of geographic proximity. Thus, it is handy, if nothing else, to members of the immediate neighborhood. In a very real sense it is also in an excellent position to feel the pulse of the surrounding area.[9]

As urban and suburban communities have become more and more complex and power sources have become diffused, neighborhood influence systems have become increasingly important, at least partly because of a perceived lack of responsiveness of certain community welfare delivery systems such as schools. More often such influence systems also reflect racial or ethnic homogeneity. Individual schools may serve as effective mechanisms to receive information from and to dispense information to neighborhood leadership. Research suggests that an individual community member's decision to support or not support any particular community issue is more often than not based on the influence of friends and neighbors rather than on the presence of any outside objective data. It would seem, therefore, that the perceptive school principal would become familiar with the leadership structure of the neighborhood the individual school serves.

Every social group has a leadership structure that, with some diligence, can be identified. The principal who wants to begin a new kind of interaction with the immediate community will do well to engage in this endeavor, for what is true of community power structure generally—that it represents some of the best thinking of the community—will also be true of neighborhood influence systems.

Old mechanisms may not suffice for a school administrator interested in developing school-community relations programs based on mutual trust and a willingness to examine issues of mutual concern. Traditional community groups often do not have a membership composed of anything approximating the real nature of the community or the neighborhood served by the schools, and there may exist, well outside these more conservative groups, a leadership structure that has not yet been recognized but that has important things to say to the schools. School administrators should not engage in self-delusion about the nature of the leadership pattern in the neighborhood the school serves. An examination of the membership rolls of the local formal parent-teacher organization and a comparison of certain characteristics of these people with general demographic characteristics of the student body of the school may reveal that certain people are missing. If different kinds of people are missing, many key neighborhood influentials will not be reached.

Blut und Bod

The most intense memberships are held in groups that could be classified as *Blut und Bod*, those groups with kinship and territorial bonds rooted in certain ethnic or racial ties.

> A common language, a common dietary, a common neighborhood, common experience with outsiders, a common history, make people feel more comfortable with one another, more at ease. They understand one another, they read one another; they get one another's messages. They feel they can count on one another for support. They constitute an in group; everyone else is an out group.
>
> The bonds that hold people together also separate them from others; invisible lines are drawn to protect the boundaries between them and outsiders.[10]

People in the community are also often members of an array of different formal and informal groups that may impinge upon the schools. They are members of clubs and associations as well as other more general self-help groups such as the American Indian Movement, the League of United Latin American Citizens, the N.A.A.C.P., the A.C.L.U., B'nai Brith or groups such as the DAR or the less definitive "moral majority," for example. All of these organizations will demand loyalty from their membership and may oppose certain school system procedures and policies. Membership in what may at times be adversary groups may be the source of much community-school conflict.

In sum, then, characteristic of our complex society are communities which are more generally reflective of cultural pluralism. The fact is that many people in the community will not derive their normative behavior from white, middle-class heritage— and by extension, of course, neither will the student body; nor the teaching staff. Responses to traditional control and decision systems in the school and the community may vary from hostile acquiescence to open challenge. Teachers and administrators must learn to cope with this great diversity.[11]

School leaders need to identify the influential people and groups in the community or neighborhood. Power structure and influence systems vary from community to community and neighborhood to neighborhood. There is an indeterminacy and amorphousness about power structure and influence systems, but the degree to which various leaders in a community are able to agree on the direction schooling ought to take and the degree to which they are able to accept certain principles and guidelines that school leaders determine, in great part, will determine the extent of reform, modification, and growth of the educational institution in the community.

The school administrator should subject the area that the school serves to a community analysis to utilize the resources and problem-solving ability manifest in neighborhood or community influentials. This will provide a foundation for cooperative development and growth of both school and community.

Pressure Groups

No discussion of community influence systems would be complete without some discussion also about the nature of pressure groups. Pressure groups must be distinguished from a normal community decision system because of the somewhat temporal nature of their activities and their tendency to form and reform around single issues or causes, or because of a specific decision made by the school leadership.

Pressure groups should not be dismissed lightly. They have been a source of great disruption in many communities as well as a source of productive change. It is difficult to think of the term *pressure group* in a noninflammatory context. Immediately, thoughts of book burnings, witch hunts, placard-carrying demonstrators, impassioned pleas from the pulpit or the podium come to mind. One also gets the picture of school boards and the superintendents hastily capitulating to the onslaught of such charges that the "schools are Godless," that the English department is assigning lascivious literature, that sex education should not be taught in the schools, among a host of similar kinds of charges, emotion-ridden in context and within which rational thinking often goes out the window.

There is another side, however. Schools are a "public business" and permeable. A pressure group may be composed of parents arguing persuasively for the return of an art program or it may be collection of citizens raising important issues of equity. It may be a group raising questions about district employment practices, or a lack of bi- and trilingual programs, or insisting that there be compliance with OSHA regulations and equal access to school buildings. The fact is that most of the legislative acts and court orders ensuring or extending rights at local, state, and national levels have occurred because, early on, persistently and insistently, a small group of concerned citizens organized to call attention to an undesirable condition.

It is clearly the right of a citizen to protest when he or she is disappointed with the performance of public agencies. Conflict may not be inevitable, but it is frequent in any society. Often, it is out of conflict that productive change occurs, provided the conflict is managed sensibly and sensitively. Such situations are characterized by openness, a willingness to compromise, and well-understood and agreed-upon procedures for resolution.

Negotiating with Pressure Groups

From time to time, all school administrators will be confronted with requests from organized groups of people who represent a particular point of view about a school-related issue. Frequently, such pressure groups begin their inquiry at the individual school level in the principal's office. The issues may run the gamut from complaints about teachers, textbooks, or specific courses of study to alleged institutional racism and demands for more equitable staffing or pupil personnel decisions. The following guidelines may help a besieged principal:

1. An early identification should be made of the group that is in opposition or is likely to be in opposition to certain school programs. Who are they, and more important, who are their leaders?

2. Can the leaders be talked to? Once the leaders have been identified, it is appropriate to contact them for a closed-door session to explore the elements of the issue. The principal may gain some more definitive notion of just what it is that is troubling the group. This meeting or series of meetings may develop ways, if the cause is legitimate, for the school to help the group achieve its goals. It may require great insight to find out what the real issue is, because stated "reasons" for opposition to this or that school issue are often at variance with the real causative factors. It is important to know what the real reasons are if the group is to be dealt with effectively and if subsequent negotiations are to be successful. At this point, it is also important to apprise the central office of the potential hostile situation and to seek counsel.

3. Following these informal meetings, it is important to reach a decision. Some important points must be determined at this time, including the question about how strong the opposition really is. Do they have a good chance to beat the school in its present position? Most important, do they have a solid point on which to differ with the school? It is at this time that the principal must decide whether or not the issue will be fought on the basis of the initial position of both sides or whether some areas of accord are possible. Before a decision is made to fight it out, there is usually an alternative.

4. Is there room for compromise? The political system under which we operate functions on compromise. The greater good sometimes demands compromise solutions where desirable changes can be achieved without compromising principles or without loss of integrity.

Of course compromising may not be necessary. Perhaps simply sitting down with members of the pressure group and explaining the school's position and the facts may dissuade the group from further action. Administrators who have engaged in potential community-conflict situations over the years would suggest that compromise through negotiations may be the more likely result. The pressure group's motives may be highly complex. Its needs and goals are every bit as important to its membership as the needs and goals of the particular administrator or school system in question.

In any effort to influence or achieve compromise, timing is important. The time to influence a pressure group is before the particular group has launched its initial fusillade and before the school or the administrator is totally committed to a position. Common sense says that it is increasingly difficult, if not impossible, to change someone or some group when there will be much loss of face, real or imagined, by doing so.

5. Seek help from other community members. Assuming that all efforts to appease the opposition are unsuccessful, what does the administrator try next? The first step is to find out who is on the school's side, or who it appears ought to be on the school's side. Some community analysis can be conducted even at this stage and may prove fruitful. Who besides the school really stands to lose? School principals should not forget about other less-organized neighborhood groups of people who, though they seemingly have a low potential for power, might have a high potential for unity on the particular issues and who could be called upon for counsel and other help. Community advisory councils can help with this.

In all situations, it is crucial to determine what the real goal is and what results or gains can be expected from the achievement of that goal. In other words, is the school's position or is the school administrator's position on the issue tenable? If so, evidence must be presented to substantiate why it is tenable. Many school administrators have ended up in worse difficulty because of a refusal to negotiate or compromise or because of a determination to stick to their guns on irrelevant points of contention.

Is the Criticism "Legitimate"?

Not all criticism is legitimate and vigilance against individuals and groups that form from time to time to advance spurious or selfish interests is necessary. What is legitimate? One of the best ways to determine legitimacy is to observe the behavior of the group and its leaders. Is the group willing to meet with appropriate school personnel without the glare of TV lights or without benefit of newspaper rhetoric? Will the group look at other sides of the issue? Will the critics accept demonstrable fact and reasonable inferences? Is the criticism characterized by great emotion, more so than rational thought? If the answers to these questions don't add up to reasonable discussion, then the only choice is to do battle. It is a worthy battle.

Need for Well-Developed Policies

If conflict can be expected on educational issues, if ideological unity is not characteristic of very many complex communities, and if criticism can be expected as a part of the normal life of the administrator of any public institution, what can be done to modify the divisive effects of such actions and instead capitalize on the rich diversity of views and opinion to improve the schools? Foremost is to provide a broad set of policies, both at the school-district level as well as at the school-building level, that establish a framework within which diverging views can be heard in a regular and systematic manner. Such a framework provides, in effect, procedural due process whereby dissident factions in a community can formally register their views.

Figure 4–2 is a sample form that some districts provide to those individuals who are objecting to the use of certain educational material. Such a complaint form could be adapted to other issues and, if used judiciously, provide a vehicle for citizens to make their views known in a rational and systematic way.

CITIZEN'S REQUEST FOR RECONSIDERATION
OF EDUCATIONAL MEDIA

Title of Media _____
Type of media: (circle)
   Book   Film   Filmstrip   Recording _____
                                                        (other)
Author/artist/composer/other _____
Publisher/producer (if known) _____
Request initiated by _____   Phone _____
Address _____
Complainant represents _____
_____ Self
_____ (Name of organization) _____
_____ (Identify other group) _____
1. After having read/viewed/listened to the item in question, to what do you object and why? (Please be specific; cite pages, frame, other) _____
_____
2. What do you believe is the theme of this item? _____
_____
3. What do you feel might be the result of students reading/viewing/listening to this item?
_____
_____
4. For what age group would you recommend this item? _____
_____
5. Other comments _____
_____
_____

_____   _____
         Date   Signature of Complainant

FIGURE 4–2.

Using Review Boards

Individual principals would be wise also to establish some kind of review body on whom the principal could rely for advice, counsel, and the development of criteria for judging potentially controversial instructional materials.

The importance of involving a wide array of appropriate personnel in the development of policies to anticipate problems is important because it provides the basis for information sharing and good decision making. Principals cannot be expected to know everything. No principal should expect to be able to respond instantaneously to a critic. The advice and counsel of the school staff, as well as the community, and the development of broadly based policies and policy review boards are needed to provide for effective decision making and intelligent responses to questions that may issue from the community.

Working with Other Community Agencies and Organizations

Many community agencies and organizations in addition to schools have—or could have—an impact on the quality of children's lives. The school principal is in an uncommonly good position to coordinate the efforts of these agencies.

It often happens that the principal serves in that role anyway because, as we wrote at the beginning of this chapter, the elementary school is most often the closest social agency available to patrons. And, patrons look to their schools for all sorts of help that has to do with their families' well-being. The "closeness" of the school is for many as much a matter of psychological proximity as it is a physical proximity. Many community members look to the school for help in matters neither of the school's doing nor jurisdiction simply because they know of no other place to turn.

The sad fact is that in our complex society the important and varied welfare delivery agencies often operate in a most uncoordinated way. Principals frequently find themselves dealing with court orders, child protective services, police departments, city and state health and human services departments, and businesses and industries in an effort to help just one particular child or family. Sometimes these agencies even conflict with each other in their efforts and in their policies.

We are not aware of any administrator training programs that specifically prepare principals for this "add-on" role. But it is there, and while it may not be a part of the job description, effective principals recognize the importance of developing good contacts with these outside agencies and providing referral and follow-up services to their patrons who may be in need.

Developing close relationships with the police department, for example, to assist in such programs as Drug Abuse Resistance Education (DARE), where police officers work in the schools, only makes good sense. Becoming personally connected with child protective services directors and counselors among other welfare delivery agencies will pay rich dividends. Business partnerships such as "adopt-a-school" can provide an enriched educational offering as well as create an intimate involvement of the private sector in community service and an important support base.

Outreach efforts do not need to stop with these latter more obvious activities. Concerned about student achievement, as well as the negative impact of transience on students, school officials and individual principals in such school systems as Kansas City, Missouri and Spring Branch Independent Schools in Texas are working directly with housing project managers and apartment managers to provide study rooms in their buildings for students and parents alike. Spring Branch has gone a step further. There, principals have worked with these same managers to provide "school-year" leases with the last month's rent free, rather than the usual "first month free" enticement that had formerly been offered, thus encouraging parents to remain the full year in a single attendance area.

In Chapter 19 we will discuss other sorts of partnerships and ways to engage community members in sustaining productive schools.

Summary

The focus of this chapter has been on the nature of the communities served by the schools. There are a multiplicity of social forces that interact with and act upon the schools. Neighborhood influence systems, pressure groups, and the differing characteristics of power structures impinge on the life of the elementary school principal. The need to be sensitive to the outside demands and to analyze the very nature of the school community is apparent. The successful school administrator develops a wide range of response patterns, problem-solving mechanisms, and information-seeking devices so that the school can be at once responsive but also true to its obligation to serve all of the people.

Working with other community agencies is an important task of the principal. In this chapter we have described some ways in which that task may be best accomplished.

Endnotes

1. The salesman's refrain in Meredith Willson's *The Music Man.*

2. For insight about the nature of an ideologically unified community, the reader is referred to *Fiddler on the Roof.* In this musical play, the opening number, "Tradition," lyrically describes just such a community, with carefully spelled-out rules and ways of behaving—understood by all. The play goes on to detail the dissolution of this community because of forces within and without.

3. Thomas J. Sergiovanni and Fred D. Carver, *The New School Executive.* New York: Harper and Row Publishers, 1980, p. 252.

4. Larry W. Hughes, *Informal and Formal Community Forces: External Influences on Schools and Teachers.* Morristown, NJ: General Learning Press, 1976, pp. 2-3.

5. See Leslie Kindred *et al.*, *The School and Community Relations*, 4th edition, Englewood Cliffs, NJ: Prentice-Hall, 1990 for a good discussion of the nature of "the publics" and the implication this has for the school administrator.

6. Robert Dahl, *Who Governs*. New Haven, CT: Yale University Press, 1961, p. 7.

7. Floyd Hunter, *Community Power Structure*. Chapel Hill: University of North Carolina Press, 1953. C. Wright Mills. *The Power Elite*. London: Oxford University Press, 1959.

8. Dahl, *Who Governs.*

9. An especially good approach for working within the various neighborhood social structures is described in Donald J. Warren and Rachel B. Warren, "Six Kinds of Neighborhoods." *Psychology Today*, 9:1 (June 1975): 74-80. A "neighborhood organizers" guide is provided and techniques to best communicate are described.

10. Jesse Bernard, *American Community Behavior*. New York: Holt, Rinehart, and Winston, 1965, p. 358.

11. Hughes, *Informal and Formal Community Forces*, p. 19.

Selected Readings

Agger, Robert, Swanson, Bert E., and Goodrich, Daniel, *The Rulers and the Ruled: Political Power and Importance in American Communities*. New York: John Wiley and Sons, 1964. Still the best single source for understanding the nature of power and influence in communities.

Hughes, Larry W., *Informal and Formal Community Forces: External Influences on Schools and Teachers*. Morristown, NJ: General Learning Press, 1976

Hughes, Larry W.; Gordon, William M.; and Hillman, Larry W., *Desegregating America's Schools*. New York: Longman, 1980. See especially Chapter 11.

Kindred, Leslie, Bagin, Donald, and Gallagher, Donald, *The School and Community Relations*, 4th edition. Englewood Cliffs, NJ: Prentice-Hall, 1990.

National School Public Relations Association, *Building Confidence in Your Schools*. Washington: The Association, 1982.

Warren, Donald J. and Warren, Rachel B., "Six Kinds of Neighborhoods." *Psychology Today*, 9:1 (June, 1975), 75-80.

Wayson, W.W., Achilles, C.M., Pinnell, G.S., Litz, M.N., and Cunningham, L., *Handbook for Developing Confidence in Schools*. Bloomington, IN: Phi Delta Kappa Educational Foundation, 1988.

Part 2

Leadership and Management Tasks and Functions

Part 2 is composed of fifteen chapters, each of which contains descriptions and guidelines to implement the leadership and management functions of the principalship.

Chapters 5 and 6 focus on goal setting and goal implementation. Strategies and proven practices for engaging staff, students, and community in problem identification and problem solving are discussed.

The focus is the student in Chapters 7, 8, and 9. Grouping, establishing positive learning climates, and meeting the needs of all students are the subjects.

In Chapters 10, 11, 12, and 13 curricular and instructional issues are paramount. Research and effective practice in scoping and sequencing learning events, deploying instructional personnel, and scheduling staff and students are presented and guidelines for action suggested.

Issues that have to do with personnel are the subjects of Chapters 14, 15, and 16. Personnel selection, appraisal, and development are subjects of the first two of these chapters. The principal's role in contract administration is the subject of Chapter 16.

Chapters 17 and 18 get at the "nuts and bolts" of school operation. Fiscal planning and budget development from a site-based approach and sound accounting practices are included in one chapter. The other encompasses building and facilities management.

The final chapter in Part 2 is about the role of the principal as a public relations specialist. Processes and practices to help establish and maintain good relationships with the community are presented. This chapter might best be read in conjunction with Chapter 4.

$$C\ h\ a\ p\ t\ e\ r\quad 5$$

Guidelines and Goals for Planning School Programs

If you don't know where you are going,
it doesn't much matter what you do.[1]

Introduction

What is the purpose of schooling? What do you believe should be the major goals of education? What should a school do in order to accomplish these goals? What is the nature of educational excellence? Where should the line be drawn regarding the inclusion of activities and programs in the school? What can we do to ensure excellence in our programs? These are difficult questions to answer but a school must have some sense of direction and should consider what guidelines to follow if it is to be an effective school. This chapter provides a framework in which the principal and staff can outline their beliefs and establish goals and objectives for the school.

Beliefs, Goals, and Objectives

Sense of Direction

Every school today must strive for excellence. When improvement is seen in a school's quality, it is usually because the school has a sense of direction toward creating a quality program. A sense of direction can be provided for a school in the form of a statement of beliefs, a set of goals, and specific objectives to be achieved. Each of these three levels, beliefs, goals, and objectives, has a specific purpose in the planning process and each contributes in determining direction and showing interrelationships. A planning hierarchy of beliefs, goals and objectives can be established (Figure 5–1).

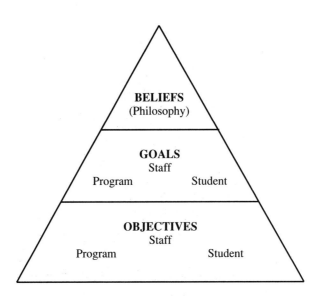

FIGURE 5–1. Determining Purpose and Direction for the School

Source: Gerald C. Ubben and Larry W. Hughes, *The Principal: Creative Leadership for Effective Schools* (Boston: Allyn and Bacon, 1992), p. 122.

A *statement of beliefs* can be thought of as a foundation or a philosophy for the school and should represent the collective thinking of the staff and community representatives. For example, the statement "Every child can learn and achieve mastery" is a statement of belief. It is part of one's philosophy of education.

A *goal statement* is a statement of intended direction relative to a belief statement. For example, a school goal could be "Successful learning experiences will be provided for every child each day." This is a specific statement of intent. A goal, however, is often something that a school strives toward but may never totally achieve.

Just as goals should be an outgrowth of a philosophy or belief, *objectives* should be extensions of goals. Objectives are more specific than goals and should be obtainable, often within a stated period of time. An illustration of a program objective is "Instructional objectives will be developed by the staff for the reading and math curricula this year."

Total Quality Management (TQM) speaks of performance goals or process goals.[2] These suggest that some goals or objectives will be stated in such a manner that they are measurable in some meaningful way. An example might be "that unit test scores when charted over time will show overall class improvement." However, Deming, in laying out the principles of TQM, also cautions against setting work standards that prescribe numerical quotas.

Much of the literature on effective schools refers to their being both loosely and tightly coupled.[3] In excellent schools there exists a strong common sense of purpose (tightly coupled) while at the same time a great deal of freedom (loosely coupled) is given to teachers as to how this purpose is to be achieved. Well-articulated goals to which the faculty "buys in" are the keys to the loosely coupled-tightly coupled concept.

This loosely coupled-tightly coupled concept also applies to the restructuring ideas of site-based management. Properly done, the higher authority (school district or state department) should establish fairly specific goals with a school (tightly coupled). The method or process by which those goals are attained should be left with the local site to determine based on what works best for them (loosely coupled).

Focus on Purpose

A second consideration, a focus on purpose, must be made relative to beliefs, goals, and objectives. There are basically three types of goals used in the school: (1) program goals, (2) staff goals, and (3) learner goals. *Program goals* focus on the overall collective expectations for the curricular and instructional program of the school. Examples of program goals are "to improve the reading test scores in the second grade" or "to improve the articulation between science programs in the fourth and fifth grades."

Staff goals focus on specific improvements to be sought often by the individual staff members. Examples of a staff goal are "Developing procedures for increasing the amount and quality of student-teacher verbal interaction in my classroom," or "To tailor my questioning style to a different ability level in my classroom," or "To increase the involvement of students through the use of more student-centered teaching techniques."

Learner goals focus on the specific outcomes expected of students. An example of a learner goal is "At least eighty percent of the students will be able to answer correctly at least eighty percent of the problems on a four-place multiplication test."

The focus of this chapter will be largely on program goals. Using the concepts of TQM these would be thought of as process goals. Staff goals will be discussed at greater length in Chapter 15 on staff supervision and evaluation, and learner goals will be discussed in Chapters 10 and 11 on curriculum and instruction. The use of goals and objectives as a basis for systematic planning is discussed in greater length in Chapter 6.

Principal's Role

Schools really can make a difference in the achievement levels of students, but a school is most often only as good or bad, as creative or sterile, as the person who serves as the head of that school. The research on effective schools highlights the role of the principal in establishing goals and objectives for the school.

What do effective principals do?

> Principals of effective schools are strong instructional leaders who know how to manage time and money effectively . . . they concentrate on priority goals . . . they set as their main goal the acquisition of basic skills . . . effective principals have high expectations for all students and they will enlist the support of others in meeting common goals.[4]

The principal is the one person in a school who can oversee the entire program because of his or her interest in the success of the entire school and all of its parts.

Therefore, the principal is in the best position to provide the necessary sense of direction to the various aspects of a school. Research has shown that the most effective principals have a clear sense of purpose and priorities and are able to enlist the support of others toward these ends.

Many of the problems of direction within a school organization are very subtle, will be difficult to solve, and require great conceptual and technical knowledge of curriculum, instruction, and learning. The principal must have the necessary understanding to find proper and just solutions to these problems and many others like them.

Framework for Establishing Beliefs or Philosophy Statements

The beliefs and philosophy for a school should relate to societal expectations, wants and needs, and the individual differences of children. Such a list can best be organized with an outline or framework of concepts and ideas to be included. There are many different ways such a framework can be organized. Three different frameworks or structures are included in this chapter for consideration.

School Structural Framework

The structure of a school program requires that specific thought be given to each of several organizational components of the program: (1) curricular organization, (2) instructional processes, (3) student grouping practices, (4) staff organization, (5) the scheduling of learning time, and (6) facility utilization and design. Although the six components can be separated for discussion purposes, the program that results for any particular school must give detailed attention both to the contribution that each component makes to the achievement of the goals and objectives of the school and the development of each component in such a way that it is compatible with the other five components. For example, a belief statement may speak to the importance of meeting the individual needs of each child. From this belief statement a goal of individualizing instruction might be selected. This instructional format must then be supported with a student grouping plan, staffing plan, and schedule. In turn, if the staffing selection proposes team teaching, the facility utilization design should provide appropriate work spaces for teaching teams.

The organizational components are not equally important and should not be considered as equals, nor are they independent entities. Decisions regarding the organization of the curriculum and instructional program should be made first. These must logically be based on the beliefs and goals for the school. The other four components serve the first two.

Evaluative Criteria Framework

A second perspective of what approach should be used in developing a statement of philosophy or beliefs is drawn from the *Evaluative Criteria* guidelines of the national accrediting associations. They suggest considerations should be given to the following:

1. Relevance of the statement of philosophy to the larger purpose of the American democratic commitment.

2. Attention to intellectual, democratic, moral, and social values, basic to satisfying the needs of the individual and his culture.

3. Recognition of individual differences.

4. The special characteristics and unique needs of elementary school children.

5. Concern for the nature of knowledge and for the nature of the learning process as they apply to learners and their total development.

6. Consistency of philosophy with actual practice.

7. Identification of the roles and relationships expected of the community, the student, the teacher, and the administration in the educational process of the school.

8. The role of the elementary school program of the school district and the importance of the articulation with other elements of the overall educational program.

9. The responsibility for making a determination as to a desirable balance among activities designed to develop cognitive, affective, and psychomotor demands.

10. The relationship of the school and all other educational learning centers.

11. The responsibility of the school toward social and economic change.

12. The accountability of the school to the community it serves.[5]

Effective Schools Framework

The research on effective schools also suggest specific areas that might be considered for inclusion in a beliefs and goals listing. A summary of major areas includes

1. School-wide measurement and recognition of academic success

2. A positive student climate emphasizing an orderly and studious school environment

3. A high emphasis on curriculum articulation

4. High support for good methodology

5. High expectations and clear goals for performance of students

6. Parental support for the education of students

These three frameworks for identifying beliefs statements obviously have some degree of overlap. But each also has a certain rationale for its own structure. The school might elect to use one of the three frameworks or create its own structure from a combination of them. One or more belief statements can be written for each of the areas on the outline.

Beliefs Development

The process of establishing a sense of direction in a school must be a dynamic one involving teachers, community members, and, in some cases, students. In reality, the interaction and debate of the processes in determining what the document is to include is more important than the product itself in that the beliefs and goals are important only if they are alive. Beliefs must be kept alive in the minds of staff and community and those people must feel that the goals and objectives relative to those beliefs are appropriate.

The initial formulation as well as the annual reviews and updates of the belief statements should be done using some type of staff, community, student consensus model. An example of this process model is described in the following paragraphs.

The participants are divided into writing teams consisting of three to five members including all members of the faculty. Each writing team is structured to create maximum internal variability with each team having teachers from different grade levels, subject areas, and experience backgrounds. If community members and students (secondary) are participating, one or more should be assigned to each writing team.

Each writing team should be given a complete list of the belief framework or an outline of topic areas. Their task is to write one or more statements regarding what they believe for each of the topics. For example, if one of the topic areas asks them to state their beliefs regarding curriculum, they might ultimately write a statement such as: "We believe that the school staff should collectively review the basic objectives and strategies for teaching and learning and periodically reexamine and reconstruct objectives in view of current curricular priorities." Several sample statements can be provided to give the group the idea of what is wanted. Each writing team should develop statements for each area of the belief framework. This may require six to twelve or more statements from each writing team. Upon the completion of their initial writing task, each writing team selects one representative member of their group to meet with a similar member from each of the other teams to form a consensus team to discuss the statements written down by each team on the first topic. A second representative should be identified for the second topic as well as a third and fourth until all writing team members are representing their team to a consensus team consisting of one member from each of the other writing groups.

These newly formulated consensus teams review the written statements on their assigned topic from each of the writing teams and select, combine, and rewrite the submitted statements until they have developed a series of statements on the assigned topic that their group accepts. Each writing team representative then takes the newly combined set of statements on their topic back to their original writing team for discussion, additional modification, or ratification.

If the original writing team feels that the rewrite of the consensus team does not reflect their beliefs, they modify its work. The consensus team then is reconvened to consider the recommended modifications. If necessary, the statements may go back and forth several times before agreement can finally be reached. The other consensus teams are carrying out the same procedures for their topics. Figure 5–2 illustrates the writing team–consensus team structure. An example of the final set of belief statements developed by a school using this process is shown in Figure 5–3.

Developing Goals for Improvement

Once the school's belief statements or philosophy has been developed, the next task becomes one of determining how well the beliefs are presently being implemented. Belief statements provide a sense of purpose for the school, but they often do not provide a specific sense of direction. For that reason, goals need to be stated to help the organization focus on improvement. One way to select goals is to conduct a needs assessment and dis-

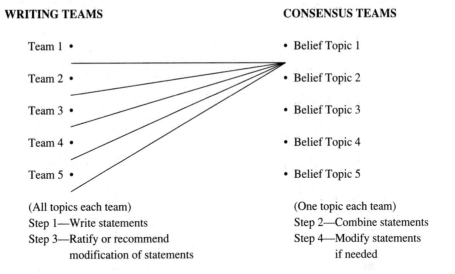

FIGURE 5–2. Writing Team–Consensus Team Structure

Source: Gerald C. Ubben and Larry W. Hughes, *The Principal: Creative Leadership for Effective Schools* (Boston: Allyn and Bacon, 1992), p. 126.

crepancy analysis to determine the extent to which those involved feel the stated beliefs are being carried out by the organization. The needs of the organization for improvement can then be defined by focusing on those beliefs that are being least successfully achieved.

Developing a Needs Assessment Instrument

An easily developed needs assessment instrument can be created by using the belief statements as a base. A series of statements that can be rated on a five-point Likert-type rating scale, ranging from strongly disagree to strongly agree, are developed for each belief statement. An illustration of a needs assessment statement is as follows:

SA	A	N	D	SD	
1	2	3	4	5	Programs and varied instructional techniques are provided in order to respond to each child's individual needs and differences.

Statements can be grouped into logical categories, weighted, and scored. For example, if belief statements were organized around concepts from the effective schools research including time, climate, basic commitment, staff, curriculum, leadership, and evaluation, several assessment items could be written for each of the categories. Responses can be divided by the number of items in the category in order to be weighted equally. This will allow comparison between categories for later priority determination.

FARRAGUT MIDDLE SCHOOL PHILOSOPHY

We believe that each child is a unique individual, and the school exists for the benefit of the students. We will strive to meet the needs of each individual child. The curriculum of Farragut Middle School should focus not only on basic skills, but also in the development of the total child. The environment of the school should foster positive attitudes and values, helping students to become responsible citizens and to respect the rights of others. Many people will be involved in the total instructional process, working as a team. Teachers from various disciplines, administrators, parents, aides, and volunteers will participate in the school program, maintaining open lines of communication. We believe that success helps to promote increased interest in succeeding in other areas of learning.

Goals

I. With faculty assistance and guidance each student will have an opportunity to:
    a. Gain knowledge of basic skills
    b. Use intelligently and fully appreciate our natural resources
    c. Develop an awareness of the interdependence of cultures
    d. Expand cultural and aesthetic values
    e. Realize how current events affect the environment
    f. Receive guidance and career information
    g. Discover and develop special talents, interests, and capabilities
    h. Develop basic communication skills
II. In order to function and interact successfully in society the student should:
    a. Recognize the importance of self-discipline
    b. Accept responsibility for his or her own behavior
    c. Develop a positive self-concept
    d. Respect the worth, dignity, and feelings of others
    e. Participate as an effective citizen in society
    f. Clarify personal values and beliefs
    g. Become aware and concerned about others
    h. Respect the rights of others
    i. Prepare for and cope with change
    j. Become more self-directed
    k. Develop thinking skills
    l. Develop skills of problem solving and decision making
III. Each staff member should strive to:
    a. Provide and maintain an environment conducive to learning
    b. Maintain open lines of communication with the community
    c. Recognize individual differences and identify special needs of students
    d. Create a learning environment that will develop in the student the ability to direct his or her own learning
    e. Use a variety of instructional approaches including large group presentations, small group discussions, and a variety of individual approaches

(Continued)

FIGURE 5–3. Belief Statement

III. Each staff member should strive to (*continued*):
    f. Evaluate each child on the basis of his or her own ability and each program based on its contribution to the total school
    g. Develop a climate in which the student can develop appropriate attitudes toward himself or herself, peers, and society
    h. Help each child achieve his or her maximum potential in the various areas of the curriculum
    i. Involve the community in the school and the school in the community
    j. Become involved in the decision-making process of the school, including teaching teams, curriculum committees, advisory groups, student organizations, and community organizations

FIGURE 5–3. Belief Statement   *(Continued)*

Figure 5–4 gives a complete illustration of a needs assessment instrument including a weighted scoring sheet that is organized around effective schools concepts.

Although the development of the needs assessment instrument should be a major responsibility of the principal, other staff members should be contributors to the items included. Be sure the completed instrument offers the opportunity for written comments also.

Upon completion of the newly developed needs assessment instrument, it should be administered to all faculty members and also be completed by other interested parties who are knowledgeable about the school. Certainly include supervisory staff, but also include teacher aides, volunteers, and knowledgeable parents. Don't give it to just your supporters; school critics often are very insightful.

When an ample number have been returned, they should be scored, weighted, and ranked by category. Areas of lowest weighted scores on the returned needs assessments are candidates as priority goal areas for the new planning period.

Selecting Goals

The principal has the responsibility to provide the leadership to the faculty and the community for the development of annual educational goals as well as the specific objectives that support them. It is important to keep the current goals and objectives in the minds of the staff in order to maintain direction and momentum in the school improvement program.

Annual program goals should be prepared for only selected areas of the school program. The needs assessment described in the previous section becomes the means of identifying those areas believed by the staff and others to be most in need of improvement. It should be in these areas of need that immediate attention should be focused by the formulation of program improvement goals.

It should be remembered that a goal statement is a statement of intended direction indicating a desired result even if certain goals may not always be fully attainable. Goal statements are to be supplemented by specific objectives that are attainable and can be

SCHOOL EXCELLENCE INVENTORY

Directions—Rate the following items on a scale of 1 to 5 to reflect your opinion of your school. (1 = Low . . . 5 = High)

	(Low)				(High)
1. Students have favorable attitudes toward school and learning.	1	2	3	4	5
2. Student learning is frequently evaluated using curriculum referenced materials.	1	2	3	4	5
3. The staff has high expectations for the students and adults with whom they work.	1	2	3	4	5
4. Student time on-task behavior is maintained at a high level because:					
a) A climate of order and discipline has been established.	1	2	3	4	5
b) Limited time is used in maintaining order.	1	2	3	4	5
c) Classroom management tasks have been "routinized" to maximize available instructional time.	1	2	3	4	5
d) The school staff has made a commitment to maximize learning time by reducing impediments to learning and interruptions of the school day.	1	2	3	4	5
5. Students and parents receive regular feedback regarding the student's progress.	1	2	3	4	5
6. Student attendance rates are high.	1	2	3	4	5
7. There is a clear understanding of what the school believes in and stands for which includes:					
a) An academic focus.	1	2	3	4	5
b) A belief that all students have the ability to learn.	1	2	3	4	5
c) An expectation that each student will learn.	1	2	3	4	5
d) High expectations for each student.	1	2	3	4	5
8. Teachers regularly utilize techniques to assure that all students are learning.	1	2	3	4	5
9. Staff members are evaluated regularly.	1	2	3	4	5
10. Programs and varied instructional techniques are provided in order to respond to each child's individual needs and differences.	1	2	3	4	5
11. Students feel valued and successful.	1	2	3	4	5
12. Individual help is provided to students when needed.	1	2	3	4	5

FIGURE 5–4. Needs Assessment

Source: Gerald C. Ubben and Larry W. Hughes, *The Principal: Creative Leadership for Effective Schools* (Boston: Allyn and Bacon, 1992, pp. 129–131.

13. School staff members exhibit a high degree of concern and commitment for the achievement and well-being of each student.   1 2 3 4 5

14. The principal is effective because:

  a) He/she understands the process of instruction, and accepts the responsibility for being an instructional leader.   1 2 3 4 5

  b) He/she is an able manager.   1 2 3 4 5

  c) He/she has high attainable expectations for the students and adults with whom he/she works.   1 2 3 4 5

  d) He/she has goal clarity (a clear sense of purpose and priorities) and is able to enlist the support of others in understanding, accepting and accomplishing those ends.   1 2 3 4 5

  e) He/she recognizes the importance of (and actively involves) the people who work in, and who are served by the school.   1 2 3 4 5

  f) He/she assists the school staff in implementing sound instructional practices.   1 2 3 4 5

15. Students receive prompt feedback on their work.   1 2 3 4 5

16. A high level of staff and student morale exists.   1 2 3 4 5

17. Members of the school staff are cooperative and supportive of each other.   1 2 3 4 5

18. The curriculum:

  a) Emphasizes mastery of basic skills.   1 2 3 4 5

  b) Is well-defined.   1 2 3 4 5

  c) Is appropriately sequenced and articulated from grade to grade and from subject to subject.   1 2 3 4 5

  d) Includes clearly defined learner goals.   1 2 3 4 5

  e) Is regularly evaluated.   1 2 3 4 5

19. Techniques are used to pinpoint individual students' strengths and weaknesses.   1 2 3 4 5

20. The staff is competent and continues to grow and learn.   1 2 3 4 5

21. The school is open to and encourages participation and involvement by parents and other citizens.   1 2 3 4 5

22. Parents, students, and staff place a high priority on learning.   1 2 3 4 5

23. Students are instructed at the appropriate level of difficulty.   1 2 3 4 5

(Continued)

FIGURE 5–4. Needs Assessment *(Continued)*

Summary Sheet
School Excellence Inventory

Time	Climate	Basic Commitment	Staff	Curriculum	Leadership	Education
#4a = ___	#1 = ___	#7a = ___	#3 = ___	#10 = ___	#14a = ___	#2 = ___
#4b = ___	#6 = ___	#7b = ___	#9 = ___	#18a = ___	#14b = ___	#5 = ___
#4c = ___	#11 = ___	#7c = ___	#13 = ___	#18b = ___	#14c = ___	#8 = ___
#4d = ___	#16 = ___	#7d = ___	#17 = ___	#18c = ___	#14d = ___	#12 = ___
Total = ___	#21 = ___	#22 = ___	#20 = ___	#18d = ___	#14e = ___	#15 = ___
÷ 4 = ___	Total = ___	Total = ___	Total = ___	#18e = ___	#14f = ___	#19 = ___
	÷ 5 = ___	÷ 5 = ___	÷ 5 = ___	Total = ___	Total = ___	#23 = ___
				÷ 6 = ___	÷ 6 = ___	Total = ___
						÷ 7 = ___

FIGURE 5–4. Needs Assessment *(Continued)*

reached within a specific period of time. Three examples of priority goal statements for attention this year are as follows:

Goal I.   All students will attain mastery of identified instructional objectives.

Goal II.   The staff will identify standards for mastery of instructional objectives for all students as well as procedures for certifying the attainment of those standards.

Goal III.   The instructional climate of the school will be developed and maintained at a high level.

Program Improvement

Improvement Objectives

Objectives represent the basis for a plan of action. They should be written for a specific time period—in most cases a year or less is appropriate. They should be written in a form that will allow the results to be observable or measurable.

Objectives should be written with major participation by the faculty. If teams or departments are operating, they can form a basic working unit to develop objectives from the needs assessment and goals. Representatives from each team can review and modify the statements to develop a schoolwide list. Objectives can apply to the entire school, to a particular team or department, and to individual staff members.

Staff attention can be focused on objectives in several ways. Objectives can be made the focus of staff and inservice meetings. Team and school objectives can become part of the staff evaluation plan for the school when an evaluation-by-objectives model, such as the one discussed in Chapter 15, is used.

Examples of program improvement objectives are as follows:

Objective 1.   To implement and evaluate the new objectives for the mathematics curriculum developed by our system for grades kindergarten through six.

Objective 2.   To continue the Holt Reading series and skills management program in grades one through four and to implement this program in grade five.

Objective 3.   To continue to stress school discipline and enforce stated school rules to further enhance the school's instructional climate.

Objective 4:   To increase our academic learning time by making more use of our allocated time and motivating more students to stay on task.

The achievement of objectives should be regarded and reviewed periodically as a measure of the progress of the school. Annual self-evaluations should reflect an objective achievement, goal attainment, and a new needs assessment for planning of the next cycle. In keeping with the concepts of TQM, as many of the short term objectives as possible should be stated in some measurable manner. Frequent assessments of progress should be made and shared among staff members and students. Care must be taken of course that the items measured and shared represent a true reflection of what you are really trying to accomplish.

Summary

The beliefs of the school represent the philosophy of the faculty and hopefully the community toward the school. The goals of the school are statements of intent or direction for the organization and should be prioritized through a needs assessment for immediate or long-term action. Goals are important to the organization because every objective and every action should be planned to move the organization toward the goals. It is important that all members of the staff and school community be cognizant of the goals, and it is preferable that many have a hand in their development or modification. Goal understanding on the part of the members of an organization is a sound basis for their coordinated action in moving the organization in the desired direction.

Objectives are detailed plans for goal attainment and suggest the specific tasks to be carried out if goals are to be realized. Completion of objectives should be reviewed annually as part of the school's self-evaluation.

Endnotes

1. Comments of the Cheshire cat to Alice (*Alice in Wonderland*) upon her request for directions after admitting she didn't know where she wanted to go.

2. Chapter One outlines the concepts of Total Quality Management (TQM) and the fourteen principles for TQM proposed by Edwards Deming.

3. T.E. Deal and L.D. Celotti. *Loose Coupling and School Administrators: Some Recent Research Findings*. Stanford, CA: Center for Educational Research, 1977.

4. *Good Schools—What Makes Them Work.* Washington, DC: National School Public Relations Association, 1980.

5. *Elementary School Evaluative Criteria.* Arlington, VA: National Study of School Evaluation, A Guide for School Improvement, 1973, pp. 39–40.

Selected Readings

Adler, Mortimer J., *The Paideia Proposal: An Educational Manifesto.* New York: Macmillan, 1982.

Buell, Nancy A., "Building a Shared Vision—The Principal's Leadership Challenge." *NASSP Bulletin, 76,* 542 (March 1992): 88–92.

Chance, Edward W. and Grady, Marilyn L., "Creating and Implementing as Vision for the School." *NASSP Bulletin, 74,* 529 (November 1990): 12–18.

Cohen, Michael and Manasse, A. Lorri, "Effective Principals." *School Administrator, 30,* 10 (November 1982): 14–16.

Duke, Daniel L., "What is the Nature of Educational Excellence and Should We Try to Measure It?" *Phi Delta Kappan, 66* (June 1985): 671–674.

Goodlad, John I., "A Study of Schooling: Some Findings and Hypotheses." *Phi Delta Kappan 64,* 7 (March 1983): 465–470.

Herman, Jerry J., "School-Based Management: Sharing Resource Decisions." *NASSP Bulletin, 76,* 545 (September 1992): 102–105.

Holt, Maurice, "The Educational Consequences of W. Edwards Deming." *Phi Delta Kappan, 74,* 5 (January 1993): 382–388.

McGread, Thomas L., "Helping Teachers Set Goals." *Educational Leadership, 61* (February 1980): 414–419.

Rankin, Stuart C., "Total Quality Management: Implications for Educational Assessment." *NASSP Bulletin, 76,* 545 (September 1992): 66-76.

Rhodes, Lewis A., "Beyond Your Beliefs: Quantum Leaps Toward Quality Schools." *The School Administrator* (December 1990): 23–26.

Rhodes, Lewis A., "Why Quality is Within Our Grasp . . . If We Reach." *The School Administrator* (September 1990): 31–33.

Sapone, Carmelo V., "Planning and Implementing Principles of Changes." *Catalyst for Change, 13,* 2 (Winter 1984): 9–11.

Snyder, Karolyn J. *et al.,* "School Improvement Goal Setting: A Collaborative Model." *NASSP Bulletin, 67,* 465 (October 1983): 60–65.

Sullivan, Keith C., *"The Importance of Goals to Effective Schools and Minority Groups."* Paper prepared for the annual conference of the American Educational Research Association, New Orleans, April 1984. ERIC ED245008, p. 34.

Wilson, Richard B. and Schmoker, Mike, "Quest for Quality." *The Executive Educator* (January 1992): 18–22.

Chapter 6

School Improvement Through Systematic Planning

A goal without a plan is a wish—a wish that won't come true.

Introduction

The emphasis of this chapter is action planning at the school site. That is, after all, where the "action" is. Systematic processes by which the principal, staff, and community can engage in both short-term problem solutions and long-term goal accomplishment will be described and addressed. Problem identification, analysis, and principles of project management that lead to problem solution are the subjects. Guidelines to engage a school staff in the planning and problem resolution process are well established and a case in point is presented.

Systematic planning involves the translation of long-term goal statements into more specific, more measurable objectives which, when reached, will lead to the realization of the goals.[1]

Needs Assessment/Problem Identification/Campus Planning

Whether or not the school system is operating on management by objectives, it is important that the principal be using such a process with building staff. It is not necessary that an entire organization avowedly endorse the process in order for a principal to implement a management system that will result in goal identification, target setting, and understood performance standards.

Two elements are important: the needs assessment to uncover deficiencies and establish building goals and the campus plan to address these.

The Needs Assessment

A fundamental step in the planning process is the needs assessment. It requires a review of existing data and may require some surveying of clients and other appropriate reference groups.

There is always a certain risk in a needs assessment. In the process of uncovering needs, one may also raise expectations that all of the respondent's concerns will be addressed—and soon. Fundamental to good planning is priority setting and focus; thus, not all needs can be met immediately. Resources are in short supply and difficult, sometimes painful, decisions have to be made about which of an array of "pressing" needs requires attention.

Three reference groups are especially important to the needs assessment and planning process: students and parents, professional staff, and educational policy makers.

Students and Parents

Much information about students is readily available in the myriad of reports a typical school system generates. Standardized test scores, attendance records, free lunch recipients, handicapped students analyses, transportation reports, among a host of other official and unofficial sources, serve as basic data sources when it comes time to develop a profile of the students in a school or school district. Informal discussions with colleagues, other professionals, and parents and community members about how former students are doing is another source—less objective perhaps, but nevertheless helpful for uncovering possible problem areas.

Judicious use of community and parent surveys can be very helpful to the school principal, as can community advisory groups. Such surveys are invaluable in the determination of parent and community expectations and attitudes as well as perceptions of educational needs of the community's young people. The diverse nature of most communities requires that in any survey care needs to be taken that the necessary degree of randomness exists. Concern for complete information as well as diversity of opinion should also be reflected in the composition of advisory groups.

Professional Staff

The professional staff of the school is another primary source of information about school needs, both with regard to instructional and curricular shortcomings as well as specific observations about the nature of the student body. Staff surveys, or any of a number of rational problem-solving processes, are useful in needs assessments. Good results frequently can be obtained by using some of these methods in combination.

For example, a faculty meeting—school-wide, department, or grade-level—may be given over to "brainstorming" such a topic as "This is a good school, but it could be better if . . . ," following which the information is culled, recurring themes noted, and items generated for a survey to determine the perceived intensity and importance of the issues identified. The "nominal group" technique and the "structured group creativity" technique discussed in Chapter 20 also offer possibilities.

Educational Policy Makers

Some central office personnel of the school district may fall into this category. Local and state school board members, state departments of education, legislators, the federal

Department of Education, among other agencies and agents that might come to mind, including the periodically constituted special education commissions, are policy makers.

Campus Planning

The next step after the needs assessment is the development of the campus plan. A campus plan translates the results of the needs assessment into *targeted* areas for improvement. The word *targeted* is emphasized because it is frequently at this point that good intentions and good sense and a lot of heretofore energetic persons disperse and collapse in a gigantic pile of paper covered with statements of low-level objectives and quantifiable measures of attainment of low-level objectives. Care must be taken to focus on those aspects of improvement that carry the most impact on the quality of schooling. This requires priority setting and a recognition that not all things can be addressed. The limitations of resources—human, time, physical, and fiscal—must always be reckoned with.

Displayed in Figure 6–1 is a format for a campus plan. Each of the five functional aspects of the school operation is subjected to analysis. In the example, six aspects are revealed because "building maintenance" is most conveniently separated from "finance and budgeting." An analysis is made of the strengths and weaknesses of these aspects at the various levels of the school organization. It is here that the product of the needs assessment, such as the one suggested in Chapter 5, is most useful. The final column is designated for statements of proposed actions, most often stated as outcomes or objectives to be attained, to address targeted deficiencies.

What remains is to develop the proposed actions, outcomes, or objectives into an action plan. Action planning to achieve measurable results is the subject of the next part of this chapter.

Action Planning/Project Management

Action planning is what professional planners label programming an objective, and that label is descriptive. The action plan contains

- A description of the several activities necessary to achieve an objective
- The relationship of these activities to each other
- The assignment of specific responsibilities to individuals who will see to the implementation of the activities
- A timeframe and chronology of activities and events
- An evaluation process

There are no guarantees that the plan will succeed in solving the existing problem, of course, and that is why the last element of the plan provides for an evaluation. The activities in the plan may be best thought of as "hypotheses"—more than a hunch, perhaps, certainly more than a hope, but nevertheless, not certainties. Therefore, it is necessary to evaluate the efficacy carefully, not only of the total project, but also of the specific activities comprising the project.

Campus_____ Grade / Department_____			
Aspects Studied	Strengths	Deficiencies	Action to Take
Instructional Program			
Staff			
Pupil Achievement			
Parent and Community Relations			
Finance and Budgeting			
Building Maintenance			

FIGURE 6–1.   School Self-Study

Once the action plan is developed, project management is in great part a monitoring process. The project manager may be the principal but not necessarily so. Any person on the staff with good administrative skills and an interest in the project may be a likely candidate to become the manager.

This becomes an excellent way for the principal to develop and capitalize on the leadership skills of staff members, including assistant principals, faculty, and resource or support personnel. It is important that adequate resources be provided to the person put in charge of managing a project. This may include released time and secretarial service, as well as a budget.

Problem Analysis

Care must always be taken that the presumed problem is adequately analyzed before moving into an elaborate action plan. It is at the problem analysis point that a force-field analysis proves helpful.

Force-Field Analysis

Kurt Lewin, applying certain physical laws to the organizational setting, concluded that things stay the way they are in organizations because a field of opposing forces is in balance.[2]

One way to think about a problem situation is to regard the situation as being as it is because of positive ("driving") and negative ("restraining") forces that are equal in strength. The driving forces are current conditions and actions present in the organizational environment (or in the community, or even in society as a whole) which are such that change is encouraged. Restraining forces are conditions or actions which are such that change is discouraged or inhibited. These can be thought of as negative or "minus" forces in the developing equation.

The force-field concept issues from the physical law that a body at rest (in equilibrium) will remain at rest when the sum of all the forces operating on it is equal to zero. The body will move only when the sum is not zero, and *it will move only in the direction of the unbalancing force*.

It is not difficult to observe this phenomenon in organizations. The productivity of a school staff, the state of the school-community relations program, the success level of the intramural program, among any number of other observable situations are all subject to explanation (and change) by force-field analysis. A thing is where it is because the sum of the *power* of the counterbalancing plus and minus forces is equal to zero—and the situation is "frozen."

*Powe*r is a key word here because equilibrium is not achieved by a simple equal *number* of forces. It is the strength of the force that is important. One overwhelming positive force (e.g., the infusion of huge amounts of federal or state dollars) may be quite sufficient to change dramatically the nature of a science program, which had suffered from lack of equipment, inadequately prepared teachers, and lack of community concern. Similarly, a large, vocal, and interested religious group might impact mightily on the nature of a science curriculum in any particular community, despite research evidence about inquiry methods, adequate budget, well-trained teachers, or bright students, among any number of other forces that would otherwise be generative of good programming.

Movement, that is, change, will take place only when an imbalance is created. An imbalance will occur by eliminating forces, by developing new forces, or by affecting the power of existing forces. The imbalance "unfreezes" the current situation and the situation will change and a new state of equilibrium achieved. To recapitulate, an imbalance may be created by:

- The addition of a new force(s);
- The deletion of a force(s);
- A change in the magnitude or strength of any of the forces.

Any plan that is developed after the force-field analysis is conducted will probably make use of all three ways of creating an imbalance.

There is evidence, however, that attempting to increase only positive forces creates much tension in the system and often the intensity of the restraining forces correspondingly increases. This leaves the organization no better off, and sometimes worse off, because of new tensions. The best results occur when the first effort is directed to reducing the intensity of the restraining forces. Also, there may be little or nothing that can be done about some of the forces—a few may be imponderables; others simply may be outside of the control of organization members.

Engaging in force-field analysis focuses thinking and may result in a restatement of the problem. Often, what appeared to be the problem is really a symptom; one of the identified "restraining forces" is actually the problem that requires attention. Thus, a principal, project manager, and staff must have open minds at the early stages in order that energies are ultimately focused on the right issues and not dissipated on things that are only symptomatic.

A Case in Point

You are the principal of an elementary school with an enrollment of 450 students. The composition of the student body is racially and ethnically heterogeneous, with perhaps a few more children from families at the lower end of the community's economic continuum. The following describes the current state of affairs:

Case Study

You have become aware that all might not be well with the reading program in your school. The students in grades four through six do not seem to be reading as well as might be expected. There are a number of troubling indicators.

As you review scores on standardized tests, the Iowa Test of Basic Skills among these, you observe that your students, in the main, are well below norms for the system as a whole and for the nation. Several of your teachers have also expressed concern about the reading skills of their students. The librarian has commented about a low circulation rate even among the usually more popular children's books. Junior high school and senior high school principal colleagues have remarked to you that the incoming students from your school seem to have less well-developed reading skills.

As you examine the situation you reach the conclusion that something is functionally wrong with the reading program, and the anticipated outcome—an adequately skilled reader—is not being realized.

An example of a partial force-field analysis of this problem appears in Figure 6–2. In any given real situation, many forces beyond those suggested in the example could exist. When conducting such an analysis, it is important to focus only on *what is*, not on what *might be* or on what one "wishes" were so. The purpose of the force-field analysis is to get the problem under an analytical lens, so that a feasible solution (action plan) can be developed either to solve or ameliorate the problem.

Generating Action Plans

Once the force-field analysis has been completed, it is time to generate ideas for activities that, if accomplished, could be assumed to help solve the problem. Creative thought is what is sought. To do this, a principal could lead the staff in any of the three techniques for "unstructured" problem solving described in Chapter 20. Brainstorming or the "nomi-

PROBLEM: The pupils in Hughes Elementary School are not developing good reading skills.

Facilitating Forces (+)	Restraining Forces (−)
Instructional Materials Center	Student transiency (over district average)
Full-time librarian	
Budgeted for 3 aides	Bilingual population
Funded ESL program	Bimodal distribution of teachers (many first year)
New reading series	
Assistant principal is a reading specialist	New reading series program; no inservice
State mandated and funded tutorial program	Parental involvement in school activities slight
Most children walk to school (no bus students)	Little study room in homes—high number of apartment and project dwellers
Expressed teacher concerns	
Flexible schedule	Teacher turnover above district average
	Single-parent and two-wage earner homes (people not readily available)
	No role models
	Staff overloaded

FIGURE 6–2. Example of a Force-Field Analysis

nal group" techniques most easily lend themselves to this. There is one caveat. If the solutions generated do not relate in any way to the pluses and minuses in the force-field analysis, it probably should be discarded. Unless the activity is such that it would seem to reduce a negative or strengthen a positive, then that activity cannot be expected to help solve the problem. All project activities must be related to the force field. Figure 6–3 illustrates this.

The Project Planning Document

Complex problems require the use of a planning document. The resolution of simple problems may not require an involved procedure, but the logic and steps in the project planning document are nevertheless applicable and should at least be a mental process. The document is the project manager's guide, and serves also as a monitoring device.

Figure 6–3 illustrates a comprehensive problem resolution document. Using the previous case as an example, the project goal is stated, activities are delineated, target dates are established, and specific persons are identified who have assigned responsibilities for the implementation of the activities.

Project: Improving the reading skills of fourth-, fifth-, and sixth-grade students at Hughes Elementary School
Project Manager: Kay Weise, Assistant Principal
Completion Date: June 1*
Start Date: August 15

Actions	Start/ Complete	Relation to Force Field (What +/–?)	Coordinator
Volunteers Program	10/1-cont.	#5 (–)	Holland
After school study program	11/1-cont.	#6 (–)	Norris
"Why I Read" speakers	11/1–6/1	#9 (–)	Carspecken
New teacher in-service program: Reading in subject areas	8/15–2/15	#6 (+) #9 (+) #3 (–)	Craig
Reader of Month Award	9/15–6/1	#1 (+) #2 (+)	Tanner
"Here's an Author"	2/1–3/1	#9 (–)	Strahan
Story Telling Hour	10/5–5/15	#2 (+) #3 (+) #10 (+)	Miller

* Actions #1 and 2 continue beyond June.

FIGURE 6–3.   Action Planning: The Problem Resolution Document

In many instances a specific activity may be especially complex and composed of several components to be carried out before the activity is accomplished. The responsible person would develop a similar document for use with his or her team and the project would be disaggregated to another level. The point is, with such a document tasks are clearly spelled out and all are made aware of precisely what it is that is being attempted, how, who is responsible, when, and for what.

Putting the Plan into Operation

The project has now been separated into a series of activities—complex activities have been subdivided into elements or events, the completion of which will conclude the activity, and responsibilities have been assigned and accepted. Before proceeding, there is need to establish realistic target dates, develop the project calendar, and put into place a monitoring and evaluation process.

Establishing Target Dates

Establishing precise starting and completion times for the project as a whole, as well as for each of the separate project activities, is critical.[3] In order to establish realistic completion dates, it is essential that those involved in the project understand: (1) the nuances of the problem; (2) certain organizational realities, including, for example, requisitioning and purchasing procedures and time lines; and (3) the capabilities of the staff. If these conditions are met, then it is possible to set realistic target dates. To do this the project team raises two questions: "If unanticipated problems arose—strikes, floods, a championship basketball team—what is the most pessimistic date by which this project could be completed?" Then the question is asked: "If all went well—no one became ill, adequate resources were available, the purchasing department finally got its act together—what is the most optimistic date by which this project could be completed?" The realistic target date is a point midway between the pessimistic and optimistic dates.

The Project Calendar: Gantt Charting

Once the activities and tasks have been delineated, the specific elements of the more complex activities detailed, and responsibilities assigned, the master schedule needs to be developed and posted. This is developed in the form of a *Gantt chart*. Figure 6–4 depicts a Gantt chart for the case study presented earlier.

In the Gantt chart each project activity is listed, along with the elements or tasks composing each activity and an indication of the targeted starting and completion dates of every entry.

The Master Project Document

The preparation of a master project document is an important responsibility of the project manager. The document may simply be a looseleaf binder within which is placed the comprehensive problem resolution document, key personnel checklist, Gantt chart, minutes of team meetings, and any "diary" entries, or other notes that might help future project managers. Such a document is of great assistance in the monitoring and evaluation process.

Monitoring and Evaluating the Project

The project manager's responsibility is to help the project team stay on schedule. This does not mean daily, or even weekly supervision; it does mean frequent conversations with individual activity coordinators and regular team meetings for the purpose of information sharing and "midpoint corrections."

Other monitoring devices are available to the principal or project manager to help keep the project on target, or to adapt to changes in the environment. Prominent posting of the Gantt chart will serve as both advertisement and stimulator.

Summative Evaluation

If regular monitoring has been occurring, then formative evaluation has been taking place. What remains to be developed is the summative evaluation. That is, how will the principal know if the project resulted in the desired outcome? Are things better? What worked? What did not work? What should be continued? What should not be continued?

To lend specificity, clarity, and form to the evaluation process, it is useful to think of the several activities as "hypotheses." In the case study it was believed that if certain

Project: Improving the reading skills of fourth-, fifth-, and sixth-grade students at Hughes Elementary School

Target Date: June ___, 19___

Activity Description	Aug 1	Aug 2	Aug 3	Aug 4	Sept 1	Sept 2	Sept 3	Sept 4	Oct 1	Oct 2	Oct 3	Oct 4	Nov 1	Nov 2	Nov 3	Nov 4	Dec 1	Dec 2	Dec 3	Dec 4
Volunteers' Program									X→											↑
After School Study													X→							↑
"Why I Read"													X→							↑
Reading Inservice			X→																	↑
"Reader of the Month"							X				X				X				X	
"Here's an Author"																				
Story Telling Time									X→											↑

FIGURE 6-4. The Project Calendar: Example of a Gantt Chart

activities were carried out, students would evidence better reading skills. These hypotheses must be tested, for it is pointless to engage in a series of activities if there are no provisions to determine whether the results were sufficient to justify continued expenditure of resources.

At the beginning of any project it is important to state the indicators of achievement that the project staff is willing to accept as evidence of movement in the direction of the desired outcome. These indicators best come from restatements of the symptoms of the problem as originally stated. In the case study some of those symptoms were

1. Standardized test scores were below system norms;
2. Low circulation rates of library books;
3. Caustic comments from junior and senior high school principals;
4. Expressed concerns of teachers in the building;
5. High teacher turnover.

Changes in these conditions provide a basis for evaluating the effectiveness of the project. A review of test data, surveys of teachers and administrators, circulation rates, and formal and informal feedback from students and parents are all available tools for determining whether the project was successful. Moreover, it may be that certain of the activities were more productive than others. This, too, needs to be investigated and any changes made so that energies and other resources are focused for maximum benefit.

There are numerous computer tools available to assist in the development, organization, displaying, monitoring, and evaluating of major projects.

Getting Started with a New Staff

What follows is an description of how a newly appointed principal approached a new school year. The school was in a system that provided four days of "staff preparation" prior to the beginning of an academic year. Principals had latitude in the planning of these days although one half-day session was district-wide and held at a central location. The remaining days were to be locally organized and directed.

The previous principal had left on a sour note. An inservice committee composed of teachers had been appointed, but with the changeover this group had never met. Staff attrition was such that approximately 20 percent of the 58-person professional staff was new to the school, although not all were new to the district. Seven persons were beginning their teaching careers.

The incoming principal felt a need to get up to speed quickly. There was little personal knowledge about the faculty, beyond the information in personnel folders. There was an awareness that the school did not enjoy a stellar reputation, but neither was it considered to be in desperate condition.

Because of the lateness of the appointment, there had been no opportunity to reactivate the inservice training planning committee. A modest discretionary budget existed, which did permit the use of a process consultant to facilitate many of the activities. What follows is a description of how this person proceeded to organize, develop, and implement the staff preparation days to best advantage.

A week before the preschool inservice activities were to begin, all staff members received a letter of personal introduction from the principal, an agenda of upcoming events, and the intended outcomes of the three-and-one-half-day preschool program.

The principal had five outcomes in mind:

1. A staff that was well informed about current district policies and about issues confronting the district as a whole. This outcome was to be achieved in the half-day all-district meeting.

2. The establishment of the overall school goals for the academic year and the development of priority projects.

3. Enhanced communication within and across workgroups.

4. An increased level of awareness of the school's administrators about factors that might be keeping the school from achieving a maximally productive state.

5. A list of strategies for achieving a maximally productive state in targeted issue areas.

After the customary refreshments, introductions, and opening ceremonies characteristic of any such workgroup gathering, there was an overview by the consultant of the activities to occur over the next three and one-half days. The intended outcomes were again presented. A brief presentation was made by the consultant about the nature of productive organizations and productive workgroups. Then it was time to get to work.

Chairs were pushed back and a "mall walk" was conducted as a warmup. The charge was for individuals to meet and greet as many of their colleagues as possible in the minute allowed for the exercise. As time was called, individuals were advised to remain standing and wait for further instructions.

The instructions were to locate some other person in the room whom they did not know (or did not know well), to seat themselves facing that person, remain silent, and wait for further instructions. A team-building exercise began, with the instructions that participants were to have one minute to deliver, in timed turn, a mini-lecture about themselves to their "new friend." This activity continued, using a typical team-building framework until several teams of eight had been formed.

Such an activity almost always results in groups composed of individuals from a cross-section of departments and/or grade levels, and in a large organization these will be persons who have rarely had an opportunity to work together even though the veterans may "know" each other. The purpose of the exercise was to get persons talking across workgroups and to prepare participants for the information sharing about the workplace that was to come next.

Problem Identification

The group was informed that they would be working together over the next few days, and perhaps in some instances throughout the year. The initial focus of the groups was to be on issue identification, or "surfacing conditions that might be impeding greater school effectiveness."

Flip chart paper and marking pens were distributed. What followed were two eight-minute brainstorming sessions, separated by an activity that focused on the product of the first brainstorm.[4]

The topic of the first round was: "This is a good place to work but it could be better if. . . ." The purpose here was to identify problems, constraints, irritations large and small, and training needs that might be getting in the way of a productive work environment. The groups responded with much enthusiasm and the ideas were recorded in each group on the flip charts.

After time was called, groups were instructed to distill and summarize the product. To facilitate this process, groups were charged with achieving consensus on the most important six issues and rank ordering these. Each issue was to be taken in turn and two questions answered: Can we control it? and, Can we influence it?

The effort was to keep things in a productive mode. There might be some short-term positive effect from simply "venting" about job annoyances, but the principal was after long-term development, not venting. Thus, there was the effort to focus more on "controllable" or at least "influenceable" issues. This also encouraged the group to own the problem and avoided the "somebody ought to do something" syndrome.

All issues were made public, of course, and in some instances a basis for immediate action at a superordinate level was provided by the principal. The issues that became a part of the problem-solving process that followed were those that the group thought they could either influence or control. Time was spent circulating throughout the room, examining the product of other groups before moving into further analysis and problem solving. Figure 6–5 is a representation of the effort of the several groups.

The next task confronting each group was to engage in another idea-generating session—this time focused on what might be done either to solve the problem or reduce its intensity.

This processing continued throughout the remainder of the preschool period, with time off for the all-district meeting. Groups continued their problem-solving activities, learned some elements of systematic planning, and ultimately several quality circles developed.

A proposal for the establishment of a district-wide task force to examine the teacher appraisal system was reacted to favorably from the central office, as was a similar proposal to establish a system-wide staff development program. These were other district reforms that occurred as the problem-solving process continued into the year.

And what about the intended outcome with regard to school goals? A task force was created to conduct a needs assessment, and operating on a severely tight six-week deadline, they developed a list of priority goals ready for administrator and staff reaction by mid-October. Action planning began immediately thereafter.

What the Principal Needs to Know about Managing Major Projects

Campus improvement plans need not be difficult to manage. Nor does the principal have to be the project manager. There are, however, three distinct characteristics that set major projects apart from normal, ongoing school activities.

Group I

Better benefits
Training needs
Communication
Computerization
Administrator-staff relations

Group V

Competitive salaries
In-house training
Better equipment
Better communication
More qualified leadership
Student control

Group II

Teacher-principal relationships
Pay/benefits/rewards; incentives
Automation
Excessive paperwork
Need for communication
Need for better in-service training

Group VI

Automation
Better facilities
Better training
Promotion and opportunities
Community relations

Group III

Benefits and pay
Better and more communication
Automation
Training opportunities
Operational procedure revision
Better image

Group VII

Better parent relations
Communication
Better room arrangements
Staff development programs
Computers
Tutoring program

Group IV

Lack of communication
Working environment
Positive and cooperative attitudes
Lack of modern equipment and
systems
Paperwork burdensome

Group VII

Discipline
Principal-staff relations
Leave policy
Communication
Physical facilities
More operational money

FIGURE 6–5. High Priority Issues from Brainstorm Groups: "This is a good school but it could be better if. . . "

Source: Gerald C. Ubben and Larry W. Hughes, *The Principal: Creative Leadership for Effective Schools* (Boston: Allyn and Bacon, 1992), p. 302.

An Established Life Cycle

Major projects have a defined life cycle. They have a beginning and an end after which they have either become a part of the normal operation *or* they have been evaluated as not being effective and are discarded. How long is a life cycle? Three years probably is the shortest length of time before which the results of a major project could be reasonably summatively evaluated. The complexity of the project and other variables will make the difference with regard to the timing of the summative evaluation. Formative evaluation and subsequent "mid-course corrections" occur throughout the life of the project.

An Early, Thorough, and Flexible Plan

In contrast to the ongoing programs of the school, a major project is a concentrated effort to address an issue of great importance. A premium must be placed on sound planning, timely decisions, and flexible communication channels.

A Well Functioning Project Team

The key to successful major projects is the quality of the persons on the project team. The team must be staffed with persons of sufficiently diversified talents and given some freedom from routine duties. Team membership will probably begin with a relatively few key people, and grow as the project grows and as some project functions become more important. The team is, however, *ad hoc* and disbands once the project is completed.

The Project Manager

Much care must be given to the selection of this person. He or she should be chosen because of demonstrated or potential management abilities, not primarily on the basis of technical ability. This is the person who must provide direction to the project team and coordinates its activities.

Other Team Members

The specific nature of the project, initial and demonstrated personal commitment, and any needed technical ability or special expertise are membership criteria. The principal should be an active member of the team as well, but usually does not serve as project manager. It is essential that the project team take part in the planning process. It may be necessary for team members to increase their expertise by getting special training, engaging in research, and by systematically visiting other schools or school districts that have implemented similar projects. Adequate released time for this and a budget will be required.

A hard-working project manager, a team supported by the principal, good information, and a decent budget *can* plan, decide, execute, and control major projects that will lead to maximum school effectiveness.

Getting Started

What is the problem? What needs to be done to improve the school? What is it that seems to be getting in the way of maximum school effectiveness? Important questions, these. And the answers to these questions will form the basis of the school improvement plan. Figure 6–6 illustrates how to get started.

How to Get the Staff Going
A Protocol

- State an issue or problem that something needs to be done about.
    1. Something is not right. Or something is not as good as it might be. State that "something" and state it in the negative. For example, "Sixth graders don't read well," or "attendance is not good," for example.
    2. Think of that "something" as "X." "X" is where you are. Now think of "Y." "Y" is where you want to be.
    3. Describe "Y" specifically. What conditions would have to be present (what would the school look like) if "Y" existed? State some things that would have to be evident in order to say "Y" has been obtained? These become points of evaluation.
- Why isn't it worse? What's going on that is good? It's not right; maybe it is really bad, but it is not a disaster and it is not hopeless. Be specific. Label these "pluses."
- Why is it like it is now? Why is the school not closer to "Y"? List those things that are keeping the school from being what it could be. Be specific. Label these as "minuses."
- How might the minuses be lessened? How might the pluses be enhanced? These become possible activities for the project team to implement.

FIGURE 6–6. Beginning a Force Field Analysis

Summary

The subject of this chapter has been systematic problem identification and resolution. Schools exist in an environment of change. The productivity of any particular school organization will depend in great part on the ability of leaders to analyze current conditions and future challenges, develop goals, and implement strategies for attaining the goals.

Instituting a process for identifying needs, and developing a campus plan to resolve these needs in a manner consistent with system needs is critical to effective building level leadership. Action planning and project management are fundamental skills that must be employed to meet this challenge satisfactorily.

Endnotes

1. Richard Saxe presents a good discussion of this distinction in his chapter in James Cooper (ed.) *Developing Skills for Instructional Supervision*. New York: Longman, 1984, Chapter 2.

2. See Kurt Lewin, "Quasi-Stationary Social Equilibria and the Problems of Social Change," pp. 235–238 in Bennis, Benne, and Chin, *The Planning of Change*. New York: Holt, Rinehart, and Winston, 1961. In the same volume is another relevant entry: David H. Henkins, "Force-Field Analysis Applied to a School Situation," pp. 238–244.

3. In not all cases will the completion of one activity, or one component, depend on another but sometimes this will be so. Even when this is not so, it is nonetheless vital that activities be completed on

time. When a project is very complex and has many interrelated parts, it may be necessary to institute the Program Evaluation Review Technique (PERT). PERT will depict the order in which each of the activities and any subactivities must occur, as well as the relationship of one activity, event, or element to another. Especially good treatments of this technique applied to problem solving in the educational setting can be found in Saxe, "Planning and Goal Setting," pp. 36–39.

4. Either brainstorming or the nominal group technique could have been used. (See Chapter 20). With either technique, groups may need some training in the process. This is the facilitator's or principal's responsibility.

Selected Readings

Gaynor, Alan K. and Evanson, Jane L., *Project Planning: A Guide for Practitioners*. Boston: Allyn and Bacon, 1992.

Hughes, Larry W., "Organizing and Managing Time." Chapter 3 in Cooper, James (ed.), *Developing Skills for Instructional Supervision*. New York: Longman, 1984.

Lewis, James, Jr., *Long-Range and Short-Range Planning for Educational Administrators*. Boston: Allyn and Bacon, 1983.

Saxe, Richard, "Planning and Goal Setting." Chapter 2 in James Cooper (ed.) *Developing Skills for Instructional Supervision*. New York: Longman, 1984.

Sergiovanni, Thomas J., *The Principalship: A Reflective Practice Perspective*. Boston: Allyn and Bacon, 1987. (See Chapters 4 and 6 especially.)

Ubben, Gerald C. and Hughes, Larry W., *The Principal: Creative Leadership for Effective Schools*, Second edition. Boston: Allyn and Bacon, 1992. (See Chapter 6 especially.)

C h a p t e r   7

Individual Differences and Student Placement

Introduction

The dilemma of how to deal with the vast array of individual differences in our schools continues. We have a variety of programs such as special education or English as a Second Language (ESL) designed to deal with some of the obvious differences, but what about those that are not quite so obvious. Individualized instruction, which received much attention during the 1970s, is experiencing a resurgence under the new banner of restructuring. Nevertheless, underlying all of these efforts to cope with a diverse student population is the knowledge that children come to school with a great variety of experiences and are growing and developing in different ways and at different rates.

What differences count when organizing a school? Differences can be found in children's abilities, height, weight, age, sex, interests, needs, ethnic background, learning styles, achievement, and personalities. But before determining which differences matter in school organization, we should consider what these differences really are. Obviously, as children mature, differences increase. Many characteristics can be measured against accepted fixed scales and spoken of in fairly concrete terms. Items such as sex or ethnic background remain fixed and can usually be described in specific terms, also. However, factors such as ability, interests, needs, learning style, and personality are far more difficult to assess, for they are far more complex, varied, and changeable. As a result, our efforts to classify people become more dependent on other constructs for definition and therefore less exact. For example, rarely will a single continuum suffice in a description of ability. Ability to do what? To be meaningful, ability descriptions must also be scaled in some way. Ability compared to what or to whom? Ability to do something or do something better than someone else? Comparative information, then, is necessary in studying or determining differences in abilities because of the abstract nature of terms such as ability.

Achievement vs. Ability Differences

One reason for looking at individual differences is to determine the conditions they may set for organization. Individual differences obviously affect the way instruction and curriculum are organized. Contributing to these organizational decisions will be decisions relating to grouping children. Achievement is most often used as a basis for predicting ability. As a result, the two terms often become inappropriately interchanged. Achievement can be measured with a fairly high degree of accuracy, but translating achievement into ability is fraught with dangers because of our inability always to know of, or adequately place in the formula, those factors contributing to a student's opportunity to achieve.

For example, a child may have the ability to be an excellent fisherman, but if he or she has never been fishing, future performance is uncertain. Thus, to take past achievements in fishing as a predictor of future success would be erroneous. More thought about the conditions or circumstances under which past achievement occurred needs to take place before making instructional decisions.

If one is not going to look at ability but rather at achievement as a determinant for organizing children for learning, what kind of differences should one expect to find in a school population? Studies done at the University of Minnesota in the early 1940s established a simple rule of thumb to indicate an achievement range:[1] "The achievement range of an age group of children is equal to two-thirds of their chronological age." A group of six-year-old children will have an achievement range of four years; a group of nine-year-olds will have an achievement range of six years. In other words, on achievement tests the slowest nine-year-old will appear to be approximately equal to an average six-year-old (three years below) and the fastest nine-year-old will be approximately equal to an average twelve-year-old (three years above). Figure 7–1 illustrates the formula for school-age children. Note particularly the overlap of achievement over any three-year age span. A group of six-year-olds, a group of seven-year-olds, and a group of eight-year-olds have a broad range of achievements in common. The extremes contribute only fractional difference across the several years. One could rightly question the need for age-level grouping if its major basis is achievement differences.

Differences in Learning Styles

A second factor in individual differences that merits attention for organizational progress is learning styles. How do children learn best? An identification of how children learn may have implications for how we teach. If there are different learning styles, should different teaching styles be developed when instruction is organized?

There have been numerous theoretical models developed to assess learning styles or modalities and much writing in the professional journals. However, the research on instruction has not demonstrated improved achievement occurs when learning style is taken into account in instruction. In a meta-analysis review of thirty-nine studies searching for aptitude treatment interactions, neither the value of modality assessment nor modality instruction contributed to improved achievement of students.[2]

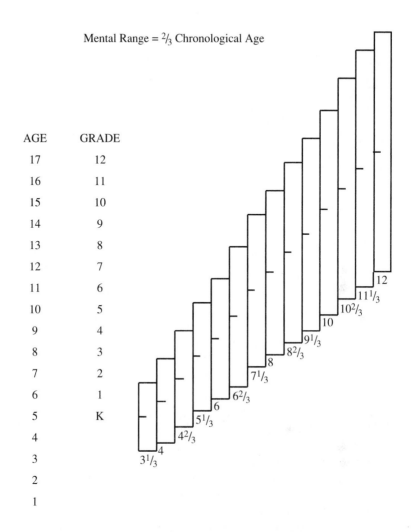

Mental Range = $\frac{2}{3}$ Chronological Age

AGE	GRADE
17	12
16	11
15	10
14	9
13	8
12	7
11	6
10	5
9	4
8	3
7	2
6	1
5	K
4	
3	
2	
1	

FIGURE 7–1.   Achievement Formula for School Age Children

Learning Interests

Student interests represent another area of important individual differences. Many factors from a child's life affect interests in school. Only a portion of a child's interest is created within the school environment; the balance is generated from the home environment, the community, and differences in children's basic nature.

The activity curriculum of John Dewey's day was organized around interests, or "impulses" as he called them. Dewey identified four such impulses: (1) the social impulse shown by a child's desire to share experiences with others; (2) the constructive impulse manifested at first in play, in the rhythmic movement in make believe and then in more advanced forms in the shaping of raw materials into useful objects; impulse to investigate and experiment, to find out things; and (4) the expressive or artistic impulse that seems to be a refinement and further expression of the communicative and constructive interests.[3]

John Dewey referred to students' interest as uninvested capital. Dewey, of course, was looking to the strong motivating force that interests can contribute to learning. This motivation can be further supported by some of the more recent work of Taylor,[4] who identified six talents that he believes are significant in our culture: (1) academic, (2) creative (productive), (3) evaluative (decision making or wisdom), (4) planning, (5) forecasting, and (6) communicating. Studying these talent areas, Taylor found that people were more self-directive (motivated) in the areas of their greatest talent. Interest, therefore, seemed to be positively correlated with talent.

Significant implications for Taylor's work exist in viewing individual differences in relation to interests if these talents are distributed evenly across a population but unevenly in relationship with one another. In other words, a high rank academically says nothing about one's creative ability. In fact, when a population is considered across all six variables, 90 percent of the people will be above average in something. In any one area, of course, by definition only 50 percent can be above average. A close tie, therefore, can be seen among interests, motivation, and talents, with definite implications for curriculum and instructional organization. Some of the recent successes with accelerated learning for the slow learner appear to support this motivation concept. Accelerated learning moves the slow learner out of the repetitive drill type activities which emphasized basic skills into ideas and concepts that are more advanced. While the student's abilities might prevent the depth of understanding achieved by another student, the interest in the material motivated the student to want to learn.[5]

Student Growth and Maturity

Any discussion of individual differences must obviously pay heed to effects of maturation on changes in student interests and needs. Several notions in particular are significant when considering the organization of a school. The first is that all children do not mature at the same rate. The difference in maturation of boys and girls is quite obvious, both physically and mentally. The same variation in size, mental capacity, interests, and needs also exists within children of the same sex at a given age, only to be in a different balance or relationship after several more years of maturation. These differences, of course, should have a bearing on instructional techniques and curriculum offerings, as well as on ways of grouping students.

As children mature, their interests and needs as well as their mental capacities expand and change. Interests begin to broaden as they come into contact with more and more of the world. Curiosities continue to expand. Needs change and children's requirements for safety, security, love, affection, and self-esteem take on new dimensions. The source of need fulfillment transfers successively from the home and parents to the teacher and then to peers, first of the same sex and finally to a peer of the opposite sex.

Quite often in organizing schools we tend to resist responding to these basic drives. The child who seeks attention, the child who needs a friend, the child who comes to school hungry, the child who needs status often cannot find solace in school because the adults there feel that since fulfilling these needs is not listed anywhere in the curriculum outline or specifically mentioned in someone's lesson plan, they are inappropriate concerns of the school.

Psychologists believe that every human being has needs that are constantly seeking fulfillment. Some theorists suggest that these needs can be classified into categories such as physiological (food, warmth), safety and security (safety from bodily or mental harm now and in the immediate future), love and belonging (a need to be wanted, appreciated, and understood, and a sense of being part of a group), self-esteem (a sense of self-worth, a good self-concept), and, finally, a need for self-actualization (the opportunity to be or become what one wants to be or become). Some motivation theorists such as Maslow[6] believe there is an ascending order to these needs and that basic needs (those first on the list) must be satisfied before an individual will consider higher-order needs. In other words, needs for food or warmth (physical) must be met before needs for safety and security, which in turn must be fulfilled before a concern for love and belonging surface. Need fulfillment also operates on several wavelengths. Hunger, obviously, is a recurring need that demands satisfaction several times daily. Other needs, once fulfilled, may sustain themselves for an extended period of time without reinforcement.

Several important lessons can be found in the application of needs theory to school organization. Most desired educational outcomes occur in the realm of the higher-order needs of self-esteem and self-actualization. If lower-order needs must be satisfied before higher-order needs, then as educators we must create an environment that satisfies the physiological, safety and security, and love and belonging needs of the student. The hungry, the fearful or insecure, and the left-out will all experience a great reduction in learning if those needs are not fulfilled.

Second, since a need creates a drive or motivation on the part of the individual, planners should create learning environments that emphasize rewards of love and belonging, self-esteem, and self-actualization. Group learning, praise for achievement, and opportunity for self-direction can all be directed to achieve both personal and school goals. Finally, knowing that needs change as children mature, we can design curriculum using needs theory. The curricular organization, through the establishment of course sequences, has become more responsive to changes in mental capacity, but in the area of matching school organization to student interests, the school has been only partially successful.

For example, the graded curriculum represents an effort to adapt the content to the levels of student capacity. It is possible to look at various curriculum materials and make a fair judgment of their appropriate intended maturity level through the degree of difficulty of the materials. On the other hand, instruction tends to look very much alike from the lower elementary grades through college. The way children are grouped, the way school staffs are organized, and the way facilities are used look very much the same at all grade levels. It would seem that if varying interests and needs motivation of students were being considered, differences would be apparent. Our lack of adequate attention to school program organization and to developing needs and interests to motivate students may be partly behind the year-to-year increased disenchantment with school on the part of children. If the activities and outcomes educators have planned for schools are not congruent with the needs and interests of the students, the increasing disinterest on their part is only natural and leads to a greater turning away to activities outside those planned by the school. The problem of lack of congruence between school programs and student interests and needs is illustrated by Figure 7–2. Circle A represents the planned activities and outcomes of the school such as social studies, language arts, math, science, health, physical education, music, and art. Circle B represents those things that actually occur for children through their interaction with the school environment such as frogs, rubber bands, paper airplanes, bicycles, girls, boys, stories, graffiti on restroom walls, fights on the playground, motorcycles, hot rods, sex, drugs, questions about what they are going to do when they finish school, and so on. Area C represents the area of congruence or the area in which what was planned actually occurred.

A school with a program highly attuned to students' needs, interests, and differences will have a high percentage of congruence between Area A and B, resulting in a large Area C. This congruence will probably not exist for the school that pays little attention to these factors.

It is important to give adequate attention to individual differences and varying maturity rates and levels and to recognize that student interests and needs are broadly based. The organization of a school program must account for these needs, interests, and capabilities in all their diversity and provide learning experiences that will motivate all students.

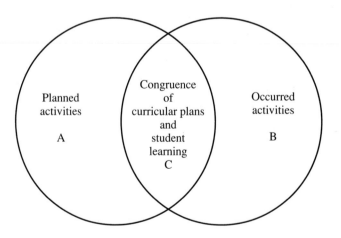

FIGURE 7–2. Planned versus Occurred Student Activity

Grouping Students

Instruction in any normal school setting requires numerous decisions about the grouping of children. Basically, these decisions will relate to three variables: group size, group composition, and group tenure. The basic purpose of grouping students is to bring about the highest quantity and quality of instruction possible. Grouping practices should be consistent with curricular decisions and should be compatible with each student's needs and interests. These lofty goals must be tempered by two factors. The first is the complexity of the individual learner. The second factor is the practical consideration of the cost of a particular organization design in comparison to its related effectiveness. For example, group size usually suggests certain staffing patterns that can be converted into dollar costs. A school might conclude that a staffing ratio of three-to-one would give the best quality and quantity of learning per student but that it would be too expensive. Instead, grouping designs must consider more economical staffing ratios, most likely in the range of fifteen to thirty students per one staff member.

Group Size

Over the years research studies on class size have produced mixed results. Two meta-analyses of class-size research by Gene V. Glass and Mary Lee Smith, published by the Far West Laboratory, have been widely interpreted as providing convincing evidence that smaller classes are better than larger ones. The basic finding of analyses on class size indicated that smaller classes resulted in increased achievement. However, the study showed that in classes ranging from twenty to forty pupils, class size made little difference in achievement. The major benefits from reduced class size were obtained as size was reduced below twenty pupils.[7]

The Educational Research Service (ERS), somewhat alarmed at some of the conclusions of the Glass-Smith studies, published a response and further explanation in 1980, stating, "The conclusions from these meta-analyses only confuse the class size issue; . . . What is needed are practical guidelines for flexible class size policy. Flexibility allows decision makers to vary the size of classes to fit the needs of pupils, teachers, and diverse school situations."

ERS had previously found that smaller classes can have a positive influence on pupils in the early primary grades (achievement in reading and mathematics) and also on low-achieving and economically or socially disadvantaged students. However, few pupil benefits can be expected from reducing class size if teachers continue to use the same teaching methods that they used in larger classes.[8]

A more recent study in Tennessee[9] using over 70 classrooms in a well-designed four year study of primary classes (K-3) size 13–17, 22–25, and 22–25 with an aide produced conclusive results. Students in the small classes made higher scores on both the achievement and criterion-referenced tests. The greatest gains were made in inner-city small classes. The highest scores were made in rural small classes. Teachers reported that they preferred small classes in order to identify student needs and provide more individual attention as well as to cover more material. The findings also suggest a cumulative and positive affect of small classes later grades. Students in grade four who had previously been in the project's small classes demonstrated significant advantages on every achievement measure over students who had attended regular classes.

Teachers who had the smaller classes were observed to cover their basic instruction more quickly, providing increased time for additional material. They used more supplemental texts and enrichment activities. There was more in-depth teaching of basic content. More frequent opportunities were available for children to engage in firsthand learning activities using concrete materials. In summary, teachers were better able to individualize instruction.

Administrative Instructional Decisions about Group Size

In the past, administrators have used group size as a constant and made instructional decisions based on group size. However, instructional decisions should be dominant, and decisions regarding group size should be secondary in nature. Therefore, if the instructional decision demands a tutorial approach, a staffing ratio of five to one would be both effective and efficient. For purposes of group discussion and maximum interaction among all members or for intensive skill work, a group size of fifteen is about the maximum. If the instructional demand on teachers includes individualization of instruction, a ratio of not more than twenty-five to one apparently is needed. Finally, if instructional plans require the presentation of basically the same material to all members of a group with the need for only one-way communication, a group of any size is appropriate. The limiting factors become those of space and the number of children. Further discussion of variability or flexibility in group size requires a discussion of variations in staff utilization.

Group Composition

What should be the basis for organizing children into groups? Obviously efficient instruction requires groups. The question of group composition has intrigued educators for years. This section will deal first with some of the more controversial grouping practices such as homogeneous ability grouping and retention and their accompanying problems. Then, on a more positive note, alternative grouping patterns based on interest, age, skill, and achievement as well as group flexibility and tenure will be discussed.

Ability Grouping

A common practice is to organize or group students on the basis of their supposed ability, creating a tracking system with a two-, three-, or four-group continuum consisting of the high-ability, average-ability, and low-ability students. The basic assumption underlying this pattern of student organization is that by subdividing children from the extremely broad ability continuum found in any normal school population, teachers will better be able to focus instruction on the needs of the children in any particular group. Thus, ability groups supposedly narrow the range of abilities within any group and make it more possible for the teacher to organize and prepare materials for a narrower range of abilities.

Factors used to determine group composition have included achievement test scores, I.Q. scores, previous grades, and teacher opinion. Serious problems develop when any of these criteria or combinations are used as the basis of organizing students on a permanent basis or for long periods of time. This method of grouping is usually not very effective. Differences exist from child to child on many variables. The pattern for each child is different. No common denominator can be found for long-term grouping across disciplines or even within disciplines. For example, a child's interest can greatly affect productivity within a discipline, overriding previous supposed ability measurements.

Children can be successfully grouped according to one factor to obtain a degree of homogeneity, but the group remains heterogeneous on all other aspects of curriculum and instruction. For example, homogeneity in mathematics can be obtained by placing in a group all children who know their multiplication tables through twelve, but they remain a heterogeneous group for the rest of the curriculum, including other areas of mathematics.

When the descriptors of homogeneity are based on previous math achievement, an I.Q. test score, or all previous grades, almost all useful definition of homogeneity is lost, for in almost any specific skill or knowledge some children placed in the lowest group on one basis will exceed the knowledge level of other children placed in the highest group on another. Therefore, homogeneous grouping as a broad-based or permanent grouping design simply does not work, and the homogeneity is a figment of the imagination of the staff (Figure 7–3).

Many teachers and administrators have argued strenuously that ability grouping does work and that definite differences exist among students. Of course, differences can be seen, but the point is that the overlap in abilities is far greater from group to group than most of us imagine, and, most importantly, homogeneous grouping overlooks the individual child.

Several attitudinal factors must also be considered in a discussion of homogeneous grouping. The phenomenon of the self-fulfilling prophecy enters into the ultimate outcomes of ability grouping. This prophecy says that children become what we say they are or what they think they are.[10] Research about self-concept has shown that children's own attitudes toward themselves as people and their assessment of their own abilities represent major factors in their ultimate success or failure in school. Teacher attitudes as well as the student's self-concept contribute greatly to the child's ultimate success or failure in school. The placement of a child in a group on the basis of perceived ability can seem to prove itself correct by adjustments in productivity on the part of the child that in fact take place as a result of the placement, thus fulfilling the prophecy. Over the past fifty years numerous research studies have considered ability grouping. A massive review of many of these studies was reported in 1973 with the following conclusions:[11]

1. Homogeneous ability grouping as currently practiced shows no consistent positive values for helping students generally, or particular groups of students, to achieve more scholastically or to experience more effective learning conditions. Among the studies showing significant effects, evidence of slight gains favoring high ability students is more than offset by evidence of unfavorable effects on the learning of students of average and below average ability, particularly the latter.

2. The findings regarding the impact of homogeneous ability grouping on affective development are essentially unfavorable. Whatever the practice does to build or inflate the self-esteem of children in the high ability groups is counterbalanced by evidence of

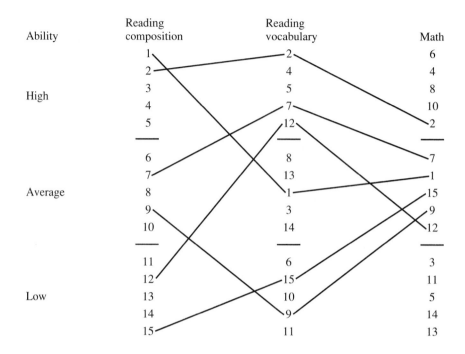

FIGURE 7–3.   Homogeneous Grouping—Student Rankings

the unfavorable effects of stigmatizing those placed in average and below average ability groups as inferior and incapable of learning.

3. Homogeneous ability grouping, by design, is a separative educational policy, made ostensibly according to test performance ability but practically according to socio-economic status and, to a lesser but still observable degree, according to ethnic status.

4. In cases where homogeneous or heterogeneous ability grouping is related to improved scholastic performance, the curriculum is subject to substantial modification of teaching methods, materials and other variables that are intrinsic to the teaching-learning process, and that, therefore, may well be the causative factors related to academic development wholly apart from ability grouping per se. Similarly, with respect to social development, evidence that points to variables other than ability grouping tends to relate substantially to personal growth or lack of growth.

More recent studies continue to support this position.[12]

Retention

Retention in a particular grade for a second year is one form of ability grouping that is often overlooked. Retention places a child with a less intellectually and socially mature group based on the child's demonstrated ability or achievement. Therefore, it is actually an instance of ability grouping—adjusting the placement of the child to fit a curriculum and instructional level thought more appropriate, rather than bringing the appropriate curriculum and instructional level to the child.

Retention is also shown to be an ineffective approach to the grouping of children. A poorly achieving fourth grader is not more like third graders. That student is still more like his or her peers and will be more successful with them than if retained and placed with a younger group of children. At any grade level the achievement range will spread over a number of grade levels. The Cook studies of the early 1940s concluded that:

When pupils in the lower 10 percent of the classes are failed because of low achievement, they do not become better adjusted educationally or socially in the retarded position. The available evidence indicates that, on the average, they achieve as much or more by being given more regular promotions.

The study goes on to point out that:

When attempts are made to reduce the range of abilities and achievement in a school by retarding slow learning pupils and accelerating fast learning pupils, there is an increase in the proportion of slow learning pupils in each grade. Average grade achievement is lowered.

The study concluded, somewhat tongue-in-cheek, that:

If the major concern of the teachers is to maintain grade level standards, the most effective way of increasing achievement standards in a school is to retard the bright and accelerate the dull pupils.[13]

Recent research on retention continues to show its inappropriateness as a means of adjusting for individual differences.[14] Nevertheless, it continues as a very popular policy in many schools. It is much better if a school uses other solutions to adjust to the individual differences of children.

Alternate Solutions for Grouping Children for Instruction

Groups are necessary for school organization, but retention and homogeneous ability grouping as semipermanent forms of student organization are not effective. What should be the basis for grouping? The following principles and techniques for organizing students are sound:

1. Regular classrooms and teams should be based on heterogeneous grouping. Some means should be taken to ensure that all teams have an equal portion of students on various achievement and ability levels.

2. Achievement grouping for math and reading is appropriate, particularly if these subjects are taught from a skill continuum. However, achievement groupings should not result in tracking. Primary identity for a student should still be with the heterogeneous grouping pattern.

3. The principal has the responsibility of sharing with teachers the research on retention and grouping practices. "Conventional wisdom" misleads in this case. The principal also needs to be responsible for developing grouping patterns that serve the needs of the unique student population and should monitor teacher implementation of these grouping plans.

4. Grouping patterns must be flexible and, as a result of individual student assessment, allow change in student placement as needed.

5. Within each classroom setting, subgroupings should be kept small enough to ensure individual instruction.

6. Children of various ages may be grouped together if some other appropriate criteria such as skill development is utilized.

7. Particular care should be taken so that grouping practices do not become damaging to the self-concept of the child or create stereotypes in the eyes of other students or teachers toward particular children.

With these criteria in mind, a tremendous variety of grouping bases is available. Possible designs include the following:

Heterogeneous Grouping

A heterogeneous group is a group created to represent a cross-section of the available student population. Planned heterogeneity is not the same as that which may occur by simply placing together an available group of children. Many factors within a school can indirectly affect the availability of children for heterogeneous groups. Care must be taken if true heterogeneity is sought to ensure the distribution of children in some uniform fashion across the various groups being created. By definition, unlimited heterogeneity would even include a proportionate number of children from each age group within the school. In other words, if the school consisted of grades one through six, the group would consist of children from each of those age categories.

Age Grouping

Children of a particular age or range of ages are placed into a single group. The group may still be heterogeneous in all other factors except age.

Multiage Grouping

A common practice is to not limit age groupings to a one-year span but to group children over a two- or three-year span. Therefore, children between ages five and seven, six and eight, ten and twelve, or fifteen and eighteen are eligible for membership in particular groups.

Interest Grouping

This technique brings students directly into the decisions regarding grouping. Based on individual interests, the child selects the group according to whatever criteria have been established for group organization. Learning centers at the elementary level and mini-courses at the secondary level would be compatible curriculum components to accompany interest grouping.

Skill Grouping

Children are grouped on the basis of possessing or not possessing particular skills that are usually quite narrowly defined. Skill grouping is often used in conjunction with a curricular area of a skills nature that lends itself to a detailed continuum of learning with a logical sequence and order. By diagnosing previous student skill acquisition, a current skills placement can be identified for each student. A choice of several appropriate learning activities then is available. Instructional modules are usually short, requiring from one to five hours of student and teacher time. Students needing a particular skill are placed together in a group for instruction on that particular skill. When the skill has been learned, a new group is found for them. The new group may consist of the same children or new children, depending on the progress of the other children in the group and the availability of other children for inclusion in the new skill area. Reading and mathematics represent two elementary subject areas where such groups have been organized. With available diagnostic instruments, children can be accurately placed and organized into groups where similar needs exist. The major problem with skill grouping is that a relatively large group of approximately 100 children is usually desirable as a base group from which to create the skill groups. This allows for the creation of skill groups large enough for efficient use of teacher time but limited to a relatively narrow range on the skills continuum.

Achievement Grouping

Achievement grouping is similar to skill grouping but is somewhat less specific, covering a wider range of previous learning. It is based on demonstrated achievement, not predicted ability. It should be as narrowly defined as possible, rarely expanding outside of a single discipline and preferably representing a subset within a discipline. For example, an achievement group might be established within language arts on the basis of previous demonstrated competence in composition writing. The same grouping should not be used for spelling, grammar, reading, or literary analysis. Each of these would need their own achievement groups. Within the area of composition, a whole series of subskills could be defined for the further breakdown of groups into skill groups. Achievement groups are usually used where minute skill details cannot be adequately diagnosed, are not needed for intended instruction, or would create groups too small for efficient instruction. Achievement groups are based on previously demonstrated achievement. Achievement should not be confused with ability, a prediction of potential rather than a measure of past achievement.

Group Flexibility

How long should an established group remain intact? When groups are reorganized, how extensive should that reorganization be? At what level within the organization should decisions for group reorganization take place? These questions relate directly to the ultimate flexibility that can be obtained for grouping within any school organization.

Groups should remain intact until they have accomplished their skills objective. Once the original purpose for the grouping has been achieved, the group must be reorganized. This may be after one hour of instruction in a skills group, or it might be after three years together as a heterogeneous, multiage group. Skill groups, interest groups, and achievement groups should be designed so they can be reorganized daily if necessary.

Problems of Regrouping

The need for frequent regrouping in the school presents several problems in school organization. First, it is impractical to refer all grouping decisions to the principal since the quantity and frequency of needed grouping decisions would overwhelm that office. More significant, most of the information needed for intelligent grouping decisions is found at the teacher-student level.

To give teachers and students an opportunity to make flexible grouping decisions, a school is best organized into learning communities consisting of two or more teachers, their students, and an extended time block. With this arrangement students and teachers can group students. The unit design for school organization with a team of teachers, aides, and a group of 75 to 150 students is a good example of this organization.

Empowering Teachers to Group Students

A number of tools are available to aid learning communities in the mechanical details of internal team grouping. Skill continua and diagnostic tests are available in many subject areas to aid in the placement of students. If skills and objectives met are listed in a computer data-based management system, it is easy for a teacher or team of teachers to sort and group students quickly on the basis of skills achieved. Figure 7–4 illustrates the data base screen and how a grouping list might appear.

The important concept here is that the principal has passed on power of decision making regarding grouping directly to the teachers. Once the components of the learning community have been designated, the principal's role becomes one of giving advice to the teams for internal grouping decisions. The teachers, in turn, then organize the groups or may pass directly on to the students many grouping decisions based on interest. Students can group themselves according to whatever ground rules are established by the learning community team. The student-selected learning center is a good illustration of this technique.

Grouping Guidelines

Student grouping is necessary for all school organization.

1. For purposes of assigning students to individual teachers or teams, a heterogeneous or mixed grouping plan is usually best.

2. Homogeneous grouping should take place in the classroom and be done by teachers. The basis for internal class grouping can be interest, achievement, skills, age, or designed heterogeneity.

3. Homogeneous grouping should be kept flexible with several different grouping patterns used each day. All homogeneous groups are usually of short duration. Flexibility is necessary because of the changing nature of groups and the problems of negative student self-concept or poor teacher attitudes that can develop from rigid homogeneous grouping patterns.

4. Homogeneous groups should not be used for more than one-half of each school day.

Summary

The efficient organization of instruction requires that students be grouped in various ways. For purposes of assigning students to individual teachers or instructional teams, heterogeneous grouping is usually best. Homogeneous grouping is best attempted within the classroom by the teacher. The basis for this kind of grouping depends on the nature of the learning experience and such factors as interest, achievement, skill levels, and age. Attention to individual differences, varying rates of maturation, differing skill levels in the several subject matter areas that are a part of the elementary school curriculum require much diagnosis and a willingness to group, ungroup, and regroup as the situation demands.

Classroom Skill Mastery List

Student ID Number: 434-35-6710   Student Name: Becky Bledsoe

Skill	Date Started	Number of Attempts	Date Mastered
Skill 1	2/19/94	2	2/24/94
Skill 2	2/24/94	1	_/_/_
Skill 3	_/_/_		_/_/_
Skill 4	_/_/_		_/_/_
Skill 5	_/_/_		_/_/_
Skill 6	_/_/_		_/_/_
Skill 7	_/_/_		_/_/_
Skill 8	_/_/_		_/_/_
Skill 9	_/_/_		_/_/_
Skill 10	_/_/_		_/_/_

Skill Report

Skill #1	Date Started	Number of Attempts	Date Mastered
Bill Albright	2/19/94	1	2/21/94
Mary Baker	3/14/94	1	3/14/94
Carol Clouse	2/11/94	1	2/13/94
Jim Delors	4/12/94	2	4/22/94

FIGURE 7–4.   Computer-Based Classroom Skills List Used for Student Grouping

Endnotes

1. Walter W. Cook and Theodore Clymer, "Acceleration and Retardation." In Nelson B. Henry (ed.). *Individualized Instruction, 1962 Yearbook of the National Society for the Study of Education.* Chicago: NSSE, 1962, pp. 179–208.

2. Kenneth A. Kavale and Steven R. Forness, "Substance Over Style: Assessing the Efficiency of Modality Testing and Teaching." *Exceptional Children, 54,* 3 (1987): pp. 228–239.

3. John Dewey, *The School and Society.* Chicago: University of Chicago Press, 1900, chapter II.

4. Calvin Taylor, "Talents—Waving Good-bye to the Average Man." *Pace Magazine* (June 1969).

5. For information on the Accelerated Schools Project contact the Center for Educational Research, Stanford University, Stanford, CA 94305.

6. Abraham H. Maslow, *Motivation and Personality.* New York: Harper and Row, Publishers, 1954.

7. Gene V. Glass and Mary Lee Smith, "Meta-Analysis of Research in the Relationships of Class-Size and Achievement." In *The Class Size and Instruction Project,* Leonard S. Cahen, principal investigator. San Francisco, CA: Far West Laboratory for Educational Research and Development, September 1978.

8. *Class Size: A Summary of Research.* Arlington, VA: Educational Research Service, 1978.

9. Helen Pate-Bain, C.M. Achilles, Jayne Boyd-Zaharias, and Bernard McKenna, "Class Size Does Make a Difference." *Phi Delta Kappan* (November 1992): 253–256.

10. A study by Rosenthal investigated the concept of the self-fulfilling prophecy and found that teacher attitudes and expectations about a child do have a direct bearing on the child's performance. Robert Rosenthal and Lenore Jacobson. *Pygmalion in the Classroom.* New York: Holt, Rinehart, and Winston, 1968.

11. Dominick Esposito, "Homogeneous and Heterogeneous Ability Grouping." *AERA Journal* (Spring 1973): 163–179.

12. R.E. Slavin, "Grouping for Instruction in the Elementary School." *School and Classroom Organization.* Hillsdale, NJ: Lawrence Erlbaum Associations, 1989.

13. Walter W. Cook, "Effective Ways of Doing It." In Nelson B. Henry (ed.). *Individualized Instruction, 1962 Yearbook of the National Society for the Study of Education.* Chicago: NSSE, 1962, chap. 3.

14. Margaret M. Dawson, and Mary Ann Rafoth, "Why Student Retention Doesn't Work." *Streamlined Seminar, NAESP, 9,* 3 (January 1991): 1–6.

Selected Readings

Booth, Martin and Lerpiniere, Dudley, "Humanities Courses and Mixed Ability Teaching: A Report of Small Scale Research Project with 11-year-old Pupils in a Comprehensive School." *Journal of Curriculum Studies,* 17 (January–March 1985): 99–102.

Cohen, E.G., *Designing Groupwork: Strategies for the Heterogeneous Classroom.* New York: Teachers College Press. 1986.

Cook, Walter, "Effective Ways of Doing It." In *Individualized Instruction, Yearbook of the National Society for the Study of Education.* Chicago: NSSE. 1962, chapter 3.

Dawson, Margaret M. and Rafoth, Mary Ann, "Why Student Retention Doesn't Work." *Streamlined Seminar, NAESP, 9,* 3 (January 1991): 1–6.

Dunn, Rita and Dunn, Kenneth, "Learning Styles, Teaching Styles: Finding the Best Fit." *NASSP Bulletin, 59* (October 1975).

Eder, Donna, "Peer Influence on Student Attentiveness during Classroom Lessons." Spencer Foundation, Chicago. *RIE* (January 1983).

Esposito, Dominick, "Homogeneous and Heterogeneous Ability Grouping." *AERA Journal* (Spring 1973): 163–179.

Evans, Ellis D. and Marken, Dan, "Multiple Outcome Assessment of Special Class Placement for Gifted Students: A Comparative Study." *Gifted Child Quarterly, 26*, 3 (Summer 1982): 126–132.

Evans, Ellis D. and Marken, Dan, "Multiple Outcome Assessment of Special Class Placement for Gifted Students: A Comparative Study." *RIE* (November 1982).

Gamoran, Adam, "Egalitarian Versus Elitist Use of Ability Grouping." Spencer Foundation, Chicago. *RIE* (November 1984).

Goodlad, John I. and Anderson, Robert H., *The Nongraded Elementary School*. New York: Harcourt, Brace and World, 1959.

Hamilton, Bruce and Burkholder, Sue, "A Team Approach to Grade Advancement." *Streamlined Seminar, NAESP, 9*, 3 (January 1991): 6–7.

Kulik, Chen-Lin C. and Kulik, James A., "Effects of Ability Grouping on Elementary School Pupils: A Meta-Analysis." *RIE* (August 1985).

Leiter, Jeffrey and Brown, James S., "Sources of Elementary School Grading." *RIE* (March 1984).

Oakes, J., *Keeping Track: How Schools Structure Inequality*. New Haven, CT: Yale Press, 1985.

Pate-Bain, Helen *et al.*, "Class Sizes Does Make A Difference." *Phi Delta Kappan, 74*, 3 (November 1992): 253–256.

Rosenthal, Robert, and Jacobson, Lenore, *Pygmalion in the Classroom*. New York: Holt, Rinehart and Winston, 1968.

Schultz, Tom, "Testing and Retention of Young Children: Moving from Controversy to Reform." *Phi Delta Kappan, 71*, 2 (October 1989): 125–129.

Slavin, R.E., "Grouping for Instruction in the Elementary School." *School and Classroom Organization*, Hillsdale, NJ: Lawrence Erlbaum Associates. 1989.

Smith, Mary Lee and Shepard, Lorrie A., "What Doesn't Work: Explaining Policies of Retention in the Early Grades." *Phi Delta Kappan, 69*, 2 (October 1987): 129–134.

Veldman, Donald J. and Sanford, Julie P., "The Influence of Class Ability Level on Student Achievement and Classroom Behavior." *American Educational Research Journal, 21*, 3 (Fall 1984): 629–644.

Chapter 8

Developing an Orderly and Positive Learning Climate

*We have to insure these children that while they are with us they are
safe and will be treated well. For some that may be all we can do but
we must do that. We may not be able to control what goes on in any
child's life before or after school. But here they will not be abused
and they will be treated fairly. And they will be protected and they will
be respected. And we're going to help them learn how life can be.[1]*

Introduction

Good elementary schools are orderly places, but we don't confuse orderliness with pin
drop silence and heavy-handed disciplinary practices. Good elementary schools are also
happy places. Children want to be there and so do their teachers.

Developing the Positive Environment

Schools should be inviting places. Purkey[2] writes of "invitational theory" stating that
"inviting is an ethical process involving continuous interactions among and between
individuals."[3] The assumptions of invitational theory are "trust, respect, optimism, and
intentionality [sic]." The invitation is "an intentional act designed to offer something
beneficial . . ."[4]

The "invitingness" of school is manifest in any number of ways—in the ways people
treat each other, in the nature of the rules that guide behavior, in the sheer look of the
place. Do the staff members appear to enjoy each other? Is there an air of good fellow-
ship along with a clear sense of purpose? Are there in place fair policies and rules that
are helpful and supportive of a good learning environment? Are all the needs of children

being met? Do things that need fixing, physical and otherwise, get fixed in a timely manner? Are the problem sensing/problem solving processes adequate to the task? In short, is it a nice place to be?

A Perspective

The nature of the student body in most of today's schools is quite unlike that of only a few years ago. "Latch-key" children abound. Family structures and family environments have changed dramatically from the two-parent norm of years past. The realities of a multicultural society are manifest. The makeup of school populations in some places has changed dramatically in only a few years. Teachers, almost at once it seems in some schools, are faced with learning problems, behavior patterns, and cultural orientations much different than they have ever faced before.

The birth rate of unmarried adolescents has reached an all-time high. One-fourth of those pregnant, married or not, receive no prenatal care in the first three months of pregnancy, and the impact of that on the development of the born child is significant. Two million school children receive no supervision during the late afternoon hours; another two million are being reared by someone other than a parent. Since 1976 the number of reported cases of child abuse has tripled.[5] Homicide is the second leading cause of death for young people, and in some urban areas it is the leading cause of death for young African-American males.

Where is the elementary school in all of this? For many children the school is the only stable factor in their lives—an anchor in a chaotic and very puzzling personal world. The focus of this chapter is on how to make the school at once responsive to children's needs while providing a safe, orderly learning environment.

Maintaining Positive Student Control

In Gallup poll after Gallup poll, discipline is reported to be one of the top five problems facing the public schools. What is meant by discipline as a problem in the school varies with each respondent, but it can be generally summed up as the control of student (mis)behavior.

The principal's responsibilities with respect to creating a positive learning climate may be as follows:

> There are no short cuts or easy-to-follow rules for establishing and maintaining discipline in a school. Discipline is based on the overall school purposes and program. A strong instructional program geared to individual student needs is the foundation for good discipline.
>
> The primary task of the principal is to establish a proper learning environment, one which affords the opportunity for both students and teachers to engage successfully in the teaching-learning process. The central position which the principal occupies in the school requires that he or she be aware of disciplinary problems and appropriate disciplinary procedures. Ideally, the awareness of potential problem areas affords the opportunity for the principal to prepare more effectively to deal with problems as they arise.

Schools should be dedicated to the twofold task of helping students understand that (1) every human being inherently possesses dignity and worth and (2) inalienable rights are accompanied by inescapable responsibilities. Such responsibilities, however, cannot be learned in the absence of freedom. Children generally learn better from what educators demonstrate than from what they advocate.

When it is obvious to students that administrators are responsive to the serious concerns of young people, the school administration and staff can focus upon preventive discipline rather than punitive discipline.

Development of a Preventive Program

The principal of a school has a particular responsibility to lead the staff in developing school policies to control student behavior. This does not mean that the principal personally should write the policy but that the principal should set up procedures by which the staff can establish a behavior philosophy, disciplinary procedures to be followed, and techniques for corrective action.

Fundamental to an orderly learning climate is a collection of well-understood, appropriate, and consistently applied rules and procedures. Once the rules are in place there are two equally important conditions that must be met:

- The rules must be stated in a manner that ensures understanding by all affected;
- There must be regular and systematic evaluation of the need for and efficiency of the existing rules. Times change, needs change, and response patterns change. Therefore, it is important that rules be examined in view of whether or not they continue to serve their purpose in an efficient and effective manner.

A good policy statement should include a referral system where teachers know under what circumstances they should ask for assistance, and of whom, and a statement of who accepts responsibility for the youngster's behavior after the referral. If the school is operating on a team arrangement, teacher to team to principal is a good order to follow. For example, a teacher should refer a student for discipline when the situation has gone beyond the teacher's reasonable ability to handle it. At that point, the problem is turned over entirely to the referral agent, and changes and modifications in teacher-assigned punishment can be made and understood without undermining the teacher's authority.

All extreme discipline cases should require the involvement of a second professional. This person should give advice and present a level head in treating the problem as well as provide the legal protection of a witness.

An adequate follow-through reporting system must exist so that all staff members involved will be aware of any action taken. Any policy developed at the building level must follow the policies established by state rules and regulations and local board of education policies.

Good student behavior in the school comes as a result of adequate supervision and the use of good student management techniques. There are certain areas of the building and school grounds, for example, that require appropriate supervision to maintain a good preventive program. Guidelines drawn up by teachers themselves often offer the best solution, both in ensuring that all such areas are supervised as well as providing teacher cooperation in carrying out the plan.

Nip It in the Bud

Anticipation and prevention are the primary aspects of "nip it in the bud" programs. Early identification of students who are potential failures and early intervention to prevent failure from occurring are critical to a positive learning climate.

In the fourth week of the term the principal queries teachers: "Who pops into your mind as a poor performer?" "Do you have anyone in class who is not turning in assignments, seldom has a pencil, doesn't seem to be with it?" These queries are made every four subsequent weeks. A list of those students identified is then reviewed by the principal, assistant principal, and counselor. A conference is held with the teacher and a subsequent teacher-parent conference is arranged for those on the list. If more than one teacher submits the same name, those teachers have a joint conference with the parent.

If a child's name reappears in later weeks, another conference is arranged, this one to include the principal and counselor and an "individual education plan" (IEP) is formally developed for the child. This meeting and the plan are not unlike the meetings that are held to meet the conditions of the IEP as provided in PL 94-142 and the intended outcome the same (See Chapters 3 and 9). It's a team approach and the parent or guardian is an active participant.

The attempt is to address the problem at the earliest moment when there is the greatest likelihood that recovery can occur. To the student, it is a clear indication that there is considerable concern for his or her performance.

"Time-Out" Areas and In-School Suspensions

The separation of children with behavior problems from other children often functions as a mild form of corrective behavior. Within the classroom the teacher may have an isolation booth or an area apart from the other children that minimizes contact, preferably visually as well as physically, and is used as a temporary abode for the child who is exhibiting inappropriate behavior.

For more serious cases requiring a possible out-of-school suspension, many schools are having much success with the "in-school suspension." This entails setting up an adequately supervised isolation area within the school where the child will work during the suspension. When both parents work, the in-school suspension seems to offer a good solution; in any case, it is more educationally sound.

Resolving Student-to-Student Conflicts

Gilmore Middle School in Racine, Wisconsin, has developed an effective way to manage student-to-student conflicts. The program, called "Mediated Dispute Resolution," offers a "face-saving" opportunity for both parties to find a solution to the issue. The mediator is a trained peer.

In the first six months of the program, there were 189 disputes involving 415 students. Of these, only 3 had not "held," and while in two cases no agreement was reached, a "cease fire" was called and there was no more fighting. Twenty-one different students served as mediators.

When students have serious disagreements, they can ask for a mediator, or an intervening teacher may suggest such. When the mediator approach is taken, the conflicting parties agree not to talk to each other until they can meet with the mediator. The more heated the dispute, the sooner the meeting is set up. The arguing students and the mediator meet in a private area in the school. The mediator explains the ground rules: no name calling or interrupting; each person has a chance to explain his or her side; and the disputants themselves must come up with a variety of alternative solutions.

Teachers and counselors favor the system because students learn coping skills and nonviolent techniques for resolving problems. Students like it because they feel a peer often understands their problems better and they do not end up in detention or with other formal disciplinary action being taken by the school.

Keeping Records

It is important to keep records about student misbehavior. A good record system will assist in the early identification of potential "problem" students, help locate trouble spots in the building and on the grounds, and track those techniques that seem to be effective and those that are not. It can also identify those teachers who may need special help in creating a good behavior management system in the classroom.

Maintaining such records need not be tedious; a system can be developed that will ease analysis. Computer-based management systems offer a means of recording, categorizing, and summarizing data efficiently. Some principals report that the use of microcomputers to analyze data results in a 50 to 70 percent reduction in the time it takes to generate reports. There are programs that will generate individual student profiles, summarizing the number of referrals, the offenses, and the disposition. Data such as offense-frequencies, period-frequencies, teacher-referral distribution, and location-frequencies are easily obtained.

Helping Teachers Improve the Classroom Behavior Management System

Some teachers never seem to have student control problems; others do. Five factors contribute to good classroom behavior: the establishment of classroom rules, the consistent application of these rules, regular discussion of the rules and how they might be improved, involving students in a plan to improve conduct, and positive reinforcement for positive behavior. A sixth factor, a well-organized lesson plan that provides for maximum "time on task," is fundamental to it all.

Figure 8–1 is a list of teacher-generated ideas and suggestions for reinforcing classroom rules. These are tested suggestions and they work.

Setting the Tone Is a Key Administrator Responsibility

The good behavior of students is necessary before an instructional program can be fully effective. Discipline, however, is not always easy to maintain. Environmental factors

Rewards	Consequences
Praise	Time-out area
Extra privileges	Call parents
Free play time weekly	Confer with child
Games	Confer with parent
Buttons	Child writes to parent
Conduct chart/Bulletin board	Remove privileges
Stickers and stamps	Daily/weekly conduct grade to parent
Happy face rings	Name on board
Class helper (line leader)	Remove special responsibilities
Movies	Loss of free time
Daily point system to reward class at end of 6 weeks	Detention after school (parents get 24 hour notice on this)
Visual reward system, such as filling up a jar with marbles for each orderly day	

FIGURE 8–1.   Ideas for Reinforcing Classroom Rules

outside the school's control have a major effect on the behavior of children in school, as well as the climate created by staff in the school.

There are, however, a number of functions well within the control of the school administrator that can contribute mightily to a positive learning climate. Disorder and lack of control in schools are frequently a result of the existence of large, impersonal masses of students. Students' feelings of alienation and teachers' feelings of helplessness must be recognized and addressed by the administration through reorganization of the school into smaller learning communities.

A large percentage of severe discipline problems are caused by a small percentage of the students. Special facilities and methods are needed to handle the more severe disruptive behavior of children if it cannot be handled effectively in the classroom. Much alienation and misbehavior are caused by a curriculum that is irrelevant and inappropriate for many students. A curriculum that is appropriate and relevant to the students' life can do much to improve behavior.

The principal's own behavior and activities will help set the tone. A principal who helps teachers develop good discipline practices, a principal who maintains direct contact with students, and a principal who is visible are all critical to a good learning climate. Attention to the list of procedures in Figure 8–2 will establish a positive framework.

Hoopla

Celebrate success! The efficacy of public rewards for achievement cannot be underestimated. We label such "hoopla." Hoopla is not hokey—it really is a manifestation of a

Tips for Maintaining Control

1. Be visible. The principal's presence in the halls, cafeteria, or playground serves as a deterrent to misbehavior and gives the teachers a feeling of support.
2. Develop school discipline policies consistent with school board policies and make sure that parents, teachers, and pupils are familiar with them. This may be done through a school handbook.
3. Base all rules and regulations upon whether or not the educative process is disturbed rather than on whether or not the educator is disturbed.
4. Require teachers to keep records of recurrent misbehavior. A simple card file will suffice.
5. Encourage teachers and parents to make the initial attempt to solve problems.
6. Emphasize the responsibility that parents have in regard to their child's behavior.
7. Let minor infractions be handled by the teacher, recognizing that some teachers need more help than others with discipline.
8. Ask teachers to submit a disciplinary report along with the request for help from the principal. That is, teachers should report what happened, who did what to whom, and why.
9. Use some convenient method to inform teachers of the disposition of referred discipline problems.
10. Encourage teachers to assume responsibility for school discipline. A word from a teacher to students running or scuffling is often a sufficient deterrent.
11. Identify trouble spots such as restrooms, halls, and the cafeteria, and assign faculty members to be there at specified times.

FIGURE 8–2. Maintaining Control: Tips for Elementary School Principals

"value-added" school culture (see Chapter 2). The most productive organizations—public and private—make much of individual accomplishments and group progress toward goals. Acknowledgement of achievement shouldn't be limited to just students. The entire school family—custodians and cooks, teachers and other professional staff members, contributing community members—all deserve recognition for jobs well done.

How to do this? Ceremonies, some of the moment; T-shirts; special parking privileges; standing ovations at assemblies; stars and stickers; Number One clubs; prizes; badges; friendly taps on the shoulder; all and many other devices should be frequently employed. Praise, sincerely given, works! More than that, an ethos of acceptance and pride in the organizations obtain.

But it is also important to help individuals recognize their own achievements without benefit of others' acknowledgement. Self-acknowledgement is sustaining. Teachers can help children with this by asking them to share a personal accomplishment that they are proud of but which others may not know about. Principals can do the same with the staff.

The Child Misbehaved: Being Firm, Fair, and Friendly

We discussed procedural and substantive due process at length in Chapter 3. These fundamental principles to insure a fair and equitable learning environment need to become an automatic mental process in everyone when a student appears to have misbehaved. Elaborate vestments are not needed for minor miscreance, but at the least the thought process ought to be:

Do I know this is the child who did "it?"
What is "it?"
Have I let the child tell his side?
All egos aside, how serious is this?
What is a fair response? Does the response fit the seriousness of the transgression?

Helping Children

Many things go on in a school that are not in the curriculum. The needs of children are varied and only partly addressed by the formalized set of classroom or cocurricular activities.

Students may be said to have four interacting selves: an intellectual self (an inquiring mind in need of systematic development); a physical self (a developing body); an emotional self (a psychological dimension); and a social self (a need to be accepted in groups of interacting humans). All of these selves come to school with the student and affect individual growth. If the only self educators had to be concerned about was the intellectual self, it would be a much simpler professional world, but this is not the case. The interaction of each of the other three selves precludes ignoring any one. Reams have been written about the nature of human nature and specifically about the nature of and reasons for learner behavior. What makes students act as they do? What turns students "on"? What turns students "off"? Professional educational and psychological literature abounds with research and conceptual treatment of the subject. Yet we really don't seem to know much about why some schools have a student body that evidences productive learning; why students in other schools manifest dissonance and disruption, others are deceptively quiescent, and still others are openly hostile, if not aggressively so. Of one thing we can be certain: students do affect, sometimes in dramatic ways, the climate of a school.

The real or perceived normative behavior of a student body will determine reward or punishment practices, teacher and administrator attitudes and behaviors, and even teacher and administrator attrition rates. Some schools in a community may be classified as "tough" schools, others as "good places to work;" most often the reference is to normative student behavior patterns. In all of this it is easy to forget that, normative behaviors and "mass actions" to the contrary, a student body is composed of many bodies and, while certain groups may determine in great part the "accepted" behavior, the student who walks through the door of the principal's office is an individual complex of forces that may or may not epitomize the student body.

The Counseling Program

What is usually meant by student advisement and guidance? Traditionally, the guidance program is assigned to a particular person called a counselor who is given the responsibility for everything that deals with psychological services, testing, and student programs. Elementary schools that have been able to afford an elementary guidance counselor have found that they perform roles very much like those of their high school counterpart. In many cases, however, the advisement and guidance needs of elementary school children require a different professional role and pattern or organization.

Student advisement and guidance in the elementary school should remain the function of the classroom teacher. The basic advisement and guidance functions for a particular child should be in the hands of a single professional in order for someone to have a picture of the whole child. The main problem the classroom teacher faces in organizing an effective student advisement program is usually one of time. There are ways to gain time for student counseling, however. Organizing activities and dividing some of the responsibilities with other appropriate personnel will assist teachers in this endeavor.

Advisor-Advisee Systems

A system of teacher-child advisement on a regular basis will successfully combat the problem of child alienation in an individual classroom. Each teacher assumes responsibility for the curricular decisions and learning goals for a particular group of children. The ratio of students to advisor is based on the total student-staff ratio in the school. Some schools involve every professional staff member in the school, including the principal, librarian, and specialists. Involving everyone reduces the ratio and also involves every staff member in a specific instructional role.

The advisor is responsible for meeting with the entire group of children at least once a week and with each child individually at least once every other week. Individual conferences are scheduled on an appointment basis during times convenient to both the advisor and the student. These conferences should average about ten to fifteen minutes. Commonly used times are before school, during instructional breaks common to both the student and the advisor during the day, or immediately after school. For example, an advisor having twenty-five students must see an average of three per day to complete the cycle each week. It is a good idea for an advisor to attempt to see all students in four days, leaving the fifth day each week for makeup appointments.

To a certain extent, the specific function of the advisor depends on the rest of the organization of the school program. In a traditional elementary school, the teacher in a self-contained classroom performs this advisor role. The advisor's primary role is to review with the student the learning progress in various subjects, to help set goals, and to recommend to the student and teachers any program modifications required as a result of the review.

In schools that have team teaching, flexible schedules, or individualized instructional and curricular programs, the job of the advisor is crucial. The flexibility of thoroughly individualized programs requires control functions. Someone must plan with the child a curriculum and its accompanying instructional format. In programs that allow a high degree of scheduling flexibility, the individual student will make scheduling decisions daily or at least weekly. The advisor's role is to provide competent professional assistance to the student in making these choices. The influence of the advisor is further strengthened with control of all curricular and instructional decisions.

The advisor has a better opportunity to observe the whole child than the individual staff members in the various contact subjects and the advisor can take a more neutral position as to the importance of one subject over another for that particular child. In this model, the advisor has the power to remove a student from a particular part of the curriculum and place the student in another, to recommend a different instructional format for a student, or to reschedule the student in some other way. These changes should of course be done in concert with the teachers in that child's school program. This achieves a very direct and immediate link between the student and the student's program. It provides the flexibility that is necessary, particularly in an individualized situation.

An advisor-advisee model such as the one just described obviously requires a time commitment of every staff member, usually one hour or more per day. Schools that are effectively using such a system seem to feel that the ten or fifteen minutes devoted to each individual are worth ten to fifteen hours of group instruction in increased motivation for that child.

Developmental Guidance and Counseling

Three basic development activities are group guidance, individual student counseling, and parent conferences.

Group guidance activities may be varied, but underlying them should be the advisor's responsibility to aid students develop good peer relationships, good interpersonal problem-solving skills, and a good learning-community climate.

Individual counseling accomplishes two purposes. First, it provides the opportunity for each student to interact with the advisor as a friend and confidant. Second, it provides frequent program planning and evaluation. At least biweekly conferences are necessary, and they should function as the main stage for academic planning. A teacher describes such a conference as follows:

> For each of my students, I have a file folder in a box next to my desk. Every paper completed by that student is placed in that folder, and it has been appropriately graded or reviewed, and remains there until the night before our scheduled appointment. Each night I take home the three folders of the students I plan to see the next day and regroup and review their papers according to subjects. I also review my notes from earlier conferences with each child and look at the goals we had established in previous weeks. I then write down tentative goals that I have in mind for the student for the next two week period. The next day when that student comes to my desk for his conference, I review with him his schedule of activities and the amount of time that he has spent on each subject area. We then go over his papers and I ask if he is having any particular problems. I will note for him problems I have identified from my review. Next, we look to see whether previously set goals have been achieved and begin our discussion of which goals and learning activities should come next. I prefer that each of my students sets goals for himself rather than for me to always have to suggest them. We each write down the goals agreed upon and identify some of the activities to be done toward each. As might be expected most are continuations of previously laid plans, but if new interests or needs have developed, these are to be included. Finally, a cover letter is stapled to the entire two-week collection of papers to be taken home to the parent. (Figure 8–3 is an example of a letter such as the one referred to above.)

Some teachers prefer to use a form on which to set and record goals that can also be shared with parents or at least made a part of the student's yearly diagnostic file. An example of such a form is shown in Figure 8–4. A *conference with parents* gives teachers an opportunity to hear from parents about their child and to share information with the parent.

Selection of an Advisor

The effective advisor must be able to communicate with each child on a friendly, personal basis. Thus, a good personality match between advisor and student is desirable. This can be achieved if several advisors are available. Alternative advisors exist when the school operates on a team or expanded-team basis. After staff and students have become acquainted in the fall, the team can assign to each of its members an appropriate number of advisees, keeping in mind the needs of each individual student and which team member might best meet those needs. One approach that has worked particularly well is for students to select advisors.

Another organizational technique that greatly aids the effectiveness of the advisement program is multiage grouping, which places children with a particular team for two or three years, enabling a child to keep the same advisor during that entire period. This

---

Strahan Elementary School

Dear Parent:

Here are the papers completed by your child during the past two weeks. I have reviewed with
_____ and we have made plans for the next set of activities.
    Name

Although not all items in the packet have correction marks, the general concepts have been reviewed.

If you have any particular questions, please call me at school (743-5035) and leave a message for me to return your call.

Richard L. Hooker,
Teacher

FIGURE 8–3.

ADVISEMENT CONFERENCE

Student Name _____ Term _____

Advisor _____ Date _____

  A. Goals set by student and teacher
  B. Adjustments and accomplishments toward previously set goals
  C. Additional teacher comments
  D. Additional student comments
  E. Next conference date _____

FIGURE 8–4.

long-term arrangement gives the teacher a much better opportunity to become acquainted with each child and to apply that knowledge over an extended period.

An excellent opportunity to reduce the student-teacher ratio can be created by using the expanded-team concept for student guidance. This concept calls for participation in the guidance program by professionals within the school not ordinarily assigned to teams for purposes of instruction. Included would be teacher specialists, resource teachers, the librarian, and the principal. By expanding each team with one additional professional for purposes of guidance, each regular teacher's advisement load can be reduced by five or six students.

If persons outside the team act as advisors, they must have adequate time. This includes time for individual as well as group activities with the children as well as some planning time with the team in order to coordinate adequately with team instructional operations.

Establishing a Good Advisement Program

Try for maximum flexibility in advisor assignments so that more than one teacher could logically be assigned as a child's advisor. Keep the advisor-student ratio as low as possible. The concept of using *all* professionals in the school as advisors helps. Have advisors schedule meetings regularly with advisees, both on a group as well as individual basis. Figure 8–5 shows four different types of advisor-advisee activities, with their group and individual application. It assumes each advisor has twenty-four children. The total weekly commitment by the advisor to individual conferences is approximately four hours per week during the school day and two hours after school. Group guidance activities can be built into the regular school schedule, requiring approximately thirty minutes each day for a total of two and one-half hours each week. (See Figure 8–6 for a sample schedule.)

Teachers should schedule individual conferences as well as group activities in advance. If time is not set aside, conferences tend to be easily forgotten in the press of time. A regular appointment calendar on a two-week rotation should be established, and each child should know the designated time in advance.

A teacher with an advisee load of twenty-four students should plan to see approximately three advisees each day, leaving Fridays open for makeup appointments. Most appointments can be scheduled during noninstructional hours, either immediately before or after school, or during a noon-break recess period.

Each advisor should collect and file information about each child in a systematic manner. Diagnostic information collected from the student and parents, personal data sheets, interest information recorded by the teacher, learning style observations, as well as reports on academic progress are all appropriate. Forms such as those shown in Figures 8–7 and 8–8 offer systematic ways to gather such data.

Total Quality Management and Group Guidance

We wrote about Total Quality Management (TQM) in the first chapter when Deming's work[6] was discussed. Children quickly pick up on the elements of this especially in

	Academic	Personal Development	Parent Reports	Administrative
Individual applications	Diagnostic prescriptive Goal setting evaluation 1 15-minute conference every two weeks	Counseling as needed Average of 10 additional minutes every four weeks per child	Pupil / Teacher / Parent } Conferences Phone contact 1 30-minute conference each semester plus 30 minutes planning time for each conference 2 conferences per week (2 hours) beginning after first six weeks of school	*Unscheduled*
6 hours per week (4 during school day, 2 after school)	3 hours per week total	1 hour per week total		
Group applications	Standardized tests Orientation of advisor-advisee relationship General goal setting	Group process problem-solving class meetings	Parent orientation	Administrative announcements records completion, attendance
2¹/₂ hours per week in school	(2 30-minute periods per week) 1 hour per week	(2 30-minute periods per week) 1 hour per week	(1 1-hour after school or evening session each semester)	(1 30-minute period per week)

FIGURE 8–5. Guidance Activities and Suggested Average Times Needed

STUDENT ADVISEMENT SCHEDULE

Week 1 of a two-week cycle
15 minutes each conference

8:00 Early bus arrivals........... Susan D.	Pat M.	Pete H.	Elizabeth S.	Makeup
8:30 Classes begin				
Lunch and Playground				
12:15 Henry D. Walkers	Daryl P.	Ellen T.	Shirley B.	Makeup
3:00 Classes end				
3:10 Late bus departures........ Larry Z.	Brenda M.	Bill T.	Earl H.	Makeup

FIGURE 8–6.

group guidance sessions. McAuliffe Elementary School in Prince William County, Virginia is a TQM school and TQM is pervasive there, including the students in the process.

> At McAuliffe, all meetings follow quality guidelines. They start and end on time. Participants are punctual, participate actively, and listen to one another with no interruptions or side conversations. . . . [Students] strive to do things correctly from the start. They know and use interactive skills, especially brainstorming. They love to assign roles for meetings. In a cooperative learning session, for example, a first grader will say "I'll be the one who keeps us doing what we're supposed to do," while another volunteers to be the timekeeper.[7]

The Role of the Guidance Counselor

An individual trained as a guidance counselor has a particularly important role to play in the advisement structure of an elementary school. The elementary school guidance counselor should assume five different responsibilities:

1. Become attached to a team and assume an advisor responsibility along with the other specialists within the school.
2. Function as a school referral agent to handle problems identified by the teacher advisor and team. A major role for the guidance counselor is doing the diagnostic work the teacher cannot do.
3. Administer and supervise the advisement program.
4. Provide and direct staff development activities in the techniques of advisement for both group guidance functions and individual diagnostic work. A major portion of the guidance counselor's time should be spent directly on staff development activities.

STUDENT EXPERIENCE RECORD

Name _____

Instructions: List experience, date and period of time.

READING LANGUAGE ARTS	MATH	SCIENCE	SOCIAL STUDIES	MUSIC	ART	PE
		Example: 5–78 3rd grade completed. Science fair project on leaf classification 2 months study.		*Example:* 3–78 participated in spring musical production—USA song solo.		

FIGURE 8–7.

OBSERVATION AIDE

Name of Child	Behavior Exhibited	Creative	Name of Friends	Interests	Clues to Sensory

FIGURE 8–8.

5. Assist the teachers in establishing and maintaining a good record system.

In sum, the role of the guidance counselor in the school should be one of accepting student referrals, conducting staff development activities, and providing overall supervision for the advisement program. If no guidance counselor position exists, the program becomes another one of the many responsibilities of the principal.

Referral Services

Most school systems provide a complement of specialists to meet needs beyond those that can be met by the regular school staff. Each school should have someone designated to coordinate special service needs of the school. A guidance counselor is an appropriate referral agent initially to determine the need as well as to identify the proper source for available services. If a guidance counselor is not available, this responsibility falls on the principal and the classroom teachers.

A good pupil-personnel service program does not attempt to replace the need for teacher interest in the development of each of the selves of students. Pupil-personnel services are meant simply to augment the role of the teacher through the delivery of expert technical and professional services where needed.

Thus, pupil-personnel services include all of those special classroom supportive services outside of the curricular and cocurricular offerings that impinge upon the maturation of the four selves of the student. The pupil-personnel services professional becomes a member of the instructional team, providing technical services and additional professional insight in the diagnosis, prescription, and treatment of individual learner difficulties as well as in the design of balanced programs for all learners.

Each school should prepare a list of available services and persons to contact for those services so that teachers and parents will know who to contact for particular problems. Included on such a list should be guidance, special education, and attendance counselors; the school psychologist; special education resource teachers; pathologists; homebound teachers; and reading specialists. An example of such a list provided for an elementary school staff is shown in Figure 8–9.

The School as a Coordinating Social Agency

The schoolhouse is "just around the corner" in the minds of many patrons. It is a source of both knowledge and well being. Principals—teachers, too—are often asked for help in matters well outside their spheres of expertise but which are matters that affect the general well-being of children and their families. A host of general welfare delivery systems exist in a community, many of which are not known or felt to be readily accessible to the clients they were created to serve.

SPECIAL HELP AVAILABLE AT HOLLAND ELEMENTARY

1. *Holland Guidance Counselor* Mr. Richard Hamilton is a full-time staff member at Holland offering counseling, testing, and referral help to parents and students. Telephone 699-3194.
2. *School Psychologist* Dr. Robert Williams is available to all Holland parents and students. His services are available by referral through the Pupil Services Department. Telephone 699-2860.
3. *Special Education Counselor* Dr. Michael Brady is the school counselor responsible for coordinating placement and for assisting parents and students in disability classes. Telephone 699-2860.
4. *Special Education Teacher* Mr. John Fredricks is a full-time Holland staff member who teaches students experiencing learning problems.
5. *School Pathologist* Miss Gladys Haines is a full-time Holland staff member. She is responsible for diagnosis and treatment of speech and hearing problems in our school.
6. *Homebound Teacher* Mrs. Laurel Tanner is available at the physician's request to every pupil who is unable to attend school for a period of four weeks or longer. Requests are made through Pupil Personnel Department.
7. *Diagnostic Center* This center is being operated by Mrs. Betty Larson to fully diagnose and prescribe educational programs for students experiencing problems in school. Contact your school counselor.
8. *Home-School Coordinator* Miss Phyllis Selter serves as liaison between the home and school. Telephone 699-2860.
9. *Attendance Counselor* Mr. Allen Warner coordinates all attendance and data processing. He is responsible for attendance problems, juvenile court contacts, enrollment projections, report cards, secondary and junior high scheduling, and processing of test data. Telephone 699-1658.
10. *Reading Specialist* Holland Elementary School has $1^{1}/_{2}$ reading teachers who work with students needing extra help with their reading. The teachers are Mrs. Helen Dansby and Dr. Richard Abrahamson.

FIGURE 8–9.

Summary

Children entering schools do not enter with the same abilities or with the same inclination to do schoolwork. Not everyone will have the support of a caring family, nor will all enjoy good health. More and more children come to school with emotional problems and from dysfunctional families. Some are poverty stricken. All who enter our schools require a safe, orderly and nurturing environment if they are to become what they must become—learning, growing, contributing members of society.

This chapter has focused on processes and practices that can make a difference in children's learning. Basic to a well-functioning school is an understood framework of rules and regulations so that students and teachers know what is expected of them. Each school should develop a discipline philosophy and policy acceptable to the staff, administration, and community, outlining the basis procedures to be followed when behavior problems occur. A good discipline policy will outline the basic steps to be used in severe discipline cases, indicating the referral procedures for the involvement of other professionals.

Moreover, students have special needs that can only be attended to by an effective counseling program. The elementary school counseling program must be a total school program. The classroom teacher is responsible for most day-to-day counseling. A structured program including both individual and group counseling should be built into the schedule. The guidance counselor in the school administers the teacher-counseling program and coordinates referral services and staff development as they relate to the guidance program.

With respect to the delivery of these other pupil-personnel services, the principal is a person in the middle—not as a gatekeeper but rather as a facilitator. While an organizational structure is frequently developed to deliver many of the student personnel services, it is still incumbent on the principal to take the lead in the orderly provision of these services to teachers and students in the school building.

Research about effective schools invariably reveals that such schools are orderly places. They are characterized by high standards, high expectations, and a caring environment. Misbehavior is dealt with quickly, fairly, openly, and without recrimination.

An analysis of leadership style and support behaviors revealed that principals in effective schools were perceived to be more assertive and more task and academically oriented. Principals in the ineffective schools were seen as permissive and maintained a "decentralized" posture; teachers operated their classes "independently."

The main difference in the discipline policies was that in effective schools the discipline code was clear and the principal was viewed as "firm and friendly" but not as a "pal." Punishment for breaking the rules was certain. Principals in effective schools were more mobile and highly visible in the halls, classrooms, and cafeteria. They spent much time monitoring behavior, trouble shooting, and conferring with teachers. Such was not the case in schools deemed to be ineffective. Attention to behavior in these schools was more casual and inconsistent, and sanctions for rule breaking were not certain.[8]

Endnotes

1. Dr. Karon Crow-Rilling, Principal of Humble Middle School, Humble (Texas) Independent School District, to a graduate class of aspiring principals (May, 1990). Dr. Crow-Rilling was speaking about "at risk" students, deprivation, and home environments.

2. W.W. Purkey, "An Introduction to Invitational Theory." *Journal of Invitational Theory and Practice*, *1*, 1 (Winter, 1992), 5–16.

3. *Ibid*, p. 5.

4. *Ibid*, p. 9.

5. Harold Hodgkinson, "Reform Versus Reality." *Phi Delta Kappan, 73*, 1 (September, 1991), 8–16.

6. W. Edwards Deming, *Out of Crisis*. Cambridge, MA: Massachusetts Institute of Technology, Center for Advanced Engineering Study, 1986.

7. Dorothy Mulligan, "Quality Management for Schools." *Streamlined Seminar*, National Association of Elementary School Principals, *11*, 2 (October, 1992) p. 3.

8. S.A. Jackson, D.M. Logsden, and N.C. Taylor, "Instructional Leadership Behaviors: Differentiating Effective from Ineffective Low Income Urban Schools." *Urban Education, 18*, 1 (April, 1983) 59–70.

Selected Readings

Achilles, Charles M. and Smith, Penelope, "Stim-ulating the Academic Progress of Students." Chapter Ten in Hughes, Larry W. (ed.) *The Principal as Leader*. Columbus: Charles E. Merrill, 1994.

Helen, Owen, "Is Your School Family-Friendly?" *Principal, 72*, 2 (November, 1992), 5–8. Note: Most of this issue of *Principal* is devoted to the theme "Family Involvement."

Koch, Moses and Miller, Suzanne, "Resolving Student Conflicts with Student Mediators." *Principal, 66*, 6 (March, 1987), 59–62.

Menacker, Julius; Hurwitz, Emmanuel; and Weldon, Ward, "Discipline, Order, and Safety in Elementary Schools." *Streamlined Seminar, 8*, 4 (March, 1990). Washington, DC: National Association of Elementary School Principals.

Mulligan, Thomas, "Quality Management for Schools," *Streamlined Seminar, 1*, 2 (October, 1992). Washington, DC: National Association of Elementary Principals.

Purkey, W.W., "An Introduction to Invitational Theory." *Journal of Invitational Theory and Practice, 1*, 1 (Winter, 1992), 5–16.

Railsback, Charles E., "Promoting Good Classroom Management." *Here's How, 10*, 6 (July, 1992), National Association of Elementary Principals.

Wayson, William W. and Lasley, Thomas J., "Climate for Excellence: Schools that Foster Self Discipline." *Phi Delta Kappan, 66* (1984), 419–21.

Chapter **9**

≡≡≡≡≡≡≡≡≡

Special Students;
Special Services

*Historically, special education has been synonymous with separate education.
Fundamental changes in America's schools have resulted in education for special children becoming an integral part of the total schooling picture. And, all
educators now share responsibility for teaching all children.*[1]

Introduction

Children may come to school with many problems that will make learning difficult.
Some are hungry, some need clothing before they can come to school and not be
ashamed, some have been abused at home physically or psychologically, and others have
physical or mental handicaps that make learning difficult. Often the need for special
assistance is first signaled by low attendance. In many cases school personnel have a
legal responsibility to provide the resources to improve students' learning opportunities.
In other cases, school personnel may feel a moral responsibility to function as a quasi-
social service referral agency in order for some of the children of that school to have an
adequate "quality of life." This is often necessary before learning can take place.

The principal or designated members of the staff need to develop a network of contacts in the community where assistance can be obtained. Many communities are fortunate to have governmental agencies both within and outside the school system available
to provide most needed services to children. Special education services are mandated
nationwide by the Individuals with Disabilities Education Act (IDEA).[2] All states have
child abuse laws administered most often as part of a social service agency or welfare
department. Public health departments often are charged with providing special health
services to needy children as well as providing health screening and immunization moni-

toring of school age children. Many private agencies also have available services for needy children, such as the Lions clubs that provide eye care or church groups that have emergency food or used clothing available.

While some will argue that these needs of children should not be the responsibility of the school, often the school—the gathering point for all children—is the first to become aware of problems. When the physical or emotional needs of children get in the way of learning, the school has a direct stake in seeking a solution. The principal, the guidance counselor, the school nurse, the social worker, the special education staff, the regular classroom teachers as well as others, all have a part to play. But when reaching beyond those activities required by law, or when taking fullest advantage of services from available agencies, the leadership of the principal in setting the direction for the school in providing services to special children is critical.

Special Education and Related Services

The IDEA requires school districts to provide a free appropriate public education (FAPE) including special education and related services, in the least restrictive environment (LRE), as determined by a multidisciplinary team (M-team) and written in an individualized education program (IEP). These services are mandatory for all children between the ages of four and to the end of the school year in which the student turns twenty-two or, in the case of a deaf child age twenty-three, who can be certified by an appropriate specialist as having a disability or exceptionality and verified by a multi-disciplinary team of educators as needing special education services. Exceptionalities include:

Mental retardation	Serious emotional disturbance
Learning disabilities	Visual impairment
Hearing impairment	Other health impairment
Orthopedic impairment	Speech impairment
Autism	Deaf-blind
Multi-handicapped	Traumatic brain injury
Developmental delays	

Due Process

The law requires that certain due process procedures be followed, assuring the right of the parent and child to be fully informed and included in the decision making at all steps in identification, child evaluation, planning, programming, and program evaluation. (See Chapter 3 for a more complete review of the law regarding special students.)

Step One: Screening
The school has the responsibility to monitor the development of each child in order to know as early as possible if any child is having problems with his/her school work. Screening checks are to be made for the child's medical health record as well as the

child's progress in school. Medical screenings are usually scheduled by the district special education departments or appropriate health agencies. Educational checks are initially the responsibility of the regular classroom teacher to observe and identify potentially handicapped children.

Step Two: Prereferral Actions

When a student presents a particularly unique problem, the classroom teacher often needs somewhere to turn for help. The problem may surface as a disciplinary problem, a learning difficulty, poor attendance, or what seems like a lack of interest in planned classroom activities. None of the strategies tried by the teacher have seemed to work. If the child is referred to special education, weeks can pass before a formal assessment is completed and a staff meeting is held to recommend a plan. In some cases, a formal referral may identify a student as handicapped and recommend placement in a special education instructional program. Other students may be identified as mildly disabled, but not in need of special education programming, while others will not be identified as disabled at all. For these last two groups, the delay in providing immediate support to the teacher and student may not have been necessary at all.

It is suggested that prereferral procedures be developed that will allow for more immediate action and assistance in most cases and that would be less costly than the formal referral and assessment process. The prereferral procedure should begin with the collection and review of classroom data gathered by the teacher. Included should be attendance information, available standardized and classroom test data, teacher observations of student effort, attention, ability to follow directions, listening, social skills, self-confidence, peer relationships, etc. Teaching strategies attempted should also be documented.

Step Three: Support Team Review

Each school should organize a school support team (S-Team) to function as an intermediate step between the recognition of a problem by a classroom teacher and a formal referral for a comprehensive educational evaluation. For students who are obviously handicapped, this support team review is bypassed and a formal referral is made immediately. On the other hand, the teacher who is experiencing less severe difficulty with a student should request the team's assistance. The information gathered through the prereferral action is received by this team. The team that meets regularly to discuss such cases considers the problem, generates possible remedial actions, and recommends specific intervention strategy. The support team (S-Team) should be made up of experienced teachers qualified to teach that age child, possibly the special education teacher, and other appropriate staff members such as a Chapter I teacher or guidance counselor. One member should function as the S-Team coordinator to schedule meetings, organize records, and insure that the teams recommendations are implemented.

The S-Team should be viewed as problem solvers, bringing to focus the expert resources of the school on those issues that fall just short of resulting in a formal special education referral. Those students deemed to have educational or emotional problems beyond the normal capability of the school staff and program to adequately address ultimately will be given a formal referral to the other education specialists for further evaluation.

Step Four: Formal Referral for a Comprehensive Evaluation

An evaluation to specifically determine the severity of a child's deficits is scheduled. An assessment team may include all or any of the following: school psychologist, occupational therapist, physical therapist, other special educators, physician, regular classroom teachers, and/or medical specialists. Parents have the right to obtain an independent evaluation at their own expense if they so choose; however, depending on the nature of the events, the school must sometimes eventually assume these costs. Ultimately, the assessment team determines if the student is eligible for special education. Eligibility is based on the child fitting the certification requirements for a particular special education category.

Step Five: The Multi-Disciplinary Team

The multi-disciplinary team (M-Team) is made up of a group of at least three school professionals and the parent/guardian and is responsible for developing an appropriate educational program for the student based on a careful review of all diagnostic data. The M-Team's responsibilities include: (1) reviewing the present level of educational performance as derived from the assessment data; (2) developing the individualized educational program (IEP), and (3) making a recommendation for placement.

The M-Team approach is designed to ensure that decisions concerning a student's program will be made by a team of persons whose primary goal is to accommodate the interests, needs, learning styles, and abilities of that student. Careful consideration should be given to the selection of M-Team members who are most qualified to contribute to the development and implementation of the IEP. Those individuals who must be part of the initial M-Team include the principal or his/her designee, the teacher who recently or currently has the student in class, the assessment specialist(s) such as psychologist, audiologist, etc., who conducted the assessments as part of the evaluation, the parent/guardian of the student, and the student, when appropriate.

Principal's Role

For the principal, the M-Team represents a very visible form of involvement with the special education program and the special-needs children in the school. While it is possible for the principal to designate a representative to serve on M-Teams, direct participation by the principal in the M-Team process signals an interest in this program to students, teachers, and parents. It also provides to the principal very direct feedback regarding the adequacy of the special education program in meeting the needs of the children in the school and an opportunity for leadership in improving the program where needed.

Individual Educational Program (IEP)

The individualized educational program, or IEP, or for preschool children an individualized family service plan (IFSP), is a written record of the decisions reached by the members of the multi-disciplinary team at the IEP meeting. It sets forth in writing the commitment of resources necessary for the disabled child, functions as a management tool to insure services, is the compliance/monitoring document for government monitoring of the law, serves as the evaluation device in determining the child's progress, and functions as the communication document with the parent.

The IEP must contain the following components:

1. The present level of educational performance.
2. Certification that student meets disabled requirements.
3. Annual program goals and interim program objectives.
4. Regular program participation and modifications.
5. Special education placement and justification.
6. Multi-disciplinary team signatures of participants.
7. Parent signature and statement of review/appeal rights.
8. Indicated date for annual review.

Recommendations for Placement

It is required by the IDEA that the individual educational program developed by the M-Team be provided in the *least restrictive environment*. This means that each child should be placed in a setting where he/she can be with noneligible children as much of the time as possible. The act allows for ten different placement options but demands that the least restrictive option appropriate for the child be used. The act requires that a continuum of service options be provided. A typical sequence of options would include the following:

1. Full-time in the regular classroom with special supplies and/or equipment.
2. Full-time in the regular classroom with consultative services for the teacher.
3. Full-time in the regular classroom with additional instruction by a special education teacher in the regular classroom.
4. Part-time in the regular classroom (as much as is appropriate) and part-time in a special *resource program* coordinated with the regular classroom activities.
5. Full-time in a special *comprehensive development classroom* (CDC) provided to meet the needs of the severely/profoundly involved students who require intensive planning and programming.
6. Part-time in the regular school program with a special education aide supervising the child with disabilities while in the regular classroom.
7. Other related services including transportation, speech pathology and audiology, psychological, physical and occupational therapy, recreation, counseling, medical (for diagnostic and evaluation purposes), school health, social work, parent counseling and training, assistive technology devices and services, transition, nursing, interpreter, as well as others not specified.
8. Ancillary services provided by agencies outside the school to provide services a minimum of four hours a day in order to maintain the child in the regular program.
9. Residential services to provide for a child whose disabling conditions are so profound or complex that continuous intervention is required to meet his/her educational needs and no special education services offered in a CDC or self-contained program can meet these needs. While these programs are very costly, if the IEP calls for this service, the school system is responsible for the total program.

10. Home or hospital instruction may be provided to continue the educational advancement of eligible students who are unable to attend school.

Step Six: Implementing the Plan

Options numbered one through six from the list above are often implemented in the regular school while the services of options seven through ten are more often provided by school district staff, by special schools, or by contract with outside agencies. The concept of "least restrictive environment" is being applied to greater and greater numbers of special education children, bringing more low-functioning and disabled children into contact with the regular education program. As a result, many more severely handicapped children previously housed in segregated special schools are becoming part of the regular school and are spending at least a part of their day in regular classrooms, often accompanied by an attendant.

In some cases, building modifications are required to provide access for wheelchairs, and health-related and other equipment required to support these special students and their program needs. Special Education Vocational Rehabilitation Laws (PL 93-113, sec. 504) require that buildings be made accessible to all children.

Often, the initial reaction of the staff to students with severe disabilities in their classrooms is one of fear because of the health concern for the disabled child and the concern that they will disrupt the normal classroom environment. A good in-service training program for the staff frequently turns the fear of special students into a learning opportunity. This is especially true when regular classroom children are taught about the disabled classmates who are joining them. Often a compassion and understanding develops in children that could not be taught as effectively any other way. Rather than disabled children detracting from the learning of other children, they often enrich it with the development of new values and understanding for all children.

The principal should take advantage of the opportunities provided by the special education program and its integration into the regular education activities and be very careful not to allow these to develop into separate programs.[3]

Program and Assessment Reviews

Each special education student's IEP is reviewed annually by the M-Team for the purpose of determining the continuing appropriateness of the program placement, goals, and objectives. These review dates must be monitored so that these annual reviews take place on schedule. The intent of the review should always be to move the child toward a less restrictive environment with less special education assistance if this is appropriate. The effort should be to try to move the child back toward the regular program whenever possible.

The evaluation process for each special education student must be repeated every three years. A new assessment plan must be developed and carried out, recertification must take place, and the M-Team must once again develop a new IEP.

Safeguarding Special Education Records

Special education records must be maintained separate and apart from a student's regular school cumulative record folder. Access to the special education records is to be carefully controlled, with availability restricted to only those school personnel who have direct contact with the child or to whom the parents have given written permission for access, such as an outside psychologist. Sign-out sheets should be used and permission letters kept on file. Regular education records are not supposed to reference the existence of a special education file. The purpose of this regulation is to protect the special education student from later discrimination that might occur if it became known the child had some type of disability. This makes it extremely difficult for records maintenance, however, and it is easy to misfile or not be able to locate information. Some schools code their regular cumulative folders with some special mark to indicate the existence of a separate special education folder.

Rights of Parents and Due Process Requirements

The requirement of involvement of the parents of the potential or verified special education student has been noted through this entire section describing special education procedures. From the notification of the initial referral, through the assessment process, to the writing of the IEP,[4] and finally to the approval for placement, as well as future access to their child's records, parents must give their informed consent as participants in the process. Failure to notify or obtain this consent is a violation of the rights of parents under the law.

Disciplining Students with Disabilities

Discipline of children in school is an important concern of all principals. In most situations, the day to day decisions regarding the control of children has been the prerogative of the principal supported by the staff. However, in the case of children with disabilities, intricate federal and state regulations govern the administration of punishment of these students; these regulations are based solely on federal court cases interpreting the IDEA.

The results of these cases clearly establishes a double standard. One cannot discipline children with disabilities in the unilateral fashion we generally use for our regular students. In 1989, in *Honig* v. *Doe*,[5] the U.S. Supreme Court ruled that students with disabilities cannot be unilaterally suspended or expelled for more than 10 days without provision of due process. This case triggered a array of procedural restrictions on local schools. Figure 9–1 summarizes basic disciplinary actions often used in school and indicates under what conditions they may or may not be used for children with disabilities.

Dealing with Parents of Special Children

The identification of a child as a potential special education child is always stressful for parents, and the principal and staff must be prepared to deal with a variety of reactions from parents. The parent has probably been aware for some time that a problem exists for his/her child. This knowledge may have been suppressed or the parent may already have a long history of dealing with the child and the school about the problems. There are at least four general patterns of parental reaction for which the school, the M-Team and the principal, whether part of that M-Team or not, must be ready.

DISCIPLINARY ACTION	CONDITIONS OF USE
Verbal reprimand	OK
Written warning	OK
Payment for damages	OK as long as the child's behavior does not suggest IEP changes.
Time out	OK
Detention (lunch, recess, after school)	OK
In-school suspension	OK if supervised by a certified special ed. teacher and/or the child's IEP is being carried out.
Corporal punishment	Many states prohibit its use. If permitted, it must be administered fairly. It is not recommended for children with disabilities.
Aversive therapy/Devices	Only if specified in IEP.
Bus suspension	Counts as part of 10 day maximum if bussing is included in child's IEP.
Exclusion from extracurricular activities	OK as long as it is not central to IEP goal.
Suspension/Expulsion	OK for 10 school days per offense so long as "pattern of exclusion" does not exist.[6] For longer periods, the M-team must determine the offense not to be related to the child's disability.
Alternate school placement	OK as long as the change is made through the regular IEP process.

Any disciplinary action must have no adverse effect on IEP goals and objectives and must not be applied in a discriminatory manner.

FIGURE 9–1.   Conditions of Disciplinary Action for Children with Disabilities

The Supportive Parent

This parent is understanding of his or her child's problems, is concerned about the child's education, and respects and appreciates the efforts of the school to develop an appropriate educational plan for that child. He or she generally is most supportive during M-Team meetings, attending faithfully, and asking how he or she might best support the school's efforts at home. Some always accept the recommendations of the school staff without question, while others may begin to question M-Team recommendations if they feel services are not adequate. This latter type may become a demanding parent if the school fails to carefully present a rationale for its recommendations.

The Denying Parent

This is the parent who is unaccepting of the possibility that his/her child has a handicap. He or she is offended by the request for a referral, often initially refusing to sign the permission for testing, and frequently demanding to submit outside independent evaluations to refute the school's claim that the child is handicapped. In some cases, he or she begins to resist actions of the school by not attending meetings, by refusing to sign documents, and generally by becoming purposefully nonresponsive. The denial of the disability may be due to a feeling that the child's handicap is a reflection on his or her own intelligence or on his or her ability as a parent to raise the child. In these cases, parent education must often be an additional consideration before meaningful assistance can be provided for the child.

The denying parent is often extremely frustrated with the child and demands of the child the impossible, given the identified disability. It is sometimes helpful to counsel with the parent privately, reviewing assessment data and pointing out that disabling conditions know no social or intellectual bounds—Albert Einstein had a learning disability; the Kennedy family has a retarded sister, and President Roosevelt was confined to a wheelchair. Additional support needs to be provided to these families because these feelings of denial die slowly and new strategies for dealing with the handicap at home must be learned if the home is to be a supportive environment. Parent education and counseling is an appropriate consideration in the development of the IEP for these situations.

The Nonresponsive Parent

The problem of the nonresponsive parent is probably the saddest of all. Notices are sent out, phone calls are attempted, and certified letters are sent in order to meet the due process informed-consent legal requirement for parent notification. Some schools will even attempt to arrange a home visit in order to elicit a parental response. In some cases, the work schedule of the parent interferes; in others, child care makes school visits difficult. If these are really the problems, the school should make every effort to arrange a schedule or situation that will allow the parent's participation. However, there are situations where there is little or no interest on the part of the parent in the child's schooling. In these cases, it is often appropriate to identify some other responsible adult to work with this child and to provide an adult advocate and educational support system outside the classroom environment.

The Belligerent, Demanding Parent

This parent is going to attempt to obtain more than the school, through the M-Team, believes is necessary to provide appropriate options for program placement. He or she will question the assessments provided by the school staff to the point of demanding independent evaluation or bringing in his or her own psychologist. He or she will challenge the recommendations of the M-Team, and if his or her demands are not met, will threaten to or actually will bring his or her lawyer to the M-Team meeting. He or she will sometimes contact EACH[7] and bring a representative of that organization to the M-Team meeting. As might be expected, this parent is very aware of his or her due process rights and will demand a hearing to contest the recommendations of the M-Team if his or her demands are not satisfied.

When, as a principal, you see this type of parent, be prepared to participate fully in the M-Team process yourself. Don't leave your teachers to deal with this situation without strong support. If you can see that a particular staffing is going to be very difficult or complicated, request that someone from the district level special education office join the M-Team. Remember, you must keep in mind the best interests of the child, tempered by the needs of the parents, staff, administration, and other children in the school. Your goal is to provide each child with an appropriate educational program in the least restrictive environment possible, given that child's disabling conditions.

Special Education and the Regular Classroom Teacher

Many students with special needs are in regular classrooms. The teachers in these classrooms have certain responsibilities for these children including the following:

> Identifying and referring potentially disabled children.
> Taking part in due process and M-Team procedures.
> Collecting assessment data about children with disabilities.
> Assisting children with disabilities with special equipment.
> Participating in a team effort with special education staff.
> Helping all children work and play together.
> Communicating with parents.

Whenever a child with disabilities is placed in the regular classroom, the responsibility of the regular classroom teacher for that child is the same as for any other child in the room. Because all children differ with respect to the amount, rate, and style of learning, minor modifications in methodology, curriculum, or environment are often necessary for both disabled and non-disabled children. When a child's IEP specifies modifications in methodology, curriculum, or environment from the regular class, the development of such specially designed instruction is the responsibility of special educators. Regular educators are responsible for assisting in carrying out the program. Overall classroom management remains the responsibility of the regular educator.

Educating severely disabled children in the regular classroom can often be difficult. It is here where problems sometime arise. Given the requirement of the law for providing programs in the least restrictive environment, more children with severe disabling conditions are now being educated in the regular school setting, both in the regular classroom as well as in the special education classroom but housed in the neighborhood school. Regular classroom teachers are sometimes frightened by the responsibility they feel for children who have special physical or emotional needs. Wheelchairs and other special manipulative equipment to transport children are seen as problems. Assisting children with bodily functions—helping to place a child on a toilet, changing diapers, and monitoring catheterizations—is felt to be beyond their level of training or interest. With the onset of AIDS and the need to wear rubber gloves as a precautionary measure, additional fears are generated. When difficult physical situations exist, the IEP should specify the need for special assistance for the classroom teacher both through special training and through the provision of a special education assistant in the classroom or one who is on call and immediately available.

Children with mental disabilities provide an even greater problem for many teachers. Many of the learning disabilities, though mild in a sense, cause great difficulty for the child and require great understanding and skill on the part of the teacher. Children who we used to say were just discipline problems and should be sent to the office or who we claimed were lazy and not motivated to do their work, we now know are really suffering from a variety of learning disabilities such as attention deficit disorder, dyslexia, dysnomia, or one of a host of others. In many cases, the problem has gone undiagnosed for many years and becomes compounded by the repeated failure to succeed on the part of the student who now has advanced to middle or even high school. Teachers often have not been trained either to diagnose these problems or know how to deal with them property when they are known. Additionally, many teachers feel overwhelmed by the number of children and problems they face daily in the classroom.

Good staff development activities are needed by most school faculties in many aspects of working with children with special needs. Training in diagnosing and treating learning disabilities can be a help to virtually every classroom teacher. Knowledge in the use of supplementary aids and services such as brailled worksheets for blind students, provision of tape recorders or computer word processors for children who cannot write, or the operation of physical aids such as wheelchairs, walkers, and hearing aids is helpful. Skill in the use of cooperative learning techniques in conjunction with special educators or the management of disabilities in the classroom needs to be learned.

Maybe, most needed of all is the need for good human relations training for teachers to help them understand and deal with their own fears and biases concerning people who are disabled and how to help children in their classes to do the same.

Finally, teachers need to be trained about their role in special education, state, and national special education policies, their role in referrals, evaluations, IEP development, due process, working with parents, and working with special educators regarding such things as student grading, scheduling, and record keeping.

Outside Public Agencies

A variety of public agencies in every community have direct access to the school. Local states and communities will have different names for these agencies and offer somewhat different services, but each school must recognize the demand and need to interact with these other services. The three that are common to almost every school are public welfare or human services departments, public health agencies, and judicial systems usually represented by police departments and juvenile court systems. Each of these agencies has certain legal responsibilities and authority. The authority of each of these agencies transcends the walls of the school, and the school principal is not always "master of the house." It is important not to get into a "turf battle" with the representatives of these agencies, but rather to develop a supportive network with them to serve the children of the community better. When the police come to pick up or question a child regarding a local crime, the principal is summoned to juvenile court to testify on a matter dealing with one of the school's children, or a representative of the protective services unit of the local welfare department shows up to investigate a child abuse case, it is not only important for the principal to know his or her rights and the rights of the children, but also for the principal to have a good working relationship with the representatives of these other agencies so that all can work for the benefit of the children and the community.

The development of a network of contacts with private agencies and other public agencies is also important. Who should be in a principal's network is somewhat dependent on the nature of the local student clientele, but important network contacts for many schools would include groups that can provide clothing or food on an emergency basis, both emergency and nonemergency medical treatment, and both public and private mental health professionals.

Public Welfare or Human Services Agencies

Child abuse cases are one of the most common school-related involvements with public welfare or human services agencies today. A problem that a few years ago was normally considered "only a family matter" now is recognized as an area of responsibility for our society. Most states now require that the school report suspected child abuse cases to the appropriate authority for investigation. The classroom teacher who notices heavy bruising on a child or the pattern of absences along with extremely emotional behavior on the part of a child is required by law to report it. The school is, in fact, the one place outside the home where a child can take some refuge from an abusive home environment. Confidentiality regarding the reporter of abuse is generally guaranteed. However, it is this confidentiality issue along with the sensitive nature of child abuse investigations that sometimes causes some difficulty.

Child abuse investigators often consider the school to be an appropriate safe location to conduct initial interviews. It is a safe place to contact a child without alerting a suspected abuser, and it is a place where the child is more comfortable and hopefully willing to discuss the problem. The problem is that it can also disrupt the ongoing instruction in the school. The intrusion into the school by an outside investigator can also be taken as an interference in the school's domain.

Most state laws give authority to child abuse investigators from public agencies outside the school to interview children on school premises and, in some cases, to take them into their custody. These investigators also have the authority to conduct the interviews in private with no school official present and generally do not have to reveal the content of an interview after it is concluded. For some principals, this "flies in the face" of what they consider to be their responsibilities for their children. The first reaction may be not to want to take a child out of class, and, secondly, not to want to let an "outsider" conduct a private interview with a child for whom the principal is responsible. The laws of most states, however, give the public social service agency this authority if they choose to use it. The following suggestions are appropriate ways to manage requests from outside investigators:

1. Always ask to see their credentials.

2. Attempt to convince them of the importance of having a school representative present during any interview. Some workers will allow you to be present.

3. Control the time and place for the conference. You are generally allowed to protect instructional time.

4. Document the conference, noting date, place, names of persons present, and length of the conference.

5. Refuse to give access to student records without a signed release from the parent, guardian, or a court order.

In almost all cases, it is to the school's long-range advantage to develop a good working relationship with these outside agencies. They have a job to do and are also trying to safeguard the well-being of the children. Most often you need each other.

Working with Law Enforcement Agencies

The major school involvement with law enforcement agencies will be requests by officers to interview children while they are at school. Of course, schools also often employ off-duty officers as security guards for ball games and other evening school activities. The basic suggestions listed above for investigator procedures apply to police officers as well and are for the school's protection as well as the protection of the children.

Developing a good working relationship with the police officers that work in the school zone can be most helpful to both the school and the police. The occasional informal discussion with them can sometimes cut bureaucratic paperwork and procedures and solve a problem where formal procedures could not.

The school principal will also be called upon to testify in juvenile court in conjunction with children from his/her school. Every community has a juvenile court system ranging in size from a part-time judge in smaller communities to large buildings and multiple judges in larger communities.

School children may be brought into juvenile court for three different types of situations. The first is for felony or misdemeanor charges similar to charges brought against an adult. However, juvenile court handles the disposition of a case somewhat differently: Publicity of juvenile crimes is kept at a minimum and prescribed treatment has rehabilitation as its purpose rather than punishment.

Status offenses, the second category, make up the largest number of cases that will involve school officials. Status offenses can be defined as actions that are considered violations of laws for children but not adults. Nonattendance at school (truancy) and running away from home are the most common. For school officials, instigating truancy charges becomes the last resort among efforts to obtain regular attendance from a child. In many cases, the real problem is the parents. Juvenile courts have the power to order certain action from the parents to improve or control their child's behavior, such as requiring the parent to ensure the child's presence at school each day or be held in contempt of court. A contempt charge against the parent could result in the parent being jailed. Once again, a good working relationship between the school principal and the juvenile court can be most helpful in solving such problems.

The third type of case dealt with by the juvenile court involves the problems of neglected and/or abused children. In these cases the children are the victims rather than the offenders. School employees are often reporters of suspected child abuse and may be called upon to testify in juvenile court regarding their observations. Testifying in these situations can be particularly traumatic. Reporting child abuse is generally kept confidential, or at least confidentiality is attempted. However, when the accused are the parents or someone else closely associated with the school, testifying can be difficult.

Outside Agencies and Closed Records

In an effort to protect the reputation of children and their families, many of the agencies who work with children are required by law to maintain strict confidentiality of the records they develop and maintain. This is true, for example, with the special education records maintained by the school. When a child has been in the custody of the juvenile court or has been a ward of the welfare department's Children's Protective Services unit and is then returned or placed in your school, it is extremely difficult, if not impossible, to get any information about the child's recent history. In some cases, this makes it extremely difficult to know how to deal with a child or even if the safety of other children should be a concern. Some local areas have developed coordinating councils for the several children's agencies in an effort to improve the communication among them. The individual principal will probably find his or her efforts to develop an informal network among the workers of the various agencies to be an extremely useful communication link to information not available through the formal channels.

Drawing on the Services of Outside Social Welfare Agencies

Mental health agencies, chemical abuse agencies, civic clubs, local churches, women's organizations, etc., all have an interest and a role to play in the welfare of school children. Networking once again becomes the byword for the principal and staff. Situations always develop which fall short of eligibility for one or more of the formal service agencies to the school. It may be a parent who becomes aware that his or her child is doing drugs, or it may be the child that appears to be suffering from severe depression; however, until children take some overt act to harm themselves there is no regular agency support available. It is in these situations that it is important to have contacts with professionals from other agencies from whom the principal can get advice and learn where the school or the parents might turn for help.

What can be done for middle school age children who don't want to come to school: the boy who doesn't have any shoes, or the girl who has had a front tooth knocked out and is ashamed of her looks? The best way to solve the attendance problem is to help solve the child's personal problem. If the school is fortunate enough to have a public agency that can meet these needs, that is wonderful, but often it must be met by the principal's getting a pair of size eight sneakers from the local church clothing service or working out a deal with a local shoe store or the salesperson from whom the principal buys athletic equipment. For the girl who needs dental work, but the school does not have a formal procedure for obtaining assistance, the principal may call a local dentist, explain the problem, and ask for some free service. Obviously, a preestablished relationship with these community members and agencies is critical to the success of these attempts. Once again, the importance of establishing a network of contacts in the community is apparent.

Public Health Departments and Local Schools

The services provided by public health agencies directly to school children vary greatly throughout the country. In some states, the only contact may be to monitor immunization records to insure the health of the general public, while in other areas services may include provision for public health personnel to provide direct services to children in the school. Nurses stationed in the school, health presentations in classrooms, dental services, immunizations, and some emergency medical care may be provided. Once again, there may be more services available for the asking than the average school receives. It is up to the principal to make the contact, develop the relationship, and add these professionals to his or her network of available persons tc be called on when needed.

Summary

Our schools have many special children with many special needs. The quality of school life is dependent on the collective satisfaction of the needs of all the children. The principal cannot personally meet the needs of each and every child, but can set the tone, develop the network of contacts who can assist in providing for the children's needs, and be a facilitator of resources for its achievement. Once again the symbolic leadership of the principal in showing concern for all children will demonstrate to the staff the significance and importance of their efforts also.

Endnotes

1. Professor Michael Brady, University of Houston, Department of Educational Psychology, to a graduate class of aspiring principals, summer 1991.

2. The Individuals with Disabilities Education Act (IDEA) Part B and its amendments were passed in 1990 and 1991. It is located in 34 CFR Part 300 and 304. Section 504 of the Rehabilitation Act of 1973 also addresses children with disabilities. This law is administered by the Office of Civil Rights (OCR).

3. In Chapter 12 *supra* will be found several suggestions to aid in the development of an integrated special education and regular education program.

4. A draft copy of the IEP should be developed in advance of the M-Team meeting to be presented and explained to the parent. Following this meeting and any appropriate parental modification, refinements are made and the document executed.

5. *Honig* v. *Doe*, EHLR 559:231 (U.S. 1988)

6. In addition to the ten-day limitation imposed by *Honig* v. *Doe*, the Office of Civil Rights (OCR) reminds districts that Section 504 requires a student reevaluation prior to every significant change in placement. Therefore, any change in placement including a suspension/expulsion for more than 10 days or any consecutive 10-day suspensions must be evaluated by the M-Team.

7. EACH (Effective Advocacy for Citizens with Handicaps) is a nationwide volunteer organization that provides assistance for disabled individuals to insure their legal rights are met.

Selected Readings

Anderson, Ronald J. and Decker, Robert H., "The Principal's Role in Special Education Programming." *NASSP Bulletin, 77*, 550 (February 1993): 1–6.

Darrell, Larry D., "At-Risk Students Need Our Commitment." *NASSP Bulletin* (January 1989): 81–83.

Dixon, Virginia L. and Greenburg, David E., "Assessment in Special Education: Administrators' Perspectives." *Diagnostique*, 10 (1985): 161–75. (ERIC Document Service No. EJ 334 426).

Dubin, Andrew, "Through the Administrative Looking Glass: The Special Needs Child." *Thrust for Educational Leadership, 16*, 4 (January 1987): 36–37. (ERIC Document Service No. EJ 347 177).

Ellis, Joseph and Geller, Daniel, "Disciplining Handicapped Students: An Administrator's Dilemma." *NASSP Bulletin, 77*, 550 (February 1993): 22–38.

Epstein, Michael H. *et al.*, "Improving Services for Students with Serious Emotional Disturbances." *NASSP Bulletin, 76*, 549 (January 1993): 46–51.

Freeze, D. Richard, "Microcomputers in Special Education." *Canadian Journal of Special Education, 4*, 1 (1988): 9–22. (ERIC Document Service No. EJ 370 480).

Golden, Diane Cordry, "Discipline of Students with Disabilities: A Decision-Making Model for Principals." *NASSP Bulletin, 77*, 550 (February 1993): 12–20.

Greenburg, David, *A Special Educator's Perspective on Interfacing Special and General Education: A Review for Administrators*. Reston, VA: ERIC Clearinghouse on Handicapped and Gifted Children, 1987. (ERIC Document Service No. ED 280 211).

Hensarling, Paul R. *et al.*, *School Special Services: Organization and Administration*, 3rd ed. Bryan, TX: Demand Publishing Company, 1983. (ERIC Document Service No. ED 242 091).

Jachard, Charles, "Researching the Underchallenged, Marginal, or At-Risk Student." *Clearing House* (November 1988).

Sires, Carolyn and Tonnsen, Sandra, "Special Education: A Challenge for Principals." *NASSP Bulletin, 77*, 550 (February 1993): 8–11.

Chapter 10

Restructuring the Curriculum

Introduction

Recent years have brought about a resurgence of emphasis on basic skills, state-mandated proficiency tests, skills, continua, and additional course requirements for graduation. A number of educational writers have argued for a "no-frills curriculum," emphasizing the basic skills along with cuts in other programs, including music, art, guidance, and other areas that are not considered to be part of the three Rs.

Focus has often been placed on content acquisition and instructional objectives have been heavily biased toward knowledge acquisition in order to produce high gains on standardized achievement tests. In our desire to improve our test performance, we have too often overlooked instructional objectives that focus on teaching values and critical thinking skills. Similarly, in many schools we have concentrated so heavily on basic skills and common learning areas that we have neglected adequate attention to the fine arts. How should a faculty be guided in its development and implementation of a school curriculum? What are the important considerations for the principal in providing leadership in curriculum development?

Curriculum Development

Under the principles of site-based management, the roles of teacher and principals for curriculum development need to form a new dimension. Most schools have been in a period of highly centralized curriculum development with state government and school districts passing down what should be taught and as well as the number of minutes a day to be devoted to each subject. Now, greater autonomy must be afforded to the faculty of each school to adapt programs to fit the needs of each community and each group of children.

Curriculum development has many facets. It includes the identification of goals and objectives, selection and organization of the content, learning activities and teaching processes, evaluation processes for measuring student outcomes and measuring the effectiveness of instruction.

The process of curriculum development, when broadly defined, is very time-consuming; generally, beyond the time available to the classroom teacher unless release time or summer employment is provided. If teachers are to be expected to play a major role in curriculum development beyond adapting curricula to their specific needs, additional training will need to be done to assist them in developing the skills for writing and organizing curricula.

Teachers can be given much latitude in adapting curricula to the needs of their students. Teacher empowerment can be most effective when organized as a collective effort. Curriculum committees composed of a balance of experiences and abilities within the group can foster a sense of dialog between expert teachers and administrators.

Curriculum Organization

Organization of the curriculum is the major focus of this chapter. The local school must have a means of conceptualizing the interrelationships of the various parts of a school curriculum, whether it has been determined for the school by some central authority or is being developed by the local staff. This chapter defines a structure for curriculum with both a course of study over time (the vertical dimension) and the balance of content in which a student would participate at any given moment (the horizontal dimension), a means of organizing curriculum materials within the structure, and a model to provide a framework for curriculum balance.

Curriculum Structure

Effective schools research identifies curriculum structure as an important aspect to the development of effective schools. The recommended structure includes for each subject or course a list of topics, skills, or concepts to be covered; specific student objectives to be accomplished; lists of resources classified by objectives; and mastery levels set for each subject or course along with mastery tests for each course (Figure 10–1).

Objectives and test items developed for the various course structures should be analyzed for the depth of learning they are requiring. A classification system such as Bloom's Taxonomy[1] provides a method to determine the level of learning being expected of students. Bloom's Taxonomy of Cognitive Objectives, which includes the domains of knowledge, comprehension, application, analysis, synthesis, and evaluation, is valuable in ensuring high-order skills are developed within the various disciplines.

The course outlines, objectives, and tests should be used by all of the teachers in the school who might be teaching that particular subject at that grade level. These curricular structures, in some cases, may be based on a state-approved curriculum, organized around a particular text series, developed by district-wide curriculum committee, or constructed by the teacher or teachers in an individual building. The prescribed curriculum should be at least the work of two or more professionals and determined in concert by their joint effort.

What content is appropriate? Topics, concepts, and skills should be sequenced from year to year so that good curricular articulation occurs throughout the program with a

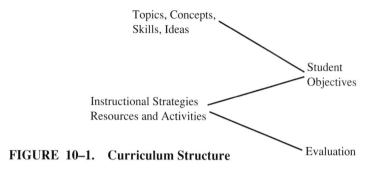

FIGURE 10–1.   Curriculum Structure

Source: Gerald C. Ubben and Larry W. Hughes. *The Principal: Creative Leadership for Effective Schools* (Boston: Allyn and Bacon, 1992), p. 191.

minimum of gaps or overlaps in content. Figure 10–2 shows a portion of a skills outline for elementary mathematics illustrating this structure.

How is school curriculum to be organized? The structural analysis of curriculum usually defines both a vertical and horizontal dimension. The vertical dimension considers what content is to be presented or what objectives are to be met at each maturity level, with sequence as an important aspect of the vertical dimension. The horizontal dimension focuses on the array of subjects or concepts available or taught to a student or group of students during a particular time period such as a semester or year.

Vertical Dimension

Many resources are available to provide suggestions to a school or systems staff in the development of curriculum guides, including objectives and test items for vertical organizations. National professional associations for the various disciplines such as the International Reading Association (IRA), the National Council of Teachers of English (NCTE), the National Council for the Social Studies (NCSS), as well as many others, have curriculum outlines available. Textbook publishers often provide curricular management systems, including skills continua, mastery tests, and tracking systems to support their materials. A number of local school-developed federally supported projects promoted through the National Diffusion Network and listed in the catalog entitled *Educational Programs*[2] also include curriculum guides. Finally, the Instructional Objectives Exchange (IOX) has compiled lists of objectives and test items organized by subject area and difficulty level that provide an excellent resource for curriculum planners in the selection of objectives in matching test items.[3] The test items, many of which are classified according to the Bloom's Taxonomy, make excellent contributions to test item banks.

Level A

Order Concept
1. WN-1 counting
2. SETS-1 description
3. SETS-2 equivalent, nonequivalent
4. SETS-3 1 more or 1 less member
5. SETS-4 numbers 1–4
6. SETS-5 zero
7. SETS-6 numbers 0–10
8. SETS-7 number comparison
9. SETS-8 ordering 0–10
10. WN-2 ordering 0–10
11. SETS-9 ordering sets
12. SETS-10 partitioning of sets

Level B

Order Concept
1. SETS-2 equivalent, nonequivalent
2. SETS-6 numbers 0–10
3. WN-3 writing numbers
4. WN-2 ordering 0–10
5. A/S-1 add sums through 5
6. A/S-2 sub, combs. through 5
7. A/S-3 add, sub., combs. through 9
8. PI V-1 ones and tens
9. WN-4 0–100, ordering skip counting
10. A/S-4 add, sub., combs. through 10
11. ME-1 time—hour, half hour
12. A/S-5 add, sub., combs. through 18
13. A/S-6 3 addends
14. FR-1 fractions—emphasis on $1/_2$, $1/_3$, $1/_4$

Level B *(continued)*

Order Concept
15. ME-3 length—inches, centimeters
16. ME-5 volume—cups, pints, quarts, liters
17. GE-1 shapes
18. ME-3 money—pennies, nickels, dimes

Level C

Order Concept
1. SETS-7 number comparisons
2. PI V-1 ones and tens
3. WN-4 0–100, ordering, skip counting
4. PI V-2 ones through hundreds
5. A/S-4 add, sub., combs. through 10
6. A/S-5 add, sub., combs. through 18
7. A/S-6 3 addends
8. ME-2 time—5 minutes
9. WN-5 Roman numerals
10. PI V-3 ones through thousands
11. A/S-7 add, without regrouping
12. A/S-8 sub., without regrouping
13. A/S-9 add, regrouping
14. A/S-10 sub., with regrouping
15. WN-6 odd or even, skip counting
16. M/D-1 mult, facts through 5
17. FR-2 fractions—emphasis on halves through fifths
18. ME-4 length—inches, centimeters, meters
19. ME-6 volume—gallons, milliliters
20. GE-1 shapes

FIGURE 10–2. Math Skills Outline

Source: Utah System Approach to Individualized Instruction. U-SAIL Project, Salt Lake City, Utah.

Horizontal Dimension

The horizontal dimension of curriculum usually includes all the subjects available to a student at a given time. When a student participates daily or weekly in social studies, English, science, mathematics, health, art, music, and physical education, one is describing the horizontal dimension of the curriculum. The horizontal structure of most of our schools is relatively uniform, and curricular areas are almost standard among schools and among grade levels. The horizontal balance remains about the same from year to year, providing students with equal doses of time in each subject area.

Schools that are departmentalized, such as some upper elementary and junior high schools, have an additional problem with horizontal organization. The departmentalization creates compartmentalization, and the several disciplines being taught are often not well coordinated or integrated for the student but are taught as totally separate and unrelated bodies of knowledge.

Interdisciplinary curriculum using combinations of subjects offer ways to reestablish the integration of school subjects. In the lower elementary grades this is best represented with so-called "whole-language" programs. There is a pedagogical movement away from discrete skills sequencing in the teaching of reading, for example. This approach integrates listening, speaking, reading, writing, and critical thinking. The whole-language approach is literature and subject-matter based and is heavily student-experience based rather than issuing from teacher-prepared worksheets and other didactic materials.

Thematic units, also often literature-based, offer interdisciplinary studies. Figure 10–3 is an illustration of an elementary school thematic unit outline. Note that it includes skill areas to be taught in reading, language, mathematics, research, and higher-order thinking. Applications to social studies, science, and art are part of the unit as well. The entire unit is organized around a book about Benjamin Franklin.

Curriculum Classification System

A curriculum materials classification system is also a desired curricular feature for all schools. School resources, the materials, the books, the pamphlets, worksheets, filmstrips, tapes, kits, software, and so on that fit the curriculum structure of the school are many and vary significantly from school to school, even in the same district. The average school has over 20,000 curricular items in its holdings. Teachers having limited memories seldom are aware of all the curriculum resources for particular topics or objectives they plan to teach, much less remember the difficulty level or instructional format of these many resources. Materials also get "stashed" away in teachers' files and closets, often falling into disuse because teachers to not know they are there.

As part of the overall effort to provide structure to the curriculum, concern must be given to organizing curriculum resources by the adoption of some type of materials classification system that matches the school's adopted curriculum and its instructional objectives. An excellent prototype to consider is the Annehurst Curriculum Classification System (ACCS).[4] There are a variety of ways this might be done. This system classifies materials on the basis of subject matter and appropriate student characteristics such as age level, perception type, and so on. A retrieval system is available for manual or computerized searches to match all available materials to particular courses, topics, and students. Many of the computerized library retrieval systems that provide for bar code identification of materials can incorporate the school's instructional materials as well. Using these systems places all school material under one cataloging system, usually under the direction of the school media program.

Curriculum Alignment

The second important aspect of curriculum organization from the effective schools research is the concept of curriculum alignment.[5] Once a structured curriculum has been adopted and supposedly implemented for each subject area, the questions become: Are

WHAT'S THE BIG IDEA, BEN FRANKLIN?
Novel Study
and
Integrated Unit for Grade Three
by Judy Rehder and Kaye Williams
Knox County Schools

CONTENT AND SKILLS COVERED IN THIS UNIT

SOCIAL STUDIES/HISTORY

1. Reading and using maps—legends, distance scales, locating places, and tracing routes, latitude equator
2. Understanding of the duties of an ambassador
3. Understanding of the causes of the American Revolution and what it was
4. Understanding of the Declaration of Independence and the Constitution of the United States
5. Cities—organization, fire departments, libraries—how people work together
6. Understanding of occupations and apprenticeships then and now
7. Understanding of how cities grow based sometimes on physical location
8. Understanding of how latitude affects climate
9. Understanding of how water and warm water currents affect climate
10. Understanding of the printing process and newspapers—understanding the effect of newspapers, etc. on people
11. Learning to work together on group projects

SCIENCE

1. Understanding what electricity is
2. Understanding how electric currents work
3. Understanding what will conduct electricity
4. Understanding dangers and safety measures related to lightning and electricity
5. Understanding how electricity has affected life
6. Understanding of seasons and earth/sun relationships
7. Scientific method
8. Inventions and inventors
9. Understanding how soap is made

ART

1. Printmaking—vegetable prints
2. Drawing illustrations for a how-to book
3. Looking at famous American artists of this period
4. Making candles

READING

1. Main idea, sequencing, details, inference, cause/effect
2. Reading to learning how to do things
3. Reading to learning information

FIGURE 10–3.   Sample Integrated Unit

Reprinted by permission of Judith J. Rehder, Kaye Williams, Chilhower School

LANGUAGE SKILLS

1. Letter writing
2. Report writing
3. Writing poetry and prose and understanding the difference between
4. Using capital letters in place of names and titles
5. Underlining titles of books
6. Use of the comma—series and dates
7. Use of a dash
8. Forming plurals
9. Forming possessives
10. Dividing words into syllables at the end of a line
11. Suffixes and prefixes
12. Oral communication skills

MATH

1. Magic squares
2. Figure distances on a map
3. Figure ages and differences in time

RESEARCH SKILLS

1. Encyclopedia
2. Almanac
3. Maps
4. Other books
5. Gathering information
6. Organizing information
7. Utilizing information
8. Sharing information

HIGHER LEVELS OF THINKING AND WORKING

1. Comparing and contrasting
2. Cause/effect
3. Productive thinking
4. Analysis
5. Synthesis
6. Evaluation—decision making
7. Drawing inferences/conclusions
8. Application
9. Working together in a constructive manner in small groups
10. Self-discipline and management skills for independent work

RELATED MINI-COURSES

1. WHAT A SHOCK!!!—Experiments and experiences with electricity
2. WEATHER OR NOT!—Observing, recording, and forecasting weather
3. BRIGHT IDEAS!!!—A look at inventions and inventors—becoming inventors

the teachers following it? Is the content being presented to the students that is indicated by the stated curriculum? The teacher who takes the student only two-thirds of the way through the prescribed topics for the year is out of alignment with the planned curriculum. The classroom teacher who spends an inordinately large amount of time on his or her favorite topic and slights or ignores the prescribed topics is out of alignment with the agreed upon curriculum.

The concept of curriculum alignment is particularly significant when accountability for learning is important. If the school's evaluation system of either standardized achievement tests or criterion reference tests is matched to the anticipated curriculum, a serious curriculum alignment problem could lower test scores significantly of children who were never given the opportunity to master the content measured by the tests. Thus, curriculum alignment is, in part, the alignment or coordination of what is taught to what is to be measured.

Curriculum alignment, however, is more global than just the match between what is taught and what is measured. It also encompasses the idea of alignment or coordination of the school's philosophy to goals, goals to objectives, objectives to instruction, and instruction to evaluation. For example, if the school's philosophy includes the statement, "We believe critical thinking and decision-making skills are important for every student to develop," then a goal should exist such as "Courses should provide opportunity's for students to develop critical thinking skills." Objectives also need to exist that speak to developing critical thinking skills, such as: "A student will be able to demonstrate critical thinking skills by (1) defining a problem, (2) identifying and judging information relative to the problem, (3) solving the problem and drawing conclusions." Instructional activities in a variety of levels of sophistication need to be incorporated into the several different courses, and finally, test items need to be utilized that are designed to measure critical thinking skills. Any of these items out of place may result in curricular misalignment.

What about the idea of teaching being an art and teachers in the classroom having the freedom to change, adapt, and take advantage of unique opportunities for learning as they evolve? This certainly is still desirable but can largely be thought of as a problem of teaching technique or strategy and should not necessarily be a problem of content or curriculum unless a teacher drifts too far from a prescribed curriculum. If that occurs, then maybe it is time to reevaluate the approved curriculum; otherwise, teachers need to review the curriculum collectively to determine if it is meeting their students' needs.

Test Item Bank

The secret of good curriculum alignment often lies with the school's ability to monitor its progress through evaluation. The development of a test item bank or collection of test items that reflect the prescribed content of the curriculum guides to be used by the staff becomes a way of providing some of this monitoring ability. The bank consists of a minimum of three or four test items for each of the stated objectives for the course. Tests are then compiled to measure the mastery of students on each objective in the curriculum outline by including one or more test items for each objective at appropriate levels of difficulty. Test item profiles reflecting the percentage of items from each of the levels of Bloom's Taxonomy can also be prescribed for each test.

Having contributed the test items to the bank and knowing their students will be evaluated in all aspects of the content assigned to their particular course study, teachers are highly motivated to maintain a high degree of curriculum alignment with the pre-scribed course of study. By having multiple items in the test bank and drawing on them randomly for particular test administrations, reduction in the opportunity to "teach the test" can also be accomplished. The major change in the system is one of making the staff collectively responsible for curriculum and evaluation instead of allowing each indi-vidual teacher to function as an autonomous agent for those responsibilities.

This technique also provides opportunity for a school to implement TQM principles. The frequent measure of student progress with teacher-made tests allows teachers to evaluate instructional processes and as a team constantly to be searching for ways to improving learning.

Curriculum Density

Curriculum density is the third area of concern relative to curricular organization. Curriculum density is defined as the quantity of content that students are expected to learn over a given period of time.[6] As a general rule, the higher the curriculum density the less well the students will be able to master the objectives or content. If high-density curriculum is to be maintained with adequate learning it must be accompanied by efforts to maintain high academic learning time (ALT) rates as well. The definition of academic learning time, it should be remembered, includes both the concept of high time-on-task ratios as well as appropriate success ratios.[7] Time can be gained by using maximum class time for direct instruction along with well-organized, out-of-class activities for reading and the review of other instructional materials.[8] Obviously a high level of stu-dent motivation is required if high levels of homework activity are to be required to maintain the desired level of curriculum density. Also recommended when high-curricu-lum density is attempted are daily and periodic reviews of previously covered material.[9]

Our common approach of reducing curriculum density for slow learners may not be good methodology. Recent studies[10] have shown that reducing the rate of coverage for many slow learners may be a mistake in that it also reduces their motivation caused by the lack of new exciting stimuli in the material they are to learn. More successful have been efforts to accelerate content coverage for slow learners (the vertical dimension of the curriculum) and where necessary reduce the expected level of content mastery. Overall motivation stays high and overall learning continues where apathy reigned previ-ously. So expected content mastery can be included as another variable in the definition of curriculum density.

Considerations for Curriculum Redesign

Student Growth and Maturity

Any discussion of curriculum must obviously pay heed to effects of maturation on changes in student interests and needs. Several notions in particular are significant when considering the organization of a school. First, all children do not mature at the same rate and thus all are not ready for the same curriculum at the same time. The difference in maturation of boys and girls is quite obvious, both physically and mentally. The same variation in size, mental capacity, interests, and needs also exists within children of the same sex at a given age, only to be in different balance or relationship after several more years of maturation. These differences, of course, should have a bearing on both instructional techniques and curriculum offerings, as well as on ways of grouping students.

Curricular Flexibility

It is important to give adequate attention to individual differences and varying maturity rates and levels and to recognize that student interests and needs are broadly based. The organization of a school program must account for these needs, interests, and capabilities in all their diversity and provide learning experiences that will motivate all students.

If individual differences are to be recognized, both the vertical and horizontal dimensions of the curriculum require flexibility. Figure 10–4 illustrates the three different rates of learning. Since most children vary from the norm, the curriculum needs to be organized to allow each child to progress individually, as shown by lines a, b, and c.

The organization must allow both child b and child c access to appropriate information as it is sequenced according to the difficulty of concepts and materials. The achievement of the student over time will depend, therefore, on the capability of the student to learn and the time committed to that subject.

In subjects such as reading and mathematics, where we traditionally have assumed that all basic skills are taught in the elementary school, we must now recognize that, because of their slow maturation rates, a large portion of our children have in fact not learned these basic skills to a satisfactory level in each grade. Therefore, these subjects must be continued through the middle school years and on into high school.

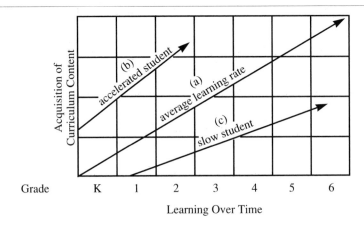

FIGURE 10–4.   Impact of Individual Differences and Rate of Learning on Curriculum Needs

Grade			Subjects Taught				
12 11 10 9 8 7 6 5 4 3 2 1 K	LANGUAGE ARTS	SOCIAL STUDIES	MATHEMATICS	SCIENCE	ART	MUSIC	P.E.

FIGURE 10–5. The Traditional Curriculum

Curricular Continuity

How much freedom should a student have to pursue needs and interests when curriculum selection is determined? Should a student have unlimited choice or should he or she be guided according to some plan? Should the student have no curricular choices but be expected to take all required subjects? How can the school arrange curricular opportunities for the student who can move rapidly up a vertical skill sequence ladder, for the student who progresses at a slower rate, for the student who wants or needs an extremely broad range of content areas, or for the student who must concentrate on basic skills? In the past we have not differentiated for individual students but have provided a very basic curriculum for everyone, allowing for little variation.

This traditional curriculum is shown in Figure 10–5. The same basic subjects are included in each year of a child's education.

A Curriculum Model

Consideration of needs and interests of students throughout the curriculum should accommodate different maturity levels. Furthermore, curriculum must be divided into priorities with different weightings for each subject. Equal amounts of all curricular areas are not necessarily appropriate for each year. For example, basic skills in language and computation are obviously needed in the early years of education. As a child matures and as interests broaden, the curriculum of the school should expand along with the child. By the middle of the elementary school years, the curiosity of most children is very broad in scope, and a child may participate in a great variety of different elective exploratory curriculum areas over the course of the year. Obviously, if the child participates in many different activities, covering most in depth is unlikely.

The pattern of elective curricular choices may need to be somewhat different for each child. For example, during one quarter, a particular child, if given the opportunity, may select sewing, leisure reading, the study of insects (basic entomology), music appreciation, spelling skills, and math games. A second child may select topics on the basis of what friends select because of a real need to belong to a specific group. The following quarter, the pattern for both children might be different. This normal variation of curricular interests among children raises the important question of what areas of learning are common to all children.

Organizing curriculum around areas of importance rather than considering all curricular areas equally offers one solution. In this way, varying emphasis can be placed on different areas as appropriate during each segment of a student's school career. One well-accepted model clusters curriculum into four major areas:

1. Basic skills
2. Common learnings
3. Exploratory areas
4. Specialization

Figure 10–6 shows the type of subjects to be included in each area. The time-on-task studies demonstrate that the amount of engaged time a student spends in a particular discipline has a direct effect on the student achievement in that subject.[11] These studies on academic learning time (ALT) are usually emphasizing the importance of the efficient and effective use of time. However, the total amount of allocated time is probably an

Basic skills	*Common learning*
Reading	Health
Arithmetic	Social studies
Psychomotor skills	Science
	Language

Exploratory	*Specialization*
Social sciences	College prep
Science	Computer science
Art	Drafting
Music	Commercial foods
Mathematics	Distributive education
Typing	Horticulture
etc.	etc.

FIGURE 10–6.   Major Curriculum Clusters

equally important factor to be considered in the formula. The most effective way to improve a student's achievement in any particular subject is simply to increase the amount of allocated time for that subject, recognizing of course that a corresponding decrease in other subjects must occur unless the school day is lengthened. In other words, if school officials are under tremendous pressure to improve reading and math achievement scores, an adjustment in allocated times, increasing the number of minutes each day spent in those subjects, assuming of course the quality of instruction is constant, will generally result in improved achievement.

Our culture demands that children learn certain basic skills. Included are skills in communication and computation and a knowledge of basic health care, including physical education. American society also requires basic familiarity with other more general areas, such as the knowledge of democracy and the way it works. A school can provide this information in many different ways. A real danger exists in curricular organization in regard to what to include as required common learning. It is easy to include so many topics that all of the available school time is utilized to teach this information and no discretionary time remains for exploratory and student-selected curriculum. Thus, areas of common learning must be kept to a bare minimum if other concepts are to have room in the program. The interrelationship of basic skills and common learnings and exploratory or student-selected activities can be diagrammed as in Figure 10–7.

Initially, schools concentrate on basic skills development. This work consumes most of a child's time during the early years of school, gradually diminishing as a percentage of the total time spent on learning as other things are added to the program. Common learn-

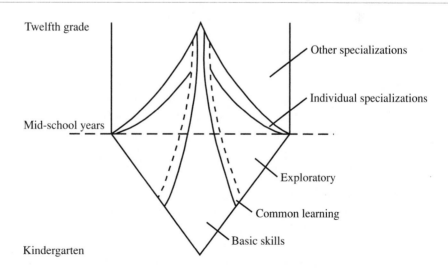

FIGURE 10–7.   Interrelationships in the Curriculum

ing curriculum may begin in small amounts during the child's early mastery of basic skills and increase as skills are learned. The exploratory or student-selected aspect of the curriculum should continue to broaden as a child matures. The curriculum will reach its greatest breadth at a point approximately midway through the school career when it is made up of many varied and diverse parts, including many of the student's own choosing.

The time involvement of the child in the several parts of the curriculum is varied while the school year contains a predetermined amount of time. The time during the early primary years has depth or concentration only in basic skills, with a relatively narrow scope of curriculum.

By the time the child has reached the mid-school point, time can be spent on more curricular areas. In other words, with so many curricular selections available during those middle years, students will spend less time on a particular subject. A child will be expected to learn a little about many things rather than a lot about a few things.

By considering the natural motivation of the child, this expanding curricular organization better meets his or her growing curiosity during the elementary and middle school or junior high school days. In high school, the needs and interests of students begin to change. Students begin to make tentative decisions relating to life as an adult. Puberty brings about emotional and psychological changes. The organization of the school system should take this into account. These changes have particular implications for curricular organization.

The interests and needs of children collectively continue to remain very broad and diverse, requiring a continued wide range of curricular offerings. On the other hand, the interests and needs of a particular child usually narrow as future life goals are sorted out. The curriculum of the school must allow students to begin to narrow their own curriculum into a specialization when they reach a maturity level that calls for it. The implications here for a flexible and active guidance program are also apparent.

During high school the individual child begins to devote more and more time and, thus, curricular scope to an area of *individual specialization*, as shown in Figure 10–7. Specialization gradually replaces the exploratory phase of a student's curriculum. This individual specialization may be the move into a specific vocational program of one type or another. It may mean preparation for a particular vocation requiring continuation into a specific college program, or it may simply mean a decision to go to college.

For example, if a particular child is not progressing in reading skill development at a rate comparable to the majority of children that age, the child should probably spend a great proportion of time in basic skills. The question, then, is: What should give way? The choices probably rest between common learnings and exploratory activities.

At first glance it would seem that exploratory activities should probably give way to common learnings. But should they? Many children need strong motivation during the middle elementary years to keep up their interest in school. If exploratory activities are diminished for an increased skills emphasis, all interest in school on the part of the student may be lost. On the other hand, if the common-learnings area is reduced instead, the interest in the exploratory areas might save the day (or the year), allowing a return to common learning later on. One might even consider the content of the common-learnings areas as appropriate material for instruction in basic skills, providing a double-barreled program with the emphasis on the skills rather than on the common learning content.

Offering Curriculum Breadth

Special Programs for Special Students

Gifted Students

Exploratory areas are one of the best opportunities to provide supplementary activities to gifted students and still have them participate with all children in the majority of curricular areas. Special programs in natural science, microcomputer science, mathematics, and other areas can be made available on an interest basis or on a selective-qualification basis while still providing other programs for all children.

Name _____   △ Two each day

Date _____

CENTERS	Mon.	Extra	Tues.	Extra	Wed.	Extra	Thurs.	Extra	Fri.	Extra
△ 1. Spelling										
△ 2. Math										
△ 3. Handwriting										
△ 4. English										
△ 5. Reading Center										
△ 6. Science										
△ 7. Creative Writing										
△ 8. Counting										
△ 9. Health										
△ 10. Phonics										
△ 11. Current Events										
△ 12. SRA										
13. Read for Fun										
14. Music										
15. Art										
16. Library										
17. Take-a-part										
18. Wendy House										
19. Math Games										
20. Sewing										
21. Listening for Fun										

FIGURE 10–8.   Breadth of Curriculum in the Primary Grades

Children with Disabilities

In a similar fashion, students with one or more disabling conditions also need the chance for exploratory opportunities. Often, when these students have difficulty acquiring basic skills, opportunity for exploration gets a low priority and is replaced by additional basic-skill activities. This presents a real dilemma in that well-taught exploratory activities often are children's major motivators in their entire school program. Thus, the reduction in exploratory activities reduces the motivation that is so desperately needed for learning the basic skills. The technique of accelerated learning mentioned earlier in this chapter can be implemented with the use of exploratory courses.

Curriculum breadth at various school levels can be illustrated in different ways. Two illustrations, one from the elementary level and one from middle-school level, are shown in Figures 10–8 and 10–9. The list in Figure 10–8 is from a primary grades classroom. This curriculum is taught through learning centers with daily skill group instruction in reading and mathematics.

First Hour Labs	*Second Hour Labs*
America's Summer Sport–Baseball	America's Summer Sport–Baseball
Basket Weaving	Cheerleader Tryouts
Chess	Chess
Chorus	Chorus
Creative Weaving	Crewel and Needlepoint
Crewel and Needlepoint	Drawing and Sketching
Embroidery	Environmental Crafts–Recycled Arts
Environmental Crafts–Recycled Arts	Good Grooming
Good Grooming	Heroes and Heroines in American History
Hiking	Hiking
4-H Club	Middle School Journalism
Model Building	Model Building
Outdoor Games	Newspaper
Picture Creativity	Outdoor Games
Putting It All Together	Picture Creativity
Rhymes and Things	Plant Power
Rock-Hounding	Putting It All Together
Rocketry	Rock-Hounding
Running and Standing Broad Jump	Rocketry
Safety and First Aid	Running and Standing Broad Jump
Science Fiction and Mystery	Safety and First Aid
Science Investigations	Say It in Spanish
Sculpture and Modeling	Science Investigation
Short Stories	Sculpture and Modeling
Softball	Short Stories
Typing II	Soccer
Volleyball	Softball
What Makes You Tick	What Makes You Tick

FIGURE 10–9.   Breadth of Exploratory Curriculum in Grades Five through Eight

The illustration in Figure 10–9 is from a middle school covering grades five through eight. During these years curriculum offerings must be broadest. Exploratory labs are offered to students twice each week, and each child selects two. Every nine weeks a new series of labs is offered, and students assist in determining topics.

Under the concepts of site-based management and TQM, curriculum organization and development become major responsibilities of the school. The principal has a significant role in implementing not only the development efforts but also the continuous review of the curriculum as it is being delivered. Teacher quality circles will need to include curriculum review in their deliberations with questions such as: Are we meeting the needs of our students with our curriculum? Are we pacing the curriculum correctly? Are we providing enough integration among disciplines? Is the curriculum interesting and motivating to our students? How are our student evaluations looking? Are there any weak areas in their learning that may require curricular revision?

Summary

A variety of curricular concepts have been outlined in this chapter. In summary, they are as follows:

1. Each content area should have developed a complete curriculum structure including concepts, topics, skills, behavioral objectives, resource lists, and evaluation instruments.

2. Curricular alignment should be maintained for all areas as well as attention being given to the density of the curriculum.

3. Improving academic learning time (ALT) is of critical importance to ensure that basic areas of the curriculum are given adequate attention.

4. Curriculum should be organized flexibly so that students can move through a sequence of learning experiences at different rates (vertically).

5. Curriculum should be organized so that more or less time can be spent by a particular student in certain aspects of the curriculum as needed (horizontally).

6. Curriculum should be organized flexibly to provide open access to meet the various needs and interests of children (exploratory, electives, specialization).

7. Curriculum should be organized so that all subjects are taught to some degree each year through high school (common learning, basic skills).

8. Exploratory areas offer a way to provide more flexibility and open access to programs for special students.

Endnotes

1. Benjamin S. Bloom *et al.*, *The Taxonomy of Educational Objectives: Effective and Cognitive Domains*. New York: David McKay Company, 1974.

2. National Diffusion Network, *Educational Programs That Work*, 10th ed. Longmont, CO: Sopris West Inc., 1984.

3. *Instructional Objectives Exchange* (IOX), Box 24095, Los Angeles, CA 90024. IOX has collections at the secondary level in the following areas: language arts—reading, comprehension, structural analysis, composition, reference skills, listening, oral expression and journalism, grammar, mechanics, usage, and English literature. Other areas include general mathematics, business education, home economics, auto mechanics, electronics, general metals, mechanical drawing, woodworking, American history, geography, biology, and Spanish. A current catalog can be obtained by writing to the above address.

4. Jack Frymier, *The Annehurst Curriculum Classification System*. West Lafayette, IN: Kappa Delta Phi, 1977.

5. D. J. Armor, P. Conry-Osequera, M. Cox, N. King, L. McConnel, A. Pascal, E. Pauly, and G. Zellman, *Analysis of the School Preferred Reading Program in Selected Los Angeles Minority Schools*. Santa Monica: Rand Corporation, 1976. D. L. Clark, L. S. Lotto, and M. M. McCarthy, "Secondary Source Study of Exceptionality in Urban Elementary Schools." *Why Do Some Urban Schools Succeed? The Phi Delta Kappa Study of Exceptional Urban Elementary Schools*. Bloomington: Phi Delta Kappa,

1980. W. W. Cooley and G. Leinhardt, "The Instructional Dimensions Study." *Educational Evaluation and Policy Analysis*, 1980. J. A. Goodlad, *A Place Called School*. New York: McGraw Hill, 1983.

6. W. Fredrick, "The Use of Classroom Time in High Schools Above or Below the Median Reading Score." *Urban Education*, 1977. T. L. Good and T. Beckerman, "Time on Task: A Naturalistic Study in Sixth-grade Classrooms." *Elementary School Journal*, 1978. J. Stallings, "Allocated Academic Learning Time Revisited, or Beyond Time on Task," *Educational Researcher*, 1980.

7. Charles Fisher *et al.*, "Improved Teaching by Increasing Academic Learning Time." *Educational Leadership, 37*, 1 (October 1979): 52–54.

8. Stallings, "Allocated Academic Learning Time Revisited." B. V. Rosenshine, "Content, Time, and Direct Instruction." In P. L. Peterson and H. J. Walberg (eds.), *Research on Teaching*. Berkeley, CA: McCutchan Publishing Corporation, 1979.

9. B. V. Rosenshine, "Teaching Functions in Instructional Programs." *The Elementary School Journal*, 1983.

10. For more information regarding accelerated schools contact the Center for Educational Research at Stanford (CERAS), CERAS Building, Stanford University, Stanford, CA 94305.

11. Fisher et al., "Improved Teaching by Increasing Academic Learning Time."

Selected Readings

Anderson, L., "Improving Instruction: Policy Implications of Research on School Time." *The School Administrator (December 1983)*. Arlington, VA: AASA.

Berliner, D., "Academic Learning Time." In R. Brandt (ed.), *Effective Teaching for Higher Achievement*. Arlington, VA: Association for Supervision and Curriculum Development, Videotape A, 1983.

Bloom, B. S., *Human Characteristics and School Learning*. New York: McGraw-Hill Book Company, 1982.

Bloom, B. S.; Engleshart, M. B.; Furst, E. J.; Hill, W. H.; and Krathwohl, D. R., *Taxonomy of Educational Objectives: The Classification of Education Goals. Handbook I: Cognitive Domain*. New York: Longmans Green, 1956.

Carnegie Task Force on Teaching as a Profession, *A Nation Prepared: Teachers for the 21st Century.* New York: Carnegie Forum on Education and the Economy, 1986.

Cook, Walter, "Effective Ways of Doing It." In *Individualized Instruction, Yearbook of the National Society for the Study of Education.* Chicago: NSSE, 1962, chapter 3.

Esposito, Dominick, "Homogeneous and Heterogeneous Ability Grouping." *AERA Journal* (Spring 1973): 163–179.

Fisher, C.; Berliner, D.; Filby, N.; Marliave, R.; Chance, L.; and Dishaw, M., "Teaching Behaviors, Academic Learning Time, and Student Achievement: An Overview." In C. Denham and A. Lieberman (eds.), *Time to Learn.* Washington, DC: The National Institute of Education, U.S. Department of Education, 1980.

Gibbons, Maurice, "Walkabout Searching for the Right Passage from Childhood and School." *Phi Delta Kappan, 55* (May 1974): 596–602.

Goodlad, John I., and Anderson, Robert H., *The Nongraded Elementary School.* New York: Harcourt, Brace and World, 1959.

Purkey, S. C., and Smith, M. C. "Effective Schools: A Review." *The Elementary School Journal, 93* (1983): 428–452.

Reavis, Charles A., "Utilizing Curriculum, Classroom Practice, Culture, and Climate." *NASSP Bulletin, 74,* 529 (November 1990): 39–44.

Rosenshine, B. V. "Teaching Functions in Instructional Programs." *The Elementary School Journal, 83* (1983): 335-352.

Rosenshine, B. V. "Content, Time, and Direct Instruction." In P. L. Peterson and H. J. Walberg (eds.), *Research on Teaching.* Berkeley, CA: McCutchan Publishing Corporation, 1979.

Rosenthal, Robert, and Jacobson, Lenore, *Pygmalion in the Classroom.* New York: Holt, Rinehart and Winston, 1968.

Silcox, Harry, "School-Based Community Service Programs—An Imperative for Effective Schools." *NASSP Bulletin, 77,* 550 (February 1993): 58–62.

$$C \quad h \quad a \quad p \quad t \quad e \quad r \quad \textit{11}$$

Restructuring Learning

Introduction

If curriculum can be defined most simply as *what* is taught in the school, then instruction is the *how*—the methods and techniques that aid students in their learning. The emphasis in instruction should be on student learning and not on teaching, but obviously both are significant.

Instruction is the lifeblood of the school. It is the process by which content or curriculum is transported to the student. Instruction, however, requires a learner who gains insight, acquires information, and forms values not only from the context of the curriculum but also through the processes by which the content is presented. Therefore, the entire learning environment of the school constantly provides content for learning. This entwining of curriculum and instruction forces school administrators to look very carefully not only at what they teach in the schools but at how they teach it, for the medium is truly the message.

Consideration of instruction as the process of providing content to the learner presents several major problems to the thoughtful organizer of the school program. These can best be presented as five questions:

1. What is the nature of the learner and how can students best be organized?
2. What instructional processes are available to be used?
3. How do these processes accommodate individual differences?
4. What are the implications of these instructional processes for the other organizational components of the school?
5. How can these processes be improved?

Answers to these questions are not always available, but principals and teachers should be aware of the implications of each.

Instructional Processes

Types of Instruction

Instruction can take place in a variety of formats. Types of instruction can be divided into several basic categories:

1. Lecture presentation or demonstration
2. Discussion
3. Laboratory activities
   a. Group or individual
   b. Independent study

Each category presents a different mode for student learning. The purpose of instruction and the expected outcomes should be major factors in determining which instructional type should be used. For example, if the purpose of instruction is to introduce or present an overview of a topic, a lecture presentation to a large group might be best. On the other hand, if the anticipated outcome is the modification of values, then an instructional

CATEGORIES OF INSTRUCTION AND MAJOR PURPOSES

I. *Presentation*
Build concepts through information
Stimulate inquiry
Enrich course
Relate course to reality
Make assignments

Usually most efficient and
effective in large groups.

II. *Discussion*
Raise questions
Report experience
Discuss ideas
Generalize
Form opinions
Plan independent study

Usually most efficient
and effective in small
groups (7–15 persons).

III. *Laboratory*

Individual Study
Student
  performed
  directed
Teacher
  directed
  planned
  evaluated
  managed

Build concepts and
  principles through
  action and viewing
Practice skills
Apply ideas
Develop investigative
  skills
Develop problem-solving
  techniques
Develop evaluation skills

Independent Study
Student
  directed
  planned
  performed
  evaluated
Teacher
  advised

These activities may be small group (2 or more) or individual in nature; can be either scheduled or unscheduled.

FIGURE 11–1.

format that directly involves the learner (such as laboratory or discussion) is usually more effective. Figure 11–1 presents the major purposes of these four categories of instruction. Note that each category also has certain group size recommendations.

Actually, in most lessons, all four types of instruction should probably be used. For example, the model lesson design proposed by Madeline Hunter uses all four types. The Hunter model suggests the following seven steps for a sequential learning model as shown in Figure 11–2.[1]

Steps 1 through 3 of the Hunter model are usually in the form of lecture to the entire group. Steps 4 and 5 are often in a discussion mode, initially with the entire group, but often with smaller followup groups as more and more children achieve mastery. Step 6 of the Hunter model is a form of group lab activity, whereas step 7 is an individual lab- or homework-type assignment.

Research about Instructional Practice

Our research approach to instruction and the development of a consistent view of teaching represents one of the major innovations in education in the past decade. Education made a major shift in its attention to research on teaching from focusing on teacher traits to focusing on instructional skills. Although we may never have a generic set of teaching skills, the research on effective teaching has produced a list of recommended instructional skills that, when implemented effectively by teachers, produces observable measurable gains in student learning. A summary of the major teaching competencies along with citations of their research are listed for teacher competencies of planning, lesson implementation, student motivation, evaluative feedback, time on task, evaluative methods, assigning grades, and individualized instruction.

Effective Planning Skills

Research on teachers' planning indicates that if teachers (1) identify instructional objectives; (2) set an appropriate level of difficulty for mastery; (3) plan for matching instructional methods, procedures, materials, and student activities; and (4) use good formative and summative evaluations techniques, the resulting preparedness can increase the probability of improving student learning as measured by test scores. Such planning also ensures teacher confidence, direction, and security.

Some of the success of this planning can certainly be attributed to the improved curricular alignment that occurs from the detailed planning around objectives drawn directly from a prescribed curriculum. However, the *planning* for instructional implementation is believed to be the major cause of the gain found in student test scores.

Research also provides a clear understanding of a stumbling block to planning.[2] Teaching for mastery demands a well-developed statement of goals and instructional objectives as well as appropriate criterion-referenced tests.[3] Although this makes good sense to administrators and many teachers, it requires a tremendous amount of work for teachers. Additionally, most teachers intuitively base their success in the classroom by student interest and attitudes and not by cognitive gain, therefore not obtaining the personal reinforcement from the results of the tests' gain.[4]

1. ANTICIPATORY SET

   The teacher prepares students for the lesson. The first five minutes of a lesson are the most critical as that is when the teacher has the greatest degree of student attention.

2. STATEMENTS OF OBJECTIVES

   The instructor should inform students of the objectives for a particular lesson: namely, Robert Mager's three elements of an instructional objective:

   a. State the task.
   b. Identify how the task is to be completed.
   c. Identify minimum level of competency to be achieved, if the teacher wishes to identify a minimal level.

   Instruction in the deductive style is recommended for students experiencing academic difficulty. The teacher would state the rule and give students adequate practice until they could demonstrate mastery prior to introducing a new concept.

   Guiding questions, prior to independent completion of an assignment, are recommended.

   The teacher should clarify for the students how one day's instruction ties into what has academically preceded it and how it will influence the next day's instruction.

3. INSTRUCTIONAL INPUT

   The teacher should move among the students while they are working, providing additional reinforcement when needed.

4. MODELING

   The teacher should illustrate concepts taught, providing many and varied examples, and responding to student questions.

5. CHECKING FOR UNDERSTANDING

   Students should demonstrate 75–80% mastery of a concept before being taught a new concept.

6. GUIDED PRACTICE

   The teacher can have children working in groups of five to seven, carefully monitoring their achievement while they are working. Particular attention should be given to those children who, in the past, have demonstrated difficulty in working independently.

7. INDEPENDENT PRACTICE

   Such practice should consist of only ten to fifteen minutes for a particular assignment. Independent practice should not be used as a teaching strategy; it should only be used as reinforcement for concepts that are understood by the students.

FIGURE 11–2.   The Hunter Model

Effective Lesson Implementation

The effective implementation of a lesson planned by the teacher is as important as the planning itself. Effective teachers use a variety of instructional methods, including drill, explanation, discussion, inquiry, role playing, demonstration, and problem solving. One important element of good lesson implementation is the use of advanced organizers which give the learner an overview of the lesson. Hunter's concept of anticipatory set is an example of an advanced organizer.[5]

Other important elements of effective lesson implementation include asking relevant questions, giving explanations, and doing demonstrations in conjunction with frequent feedback to the teacher regarding student understanding. Feedback techniques such as signing (thumbs up, thumbs down) or "if you know the correct answer raise your hand" can provide this information to a teacher throughout the lesson.

Increased wait time, the amount of time a teacher waits after asking a question, has also shown positive effects on student performance. Untrained teachers will often wait only one or two seconds after asking a question. Longer wait time produces more complete student responses, more student confidence, greater evidence used by students, the use of higher order thinking skills, a greater number of slow students participating, and reduced teacher-centered presentations.[6]

Research has also produced surprising results about questioning techniques. Many teachers seldom use questioning of students during discussion, but it has been demonstrated that the frequency of factual single-answer questions is positively related to gains in achievement as measured by standardized tests.[7] However, factual answers are only part of what is wanted.

To produce higher order thinking skills, questions must be designed to require higher order answers of application, analysis, synthesis, or evaluation, as suggested by Bloom's taxonomy. This type of questioning requires extended wait time for careful answers to be thought out.

Quizzing and reviewing have also been shown to be elements in successful lesson implementation. When teachers give regular quizzes one or more times a week, scores on final exams go up. Frequent testing influences study behavior positively.[8]

The most effective teachers also use homework to impact study habits of students. Studies support the practice that frequently assigned homework, but in small amounts to provide independent practice on what has been learned during the instructional lesson, has a positive effect on achievement.[9]

Student Motivation

Motivation concerns the *why* of behavior. Bloom suggests motivational factors can account for 25 percent of the motivation in student achievement among students.[10] In motivating students, the high-gain teacher has a classroom environment that evidences a warm acceptance of students along with consistent rules and high expectations for student behavior. A special environment or climate must be created in the classroom that ensures engagement and success. This engagement often requires student involvement in selecting curriculum of current interest to the students. Obviously, certain flexibility in curriculum choices must be available to the teacher for this to be possible. It is important to use a brisk pace, monitor all students, stimulate attention, and ensure accountability by variety and unpredictability in questioning patterns.[11]

It is a desirable motivator to use students' ideas in discussions by acknowledging student responses, repeating the responses in different words, applying their ideas, comparing their responses, and summarizing their responses.[12]

Classrooms that are organized for cooperative motivation instead of competitiveness produce a better classroom climate. Competitive organization permits aggressiveness, cheating, lowered motivation, and failure-avoiding behaviors, whereas cooperative environments are linked to positive peer relationships, higher achievement, positive self-esteem, and interracial acceptance. Cooperative classrooms can be created in several ways. Cooperative learning models have students working in supporting each other for the common learning of everyone in the group. Competition, if it is used, is among groups that have been balanced in ability by the teacher. The cooperative classroom concept can be further enhanced when students are given a stake in identifying the problems (curriculum) in which they will be engaged.[13]

Promoting students' beliefs in their own competence by carefully matching students' abilities to learning assignments is also a powerful motivator. The ALT (Academic Learning Time) studies[14] suggest materials that will allow high and middle SES students to achieve approximately an 80 percent success rate and low SES students a 90 percent success rate. Teachers need to plan for and treat all students as if they were winners.

Providing Students with Evaluative Feedback

This competency consists of several tasks, including providing written comments to students on their progress in addition to grades, returning tests as quickly as possible, holding individual conferences with students, and interpreting test results with students and parents.

The research evidence is extensive regarding the importance of the frequency and timeliness of effective feedback to students. Formative feedback, which is done while the lesson and learning are in progress, is best given orally rather than in writing and is most beneficial when correcting wrong answers, both to correct the student and to allow the teacher to modify the lesson to cope with the problem.[15]

Feedback in the form of praise should be used extensively but within certain parameters. Low-achieving students may require more explicit recognition for their classroom participation; however, indiscriminate praise may not motivate learning. What is desired is real recognition for real achievement.[16] Feedback on tests and assignments also provides information both to the students on how their work is being evaluated and to the teacher on how successful the instruction has been.[17]

A high volume of feedback is of value for reinforcement as well as its information content.[18] Immediacy of feedback and a high frequency of testing are also important.[19]

Preparation of Appropriate Evaluation Activities

The effective teacher makes the methods of the evaluation clear to students, bases the evaluation on specific goals, objectives, and content of the course, and uses both pretest and posttest in order to measure student gain. Student progress is measured through a series of formative and summative evaluation techniques.

Specific statements of instructional objectives, in measurable terms announced to the students, become the first step in preparing for evaluation. These objectives need to be closely aligned with the stated curriculum and should be reflective of some diversity as shown by some classification system such as the work of Bloom (cognitive domain), Krathwohl (affective domain), or Samson (psychomotor domain).[20] Surveys have shown that teachers generally select most of their objectives from the cognitive domain and most from the lowest level (knowledge) of that domain.[21] Greater diversity of objectives is usually desirable.

Formative evaluation, done while instruction is unfolding, should be frequent and have as its purpose monitoring and guiding students to the correct learning as well as providing the teacher with data for the monitoring of instructional effectiveness.[22] Formative evaluation needs to be linked directly with the practices of TQM. Evaluative information on groups of students as well as individual students should be the topic of discussion at staff team meetings. Teachers and principals must review instructional and learning processes and search for ways to improve the quality of learning. Data generated from student test results provides a good data source. TQM control charts can be generated from item analysis data of criterion referenced tests.

Summative evaluation should be used to determine if the student has achieved the objectives. Mastery learning is a graduated approach to summative evaluation. Here, instructional objectives are divided into small units with specific objectives whose mastery is essential for the mastery of the major objectives. In mastery learning, frequent testing and evaluation are crucial. Research indicates that mastery learning evaluation techniques produce superior student achievement, learning retention, transfer of learning, and positive affective outcomes.[23]

Assigning Grades

High-gain teachers recognize the importance of assigning grades and take the responsibility seriously. They keep in mind what parents want to learn from student report cards and they use grades to reflect student progress accurately rather than as a form of behavior modification. Teachers must test often and consistently to achieve good reliability of evaluative data.[24]

Marking systems that use a maximum of five to nine discriminations are best understood by parents, therefore a 5-point letter grade scale is probably a better communicator than 100-point scales.[25] Pass-fail grading systems appear to lead to lower achievement.[26]

Two general approaches are used by teachers in assigning grades: (1) grading students on their performance relative to their classmates and (2) using an absolute scale of some type based on a standard such as a predetermined number of objectives to be achieved. The first type, that of relative scores compared to other students, is commonly called *grading on a curve:* Students' scores may be based on raw scores drawn from posttest data only or may be gain scores based on the difference between pre- and posttest data. Gain scores logically provide a better measure of student achievement under the instruction of that teacher. However, this type of relative comparison of student scores to one another is appropriate only if there are very large groups of students included and the students are not tracked. This is rarely the case in the normal classroom setting.

The second type of grading, using an absolute scale, is common to criterion-referenced tests and mastery learning. Proficiency tests with minimum acceptable levels of performance also use this logic. Grades are based on a predetermined level of achievement necessary to obtain a particular grade, such as eight out of ten correct for a grade of B, or nine out of ten correct for an A.

Grading must reflect student performance and growth. When it reflects something other than academic achievement, it cannot be considered valid. High-gain teachers do not abuse the assigning of grades but consider it a significant part of their communication with both parents and students.

Time on Task

An effective teacher uses the time allocated for the class in a highly efficient manner. Classwork begins promptly at the beginning of each period, management time and transition time are kept to a minimum, and the teacher reinforces students who are spending time on task. Studies report that low-achieving students are off task in excess of 50 percent of the time, whereas high-achieving students are off task less than 25 percent.[27] Another study of junior high students showed that low achievers had engagement time of approximately 40 percent, whereas high achievers reached an excess of 85 percent engagement time.[28]

Research evidence demonstrates that time is a valuable resource in school and, when used efficiently, increases student performance.[29] The studies identify three levels of time used: (1) allocated time—that assigned to a particular course or subject; (2) engaged time—the amount of allocated time in which students actually are engaged in learning activities; and (3) Academic Learning Time (ALT)—a refinement of engaged time reflecting quality of learning. Factors included in the definition of *quality* are the appropriateness of instructional materials relative to the achievement level of the student and the best student's success ratio of learning (an 80 percent success ratio is suggested for most learners) and the amount of concentration the learner is actually contributing to the instructional process.[30]

The high-gain teacher is punctual and begins instruction for each class promptly, leaving management details for later in the hour if possible. During seat-work time, the teacher monitors students closely, encouraging more time on task. It is suggested that at least 50 percent of each class period be devoted to active direct instruction. This is significantly higher than found in most classes. For example, one study demonstrated that math teachers, on the average, used only 14 percent of their time for direct instruction, with 34 percent going for written work, 8 percent for review, and the balance being assigned to off-task activities.[31]

Individualized Instruction

In light of all the research findings that support direct instruction in the form of demonstration-practice-feedback, where does individualized instruction fit in? How do the findings of the need for whole-group instruction affect individualized methods?[32] Although direct instruction has shown great results for the acquisition of specific skills, it cannot do it all; in fact, for higher order learning, direct instruction may be counterproductive.[33] An effective classroom must solicit student involvement in learning activities under appropriate conditions for mastery. This demands a proper climate and opportunity for the child to achieve success. These requisites demand that teachers provide appropriate opportunities for individual differences if maximum student productivity is to be maintained. Teachers can accommodate individual differences in a variety of ways:

1. By varying the level of teaching through adjusting the level of questioning and varying the length of wait time.

2. By providing varying amounts of allocated time.

3. By grouping within or between classes, as has been discussed earlier in this chapter.

4. By considering the different learning styles of children.

5. By selecting classroom organizational methods, including learning centers, tutors, or study groups.[34]

Instructional Tools for Individualization

We have emphasized individualized instruction and the need to provide a variety of instructional activities for students in order to make a system functional. The logical question is how to organize or create materials for self-instruction.

Excellent commercial materials are now available for individualized systems, and more are becoming available each year. In areas such as reading and math, schools can purchase an entire system for a wide range of student achievement levels. Other material can be organized and coordinated for instruction by teachers using that material. Teachers, of course, should also continue to use their own material.

The real problem, however, is organizing materials in a systematic way so that they are adequately available to students when they are needed, adequately self-instructional so that teacher time can be appropriately balanced, and adequately organized to assure proper instructional sequencing, recording, and evaluation. Today's microcomputers can greatly aid in managing records for individualized instruction.

New methods have gained popularity in recent years to achieve individualization of instruction and to enhance learning. Among these are cooperative learning, improved computer-assisted instruction (CAI), and mastery learning, which often uses CAI methodology to implement its steps.

Cooperative Learning

This instructional strategy delegates some control of the pacing and methods of learning to student groups, usually composed of two to six persons. Students in the groups work together on assignments, sometimes competing with other groups. Individuals in the group assume responsibility for sharing knowledge and tutoring each other. It is an active-learning approach and has been shown to offer great opportunity for the development of higher-order thinking skills in all participants.

Classrooms that are organized for cooperative motivation instead of competitiveness produce a better classroom climate. Competitive organization permits aggressiveness, cheating, lowered motivation, and failure-avoiding behaviors, while cooperative environments are linked to positive peer relationships, higher achievement, positive self-esteem, and interracial acceptance.[35]

Step 1: A pre-test is administered to the group to be used for initial group placement or as base line data to record student progress.

Step 2: A lesson is presented using direct instruction methods.

Step 3: A post-test is administered with a predetermined minimum proficiency or mastery level established.

Step 4: The students not achieving mastery are given an alternate lesson in either another direct instruction format or an opportunity for additional learning or practice through independent materials.

Step 5: An alternate form of test is administered.

Step 6: If mastery is still not obtained, another cycle of instruction and retesting is carried out by repeating steps 4 and 5.

FIGURE 11–3. Mastery Learning Model

Source: Gerald C. Ubben and Larry W. Hughes, *The Principal: Creative Leadership for Effective Schools* (Boston: Allyn and Bacon, 1992), p. 229.

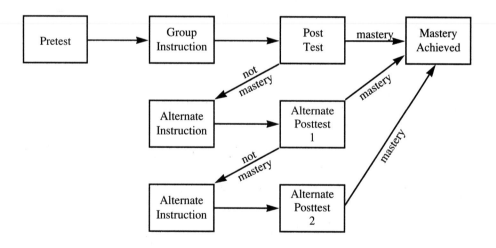

FIGURE 11–4. Mastery Learning Flowchart

Source: Gerald C. Ubben and Larry W. Hughes, *The Principal: Creative Leadership for Effective Schools* (Boston: Allyn and Bacon, 1992), p. 229.

Computer-Assisted Instruction

This methodology has been with us in theory for many years. However, new technological advances in both software and hardware make its daily use in the classroom practical and affordable. The Graphical User Interface (GUI) used now by much of the new computer software along with mass storage capabilities of compact discs make this possible with the addition of full color pictures and sound to programs. Added to this is the capability of the software to offer instruction to students on the basis of their individual needs, monitor and adjust that instruction based on progress, and maintain progress records for each student. While cost will always be a factor, it continues to drop dramatically while capability continues to rise.[36]

Mastery Learning

Mastery learning as described by Bloom[37] has been a very successful form of individualized instruction.[38] It consists basically of six steps, as shown in Figures 11–3 and 11–4.

Although this form of mastery instruction as a means of obtaining individualization has many benefits and has shown good success for certain types of learning (mainly skill development), some difficulties exist.[39]

1. Alternate instructional materials and tests are needed for those children who require recycling to achieve mastery.

2. Management problems of the increasing spread of achievements are caused by the early masters and the extended recycling of others.

Socioeconomic status (SES) also appears to interact in the success of individualized approaches to instruction. Low SES learners need more feedback and low-level questioning in order to obtain success and to stay on task.[40] Much of the effective schools research has been done with low SES learners. Less is known from that research about the effect of individualized independent materials on higher SES children. The dilemma as to how much mastery learning to use exists as high-gain teachers attempt to harness the potential of mastery systems, given their drawbacks of drain on time and materials, but still provide balance and variation to large doses of direct instruction.

Summary

A diversified system of instruction requires a new role for most teachers. Extensive preparation is needed to develop a variety of learning goals, objectives, and activities, so that appropriate instructional plans can be developed for all students.

Research on teaching indicates the importance of each teacher's having skills in lesson planning, lesson implementation, student motivation, evaluative feedback, evaluative methods, assigning grades, maintenance of high time on task, and individualization of instruction.

The principal must have an understanding of diversified instruction and exhibit an expectation of such instruction from the teachers.

Endnotes

1. M. Hunter, "Knowing, Teaching and Supervising." *Using What We Know About Teaching.* Alexandria, VA: Association for Supervision and Curriculum Development, 1984, pp. 169–192.

2. P. L. Peterson, R. W. Marx, and C. M. Clark, "Teacher Planning, Teacher Behavior, and Students' Achievement." *American Educational Research Journal, 15* (1978): 417–432.

3. J. I. Goodlad, M. F. Klein, and associates, *Looking Behind the Classroom Door.* Worthington, OH: Charles A. Jones Publishing Co., 1974.

4. T. R. Mann, "The Practice of Planning: The Impact of Elementary School on Teachers' Curriculum Planning." *Dissertation Abstracts International, 35* (1975): 3359A–3360A.

5. Hunter, "Knowing, Teaching and Supervising."

6. M. R. Rowe, "Relation of Wait-time and Rewards to the Development of Language, Logic, and Fate Control: Part II—Rewards." *Journal of Research in Science Teaching, 11* (1974): 291–308.

7. J. Stallings and D. Kaskowitz, *Follow-Through Classroom Observation Evaluation, 1972–73. Study of Implementation.* Menlo Park, CA: Stanford Research Institute, Stanford University, 1974.

8. P. Peterson and H. Walberg (eds.), *Research on Teaching.* Berkeley, CA: McCutchan Publishing Company, 1979.

9. J. D. Austin, "Homework Research in Mathematics 1900–1974." Paper presented at the 1974 Annual Georgia Mathematics Education Conference. Rock Eagle, Georgia, 1974.

10. B. S. Bloom, *Human Characteristics and School Learning.* New York: McGraw-Hill Book Company, 1982.

11. T. L. Good and J. E. Brophy, *Looking in Classrooms.* New York: Harper & Row, 1973.

12. B. Rosenshine and N. Furst, "Research on Teacher Performance Criteria." In O. Smith (ed.), *Research in Teacher Education: A Symposium.* Englewood Cliffs, NJ: Prentice-Hall, 1971, pp. 46–56.

13. D. W. Johnson and R. T. Johnson, "Instructional Goal Structure: Cooperative, Comparative and Individualistic." *Review of Educational Research, 44* (1974): 213–240.

14. C. Fisher, D. Berliner, N. Filby, R. Marliave, L. Chance, and M. Dishaw, "Teaching Behaviors, Academic Learning Time, and Student Achievement: An Overview." In C. Denham and A. Lieberman (eds.), *Time to Learn.* Washington, DC: The National Institute of Education, U.S. Department of Education, 1980.

15. "Florida Beginning Teacher Program." Office of Teacher Education, Certification, and Inservice Staff Development. Tallahassee, Florida, 1982. M. Mims and B. Gholson, "Effects of Type and Amount of Feedback upon Hypothesis Sampling Among 7- and 8-Year-Old Children." *Journal of Experimental Child Psychology, 24* (1977): 358–371. B. B. Hudgins et al., *Educational Psychology.* Itasca, IL: Peacock Publishers, 1983.

16. J. Brophy, "Teacher Praise: A Functional Analysis." *Review of Educational Research, 51* (1981): 5–32. W. Brookover, C. Beady, P. Flood, J. Schweitzer, and J. Wisenbaker, *School Social Systems and Student Achievement: Schools Can Make a Difference.* New York: Praeger, 1979.

17. M. Hunter, "Appraising the Instructional Process." Presentation for California Advisory Council on Educational Research. November 1973. Appears in *Resources in Education.* ERIC Clearinghouse on Teacher Education. Washington, DC, October 1977. B. Rosenshine, "Teacher Functions in Instructional Programs." Airlie House Paper, NIE Conference, 1982.

18. R. Bardwell, "Feedback: How Well Does it Function?" *Journal of Experimental Education, 50* (1981): 4–9.

19. Peterson and Walberg, *Research on Teaching.*

20. B. S. Bloom, M. B. Englehart, E. J. Furst, W. H. Hill, and D. R. Krathwohl, *Taxonomy of Educational Objectives: The Classification of Education Goals. Handbook I: Cognitive Domain.* New York: Longmans Green, 1956.

21. Good and Brophy, *Looking in Classrooms.*

22. Peterson, Marx, and Clark, "Teacher Planning, Teacher Behavior, and Students' Achievement."

23. J. H. Block, *Schools, Society and Mastery Learning.* New York: Holt, Rinehart and Winston, 1974.

24. Clinton I. Chase, *Measurement for Educational Research*. Reading, MA: Addison-Wesley Publishing Company, 1978.

25. G. A. Miller, "The Magic Number Seven, Plus or Minus Two: Some Limits on our Capacity for Processing Information." *Psychological Review, 63* (1956): 81–97.

26. L. A. Gatta, "An Analysis of the Pass-Fail Grading System as Compared to the Conventional System in High School Chemistry." *Journal of Research in Science Teaching, 10* (1973): 3–12. W. L. Claiborn, "Expectancy Effects in the Classroom: A Failure to Replicate." *Journal of Educational Psychology, 60* (1969): 377–383. W. M. Stallings and H. R. Smock, "The Pass-Fail Grading Option at a State University: A Five Semester Evaluation." *Journal of Educational Measurement, 8* (1971): 153–160.

27. D. Powell and M. Eash, "Secondary School Cases." In H. Walberg (ed.), *Evaluating Educational Performance*. Berkeley, CA: McCutchan, 1974, pp. 277–293.

28. C. Evertson, "Differences in Instruction Activities in High and Low Achieving Junior High Classes." Paper presented at the annual meeting of the American Educational Research Association, Boston, 1980.

29. J. Stallings, "Allocated Academic Learning Time Revisited, or Beyond Time on Task." *Educational Researcher, 9*, 11 (1980): 11–16. W. Fredrick, "The Use of Classroom Time in High Schools Above or Below the Median Reading Score." *Urban Education* (1977): 459–464. T. L. Good, "How Teachers' Expectations Affect Low Achieving Students." *American Educator* (December 1982): 22–32.

30. Peterson and Walberg, *Research on Teaching*.

31. J. Stallings and A. Robertson, "Factors Influencing Women's Decisions to Enroll in Elective Mathematics Classes in High School." Final Report to the National Institute of Education. Menlo Park, CA: SRI International, 1979.

32. W. R. Borg, "Time and School Learning." In C. Denham and A. Lieberman (eds.), *Time to Learn*. Washington, DC: The National Institute of Education, U.S. Department of Education, 1980.

33. P. L. Peterson, "Direct Instruction Reconsidered." In P. L. Peterson and H. J. Walberg (eds.), *Research on Teaching*. Berkeley, CA: McCutchan Publishing Company, 1979.

34. Good and Brophy, *Looking in Classrooms*.

35. D. W. Johnson and R. T. Johnson, "Instructional Goal Structure: Cooperative, Comparative, and Individualistic," *Review of Educational Research, 44* (1974): 213–40.

36. D. Stansberry, "Taking the Plunge." *New Media: Multimedia Technologies for Desktop Computer Users* (February 1993): 30–36.

37. Bloom, *Human Characteristics and School Learning*.

38. Hudgins et al., *Educational Psychology*.

39. Peterson and Walberg, *Research on Teaching*.

40. D. M. Medley, *Teacher Competence and Teacher Effectiveness: A Review of Process-Product Research*. Washington, DC: American Association of Colleges for Teacher Education, 1977. W. Crawford, "An Examination of the Effect of Error Rates and Grade Point Averages on Learning Gains." Paper presented at the meeting of Southwest Psychological Association, Houston, 1975. C. S. Englert, "Measuring Special Education Teacher Effectiveness." *Exceptional Children* (November 1983): 247–254.

Selected Readings

Bardwell, R., "Feedback: How Well Does it Function?" *Journal of Experimental Education, 50* (1981): 4–9.

Block, J. H., *Schools, Society and Mastery Learning*. New York: Holt, Rinehart and Winston, Inc., 1974.

Bloom, B., *Human Characteristics and School Learning*. New York: McGraw-Hill Book Company, 1982.

Bloom, B. S.; Englehart, M.D.; Furst, E. J.; Hill, W. H.; and Krathwohl, D. R., *Taxonomy of Educational Objectives: The Classification of*

Education Goals. Handbook I: Cognitive Domain. New York: Longmans Green, 1956.

Borg, W. R., "Time and School Learning." In Denham, C. and Lieberman, A. (eds.), *Time to Learn*. Washington, DC: The National Institute of Education, U.S. Department of Education, 1980.

Brophy, J., "Teacher Praise: A Functional Analysis." *Review of Educational Research, 51* (1981): 5–32.

Englert, C. S., "Measuring Special Education Teacher Effectiveness." *Exceptional Children* (November 1983): 247–254.

Evertson, C., "Differences in Instruction Activities in High and Low Achieving Junior High Classes." Paper presented at the annual meeting of the American Educational Research Association, Boston, 1980.

Fisher, C.; Berliner, D.; Filby, N.; Marliave, R.; Chance, L.; and Dishaw, M., "Teaching Behaviors, Academic Learning Time, and Student Achievement: An Overview." In Denham, C. and Lieberman, A. (eds.), *Time to Learn*. Washington, DC: The National Institute of Education, U.S. Department of Education, 1980.

"Florida Beginning Teacher Program." Office of Teacher Education, Certification and Inservice Staff Development. Tallahassee, FL, 1982.

Good, T.L., "How Teachers' Expectations Affect Low Achieving Students." *American Educator* (December 1982): 22–32.

Hudgins, B. B. *et al.*, *Educational Psychology*. Itasca, IL: Peacock Publishers, 1983.

Hudgins, Judith M., and Cone, W. Henry, "Principals Should Stress Effective Teaching Elements in Classroom Instruction." *NASSP Bulletin, 76*, 542 (March 1992): 13–18.

Hunter, M., "Knowing, Teaching and Supervising." *Using What We Know About Teaching*. Alexandria, VA: Association for Supervision and Curriculum Development, 1984, pp. 169–192.

Kean, Michael H., "Testing and the Schools: Short-Term Gain or Long-Term Investment?" *NASSP Bulletin, 76*, 545 (September 1992): 3–5.

King, Jean A., "Working for Long-Term School Improvement: Bringing Research to the Classroom." *NASSP Bulletin, 76*, 545 (September 1992): 24–29.

Ornstein, Allen C., "Making Effective Use of Computer Technology." *NASSP Bulletin, 76*, 542 (March 1992): 27–33.

Rankin, Stuart C., "Total Quality Management: Implications for Educational Assessment." *NASSP BULLETIN, 76*, (September 1992): 66–76.

Rosenshine, B., "Teaching Functions in Instructional Programs." Airlie House Paper, NIE Conference, 1982.

Stallings, J., "Allocated Academic Learning Time Revisited, or Beyond Time on Task," *Educational Researcher, 9*, 11 (1980): 11–16.

Strong, R.W., Silver, H. F., and Hanson, R. "Integrating Teaching Strategies and Thinking Styles with Elements of Effective Instruction." *Educational Leadership, 42* (May 1985): 9–15.

$$Chapter \quad 12$$

Restructuring the Deployment of Instructional Personnel

Introduction

One of the greatest responsibilities assigned to a principal is organizing and assigning staff in the school. Included in normal staffing responsibilities is the deployment of all employees and volunteer workers to the instructional program and service functions of the school. Central office administrators and supervisors often have a hand in these assignments, but especially with the advent of site-based management, the responsibility, and particularly the final decision, rest with the principal and staff.

Inherent in any good staffing design is optimal utilization of staff. Staff planning must take into account the present needs and functions of the members of the organization as well as the school's long-range goals and plans that might modify hiring practices in the future.

Professional employees in school organizations often have great insight and usually excellent ideas of how a school could be improved. They also have the need for both personal development and professional growth through interaction with other professionals in the school. School organization, however, often works against this opportunity for interaction because of self-contained classrooms that isolate teachers for up to six hours each day.

The development and vitality of the organizational climate of the school is also dependent on the opportunity and ability of the school staff to interact with each other. One way for school professionals to interact with each other is to participate in management decisions at the building level that affect the school's curriculum and instruction.

Participation by Staff

Site-based management, to function successfully, requires greatly increased participation in school decisions on the part of staff members. An excellent way to involve the faculty is through the formation of a faculty council to improve the school's curricular and instructional program. If the school has a multiunit learning community design as described later in this chapter, this faculty council should be made up of the head of each learning community and the principal, as shown in Figure 12–1; otherwise, department heads or grade level chairpersons would be appropriate. Topics appropriate for consideration by this advisory council to the principal include virtually any significant decision that will require staff cooperation and is in their field of expertise. A quality circle approach is appropriate for some of the advisory council activities.

Matrix Management

In a similar fashion to the advisory council, special coordinating committees should be organized to deal with curricular areas such as reading, math, social studies, or any area that requires cross-unit coordination. These committees may be permanent or temporary in nature, depending on the assignment.

If a multiunit staffing design is used, these committees can best be formed with one teacher from each team (Figure 12–2). The curriculum committee thus formed provides representation from each of the teams as well as communication back to each team. Each staff member also shares in the school-wide efforts to provide community and thrust to the curricular and instructional program. The major line of responsibility (vertical) in the matrix still rests with each team. The curriculum committees (horizontal) function only to coordinate the overall school program.

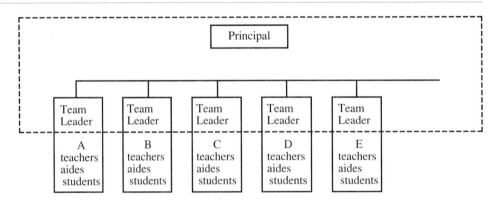

The staff within the dotted line makes up the Principal's Advisory Council.

FIGURE 12–1.   Principal's Advisory Council

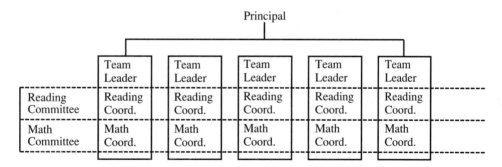

FIGURE 12–2.   Multiunit Curricular Coordinating Committees Matrix Management

     If the school maintains a more traditional staffing pattern, these schoolwide staffing designs can still be used. There will be some loss of representation, however. In any case, staffing must be viewed in the context of the total mission of the school.

Empowerment

Ultimately what is wanted of teachers is quality instruction and for learning to take place between teachers and students. There are many functions within the school organization that must be properly balanced for this to be maximized. Too little attention on the part of administration regarding what goes on in each classroom can lead to lack of coordination of the curriculum, great variation in the quality of teaching, and great variation in the motivation of teachers. On the other hand, too much control or structure over teachers or centralization of authority over the classroom might produce some uniformity but takes away teachers' autonomy, negatively affecting teacher motivation and thus reducing the quality of instruction among the better teachers.

     What is desired is a fine balance that can adequately empower teachers to exercise appropriate professional judgment while still ensuring the coordination of the curriculum and supervision of instruction. The appropriate empowerment of teachers must lie in the amount of authority granted, methods of accountability used to ensure responsibility, and the organizational structures created to maintain the proper communication flow necessary to carry out these tasks.[1]

Team Staffing

Traditionally, staffing has been by simple unit-classroom analysis, that is, one teacher, one group of students, one room, sometimes one instructional format, and sometimes one subject. Staffing plans have been built and modified from year to year using this basic classroom unit. Such a procedure is very restrictive, particularly when used in conjunction with some of the curricular, instructional, and grouping ideas presented in previous chapters. Team staffing offers several desirable alternatives to single classroom units.

Team staffing has been used with varying degrees of success in schools for years. Persuasive arguments can be given both for team staff organizations as well as self-contained classrooms. Arguments favoring team teaching are:

1. A teaching team provides variation for the children because the students have contact with a set of teachers.

2. Teacher productivity generally increases under a team arrangement since teachers tend to support each other in the achievement of goals.

3. Flexibility of grouping becomes possible and building-level scheduling can be greatly simplified when teachers are working together in a team.

4. The advantages of both specialization and generalization can be obtained when teachers specialize in either or both the curricular and instructional dimension within the team and still have the opportunity to observe the whole child as that child works with the team over the major portion of the day.

5. Individualized instruction can more easily be attained with the team of teachers sharing the variety of instructional tasks necessary to successfully implement an individualized program.

On the other hand, some still argue that self-contained classes are better. Reasons favoring self-contained classrooms are as follows:

1. Teacher training and experience traditionally has been for the self-contained classroom. Many teachers favor it because they know it best.

2. Buildings are designed for self-contained classrooms, not for team arrangements, and they simply do not lend themselves to team teaching.

3. When placed on teams, teachers develop difficulties in interpersonal relationships because of different personalities, teaching styles, or philosophies.

4. Team teaching requires a great deal of additional time in planning on the part of the teacher that could be devoted to children or to preparation of lessons in the self-contained classroom.

However, when consideration is given to the overall management of instruction, the arguments favoring team staffing patterns are clearly superior.

Staffing Patterns

An elementary staff can be organized in a variety of different ways depending on its desired result. Organizational patterns that utilize teams of teachers with responsibility for a common group of students are favored by this author. The integrated contributions of several teachers, the teacher growth enhanced by common planning and quality circles, and the collective team concern for the growth of their students generates a synergism that is difficult to match in the traditional self-contained classroom. Adaptation of the principles of site-based management and TQM strongly point in the direction of teaching teams.

Different staffing patterns are possible for any situation, from the traditional self-contained classroom to a variety of team and differentiated staffing models. Given a basic student population of 600 for an elementary school, as shown in Figure 12–3, the following examples illustrate several basic staffing designs.

Traditional Self-Contained Classrooms

A traditional staffing pattern with total reliance on self-contained classrooms based on a student-teacher ration for each classroom of approximately thirty-to-one is shown in Figure 12–4. As is often the case, tough dollar decisions determine when to exceed the thirty-pupils-per-classroom figure and when to hire additional staff to reduce the ratio. For a totally self-contained program, the only additional support staff would be the principal and possibly a librarian.

Teachers Plus Specialists

Usually, a school prefers specialists in certain areas such as special education, art, music, and physical education. Figure 12–5 illustrates a specialist staffing pattern with two special education teachers each taking a class load of ten to fifteen students, thus reducing class size by approximately one or two students in each room. The art, music, and physical education specialists, on the other hand, either come into the classroom with the regular teacher once or twice a week or take the children from the regular teacher for several periods each week, giving the regular teacher a break. The total staff size is increased by the number of specialists added, increasing the total staff in this example to twenty-eight or thirty.

Team Teaching

Teaching teams can easily be implemented as an alternate pattern to those just outlined using the same number of students and staff positions (Figure 12–5). Each team consists of three or four teachers in grade-level arrangements. The special education teachers attach themselves to either the primary or intermediate teams, dividing their time among

5-year-olds	75
6-year-olds	80
7-year-olds	95
8-year-olds	85
9-year-olds	100
10-year-olds	90
11-year-olds	75
TOTAL	600

FIGURE 12–3.   Grade Distribution of Student Population

Grade	Students	Teachers	Class Size
K	75	3	25
1	80	3	26–27
2	95	3 or 4	31–32 or 23–24
3	85	3	28–29
4	100	3 or 4	33–34 or 25
5	90	3	30
6	75	3	25

Staff Teachers		21 or 23	
	Plus	1 Principal	
		1 Librarian	

	Staff Totals	23	overall ratio 1–26.1
		25	overall ratio 1–24.0

FIGURE 12–4. Staffing Assignments for Self-Contained Classrooms

Grade	Students	Staff Team	
K	75	3	
1	80	3	
2	95	3 or 4	
3	85	3	Sp. Ed. 1
4	100	3 or 4	
5	90	3	
6	75	3	Sp. Ed. 1
Specialists, art, librarian, music, P.E.		4	
Principal		1	

	Staff Totals	28 overall ratio 1–21.4
		30 overall ratio 1–20.0

FIGURE 12–5. Staffing for Grade-Level Teams

Grade	Students	Teams		Aides
		Teachers		
K	75	3		+ aide
1	80	3	Sp. Ed. 1	+ aide
2	95	3		+ aide
3	85	3		+ aide
4	100	3		+ aide
5	90	3	Sp. Ed. 1	+ aide
6	75	3		+ aide
Specialists, art, music, P.E., librarian		4		+ aide
Principal		1		

| | Staff totals | 28 | | 8 aides |

overall staffing ratio 1–16.7

Eight aides can be hired for the salaries of two teachers

FIGURE 12–6. Grade-Level Teams with Aides

the several groups. The art, music, and physical education specialist and the librarian also form a team for staff organization. Advantages as well as disadvantages of team organization have been discussed earlier.

Team Teaching with Paraprofessionals

Grade-level teaching teams can be enhanced if each team adds a paraprofessional. In many communities, aides can be hired for a minimum wage, or in some cases volunteers can be used to support the team. The cooperative organization of a team approach permits sharing students. Teachers often prefer to employ paraprofessionals rather than additional teachers to reduce class size. If, as shown in Figure 12–5, grades 2 and 4 could function with three-teacher teams instead of four, the salary dollars saved could pay the salary for eight aides (part-time if necessary), one for each of the school's teams (Figure 12–6).

Teaching staff to support these five groups would be deployed as shown in Figure 12–7. The organizational pattern illustrated in Figure 12–8 results in the same staff requirements but distributes responsibilities more evenly. This type of team organization, coupled with multiage grouping, allows for an extremely even distribution of students. Even when the enrollment numbers vary greatly or when staffing ratios are unfavorable, balance can be provided, ensuring uniform availability of instructional services.

Utilization of Staff Specialists

The addition of specialists for special education, reading, math, learning disabilities, physical education, art, and music has been a mixed blessing in our schools. Most schools have desperately needed the extra help but have not been able to make maximum use of the talents that specialists can provide.

20 teachers (5 teams, 4 each)   5 instructional aides
 4 teacher specialists   3 clerical aides
 1 principal   —
 2 special education   8 aides
 1 librarian   overall staffing ratio 1–16.7
 —
28

FIGURE 12–7.   Staff Utilization in a Team Organization

Part of the problem of using specialists arises from single-classroom organization. The specialist in a "pullout" program is a fifth wheel and often is never fully integrated into the program. Many times, specialists have been set apart in little rooms by themselves to call children out of regular classrooms, disrupting the regular program for the child as well as using their own time very inefficiently.

A team organization leads to a variety of ways to use specialists. In some cases, specialists can best be utilized by dividing their time into fractional units and assigning them to teams for each unit. Following are three examples of how a team organization can utilize the services of specialists or the services provided by special programs.

School One: Resource Teachers

A school organized in a multiunit fashion similar to the school just discussed was allocated two additional reading and math positions out of federal funds. One was for remedial reading and the other for mathematics. The school decided to integrate these positions

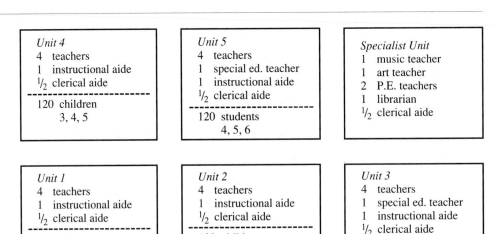

FIGURE 12–8.   A Multiunit Design for Staff and Students

fully into the teams so that no specialist would work with more than one team. In order to do this, the specialist positions were divided into fractional units and student loads were adjusted accordingly. Instead of hiring new people for these positions, interested faculty from the existing staff were identified and given the special training necessary for the new assignments. The two positions were divided into four units of time and distributed among the existing staff. Each team was assigned a one-fourth-time reading specialist and a one-fourth-time math specialist. The released staffing money was used to hire two more regular teachers. Specialist services were integrated into each team to make the available instruction relate closely to the organized program. Federal guidelines were met by assigning designated students to these specialists for the appropriate times.

School Two: Special Education—Full Inclusion

In order to provide for full inclusion for children with disabilities within this school, organized according to a multiunit pattern, these children were assigned on an age basis to the appropriate learning community. The two special education teachers for the children with disabilities in this school worked together as a team with the instructional teams in the school. They attended team planning meetings when appropriate and scheduled their visits to coincide with the skill-grouped reading program of the team. During the reading schedule they became part of the team and took the children with disabilities into expanded reading groups, thus bolstering the reading staff. The children of this school never identified and labeled these two specialists as special education teachers, even though they spent almost all of their time with certain children. A way to save time for the special education staff is to place all the children with disabilities into two or three learning communities, reducing the number of different teams with which specialists must work.

School Three: Art, Music, and Physical Education Specialists

In the third school the art, music, and physical education specialists served two major functions: (1) They served as student advisors along with each of the other four teachers on the team to which they were assigned. They did this during the early minutes of the school day, the noon hour, and the last thirty minutes of the afternoon. (2) During an approximately two-and-one-half-hour block in the morning and again each afternoon, two physical education teachers, an art teacher, and a music teacher worked on a unit-rotating basis, taking half of the children from two of the units for instruction in their specialties. Thus, for two and one-half hours once or twice a week each team had a block of time with only half of the children and could concentrate on small group instruction activities.

Team Integration

A multiunit design results in the formation of a series of learning communities consisting of three to five teachers and aides, students, and a curriculum. This design must be able to allow effective individualization of instruction and enhance the implementation of the curriculum. This can be accomplished more successfully by a team design than by single-unit classrooms, but only with proper planning.

The full integration of the team's instructional program is the key to its success. All teachers must share in organizing the curriculum, preferably with an interdisciplinary approach with each teacher carrying a specific independent assignment. The teachers must share the children and together discuss their problems. Specialization in curriculum can be used to reduce the planning required of any particular teacher, but not to the extent that it causes departmentalization of the curriculum. Figure 12–9 illustrates how one learning-community staff divided the workload after much discussion and planning. All of the children were organized into twelve skill groups for reading and eight for math. Thus, each of the four regular teachers had three reading skill groups and two math skill groups. In addition, each teacher took several other curricular responsibilities for learning-center development as well as for direct instruction. Each team member also assumed some administrative responsibility. The physical education teacher worked directly with the team only part of each day. Each week a schedule was planned.

Team Planning

Site-based management requires the active participation of staff members in decisions that affect their own areas of responsibility. This includes an expanded role in curriculum and instructional decisions, evaluation decisions and the day-by-day organizing and scheduling functions. These tasks are most effectively carried out on a team or unit basis.

One of the most crucial factors in a successful team operation is adequate planning time and efficient utilization of that time. If at all possible, team planning should occur during the regular school day. Planning should be regularly scheduled; at least two hours per week are needed in a minimum of one-hour blocks. Each team meeting should have an agenda, prepared by the team and distributed in advance, and each meeting should have a designated chairperson. A secretary for the team should keep minutes of the meeting.

Building an agenda for team meetings is an opportunity for all team members to share in the planning for the team. One good way to achieve this is to place an agenda

Teacher A	Teacher B	Teacher C	Teacher D	P.E. Specialist
25 advisees team leader advisement coordinator	25 advisees reading coordinator	25 advisees math coordinator	25 advisees learning center coordinator	20 advisees
reading (3) math (2) writing crafts language	reading (3) math (2) science spelling learning center	reading (3) math (2) social studies library learning center	reading (3) math (2) science health	

FIGURE 12–9. Learning-Community Staff Assignments

planning sheet in a central location for the team to list items they wish to discuss at the next scheduled meeting. Some principals have the teams prepare their agenda so that copies can be quickly reproduced and distributed to team members, as well as other key people such as the librarian, special education teacher, or the principal, who may want to attend the team meeting. Figure 12–10 is an example of a form to be used for agenda building.

A variety of different planning tasks of both a long- and short-term nature needs to be carried out by each team. Effective use of planning time can usually be enhanced by focusing on a particular purpose during a meeting. The following six types of planning meeting are suggested with recommendations regarding frequency.

1. *Goal-Setting Meeting.* One goal-setting meeting should be held each semester to look at the philosophy of the school, the curriculum guidelines existing for its direction, and the identification of goals for the particular group of students for whom the team is responsible. These goals would be long-range in nature and would be things to work toward over a semester or year.

2. *Design Meeting.* A design meeting is a planning meeting to select instructional topics and develop instructional units. Principles and objectives as well as general ideas for the unit are considered. After the topic has been selected, one team member is usually assigned the responsibility for drafting the unit. When the draft is ready, the team modifies and builds on the design. Specific objectives are listed, overall responsibility for each member of the team is outlined, and the calendar of events is developed with specific target dates. Methods of student evaluation are also planned. One of these meetings is necessary for each new unit, and a minimum of one each quarter or marking period is essential.

3. *Grouping or Scheduling Meeting.* This planning meeting outlines activities for the next week or two, defining specific instructional plans, organizing students into appropriate groups, and constructing the weekly calendar and daily schedule. One of these meetings is needed at least once every two weeks, if not weekly.

4. *Situational Meeting.* This meeting focuses on individual children. Various children within the group are discussed by the various members of the team to coordinate information and develop plans for learning activities for that child. The teacher-advisor for the particular child has the responsibility of carrying out team decisions. These meetings should probably be held each week, with each teacher-advisor determining which children need to be discussed by the team.

5. *Evaluation Meeting.* The major focus of this meeting should be the evaluation of the instructional program and units. Questions to be asked are: Did we achieve our goals? What were our strengths? What were our shortcomings? How well did we function together as a team? One of these meetings should be held each quarter immediately after the close of the quarter or immediately after the completion of a major unit.

6. *Team Meeting Schedule.* Assuming a planning schedule that allows for two planning meetings per team each week in a six-week instructional period, a schedule of team meetings for the period might look like Figure 12–11.

TEAM ___*4-A*___   DATE OF MEETING ___*10/14*___

I. *STUDENTS*

Name	Person presenting	Concern	Est. Time needed
Bill Fox	*Mary*	*attendance*	*5 m.*
Nancy York	*Jane*	*uncomp. assign.*	*5 m.*

II. *PROGRAM DEVELOPMENT*

Area	Person presenting	Est. time needed
Unit–election	*Gary*	*20 m.*
Unit–health	*Mary*	*to next time*

III. *STAFF DEVELOPMENT*

Area	Person presenting	Est. time needed
accelerated learning	*Pat*	*20 m.*

IV. *ADMINISTRATIVE*

Area	Person presenting	Est. time needed
lunchtime	*Pat*	*5 m.*
Friday's assembly	*Pat*	*5 m.*

FIGURE 12–10.   Form for Agenda Building

Two team meetings should be held each week.

Prior to school year	• Goal setting for the semester
	• Design of units for the first grading period
	• Initial grouping and scheduling of students assigned to team
Week 1	• Situational meeting
	• Grouping and scheduling meeting
Week 2	• Situational meeting
	• Grouping and scheduling meeting
Week 3	• Situational meeting
	• Grouping and scheduling meeting
Week 4	• Situational meeting
	• Design meeting—plans for the next period meeting
Week 5	• Situational meeting
	• Design meeting
Week 6	• Situational meeting
	• Evaluation meeting (of teaching)
Week 7 (repeats Week 1)	• Situational meeting
	• Grouping and scheduling meeting

FIGURE 12–11.   Schedule of Team Meetings

Extra grouping and scheduling meetings as well as situational meetings are scheduled early in the year to work through changes in enrollments and to place children better as more data are available.

Paraprofessionals

Many tasks performed daily in the elementary school do not require professional training. Some tasks relate directly to improving instruction, whereas others are noninstructional in nature. The move toward individualized instruction, the multiple-activity classroom, and the many additional services of a food, health, or welfare nature that are provided in schools increase the demand for nonprofessional employees.

In some schools clerical and instructional paraprofessionals have performed these functions. Other communities, without funds for additional staff, have used volunteers.[2] Paid or volunteer aides can be a great asset to the school, but schools must properly select and train these individuals to avoid problems.

Types of Paraprofessionals

There are many tasks that can be performed by the paraprofessional: the instructional or classroom aide, the clerical or support aide, the library aide—the list is long. Instructional aides usually work directly with a classroom teacher or team and assist in instructing children under the direction of a teacher or team. In addition, they fulfill a variety of clerical, support, and supervisory tasks assigned by the teacher or team. A clerical or support aide usually does not work directly in a classroom but in the office, clinic, school store, library, or resource room.

Whether the aides are paid or volunteers, the paraprofessional program must provide a sound orientation and training period as well as careful appraisal of special talents and abilities possessed by these individuals.

A first step in the utilization of any special nonprofessional in the school is the development of a policy for such a program. This is obviously necessary if the aides are to be paid, but it is also very important when volunteers are used. There are many legal ramifications of such a program, and a policy regarding the aide program should be developed in each school district and ought to include recruitment, selection, orientation, and training.

Recruitment and Selection of Paraprofessionals

Paraprofessionals can be drawn from the entire community. If most positions are established on a part-time basis—three to twenty hours per week—the potential available work force is very large. Available persons might include college students, high school students, housewives, retirees, and men or women who work evening shifts. Professional people may also be available as resource people and for short special assignments.

Recruitment can occur through newspaper articles, letters to parents, the PTO, church announcements, telephone, or any other available contacts. After a paraprofessional program has been initiated, a television news story on the paraprofessional program followed by a call for assistance may be an effective recruitment device.[3]

Each paraprofessional or volunteer should be interviewed before acceptance into the program. In the initial interview, the principal should attempt to gauge the individual's motivations, assess potential contributions, and decide the kind of responsibility the person can most effectively assume. Factors that should be considered during an interview include educational background, the use of language, appearance, poise and personality, interest in children, willingness and ability to follow directions, special interests, abilities, training, past employment, general health (a physical examination should be required), and the aide's home situation. By far the most overriding consideration is the aide's dedication to the welfare of children and a willingness to commit time and energy on their behalf.

The interview serves to inform the aide of the goals of the school and helps the aide decide if the school is a desirable place to work. The interview also can be used to determine whether a volunteer would work well directly with children. If not, the individual can receive other kinds of assignments, provided the person has the appropriate technical skills.

Orientation and Training Program

Each new volunteer or paraprofessional should attend at least one formal orientation session. Additional sessions can be scheduled as the year progresses and as needs arise. These individuals should be familiar with basic principles before they begin work. They must understand lines of authority within the school and must know where to turn in a conflict situation. An introduction to administrative and supervisory personnel will smooth relationships and give aides an understanding of who to contact if a problem arises.

Volunteers must realize that they have undertaken an important service with a fixed schedule, specific demands, and supervision of some activities. They should understand that the school expects a high quality of effort, reliability, and cooperation. They must learn to be friendly, tactful, helpful, and fair to all students. They must be instructed not to discuss children with parents and not to divulge any information from private records to anyone. They should be aware that disciplinary action is the responsibility of the teacher only, and that the teacher handles all parental problems.

A third phase of the training program for volunteers or paraprofessionals should involve a discussion of the psychological aspects of their work. This discussion should cover general characteristics of children and the implications of working with them, along with their physical, social, mental, and emotional attributes. It should focus on the procedures and attitudes that are conducive to the best psychological atmosphere and climate within the classroom. This phase of the program should help aides learn the general approach to children used by the staff.

The final phase of an aide program is continuous. It constitutes participation in the daily activities and operation of the school and is truly on-the-job training. In addition, instructional aides should participate as much as possible in teacher inservice training. The training program for clerical and support aides is similar to that of the instructional aides but also includes specific training in regard to clerical duties.

Creating a Supportive Atmosphere for the Volunteers

Volunteers and paraprofessionals, as well as teachers, must have a warm working climate within the school. They need a gathering place and time for a coffee break as well as the opportunity to share activities and responsibilities. An advisement committee of aides should meet with the principal on a regular basis to discuss improving the role of the aide within the school. Schedules for aides should be made as flexible as possible to accommodate outside responsibilities.

Administration of the Volunteer Program

If the paraprofessionals consist largely of volunteers, day-by-day scheduling becomes an important task. A principal does not have time to manage this on a daily basis and can use a volunteer to administer the work program.[4]

Liability Implications for Volunteers and Paraprofessionals

One particular caution needs to be raised regarding the use of volunteers: the legal question of tort liability. Training these individuals for the jobs they hold is important.

Specific supervisory training, as well as the development of clearly defined supervisory policies including lines of authority and responsibilities, is recommended. A training program for aides should consider techniques of supervising children, what to do in a variety of situations, how to handle the children who need disciplining, and how to handle emergency situations. If each individual, whether paid or voluntary, receives this training, the potential for a negligence charge stemming from a personal injury situation will be greatly reduced. Some states require liability insurance for paraprofessionals. Education associations usually provide this insurance in those states requiring it.

Summary

When staffing a school, consideration must be given to overall staffing patterns as well as the plans for individual classrooms. When teachers work independently, decisions about curricular responsibilities and teaching function are limited. When teachers are organized into teams, many more staffing options are available. The multiunit pattern for staffing, curricular organization, and student grouping makes maximum use of staffing potential.

The concepts of participatory management with the use of a principal's advisory council and curriculum committees can greatly strengthen decision making and faculty participation. These same committees and teaching teams should become the basis for forming quality circles.

Paraprofessionals can be used to augment a school's staff by performing tasks that do not require the professional skills of the teacher but that do demand the attention of an adult. These people may be paid staff or volunteers. In either case, it is important to provide the aides with adequate orientation and training to maximize their use in the schools.

Endnotes

1. Gene I. Maeroff, "A Blueprint for Empowering Teachers." *Phi Delta Kappan, 69*, 7 (March 1988): 472–477.

2. An excellent source of the information and ideas for volunteer aide programs can be found in the publications of the National School Volunteer Program, 300 North Washington Street, Alexandria, VA 22314.

3. One of the more successful recruitment ideas is the establishment of a volunteer-operated day care center for the children of the volunteer mothers. The day care center is extremely appealing to mothers who are home with small children, and the opportunity to get out and relate to other children and adults brings them to the school to volunteer. A free lunch for retirement volunteers also works extremely well.

4. In one case observed recently, several women who wished to work in the program but were unable to leave the home because of health reasons were used to place the calls each evening to the homes of the other volunteer aides reminding them of their hours of employment for the next day.

Selected Readings

Carnegie Task Force on Teaching as a Profession, *A Nation Prepared: Teachers for the 21st Century*. New York: Carnegie Foundation Forum on Education and the Economy, 1986.

Castetter, William B., *The Personnel Function in Educational Administration*. New York: Macmillan, 1986.

Heller, Gary S., "Teacher Empowerment—Sharing the Challenge: A Guide to Implementation and Success." *NASSP Bulletin, 77*, 550 (February 1993): 94–103.

Lange, John T., "Site-Based, Shared Decision Making: A Resource for Restructuring." *NASSP Bulletin, 76*, 549 (January 1993): 98–107.

Maeroff, Gene I., "A Blueprint for Empowering Teachers." *Phi Delta Kappan, 69*, 7 (March 1988): 472–477.

Reep, Beverly B. and Grier, Terry B., "Teacher Empowerment: Strategies for Success." *NASSP Bulletin, 76*, 546 (October 1992): 90–97.

Stimson, Terry D. and Appelbaum, Richard P., "Empowering Teachers: Do Principals Have the Power?" *Phi Delta Kappan, 70*, 4 (December 1988): 313–316.

Chapter 13

Restructuring Time: Scheduling Staff and Students

Introduction

The school schedule is considered by many to be the command performance of the principal. It is here that the ability to conceptualize, to organize, and to carry out detailed planning is most visible. If well done, the schedule will strongly support the instructional and curricular program of the school. On the other hand, if poorly designed, the schedule will be a roadblock to a balanced curriculum and instructional flexibility.

If a good structure for participatory management exists within the school and if teachers are truly empowered as professionals, then their involvement in schedule building can enhance the quality of that schedule.

Scheduling can be defined as the plan to bring together people, materials, and curriculum at a designated time and place for the purpose of instruction. Its basic purpose is to coordinate the requirements laid down by previously reached decisions regarding curriculum, instruction, grouping, and staffing.

The effective schools research has much to say about the use of time in school. The concepts of academic learning time (ALT), discussed in earlier chapters, describe scheduled time as its umbrella component from which the "actual" instructional time and "engaged" time are achieved. Therefore, it is imperative that scheduled time be maximized so that ultimately high amounts of instructional and engaged time can also be obtained.

Several important concepts in scheduling should be reviewed before actually beginning the construction of a schedule. These include the flexibility, simplicity, and complexity of the schedule, the decision level at which schedule changes are made, efficiency in the use of time, and the timeliness of the schedule. Other concepts to consider are previously made grouping patterns and space availability and utilization.

Schedule Attributes

Time Flexibility

Good instruction cannot always be bottled into one-hour classes. Time available for teaching often needs to be flexible to provide maximum benefit and efficiency. The scheduling of time in the school should have either the potential of being legitimately changed with great frequency or have the internal elasticity of meeting a variety of curricular and instructional requests within its regular structure. For example, the teacher who would like to take a group of children on a half-day field trip should be able to do so without disrupting the entire school schedule. Or the group that needs an extra hour to complete a project should be able to have that hour with an easy adjustment in the schedule.

Simplicity and Complexity

Often requests to change a class schedule must be turned down because the change will interfere with some other parts of the school program. Schedules need simplicity to prevent interdependence of the components of the schedule, so that the modification of one component does not require the modification of several others. Complexity, on the other hand, is also needed in order to meet the demands of individual differences of students. To meet individual differences, intricate schedule designs need to be constructed. This seemingly creates a paradox, but it is another application of the loosely coupled-tightly coupled concept of organization. Empowered teachers must be given control over those complex decisions at the team or classroom level. An analogy that seems fitting to describe this relationship is found in modularized electronics. The complexity of their circuitry is an amazing example of modern-day technology, but, on the other hand, this complex design is constructed in such a way that if a failure occurs or if a modification is desired, a circuit board can be removed and replaced very quickly without having to disassemble the entire set once the trouble spot has been identified or the desired modification determined. So it is with a schedule: A good schedule must permit the complex construction required for individual differences while maintaining simplicity to allow easy changes.

Efficiency and the Use of Time

The effective schools research points out the need for time efficiency. There are many ways that greater efficiency can be obtained within the schedule. Several specific suggestions are as follows:

1. Minimize the use of nonspecific study time during school hours. This means reducing—or better yet, eliminating—study halls. Too often, study halls are where we put children we cannot get scheduled into any other class. They are a reflection of the principal's inability or unwillingness to design a tight, efficient schedule. In a good schedule, study halls should be virtually eliminated. At the elementary and middle school levels, activity periods must be carefully designed so that they do not also become holding areas for children otherwise not engaged in a supervised learning activity.

2. Minimize the time used for movement from classroom to classroom. Techniques will vary greatly depending on building arrangements and instructional design. Specifics might include the use of two- or three-hour blocks of time with no student passage required, clustering of classrooms and lockers to minimize travel on the part of students, or the development of efficient hall traffic patterns and the reduction of the time between classes.

3. Available instructional time can be enhanced with the development and implementation of an efficient policy regarding the use of the intercom system. Within the school, restrict its use to the first and last few minutes of the day so as to not interrupt potential instructional time.

Other efficiencies in the use of teachers' and children's time in school may include good use of lunch time (including a duty-free lunch for teachers and the opportunity for students to relax as well) and the effective use of before and after school waiting time on the part of students (waiting for buses, parents, etc.). Every minute of the school day counts. The principal must always ask: What is the best possible use of this time?

Timeliness of Scheduling Decisions

Timeliness is part of flexibility. Schedules must be designed so that daily and weekly instructional and curricular needs can be met as they occur.

Scheduling Decisions—Involving Teachers

The decision level is the point in the hierarchy of an organization where decisions are made. A basic rule for good decision making in most organizations is that decisions should be made at the lowest level within the organization where adequate information exists for that decision (loosely coupled). The application of this rule to scheduling suggests that students and teachers should be empowered to have maximum involvement in scheduling decisions. At the building level, scheduling should be kept as simple as possible so that the various components can be changed without disrupting the entire school. Also, each building should have maximum control over its schedule and not be frequently subject to the schedules of other schools in the school system. Some traditional areas of conflict, such as coordinating bus schedules between schools or scheduling shared teacher specialists, require higher level decisions.

The major conflicts will arise over making up specialists' schedules within the school, in coordinating special areas such as gymnasiums and music rooms, and in scheduling schoolwide programs such as lunch.

Scheduling Techniques

There are several approaches to achieving a good schedule. One of the best is to provide relative large blocks of time unencumbered by outside influences to teams of teachers and groups of students, empowering them to develop a detailed daily schedule to meet curricular and instructional needs. Such a schedule would only have to accommodate special activities such as lunch, physical education, or music (Figure 13-1).

Morning	Team Scheduled Block	Team Scheduled Block	T.S.B.	P.E. MUSIC
			P.E. MUSIC	
				T.S.B.
	LUNCH	LUNCH	LUNCH	LUNCH
Afternoon	Team Scheduled Block	P.E. MUSIC	Team Scheduled Block	Team Scheduled Block
		Team Scheduled Block		
	P.E. MUSIC			

FIGURE 13–1.   Block Schedule

Inside these large blocks of time the team of teachers and students plan all of the learning activities. These internal schedules can differ from one day to the next as plans are made by the team reflecting the instructional format, curriculum, groupings, and staffing assignments. Because each of these instructional blocks stands alone, changes within them do not affect the remainder of the school.

Figure 13-2 illustrates a simple form of scheduling within the block of time that can be used by a team of five teachers following a basic rotating design. In this schedule, each teacher has access to each group of children operating in a semi-departmentalized school-within-a-school design. The schedule does not meet all of the curricular, instructional, and grouping recommendations made in the previous chapter, but it also does not preclude further development to meet the additional criteria. The team has a high degree of autonomy to plan their schedule as they see fit and can modify it as frequently as every day if they choose.

	Group A	B	C	D
Block of Time	R	SS	SS	M
	SS	SC	M	R
	SC	M	R	SS
	L	L	L	L
	M	R	SS	SC
	P.E.	P.E.	Music Alternate Days	

R Reading
SS Social Studies
SC Science
L Lunch
M Math

Four teachers responsible for groups A-D

FIGURE 13–2.   Block-of-Time Rotating Schedule

	Teacher A	Teacher B	Teacher C	Teacher D
9–9:30	Reading Group 1 10 children	Reading Group 2 10 children	Reading Group 3 10 children	90 children learning centers

FIGURE 13–3. Staffing for Small Skill Groups

Numerous schedule variations can be created from this basic design. It offers an excellent opportunity to create groups that vary in size as well as the ability to group students according to a variety of special interests and skills patterns.

At the elementary level a team might create small groups for reading instruction by assigning children to instructional groups on a skills basis. Each team member can teach a small group of children by sharing activities and placing children in several different learning activities. To have reading groups of a reasonable size, three teachers of a four-member team can each take ten children in their reading group while the fourth teacher supervises the other children in some form of teacher-planned self-instructional activity (Figure 13-3). Sharing responsibility among teachers within a schedule permits the group size variation necessary for good instruction. During additional periods, the schedule can shift so that each teacher has large group direct instruction time as well as small reading groups for skill instruction (Figure 13-4). An instructional aide can assist in supervising learning centers and independent study activities, while the regular staff does directed instruction.

Grouping patterns can remain flexible. As the team's planning develops, the internal schedule can change as frequently as needed. Variations for math; the addition of science, or social studies, or language arts activities, including independent study work; and the scheduling of field trips can be built in and designed by teachers without requesting approval from an outside authority. Only when special teachers, facilities, and services for these activities are needed must the team consult and coordinate with the principal at the building level.

Ultimately, how the block schedule is to be used depends on the decisions regarding curriculum, instruction, grouping, and staffing. If teachers are organized in teams, the curriculum has a broad base of subjects, the instructional program is individualized, and the grouping is designed to allow frequent change, the block schedule may be designed to be able to accommodate those needs with ease.

Sample Schedule

A sample internal block schedule is shown in Figure 13-5. It is designed to meet the time needs based on the following major tenets:

	Teacher A	Teacher B	Teacher C	Teacher D	Aide
9:30–10	R–4 10 children	R–5 10 children	Learning centers 90 children	R–6 10 children	Learning centers
10–10:30	R–7	Learning centers (90)	R–8	R–9	Learning centers
10:30–11	Learning centers (90)	R–10	R–11	R–12	Learning centers

Twelve groups, including those in Figure 13–3—thirty minutes directed instruction of each group.

FIGURE 13–4.   Reading Skill Group Schedule

1. A flexible curriculum (different subjects with varying amounts of allocated time for different students)
2. Individualized instruction (use of mastery learning, small skill groups, independent study, and student interest groups)
3. Varied and flexible grouping (skill groups of ten to fifteen for reading and math instruction, interest groups with student advisor direction for learning centers, large heterogeneous grouping for direct instruction—e.g., in science, social studies, and health)
4. Organization of the staff, a team of five teachers and an aide, in a learning community

This schedule is only meant as an illustration of a particular day. The reading and math schedule are fairly constant for the teachers each day, but the groups change for the children as they master their skills and are regrouped in both math and reading.

The schedules for the other subjects change frequently as instruction is planned and group sizes are determined. Students use learning centers for drill and practice activities previously assigned during directed instruction when they do not have scheduled group activity. A typical student's schedule corresponding to the above described teachers' schedule might look like Figure 13-6.

A child's daily schedule is based on skill groups. Since children are grouped in the morning on a skills basis for reading, reading then becomes the grouping basis to direct children to all other subjects during the morning. In the afternoon the math groups become the organizational block from which children are directed to the other group activities. This provides homogeneous grouping according to skills in reading

Time	Teacher A	Teacher B	Teacher C	Teacher D	Teacher E	Aide
8:00	PREPARATION FOR DAY AND FINAL TEAM COORDINATION					
8:30	Children Arrive Group Advisement					Lunch Count Attendance
9:00	Reading 1 (10)	Reading 2 (10)	Social Studies Large Group (50)	Science (50)	Learning Centers (30)	Science
9:30	Writing (25)	Learning Centers (95)	Reading 3 (10)	Reading 4 (10)	Reading 5 (10)	Learning Centers
10:00	Reading 6 (10)	Reading 7 (10)	Social Studies Large Group (50)	Science (50)	Learning Centers (30)	Science
10:30	Writing (25)	Learning Centers (95)	Reading 8 (10)	Reading 9 (10)	Reading 10 (10)	Learning Centers
11:00	Reading 11 (10)	Reading 12 (10)	Social Studies Large Group (50)	Social Studies Large Group (50)	Learning Centers (30)	Science
11:30	Writing (25)	Learning Centers (95)	Reading 13 (10)	Reading 14 (10)	Reading 15 (10)	Learning Centers
12:00	Lunch (duty free)	Lunch (duty free)	Lunch (duty free)	Lunch Supervision	Lunch Supervision	Lunch Supervision
12:30	Playground	Playground	Playground	Lunch (duty free)	Lunch (duty free)	Lunch (duty free)
1:00	Math 1 (15)	Math 2 (15)	Math 3 (15)	Health (25)	Learning Centers (80)	Learning Centers
1:30	Learning Centers (55)	Spelling (15)	Learning Centers (50)	Math 4 (15)	Math 5 (15)	Learning Centers
2:00	Math 6 (15)	Math 7 (15)	Math 8 (15)	Health (25)	Learning Centers (80)	Learning Centers
2:30	Learning Centers (55)	Spelling (15)	Learning Centers (50)	Math 9 (15)	Math 10 (15)	Learning Centers
3:00	Group Advisement Cleanup					
3:30	Dismissal	Dismissal	Dismissal	Dismissal	Room Supervision	Bus Load
4:00	PREPARATION TIME					

The number in parentheses indicates the number of children for that activity. Learning Centers are supervised by the teacher indicated but all teachers contribute to their preparation.

FIGURE 13–5.   Sample Daily Schedule (Teacher Designed)

8:15 a.m.	Arrive at school
8:30 a.m.	Group advisement, Teacher A
9:00 a.m.	SS Teacher C
9:30 a.m.	Reading, Teacher D
10:00 a.m.	L C, Teacher E
10:30 a.m.	Writing, Teacher A
11:00 a.m.	Science, Teacher D
11:30 a.m.	L C, Teacher B
12:00 a.m.	Lunch
12:30 p.m.	Playground
1:00 p.m.	Health, Teacher D
1:30 p.m.	Math, Teacher D
2:00 p.m.	L C, Teacher E
2:30 p.m.	L C, Teacher C
3:00 p.m.	Group advisement, Teacher A
3:30 p.m.	Go home

FIGURE 13–6.   Student's Daily Schedule

and math and heterogeneous grouping in all other subject areas. The only exception to this rule occurs when children are grouped on an interest basis for other activities while not in reading or math.

The schedule can be simplified or made more complex as the situation changes. Skill in scheduling these internal team activities evolves with practice and time. Adequate team planning is an essential component to making the schedule function properly.

Team Planning Time

One of the most important features of any schedule involving a team of teachers working together is the provision of adequate team planning time. Every teacher should have a minimum of five hours each week for planning and materials preparation. At least two hours of this time should be in common with other members of the team. Teachers usually prefer to arrange this time in several large blocks rather than divide it into many small segments. Teachers and aides can occasionally alternate supervision, giving each team member some time for planning or materials preparation. However, extended planning sessions where all team members are present is also a must.

Parallel Scheduling

Team planning time can usually be best arranged on a schoolwide basis using parallel scheduling. Parallel scheduling provides large blocks of planning time through the use of specialists. The elementary school or middle school staff must include three or four full-time specialists such as music teachers, art teachers, and physical education teachers. These teachers are scheduled in a design paralleling that of the regular teaching staff so the specialists can replace each of the regular teaching team members, freeing them from all of the children in their learning community for a given block of time. The specialists then work in rotation with these children from one team for a period of one or more hours (Figure 13–7). Specialists can handle additional children if there are more specialists available or if an aide can work with a specialist and increase group size. The specialists work with each group of children so that, within a one- or two-day period, they replace each team (the team organization used here is the one shown in Figure 13–1).

These examples of schedules are meant only to be suggestions to generate ideas. Many variations can be developed from these different models. Each school and each team must be empowered to develop a schedule of its own, tailored to meet individual needs. It is important to let the schedule follow the demands of the curricular and instructional program and the student grouping and staffing patterns, and not allow the schedule to dictate the rest of the program.

Middle School Schedules

Middle schools have unique problems in scheduling teachers and students. If staff members hold only secondary teacher certification, they are limited in the number of subjects they may teach. Also, since the material being taught becomes more complicated in the higher grades, more daily preparation time by the teachers is necessary. This is difficult if each teacher is responsible for a large number of subjects. On the student side, the range of differences in abilities during the middle school years becomes greater and greater (Figure 7–1), suggesting the need for more skills grouping.

The block schedule shown in Figure 13–1 is probably the best design for a school-wide schedule in the middle school, along with the following ideas to be used for the internal team schedule.

Achievement grouping is recommended for use in reading and math instruction because of the relatively large span of abilities in the middle school. The fact that curriculum tends to be organized according to skill levels in these two subjects makes them the best candidates for this technique. Most other areas of the curriculum should use heterogeneous grouping, in that the overuse of ability grouping is more damaging to stu-

	Monday	Tuesday	Wednesday	Thursday	Friday
Morning	Specialists Replace Team A	Replace Team C	Replace Team E or Specialist Planning*	Replace Team B	Replace Team D
Afternoon	Replace Team B	Replace Team D	Replace Team A	Replace Team C	Replace Team E or Specialist Planning*

*In a five-team school the specialists use an extended duty-free lunch for planning.

FIGURE 13–7. Team Weekly Parallel Schedule

dents than beneficial. If too much is used, it negatively affects student self-concept, peer roles, and teacher attitudes.

Homogeneous grouping is more successful in improving learning when the curriculum is modified for the homogeneous grouping (i.e., when reading and math skills learning continues). When homogeneous grouping is used, the criteria for grouping must specifically match the curricular area (e.g., total reading scores for reading groups, math scores for math groups). Grouping on the basis of things like an IQ score is much too general and should not be used. (See Chapter 7.)

It is almost impossible from a scheduling standpoint to group more than two subjects if each teacher teaches a separate subject. The schedule shown in Figure 13–8 will allow homogeneous grouping in reading with good flexibility in assigning and moving students, because all four teachers will be teaching reading at the same time.

Teacher Period	A	B	C	D
1	Reading Groups A–E	Reading Groups B–F	Reading Groups C–G	Reading Groups D–H
2	Math 1	Science	Social Studies	Language Arts
3	Math 2	Science	Social Studies	Language Arts
4	Math 3	Science	Social Studies	Language Arts
5	Math 4	Science	Social Studies	Language Arts

FIGURE 13–8. Middle School Team Schedule

The math teacher can homogeneously group children during periods 2 through 5 into four or eight levels for mathematics. However, this schedule may fail to meet the specification of heterogeneity for social studies, science, and language arts because the math grouping will spill over into these subjects; the good math students will stay together in science, period 3; social studies, period 4; and language arts, period 5.

The problem with homogeneous grouping, carrying over into other groups in an undesirable manner, can be corrected, however. In order to meet the correct specifications for grouping, a matrix must be designed that will undo the grouping created by a subject such as math that runs parallel in the schedule to social studies, science, and language arts. The matrix must reassign the math groups to bring about the desired heterogeneity. This is done by assigning each of the math classes a series of scheduling numbers and placing children in groups of four or five (called modules). These subgroups for the math grouping can then be disaggregated through the other classes in an orderly manner.

The first column (math) of Figure 13–9 assigns each succeeding group of five math students a number. The top five math students are assigned number 1. The lowest five math students are given number 24. This number assigned to them in math class is then used to disperse them, thus creating heterogeneous grouping in the other three subjects.

A schedule for a four-teacher middle school team might carry the following specifications. Many variations of these assignments are possible, however:

All teachers teach reading	Reading is divided into eight skill levels
One teacher teaches math	Math is divided into four or more skill levels
One teacher teaches social studies One teacher teaches science One teacher teaches language arts	These classes are to be grouped heterogeneously and not reflect either the math or reading grouping

Summary

Scheduling has as its basic purpose the bringing together of curriculum, staff, and students for the purpose of instruction. It must be kept flexible, allowing for changes in group size and instructional time. Schedules must also provide for adequate staff planning and allow major scheduling decisions to be made by the team. Block-of-time schedules assigned to the team and parallel scheduling for team planning offer good solutions to scheduling demands.

Home Base:	Heterogeneous groups	2 subjects each teacher	
Reading:	Skill groups—8 groups		
Math:	Skill groups—each math module contains 5 students—120 total		
Other Subject:	Heterogeneous groups		

Teacher → Period ↓	1	2	3	4
1	Home base heterogeneous	Home base heterogeneous	Home base heterogeneous	Home base heterogeneous
	(Heterogeneous groups are created by rank ordering on reading scores with each home base receiving every fourth card.)			
2	Reading skill groups A,E	Reading skill groups B,F	Reading skill groups C,G	Reading skill groups D,H
3	Math homogeneous groups 1 4 2 5 3 6	Language Arts 7 16 10 19 13 22	Science 8 17 11 20 14 23	Social Studies 9 18 12 21 15 24
4	Math 7 10 8 11 9 12	Language Arts 15 24 18 3 21 6	Science 13 22 16 1 19 4	Social Studies 14 23 17 2 20 5
5	Math 13 16 14 17 15 18	Language Arts 20 5 23 8 2 11	Science 21 6 24 9 3 12	Social Studies 19 4 22 7 1 10
6	Math 19 22 20 23 21 24	Language Arts 1 12 4 15 9 17	Science 2 10 5 14 7 18	Social Studies 3 11 6 13 8 16

7, 8 Lunch-activity period—Art—Music—PE—Health—Guidance—etc.

FIGURE 13–9.   Middle School Team Schedule—Four-Teacher Team

Selected Readings

Anderson, John K., "Intensive Scheduling: An Interesting Possibility." *Clearing House*, 56 (Spring 1982): 26–28.

Anderson, Robert H., "The Return of the Nongraded Classroom." *Principal, 72*, 3 (January 1993): 9–12.

Bowman, Chris, "Integrated Software Solves Scheduling Problem." *Electronic Learning* (April 1985): 22–24.

Cannady, Robert Lynn and Reina, Joanne M., "Parallel Block Scheduling: An Alternative Structure." *Principal, 72*, 3 (January 1993): 26–29.

Cannady, Robert Lynn, "Designing Scheduling Structures to Increase Student Learning." *Focus in Change 1*, 2 (March 1989).

Dawson, Margaret M., "Beyond Ability Grouping: A Review of the Effectiveness of Ability Grouping and Its Alternatives." *School Psychology Review, 16*, 3 (1987).

Goodlad, John, *A Place Called School*. New York: McGraw Hill, 1984.

Lohr, Cherie and McGrevin, Carol, "Scheduling: The Blueprint for Educational Success." *NASSP Bulletin, 74*, 529 (November 1990): 83–89.

Murphy, Joseph, "Instructional Leadership: Focus on Time to Learn." *NASSP Bulletin, 76*, 542 (March 1992): 19–26.

Shaten, N. Lewis, "Building the Schedule: Breaking from the Mold of Traditional Thinking." *National Association of Secondary School Principals Bulletin, 66* (Fall 1982): 91–95.

Toy, Steve, "Solve Your Scheduling Puzzle without a Computer." *Executive Educator, 4*, 8 (August 1982): 24–25.

Ubben, Gerald C. "A Fluid Block Schedule." *NASSP Bulletin, 60*, 397 (February 1976): 104–11.

$Chapter$ 14

Staffing the School: Recruitment, Selection, and Termination Processes

Introduction

Recruitment and selection policies of local schools vary. The principal's involvement in the recruitment and selection process will depend on local district practice and policy. Central office personnel often assume the initial responsibility for the recruitment and screening of applicants for teaching positions. The principal should maintain a major role in the process and aggressively pursue it, if necessary. Central offices, often as a means of expediency and sometimes as a policy of control, tend to limit the input of principals and staff in the selection process. Under the concept of site-based management, if the principal is to be held in any way accountable for the quality of instruction in his or her building, he or she must have a major voice, if not the final voice, in the selection of personnel.

Recruitment

The major recruitment efforts of the principal begin with good position and person descriptions. Figures 14–1 and 14–2 depict sample position and person descriptions. If the principal finds it difficult to locate appropriate candidates, central office personnel should be contacted to review the recruitment process. For example, if the principal, in an effort to diversify the staff, has asked for a teacher from somewhere other than the local college and the personnel office has not posted vacancies at other colleges, the recruitment drive will be ineffective. The principal must assume responsibility for seeing that recruitment policies are broad enough to meet personnel needs.

Lakeview Schools
219 Lakeview Ave.
Lake City

PERSON DESCRIPTION

Position: Elementary Teacher.

Sex: Prefer male.

Teaching Experience Necessary: None.

Training Requirements: BS; prefer graduates from other than local college.

Certification: Elementary, K-3.

Teaching Strength: Strong reading training, interest in social studies.

Other Skills: Prefer someone with training or experience with team teaching or cooperative learning.

Other Interests: Prefer someone with avocational interests that would appeal to young boys such as camping, hiking, model airplane making, and so on.

FIGURE 14–1.   Person Description

Lakeview Schools
219 Lakeview Ave.
Lake City

POSITION DESCRIPTION

Position Title: Teacher (team) grade level Elementary 1–3.

Purpose of Position: To plan, organize, and instruct primary children.

Starting Date:

Salary Range: Beginning teacher, B.S.—$23,000
M.S.—$25,000

Principal Duties: The teacher will be a member of a four-teacher team working with six- to eight-year-old children. Instruction is organized on an interdisciplinary basis with cooperative planning units. The team has four assigned classrooms and schedules children in a flexible manner into these spaces. Major instructional responsibilities will include reading and mathematics as well as participation in the integration of other subjects.

Performance Responsibilities:

    I. Instructional Skills

        A. Knowledge and Training

            1. Is academically competent in assigned teaching areas.

            2. Keeps abreast of new findings and current trends in the field.

            3. Remains open-minded and willing to grow and change.

            4. Provides opportunities for all students to experience success.

FIGURE 14–2.   Position Description

B. Classroom Environment and Management

1. Maintains a classroom environment conducive to learning (by using special interest areas, learning centers, units, themes, furniture arrangements, proper lighting, heating, ventilation, and structured rules and regulations understood and accepted by all).

2. Monitors individual pupil progress and adapts the pace of instruction accordingly.

3. Uses democratic procedures that show consideration for the rights of others.

C. Methods and Techniques

1. Uses a variety of stimulating instructional techniques (such as the lecture method, demonstration, self-directed activities, both small and large group activities [drill and rote activities], and community resources, audiovisual aids and individualized programs).

2. Demonstrates and fosters the growth of communication skills.

3. Presents subject matter in a functional manner.

4. Makes homework assignments for meaningful instructional purposes.

D. Planning

1. Establishes short- and long-range goals with well-defined objectives and identifies appropriate procedures to accomplish them. (Example: A minimum competency and curriculum guide.)

2. Provides opportunities for all students to experience success.

3. Has a well-defined alternative plan for substitute teachers.

E. Evaluation

1. Provides feedback to students on their accomplishments and progress with positive and effective reinforcements.
2. Uses instruments based on activity, objective, or goal-oriented criteria.
3. Guides students toward self-motivation, self-evaluation, and self-direction.

II. Student Attitudes and Performance

A. Demonstrates consistency, firmness and impartiality in dealing with students in a professional manner.

B. Appreciates individuality.

C. Shows positive attitudes toward students by helping all children experience success, possibly through the use of tutorial and counseling activities.

D. Promotes desirable standards of work and behavior within the classroom.

III. Personal Qualities

A. Demonstrates a positive and enthusiastic attitude and a genuine interest in students, colleagues, curriculum, and the education field in general.

B. Recognizes and capitalizes on his or her own assets, thereby projecting a good model for students in dress, demeanor, and speech.

C. Is able to profit from constructive criticism.

D. Shows qualities that reflect the importance of punctuality, efficiency, dependability, accuracy, and congeniality.

FIGURE 14–2. Position Description *(Continued)*

IV. Professional Growth and Development

A. Participates in enrichment activities, including such activities as study in his or her field and/or travel.

B. Actively pursues avenues of personal and professional growth through workshops, classes, professional organizations, and seminars.

C. Establishes personal goals for professional development.

V. Teacher Relationships

A. Teacher-Parent

1. Establishes an effective line of communication between home and school via notes, conferences, written reports, work samples, telephone conversations, and meetings of groups such as the PTO that stress discussion of students' strengths and weaknesses.

2. Encourages parents to form a partnership with the teacher in the total education of their child—mentally, emotionally, physically, and spiritually.

B. Teacher-Community

1. Works effectively with legitimate community organizations and identifies and utilizes community resources to augment the educational opportunities of the children.

2. Projects a positive image of the total school program to the community; liaison function is served.

C. Teacher-Teacher

1. Cooperates fully with colleagues in shared responsibilities.

2. Shows tolerance for peer differences.

3. Shares experiences, ideas, and knowledge with peers.

4. Communicates effectively with other teachers who have shared or will share the same students for the purpose of developing smooth continuity between grade levels and subject matter.

D. Teacher-Administrator-Supervisor

1. Understands and adheres to the chain of command.

2. Participates in decision making when appropriate.

3. Demonstrates cooperation in performing both classroom and extra duties.

4. Seeks advice and counsel when needed.

5. Forms a partnership to develop good public relations in the school district.

E. Teacher-Student

1. Recognizes the uniqueness of all students.

2. Guides and encourages students in a friendly, constructive, and impartial manner.

3. Initiates procedures that will invite regular feedback for students.

4. Maintains a classroom atmosphere conducive to mutual respect, one that adequately establishes appropriate roles.

FIGURE 14–2. Position Description *(Continued)*

The selection of personnel should be a cooperative effort between the district personnel office and the local school. The central-office role should be to screen applicants and then to send those best matching the position descriptions to the principal for final selection. In some large school districts, a personnel office may employ teachers unassigned to specific buildings, but even in this case, the building principal should have the final decision regarding who works in the building.

The greatest problem in the selection of new staff members often comes from the need of the central office to place "transfers." These are generally tenured employees that must be moved from a previous assignment in the district. Since they are tenured, the school district must place them ahead of any new hires. While there may be many legitimate reasons for the transfer of employees within a school district, some school districts have a bad habit of playing "pass the trash." This is the practice of allowing the transfer of poor or incompetent teachers from school to school rather than going through the process of dismissal. Once again, as a principal, you must evaluate each candidate for a position in your school on the basis of what you think is best for your school.

The principles of site-based management and the concepts of teacher empowerment strengthen your position in employing new members of your staff. Involve the leadership team in setting policies for the selection of new staff members and involve members of your teaching staff in the interview and selection process. This will increase the principal's power base in resisting undesirable placements of staff by a central personnel office.

Federal Regulations to Prevent Employment Discrimination

Care must always be taken to abide by the federal laws regarding recruitment and selection of staff. The Civil Rights Act of 1964 and the Equal Employment Opportunity Act of 1972 and their several amendments as well as the more recent Americans with Disabilities Act (ADA) of 1992 make it unlawful to discriminate on the basis of race, color, religion, sex, age, national origin, or handicapping condition.

EEOC Regulations
It is unlawful to ask about the following on either a written application or during an interview.

1. Complexion or color of skin.

2. Applicant's religious denomination, affiliation, church, parish, pastor, or religious holidays observed.

3. Applicant's sex, marital status, name or other information about spouse, or ages of children if any.

4. Whether applicant has a disability or has been treated for any of certain diseases. However, you may ask if the applicant has any physical impairments that would affect the ability to perform the job for which the applicant has applied.

5. If the applicant has ever been arrested. You may ask if the applicant has been convicted of a crime.

6. Any previous name that the applicant has used. You may ask if he or she worked for your organization under a different name, i.e., a maiden name.

7. Birthplace or birthplace of applicant's parents or spouse; birthdate or certificate of naturalization papers, and so on.

8. Require the applicant's photograph before hiring.

9. Whether the applicant or a relative is a citizen of a foreign country. You may ask if the applicant is a U.S. citizen, intends to become one, or has a legal right to be in the United States.

10. The applicant's native language. You may ask which languages the applicant speaks and writes.

11. Questions or information about the applicant's relatives. Prior to employment, you may not even ask the name of a person to contact in case of emergency.

12. The clubs, societies, and lodges to which the applicant belongs. You may ask the applicant to list organizations he or she believes to be pertinent to the job.

After the individual has been employed, many of these items of information can then legally be asked on an employee information form but cannot appear or be asked on an application or during an interview.

Americans with Disabilities Act (ADA).

The Americans with Disabilities Act prohibits employers, public and private, from discriminating against any individual with a disability. The law covers the full range of employment activities including recruiting and hiring, terminations, compensation, job assignment and advancement, and training. The law requires that employers make reasonable accommodation in the workplace to enable the individual to perform fundamental job duties of a position. This may require providing properly positioned chalkboards, or new technology to allow the disabled person to function successfully. Often the workplace itself is more of a barrier to the physically challenged than job skills and knowledge. We must be careful not to exclude anyone from consideration for employment because of his or her disabling condition if he or she is capable of performing the essential functions called for by that position.

The Selection Process

The selection process for employing staff has several steps.

Screening

The first step is application clarification. Prior to an interview, the principal should carefully review the candidate's application file, comparing the application with the personal description. Few candidates will possess all the qualifications that have been specified, but the principal should try to find candidates with most of them.[1]

Discrepancy Analysis

The second step in the selection process should be a discrepancy analysis of the application materials. Applicants present themselves in the best manner possible, minimizing weak points. One technique used to uncover discrepancies is to search the file for missing information. Common problem areas are efforts to conceal unfavorable past activities by excluding dates and not listing appropriate reference sources. Other things to check for include health and legal problems.

The reviewer should look particularly at references from previous employers to make sure each employment situation is represented. Read between the lines on health records. Look for gaps in employment or school records. The interviewer can request more detailed explanations concerning those areas where possible discrepancies have been identified. Most often, candidates will give perfectly acceptable explanations regarding the discrepancies, but occasionally interviews uncover serious problems by a discrepancy review.

Reference Check

If the job candidate has had previous teaching experience and is one of the final candidates being considered for the position, a personal telephone contact with the previous principal or some other school administrator who is acquainted with the candidate is usually helpful. Often, interviewers can obtain more information during a phone call than from a written reference.

Care must be taken, however, in the manner in which questions are asked. Similarly, you must be careful, in answering any questions asked of you regarding a previous employee. The courts have held that in cases of employee non-reemployment where no charges have been officially brought and where no dismissal hearing has been held, an employer is restricted in the negative comments he or she may make about a previous employee. This is based on the concept that such comments could limit the opportunity of that former employee to obtain employment elsewhere and therefore place a limit on that former employees "liberty," a right that is protected under the amendments to our federal constitution.[2] Therefore, employers must use care in stating opinions regarding former employees' performance.

These court decisions, however, do not prevent you from either asking for references or in answering questions. Nevertheless, they do signal that you must stick to the facts rather than delving into opinion or gossip. Similarly when asking for information from a previous employer, recognize that this individual is under the same limitation, and should hesitate in answering questions of a speculative nature. Ask for factual information about the previous employee. One very telling question that the former employer can answer is, "If the person in question would seek a job in your school again would you rehire him or her?" If the answer is anything but extremely positive it should raise a caution flag for you.

The Job Interview

The job interview has several basic functions. It provides an opportunity for the candidate to clarify any apparent discrepancies found in the written job application. The job interview, however, goes beyond the written application by allowing the principal to gather information in greater depth than can be obtained from written materials only.

The interview also allows the principal to gain insights into the personality and interpersonal skills of the applicant. Teaching is a "people" business, and teachers must be able to relate well to other adults and children. Research has shown that good verbal skills are particularly significant in determining the quality of a teacher. These skills can best be assessed through an interview. Whenever possible, an employment recommendation should be based on group interaction with the principal and the existing staff.

Interviews should be arranged to involve teachers, department heads, and team members in the process. This is one additional way to empower teachers. Some will argue that under the concept of site-based management, your local site board should also be involved. It is this author's belief that staff selection is a task to be delegated to the professional staff based on policy set by the local site board, but that board members should not be involved directly in the selection process. The one exception to this might be if the central office continues to dictate personnel placements for your school. Then the clout of your site-based management might be needed to veto unwanted placements.

When staff members are asked to participate in the interview process, they also are obligated to follow the EEOC guidelines regarding appropriate questions. It is usually wise to hold a short refresher course before staff members interview candidates to remind them of appropriate and inappropriate questions.

Interviews can be conducted using a variety of different formats. Here is an interview agenda that is well accepted:

1. *Establish the atmosphere.* Open the interview slowly, and try to create a warm pleasant relaxed atmosphere that will reduce the candidate's anxiety.

2. *Ask focused questions* designed to elicit the knowledge and information you need about the candidate. You want to learn of his or her perceptions of his or her own strengths and weaknesses, his or her understanding and philosophy of education, wish to observe his or her verbal fluency, and his or her ability to project enthusiasm. The use of "what if" questions often works well to get the candidate indirectly to share these beliefs and attitudes with you.

3. Be *an active listener.* Ask open-ended questions rather than yes-no questions. Support the candidate verbally with "uh-huhs," or "tell me more." He or she should be contributing about seventy percent of the conversation to your thirty percent during the interview.

4. *Share school information* with the candidate. Remember the candidate also has a decision to make ("Do I want to come to work for you?"). Tell him or her about the specific job vacancy; with whom he or she may be working, particularly if those individuals met the candidate; the kinds of children enrolled in the school; particular programs that the school may have; and information about the school community if the candidate is not from that area.

5. *Close the interview.* Thank the individual for his or her time and openness. Share the next steps in the selection process including when he or she might expect to hear from you or how he or she might keep up with the decision process.

6. *Write out your notes.* Gather information from the others who participated in the interview process. Often a team discussion works well. If several candidates are to be interviewed before a decision is made, the use of a checklist or some formatted method of recording your perceptions is wise so that later comparison can be more objective.

Employee Probationary Status

The selection process for staff continues through the probationary phase. Most states have a one- to three-year probationary period during which the employee is on a continuing contract before receiving tenured employment. During this period, the principal and department head must reaffirm the original decision to employ a particular staff member. Usually the contract renews automatically around April 15 unless notification is given to the teacher for nonrenewal. Through the continuation of the orientation phase and evaluation of instructional competence, which is discussed in more detail in a subsequent chapter, the emphasis for staff development is upon improving the quality of teaching. The selection process is usually considered complete only when tenure is granted. During this probationary period, the principal must consider the possibility of termination or nonrenewal of the contract when there is reason to suspect that the original selection was not wise.

Teacher Tenure

One of the most misunderstood concepts in education is tenure. It is not, as often believed, a guarantee of a job from which dismissal is all but impossible. Rather, in most states, tenure is simply a statement of the guarantee of due process assuring exercise of academic freedom for the teacher by allowing dismissal only for specific causes listed in the tenure law. Tenure does not guarantee the right to a job. If the job is abolished or a teacher is found to be incompetent, insubordinate, or guilty of a variety of socially unacceptable behaviors, that teacher can be dismissed, with proper due process.

In the last few years, federal courts have broadened their decisions regarding due process and human rights to the point that due-process guarantees, including many of the guarantees found in the tenure laws, have been extended to most employees. As a result probationary teachers are now guaranteed many of the same due-process rights afforded tenured teachers in the past.[3]

Involuntary Termination

An extremely poor or incompetent teacher should never be kept on the staff of a school simply because dismissal is difficult. The law establishes definite rights for employer and employee. Procedural due process is guaranteed, but due process does not mean that teachers cannot be dismissed. What it does mean is that teachers have specific rights, such as the right to a hearing, the right to be treated in a fair and nondiscriminatory fashion, and the right to require that just cause be shown for a dismissal action. The law may be more specific about the causes and process of dismissal for teachers under tenure, but dismissal can still be accomplished.

Every dismissal action should be carried out on the assumption that it will ultimately go to court. This attitude is the best way to prevent court action. Rarely will an attorney engaged by a dismissed teacher or provided by a teacher association take a case to court if the school district has prepared its action carefully. When the courts reject the dismissal and order reinstatement of a teacher, it is most often because of improper procedure on the part of the school district and less likely due to teacher behavior.

Preparation for Dismissal

Dismissal decisions should not be made quickly. A tentative decision not to rehire a first-year teacher for the following year should be contemplated three to four months before the deadline for contract renewal. For a tenured teacher, often two or three years are needed to build a case defensible in court to reverse earlier recommendations that were positive enough to have resulted in tenure, even though the recommendations may have been a mistake. Unfortunately, poor personnel records and poor evaluation procedures are common in school districts.

The defense attorney will often demand to see the entire personnel file for a teacher being dismissed. If positive evaluations have been given in the past, even though they were unjustified, a greater collection of data of a negative nature is required to offset them. Evidence that the teacher received specific notice of inadequacy and was offered help is important.

In a hearing, the courts will try to answer the following questions: Was procedural due process used? Is the evidence appropriate and supportive of the case? Was the employee discriminated against? Were efforts made to help the employee? Did the employee have prior knowledge that his or her work was unsatisfactory? Was the employee provided time and the opportunity to improve or correct whatever deficiencies existed?

Due Process

Teachers must be given timely notice of the decision not to rehire. If contract renewal comes on April 15, with a two-week hearing notice deadline, employees should be notified by April 1. A certified letter is the best way of assuring a record of such notification. Employees must be informed that they have the opportunity for and the right to a hearing. The hearing time, date, and place should be stated in the letter. If the teacher is tenured, the letter should also include the specific causes or charges for dismissal. Recent due-process decisions from the courts in some cases make it highly advisable to provide this opportunity for a hearing to nontenured teachers as well as to those who have tenure.[4,5,6]

Appropriateness of Evidence

Evidence should be firsthand, factual, and documented accurately with appropriate dates. If the offense is cumulative in nature, the collection of data should also be cumulative. Descriptive notes of supervisory meetings and conferences, for example, expressing agreed-upon outcomes and a statement describing the extent of the implementation or the lack thereof on the part of the teacher should be included. The statements should be objective. Rather than stating, "This teacher did a poor job of teaching today," the note should state that in presenting a lesson on the Civil War the teacher did not hold the interest of the class, the students did not understand the lesson as presented, and the class became unruly while under the teacher's direction. Include the date; the time; the events that led up to the conference, such as the previous involvement of a supervisor; and any immediate followup action that was taken. A note might simply read, "Mr. Smith arrived at school at 8:30 on December 2, 3, and 4. His designated time of arrival is 8:00. He has been notified of this deficiency." This is not a judgmental statement but a simple statement of fact. Such items, properly collected, can be used to support a claim of incompetence, neglect of duty, or insubordination. The important thing to remember is to record facts, not opinions, and to do this in a timely fashion.

Equal Rights

Was the employee treated in a fair and nondiscriminatory manner? Was anything done to or for this employee that was not done or available to other employees? Was the assignment unfair? Was the teacher asked to do more or less than the rest of the staff? Was supervision uniform? A grossly unequal schedule for supervision, for example, can be construed to be harassment. When problems arise, however, it is not unreasonable for supervision to increase as long as the time sequence can be demonstrated. Supervisory appointments and documentation included only in the file of the teacher being dismissed with no evidence of supervision included in the files of the other members of the staff, however, will often be looked upon as discriminatory action by the courts.

Were Efforts Made to Help the Teacher?

The courts will want to know what was done to make this individual an effective employee. Was adequate supervision of a helping nature developed? Was adequate time given for the improvement effort? If not, the courts may not uphold the dismissal action but may reinstate the employee, suggesting that the supervisory staff provide assistance.

Most often, when the principal is well prepared and has central-office support, teacher dismissal, while serious, will take place quietly. A teacher who knows that school officials are well prepared most often will not request a hearing and will simply resign. Most cases resulting in the failure to dismiss are a result of poor preparation and improper procedure on the part of the school district. See Figure 14–3 for a flowchart for employee dismissal procedures.

Voluntary Termination

Each year staff members will resign from a school for a variety of reasons: retirement, transfers, better jobs, starting a family, going back to school, and incompetence. In every case the principal should hold a termination interview before that person departs. Several basic purposes exist for such an interview. Of primary concern is the help the school might offer the individual in adjusting to a new life situation.

Second, the interview should be an opportunity to investigate the perceptions of the departing employee regarding the operation of the school. At times principals have difficulty getting good information about the operation of the school and the existing climate within the staff. Often, departing employees will be very candid about their perceptions concerning existing problems. They may even identify some previously hidden reason for leaving.

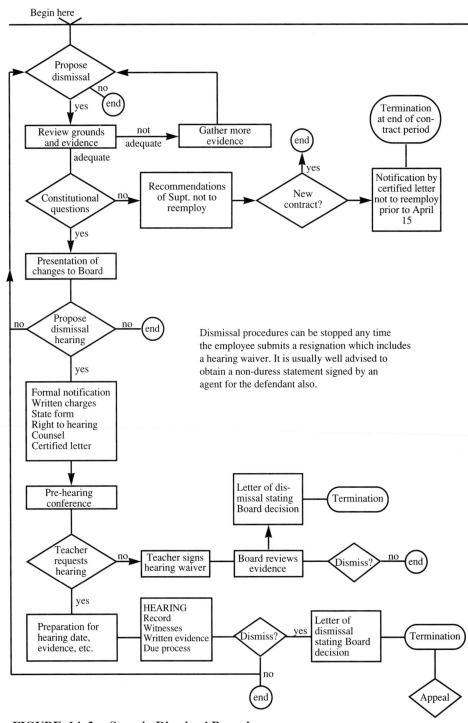

Begin here

Propose dismissal — no → end

yes

Review grounds and evidence — not adequate → Gather more evidence

adequate

Constitutional questions — no → Recommendations of Supt. not to reemploy → New contract? — yes → end

no → Presentation of changes to Board

New contract? — Notification by certified letter not to reemploy prior to April 15 → Termination at end of contract period

Propose dismissal hearing — no → (to Presentation of changes to Board)   no → end

yes

Formal notification
Written charges
State form
Right to hearing
Counsel
Certified letter

Dismissal procedures can be stopped any time the employee submits a resignation which includes a hearing waiver. It is usually well advised to obtain a non-duress statement signed by an agent for the defendant also.

Pre-hearing conference

Teacher requests hearing — no → Teacher signs hearing waiver → Board reviews evidence → Dismiss? — no → end

Board reviews evidence → Letter of dismissal stating Board decision → Termination

yes

Preparation for hearing date, evidence, etc.

HEARING
Record
Witnesses
Written evidence
Due process

Dismiss? — yes → Letter of dismissal stating Board decision → Termination → Appeal

no → end

FIGURE 14–3.   Steps in Dismissal Procedures

Finally, the interview can be useful in identifying prospects for substitute, part-time, volunteer, and future employment when the departing employee is planning to remain within the community. Retired teachers, or those who are staying home to rear a family, are particularly good candidates for part-time employment or volunteer positions.

Summary

The search for and the employment of new staff members is one of the most important tasks of a school administrator. The process begins with the determination of staff needs, including recruitment, selection, orientation, and staff development, and culminates with the placement of the employee on tenure.

Termination of employees, voluntarily or involuntarily, will occur in most schools each year. The principal needs to conduct exit interviews with all terminating employees. Involuntary termination is usually a difficult, but sometimes necessary, task. An important point in staff dismissal is following due process and insuring that the employee's rights have not been violated.

Endnotes

1. Gerald C. Ubben, "Selecting Personnel." *Principal's Audio Journal, 1* (December 1974). Cassette Services, St. Paul, Virginia.

2. *Board or Regents* v. *Roth*, 92 S. Ct. 2701 (1972). This case dealt with the non-reemployment of a non-tenured teacher who had difficulty obtaining another job because of comments made by the administrators of the non-reemploying school. The teacher charged that his right to "liberty" was violated by his inability to obtain other employment because of his lack of opportunity to defend himself against unheard charges. The Supreme Court found that his due process rights were violated and ordered that he be given a hearing and back pay.

3. See Chapter 3 for information about the steps in procedural due process.

4. See Chapter 3, especially the reference to *Illinois Education Association* v. *Board of Education*, 320 N.E. 2nd 240 (Ill. App. 1974).

5. Cases Related to Due Process—Teacher Dismissal
   a. *Board of Regents* v. *Roth*, 92 S. Ct. 2701 (1972) and *Perry* v. *Sunderman*, 928 Ct. 2694 (1972). These are the precedent-setting cases regarding due process just as *Brown* v. *Board of Education* set the precedent for discrimination cases.
   b. *Paul* v. *Davis*, 424 U.S. 693 (1976); *Bishop* v. *Wood*, 246 U.S. 341 (1976); and *Meachum* v. *Fano*, 427 U.S. 215 (1970).

   c. 7th Cir., the Court of Appeals in *Confederation of Police* v. *City of Chicago*, 547 F. 2d 375 (1977).
   d. *Codd* v. *Velger*, 97 S. Ct. 882 (1977).
   e. *Arnet* v. *Kennedy*, 416 U.S. 134 (1974).
   f. *Peacock* v. *Board of Regents*, 510 F 2d 1324 (9th Cir.)
   g. *Withrow* v. *Larken*, 421 U.S. 35 (1975).
   h. Hortonville 96S Ct. 2308.
   i. *Mt. Healthy City School District* v. *Doyle*, 97 S. Ct. 568 (1977).

6. While most state tenure laws and continuing contract laws in and of themselves do not require a hearing for nontenured staff, the federal Constitution and the Civil Rights Act of 1964 might. According to a series of court decisions over recent years, a teacher is considered to have certain rights under the First and Fourteenth Amendments to the Constitution. While nonrenewal of a contract does not require a hearing, dismissal does. If a denial-of-freedom-of-speech claim is made, a hearing is advisable, and if the case is receiving much publicity so as to endanger the individual's opportunity for other employment, a hearing should be held. Also, if discrimination is charged, a hearing should be held. If an opportunity for a hearing is not granted, the teacher may later file a complaint charging violation of due process.

Selected Readings

Beckham, J., *Legal Aspects of Teacher Evaluation*. Topeka, KS: National Organization on Legal Problems of Education, 1981. ED 207 126.

Bridges, E.M., *The Management of Incompetence*. Stanford, CA: Institute for Research on Educational Finance and Governance, 1983. Technical Report.

Bridges, E.M. and Gumport, P., *The Dismissal of Tenured Teachers for Incompetence*. Stanford, CA: Institute for Research on Educational Finance and Governance, 1984. Technical Report.

Carey, W. C., *Documenting Teacher Dismissal*. Salem, OR: Options Press, 1981.

Castetter, William B., *The Personnel Function in Educational Administration*, rev. ed. New York: MacMillan, 1986.

Dolgin, A., "Two Types of Due Process: The Role of Supervision in Teacher Dismissal Cases." *NASSP Bulletin, 65*, 442 (February 1981): 17–21.

Frels, K. and Cooper, T. T., *A Documentation System for Teacher Improvement or Termination*. Topeka, KS: National Organization on Legal Problems of Education, 1982. EDRS ED 228 725.

French-Lazovik, G., "Peer Review," In Millman, J. (ed.), *Handbook of Teacher Evaluation*. Beverly Hills: SAGE Publications, 1981, pp. 73–89.

Hooker, Clifford (ed.), *The Courts and Education, 77th Yearbook of the National Society for the Study of Education*. Chicago: University of Chicago Press, 1978, especially the chapter entitled, "Frontiers of Law."

Kaufman, H. G., *Professionals in Search of Work*. New York: John Wiley and Sons, 1982.

Larson, D. H., "Advice for the Principal: Dealing with Unsatisfactory Teacher Performance." *NASSP Bulletin, 65*, 442 (February 1981): 10–11.

Maslinowski, A. A., "An Empirical Analysis of Discharge Cases and the Work History of Employees Reinstated by Labor Arbitrations." *Arbitration Journal, 36*, 1 (March 1981): 31–46.

Martin, Cynthia, "Hiring the Right Person: Techniques for Principals." *NASSP Bulletin, 77*, 550 (February 1993): 79–83.

McDaniel, S. H. and McDaniel, T. R., "How to Weed out Incompetent Teachers without Getting Hauled into Court." *National Elementary Principal, 59*, 3 (March 1980): 31–36.

O'Reilly, C.A., and Weitz, B.A., "Marginal Employees: The Use of Warnings and Dismissals." *Administrative Science Quarterly* (1980): 467–484.

Chapter 15

Human Resource Development

*Any lasting change in a school will occur only because the staff
itself changes norms of expectations, appropriate role definitions,
standards of accountability and patterns of behavior.*[1]

Introduction

Human resource development (HRD) is a process that uses developmental practices to bring about more quality, higher productivity, and greater satisfaction among employees as organization members. It is a function of both an individual's *knowledge*, *skills*, and *attitudes* and the *policies*, *structure*, and *management practices* that constitute the system in which the individual works. The goal of HRD is to achieve the highest quality of work life for employees and to produce the highest quality of instruction and service possible for the school.

The development of human resources in the school organization is a complex process and, sometimes, not a very well accomplished one. Often, it seems, the effort lacks focus and becomes simple responses to either organizational culture expectations or spur-of-the-moment enactments of state legislatures. That being the case, no one should be surprised if any particular school staff responds unenthusiastically when issues of in-service training arise. It shouldn't be this way and it doesn't have to be this way and it isn't that way in good schools.

The focus of this chapter is human resources development in the broadest sense— from personnel in their first years to those who may be considering retirement. Our premise is that everyone wants to succeed; no one deliberately performs unsatisfactorily. We are realists too; not everyone who enters a particular workplace or workstation is suited for the job, either by personal disposition or by skills level. And, some never do seem to be able to develop the level of skill necessary to adequately perform the assignment.

But in most organizations, public or private sector, not enough is done to help persons improve their performance. Even less is done to help those who cannot improve to understand their deficiencies and find jobs where they might succeed outside of the school organization.

Human resource development (HRD) requires more than training programs, however, even though well-developed skills training events are a part of any HRD program. The most important resource in an organization is its staff. When staff are congruent with organizational needs, well trained, adaptive, and motivated, great things can happen. To achieve this requires attention to the variety of ways in which human potential can be realized and to the variety of needs that any particular person may have at any particular stage of growth.

A Human Resource Development Model

Recent years have been characterized by renewed interest and excitement about the "human dimension" of the organization.

The growing interest in W. Edwards Deming's work on TQM and his emphasis on training and cooperatively set work goals, the success of such works as *The One Minute Manager, Megatrends*, and *In Search of Excellence*, among others, has directed much attention to the human resource development focus that successful organizations maintain. If anything typifies such successful efforts, it is the diversity of programs available within any given organization.

The model we are about to present describes why the HRD program must be so diverse. Attention needs to be directed to four factors: the nature of the adult learner, the different kinds of learning required of effective staff members; the varying amounts of time required to effect different kinds of behavior change; and the application of the appropriate training or development process given factors 1, 2, and 3. Figure 15–1 displays the model.

Human resource development is a continuous process and, as suggested by the model, depending on the type of development needed, organizational responses must vary. Unsuccessful personnel development programs tend to be unfocused in approach, and the model explains why these types of programs do not work very well.

As teachers and administrators enter the school organization (point "A" in the model), they bring with them some already acquired knowledge about the nature of their work. In the instance of beginning teachers, they have been students of the technology of teaching, have acquired some degree of subject matter competence, and probably have had intern experiences as student teachers. Incoming veterans will also bring with them perceptions and skills acquired in previous positions.

Two immediate needs would seem readily apparent: a clear understanding of the formal organization requirements and certain housekeeping information, such as when payday is, room assignments, who to call when ill, etc. It is appropriate that there be "new teacher" orientation sessions and a well-developed personnel handbook.

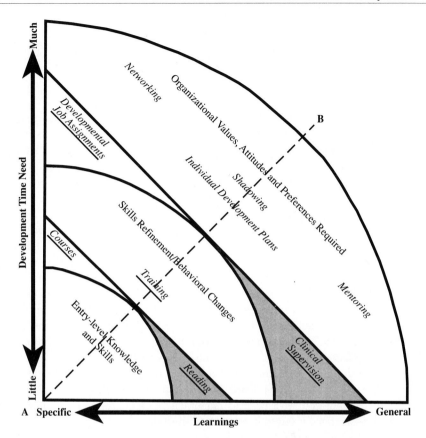

FIGURE 15–1. A Human Resource Development Model

Source: Gerald C. Ubben and Larry W. Hughes, *The Principal: Creative Leadership for Effective Schools* (Boston: Allyn and Bacon, 1992), p. 287.

Organizational Socialization

A critical but less apparent need is an organizational socialization process. This is not accomplished nearly as quickly nor as easily as other needs. Here one is dealing with attitudes, values, and organizational preferences. Mentoring and networking are among the appropriate techniques. Such approaches require careful planning, matching, monitoring, *and* time.

The use of the "buddy system" in some schools is sound and consistent with this need. When employed by the principal with first-year teachers, it does speed up the socialization processes substantially, although not completely. Judiciously applied, involving only the best veterans on the faculty, such a technique also establishes an organizational support system that will provide the basis for both a peer supervision approach and a mentoring process.

In many organizations the socialization needs are not met in any formal kind of way. The result is unnecessary blunders by new staff members as they stumble from one organization or public relations *faux pas* to another. Misunderstood directions and faulty perceptions, as well as a "survival of the fittest" mentality, send the neophyte home by Christmas and the veteran to a university placement office.

Individual Behavior Change

How should the human resource development program be organized to help individuals respond to new challenges in the system? And, how can persons be helped to improve existing skills? In other words, how can behaviors be changed? "Knowledge about" is a start, but it is unsufficient to cause or even reasonably predict behavior change. Knowledge can be acquired either by reading or taking courses. Such practices *are* efficacious with adults when they are self-directed and for the purpose of learning something the adult has decided he or she wants or needs to know.

But, knowledge about doesn't equate to ability or even desire. There is chasm between "knowing how to" and "being able to," or "wanting to." One of the most difficult human resource development problems is behavior change. This aspect requires a good appraisal system and sophisticated follow-up. It also requires a considerable investment of personnel and time. Short courses and systematic reading may help but more is required.

Commonly used successful techniques include clinical supervision, employing behaviorally anchored appraisals; on-the-job training, developmental job assignments; "shadowing," or systematic observation of another person deemed to be expert in the skill being learned; and workshops. Each of these techniques—and none is mutually exclusive from the others—requires organizational flexibility and policies which permit released time from daily duties. Once the developing person engages in the prescribed activity, there is, of course, a need to reappraise, rediagnose, and continue the development, if necessary, and if felt to be ultimately fruitful.

Our HRD model also indicates that activities appropriate to one phase in the employee's development are not necessarily to be excluded from subsequent stages (e.g., those activities suggested in the shaded areas between development stages). In any organization, new demands and new research will require updated or new skills on the part of reorganization members. Thus, there will continue to be a need for skills development workshops, taking courses, and systematic reading, among other techniques, irrespective of how long the staff member has been in the organization in a particular job.

Implementing a Staff Development Program

Assuring the quality of a school staff has always been more than a sometime concern of the successful principal. Recently, it has increasingly become a concern of "educational reformers" and state legislators as well. The result has been myriad legislative outpourings and an even greater number of literary outpourings, all designed to "improve teachers." Emphasis is being placed on "competency testing," "career ladders," and demonstrated entry-level subject matter competency; among a number of focused efforts.

While it is foolish to argue against the intent of these efforts, it remains doubtful that the quality of anything as complex as learning can be improved by legislative fiat. However, given an adequate degree of funding from these same state legislators, and given less prescriptive and categorical "advice," an uncommonly good opportunity exists for the school system and school building subsystem to implement a sound human resource development program. Certainly the external interest and influence are there and one might even presume a modicum of support from the private sector, given a reasonably persuasive principal or superintendent.

Characteristic of such programs will be the implementation of a model analogous to that presented in the first part of this chapter with a focus on subject matter expertise and on pedagogical skills. Such programs require an organized array of organizational responses: clinical supervision, peer supervision, developmental job assignments, in-house diagnostic and remedial programs, and development of systematic cooperative relationships with local or area four-year institutions of higher education and community colleges.

The model HRD program would begin with individual staff needs assessments, progress through systematic review of the demonstrated levels of individual professional expertise, and on to designated programs of remediation and development. Such practices are occurring with increasing frequency across the nation.

HRD at the Building Level

It is not the responsibility of the principal to develop an in-service program that will examine the competency of the professional staff with regard to academic skills and subject matter proficiency. This is a shared responsibility between district, state, and university, and any systematic programs designed to identify and address these needs should issue from and be administered at those levels.[2]

It is in the "higher order" staff development needs that the principal plays the most important part. This includes providing for staff needs assessments, engaging in clinical supervision, helping staff members initiate individual development plans, and organizing school-based in-service programming.

Discovering Staff Needs, Interests, and Skills

How well does the principal know the staff? In order to have a good staff development program, it is necessary to have more information than is contained in the typical personnel folder. Normal attrition of staff because of transfer, retirement, resignation, or termination makes "keeping track" of staff difficult enough. Moreover, the ordinary difficulty present in any organization of becoming professionally acquainted with all of a large staff, even over a period of years, often inhibits the effective deployment of personnel and even more so the organization of a relevant in-service program. Staff inventories can help in this.

Inventories can be used to find out special skills and interests that staff may have that are unrevealed in other sources. Such an inventory would include an array of teaching and organizational skills and knowledge areas, using any of the commonly used teaching "frameworks" and local district needs. Figure 15–2 displays a sample page of such an instrument with some representative headings and items. A similarly constructed instrument can be used to discover the skills, interests, and needs of the noncertificated support staff, as well.

Title/Position _____ Date _____
Years of Employment _____ Degree _____

Directions: Please place a check in both Columns II and III for each area. Blank columns at the end of the instrument may be used to add special areas you may wish to list.

SECTION A

I. Area	II. Experience				III. Interest		
	Expertise in: experienced and can serve as a consultant	Worked with: in many situations	Knowledge of: extends beyond definition but have not worked with	No knowledge of: extends to no more than simple definition	Desire further training in	Desire training in	Do not desire training in
(DIAGNOSTIC AND PRESCRIPTIVE TEACHING)							
Assessing the Classroom Climate							
Teacher-Made Tests							
Standardized Tests							
Grading							
(CLASSROOM M... DISCIP...)							
(MULTICULTURAL AWARENESS)							
Community Analysis Field Study							
Cultural Communication							
Multilingual Teaching Team							
(DEVELOPING INSTRUCTIONAL MODULES)							

FIGURE 15–2. Professional Staff Interest/Needs Questionnaire

Source: Gerald C. Ubben and Larry W. Hughes, *The Principal: Creative Leadership for Effective Schools* (Boston: Allyn and Bacon, 1992), p. 291.

Clinical Supervision

Clinical supervision is supervision devoted to diagnosis and prescription and formative, rather than summative, evaluation. It is behaviorally anchored appraisal consisting most frequently of established objectives and desired instructional patterns; systematic observation and recording of teaching behaviors; and post-observation conferences during which any appropriate corrective actions are prescribed and future standards of performance established.

Clinical supervision is a collaborative process. The term "clinical supervision" gained national prominence in the 1960s through the writings of Robert Goldhammer and Morris Cogen.[3] Originally, the model was proposed for use with student teachers. Its applicability in the formative evaluation of practicing teachers was soon recognized.

Five steps comprise the model. Each step helps both the supervisor and the teacher in focusing on the teaching-learning process. An examination is made of the strengths and weaknesses of a lesson and then the process involves identifying specific activities to improve future lessons or teaching practices. The final step is formal feedback to the teacher.

Step One: The Pre-Observation Conference

The purpose of the pre-observation conference is to provide focus to the upcoming observation. The teacher outlines for the principal the plans for the lesson and helps identify specific aspects to which attention will be directed during the observation. The teacher's plan is expected to contain learner objectives, the planned introductions or set, teaching strategies to be employed, resources to be used, evaluation plans, and lesson closure.

During this discussion there is opportunity for the principal to clarify the various components of the lesson and to offer suggestions about other possible approaches.

The discussion about the initial observation should desirably focus on specific areas of interest or concern to the teacher rather than areas or concerns of the principal. Later observations and discussions will provide ample opportunity to address principal concerns.

It is important that the teacher understand the purpose of each step in the clinical model. The teacher needs to know that the observer will be taking notes during the observation and that this is for the purpose of giving accurate feedback.

Before the conclusion of the pre-observation conference, both a time for the classroom visit and a time for the post-observation conference should be established.

Step Two: The Classroom Observation

The teacher's task is to teach the lesson as planned. The observer's task is to record those items specifically identified in the pre-observation conference as well as the events surrounding the lesson. Specific happenings should be scripted and in the language of the teacher. Activities relating to the lesson—student verbal and nonverbal behavior, for example—should be noted. Opinion and summary statements need to be avoided; the language of the participants and specific events are what the principal needs to provide useful feedback. It is important to be on time and to stay for the entire lesson.

Step Three: Analysis of the Lesson

To prepare for the post-observation conference, script notes need to be analyzed. Were the objectives obtained? How did the various intended teaching strategies work? What unusual circumstances were observed? What seemed to work? What didn't? What comments can you make about the teacher's verbal and nonverbal (physical) behavior? How about student verbal and nonverbal behavior? What did the teacher do well? What specific aspects might be improved? What should the teacher work on for the next observation?

Step Four: The Post-Observation Conference

The conference needs to take place in a comfortable and private location. The teacher's classroom itself is often appropriate. A good opening line, after the amenities, is "What do you think went well?" Then, the teacher should be asked to clarify the objectives of the lesson, review what happened, and assess whether or not, or the degree to which, the objectives were attained. At this point the principal will relate some of his or her specific observations supported by the notes that were taken. Discuss the successes.

Reach agreement about what went on. Together, decide on some strategies that might be worth trying. Solicit information from the teacher.

Every conference should conclude with some growth objectives and some agreed-upon plans for improving any deficiencies.

Step Five: Post-Conference Analysis

The final step in the clinical model is an evaluation of the process and the outcome. Information is solicited from the teacher. How could the process be improved? Are the growth objectives clear? What assistance is available to the teacher?

After the teacher leaves, the principal needs to reflect on the process and his or her own behavior and skill. Did the conference go well? Why or why not? The process is intended to promote both improved instruction and supportive relationships. One likely will not occur without the other.

Teacher Appraisal

In recent years many states have mandated forms and processes by which teacher appraisal will take place. Many of these mandates have resulted in standardized rating scales and designed checklists.

Care must be used in basing an entire appraisal system on this or any other specific model. There is danger that the criteria will become too narrow to encompass the teaching of subjects that incorporate higher-order thinking skills or that require a high level of creativity on the part of students.

Tom McGreal has proposed alternatives to the rating scales appraisal designs to make them more useful as a clinical tool.[4] He suggests that an appropriate appraisal be based on a cooperative goal-setting model, and that the appraiser and the teacher identify specific instructional improvement goals on which to work together. In working together the techniques of clinical supervision are used and a supportive environment established. Appraisal thus is the basis for staff development. The collaborative goal setting based on the formal appraisal that ensues at the post-observation and later conferences is critical to the development process.

Several authors[5] have suggested that supervision and teacher appraisal styles become situationally specific; that is, situational factors determine the approach used by the principal in working with each staff member. This situational approach is similar to the situational leadership model proposed by Blanchard[6] and discussed in Chapter 1. Glatthorn, describing a differentiated system of situational supervision, suggested four levels.

1. *Clinical supervision* as described in the previous section.

2. *Collaborative professional development* as a collegial process in which a small number of teachers work together for professional growth. The Quality Circle idea from TQM will integrate well with this approach.

3. *Self-direction.* A goal-directed strategy in which the teacher prepares an Individual Development Plan (IDP) with the assistance of the principal who serves as a resource person.

4. *Administrative monitoring* where the principal makes a series of brief, usually announced visits as "quality control" assurance.

The fourth approach, commonly used by administrators, is one that should not be considered a supervisory method because it does not provide improvement opportunities to the teacher being observed. However, each of these approaches has its appropriate place in certain circumstances, depending on the maturity and needs of the teacher. The chart shown in Figure 15–3 points up many of the differences in the three supervisory approaches from the above list.

Staff development and evaluation are essential activities of the elementary school principal. Just as a teacher manages student learning by using a diagnostic prescriptive model, so can the principal direct staff development using staff evaluation as a diagnostic tool and an evaluation-by-objectives approach as a prescriptive tool. For proper staff development and evaluation, the principal must take an initiating, rather than reacting, role, and the comprehensive plan for staff evaluation must be based on a sound rationale.

Staff evaluation has two basic purposes: (1) to improve the performance and provide direction for the continued development of present staff and (2) to provide a sound basis for personnel decisions such as awarding of tenure, promotions, transfers, or dismissals.

These two purposes create a dilemma for many administrators, even though both support quality education. Staff improvement is largely a helping relationship most effectively carried out when built on trust between the teacher and the principal. Personnel decisions are judgmental in nature and can cause teacher apprehension.

The Staff Evaluation Cycle

Staff evaluation and development is a cyclical process. Staff evaluation leads to a staff development prescription that is checked once again through evaluation.

Seven basic steps in the evaluation cycle focus on the ultimate purpose of improving instruction. The cycle begins when the teacher and principal plan goals and targets for

	Clinical	**Collaborative**	**Self-Directed**
Teacher Initiative	Low	Moderate	High
Supervisor Initiative	High	Moderate	Low
Approach	Formal, systematic	Collaborative	Self-directed
Goal of Learning	Create rationality/order	Problem solving	Goal directed
Knowledge	Predefined set of life-survival skills	Concrete results that "work" for individuals	That which is discovered
Learning	Condition individual by outer environment	Outcome of learner/ environment interaction	Unfolding process within learner
Foundation	Behaviorist	Cognitivist	Humanist
Learning Theory	Conditioning	Experimentation	Self-discovery
Teacher Risk	Low	Moderate to high	Moderate to high

FIGURE 15–3. Situational Models of Supervision

Adapted from: A.A. Glatthorn, *Differentiated Supervision*, Alexandria, VA: Association for Supervision and Curriculum Development, 1984

the year and include other people in the evaluation process during the year (Figure 15–4). The seven steps of the evaluation cycle are as follows:

1. Prepare an Individual Development Plan (IDP).
2. Select specific objectives or activities for observation or review.
3. Determine the observation method, time, and place.
4. Observe and collect data.
5. Analyze data and provide feedback.
6. Summarize and interpret collective observational data.
7. Report evaluation results, target achievement, and make recommendations for individual and staff development at annual conference.

Individual Development Plans (Step 1)

An IDP is a written schedule of experiences designed to meet a person's particular goals for development. It is a method of systematically planning for training and other experiences in order to develop necessary skills and knowledge. Rather than haphazardly chancing time and money on what may not be a useful learning experience, the IDP gives both staff member and administrator an opportunity to set reasonable objectives and then plan experiences that support those objectives.

The IDP is realistic and feasible because its construction includes both administrator and staff member perspectives. The staff member's personal and professional goals are

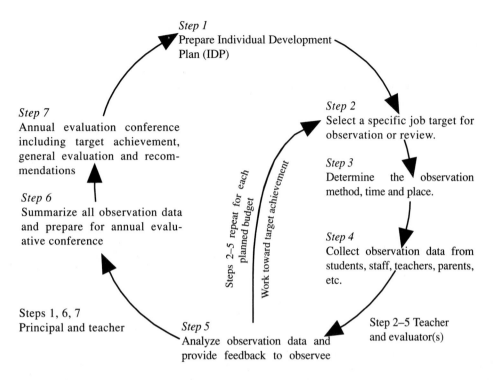

FIGURE 15–4.   Staff Evaluation and Development Cycle

considered insofar as these are organizationally feasible. And, the staff member gets information and feedback so that goals can be set that are organizationally necessary and reasonably achievable.

Individual development is a joint responsibility of the administrator and the staff member. As such, it is a logical extension of the clinical supervision and appraisal process. The principal's responsibility is to arrange the work environment to capitalize on the skills and interests of the staff so that the important tasks get accomplished in the most efficient and effective way. To do so requires that the principal and staff member work together to identify skills deficiencies (developmental needs), strengths, and professional and organizational goals. The IDP is a joint commitment to address these issues.

The IDP includes first a self-assessment. The individual staff member reviews his or her professional qualifications, skills, and interests. A personal judgment is made about how these skills may be capitalized on in the organizational setting and how any skill deficiency can be best addressed. The second step in this process is for the individual to think about his or her professional career and begin to establish long-term career goals.

The responsibility of the principal is to conduct an analysis of the staff member's strengths and weaknesses as well. This analysis is always conducted from the perspective of what is good for the school. It frequently occurs that an individual's self-assessment will overlook important organizational demands and skills needs.

Following the two analyses, a development conference is held and the IDP begins to take specific form. Important information is exchanged at this conference. The two parties may not see all things similarly. Congruence is not ever likely to be achieved without a discourse about job-related expectations. At this time, the principal becomes aware of the goals of the staff member and where possible and feasible may provide job situations, special assignments, and professional opportunities so that both individual and organizational needs can be obtained.

The conference serves two other purposes. It provides an opportunity for the principal to point out skill development areas and organizational goals about which the staff member may have been unaware. These expectations become a part of the IDP as well. It is also at this time that the principal can point out things that the organization *cannot* do to help the individual. Figures 15–5 and 15–6 display two approaches to IDPs.

Preobservation Conference

The preobservation conference has two basic purposes: (1) selecting a particular topic for observation and (2) planning the details of the observation.

Name _____   Dept. _____

   I. Instructional Target(s)
      Individualize instruction in mathematics.

      Indicators of Achievement:
        1. Develop self-instructional modules for units 1–4
        2. Revise preinstruction assessment instruments for 6th grade math
        3. Devise at least four enrichment activities or games for low-interest students

  II. Curriculum Target(s)
      Integrate one unit of first semester math and science.

      Indicators of Achievement:
        1. Initiate interdepartmental study group
        2. Develop objectives for courses
        3. Identify potential students
        4. Develop syllabus

 III. Professional Growth Target(s)
      Improve diagnostic and prescriptive skills.

      Indicators of Achievement:
        1. Review Buros, *Mental Measurements*
        2. Successfully complete EPSY 6310 at University of Houston
        3. Revise preinstruction instrument for math (same as 1–2 above)

FIGURE 15–5. School-Based Individual Development Plan

Adapted from: Gerald C. Ubben and Larry W. Hughes, *The Principal: Creative Leadership for Effective Schools* (Boston: Allyn and Bacon, 1992), p. 293.

---

1. EMPLOYEE NAME (LAST, FIRST, MIDDLE INITIAL)	2. CURRENT POSITION	3. BUILDING AND GRADE OR DEPARTMENT

4. SHORT RUN DEVELOPMENTAL GOALS
(IMMEDIATE, WITHIN A YEAR)

4A. DEVELOPMENTAL OBJECTIVES (KNOWLEDGE, SKILLS, AND ABILITIES NEEDED)	4B. DEVELOPMENTAL ASSIGNMENTS (IDENTIFY TYPE, DATES, LENGTHS, AND LOCATIONS, IF POSSIBLE)	4B. FORMAL TRAINING (IDENTIFY SPECIFIC COURSES LOCATIONS, AND DATES IF POSSIBLE)

5. LONG RANGE DEVELOPMENTAL GOALS
(NEXT FIVE YEARS)

5A. DEVELOPMENT OBJECTIVES	5B. DEVELOPMENT ASSIGNMENTS	5C. FORMAL TRAINING

FIGURE 15–6.   School-System-Based Individual Development Plan

Source: Gerald C. Ubben and Larry W. Hughes, *The Principal: Creative Leadership for Effective Schools* (Boston: Allyn and Bacon, 1992), p. 294.

Target Selection (Step 2)

A teacher's job targets are usually too many or too varied to be observed and evaluated properly all at one time. Individual job targets should be selected one at a time for observation and evaluation.

Planning the Observation (Step 3)

Once the particular target has been selected, plans should be made for data collection regarding its achievement.

Observers. A preobservation conference should include the teacher to be evaluated and those responsible for data collection. The principal should *not* attempt to conduct all observations personally. Sometimes the principal is an appropriate data collector, but students, other teachers, parents, and other supervisors are also available. Numerous research findings support the position that others besides a principal who come in contact with the teacher at work can make valid and reliable judgments about that work.[7] Also, a good data collection for evaluation takes time, usually more time than most principals have available.

Observation Tools. A variety of observation instruments are available or can be created for various types of data collection for teacher evaluation. Elementary students, for example, can provide data on certain types of teacher behavior through the use of the smiley-face questionnaire (Figure 15–7). During the actual observation students might be questioned about their degree of involvement in planning, and samples of student-planned activities could be collected. Some of the responses can be recorded directly by the students if they are mature enough.

Time and Place. The time and place for the observation also need to be arranged during the preobservation conference.

Collection of Observation Data (Step 4)

Data collection is simply the carrying out of the plan outlined in Step 3.

Observations need not be long, particularly if the job target is narrow in scope. Making separate observation cycles for different job targets is often better than trying to combine a whole series of observations into one command performance. Fifteen minutes is usually adequate time to observe one technique or activity. The observation should take place at a scheduled time and place and should maintain as normal an atmosphere as possible so the data will be reliable.

Postobservation Conference (Step 5)

The observer should report and analyze the observation and provide feedback to the person observed.

The postobservation conference should be conducted by the person in charge of data collection. In some cases it will be the principal; often it will be another teacher. Information gathered from students or parents is returned to the principal or other designated person. Confidentiality of responses should be maintained.

Appraisal Schedule

The planning schedule of the evaluation process is completed with the scheduling of the activities and the selection of dates for the completion of the various targets. Figure 15–8 illustrates the appraisal cycle time schedule. Upon completion of the planning document the staff members proceed to initiate the plan, carrying out the activities as outlined. The process of clinical supervision is often used for this. As the first target date approaches, the teacher plans for an evaluation of that target, beginning with a preobservation conference.

ELEMENTARY STUDENT CLASSROOM
ATMOSPHERE EVALUATION FORM

Categories of the Evaluation
     This evaluation was designed to evaluate the role of the teacher in setting a classroom atmosphere in which the child feels important and has an active part. It was designed to check those areas that make a child either like or dislike the classroom. The statements cover these categories:

   I. STUDENTS' ATTITUDE TOWARD TEACHER: Statements 1, 4, 10, 13, 25.

   II. TEACHER'S ATTITUDE TOWARD STUDENTS AS PERCEIVED BY THE STUDENTS: Statements 7, 17, 19, 22.

   III. TEACHER'S INTEREST IN STUDENTS' OUT-OF-SCHOOL LIFE: Statements 2, 8, 15.

   IV. TEACHER'S ROLE IN CREATING STUDENT PARTICIPATION IN CLASS: Statements 9, 14, 16.

   V. TEACHER'S INTEREST IN STUDENTS' PROBLEMS: Statements 3, 6, 18, 20.

   VI. TEACHER'S FAIRNESS IN DEALING WITH STUDENTS: Statements 12, 21, 23.

   VII. TEACHER'S AWARENESS OF THE CLASSROOM ENVIRONMENT: Statements 5, 11, 24.

ELEMENTARY STUDENT CLASSROOM
ATMOSPHERE EVALUATION FORM

Fill in the face
  1. When my teacher helps me with my work, I feel . . .

FIGURE 15–7.

2. When I talk to my teacher about my family, she looks . . .

3. When my teacher is busy and I raise my hand to tell her about a problem, she looks . . .

4. When my teacher talks to the class, it makes me feel . . .

5. When I walk into my classroom and look around, I feel . . .

6. When I do not understand something and I ask my teacher about it, she look . . .

7. When I talk to my teacher about my work, she looks . . .

8. When I talk to my teacher about what I do at home, she looks . . .

9. When I have a good idea and I tell my teacher about it, she looks . . .

10. When my teacher talks to me, I feel . . .

11. When I tell my friends how my classroom looks, I feel . . .

FIGURE 15–7. *(Continued)*

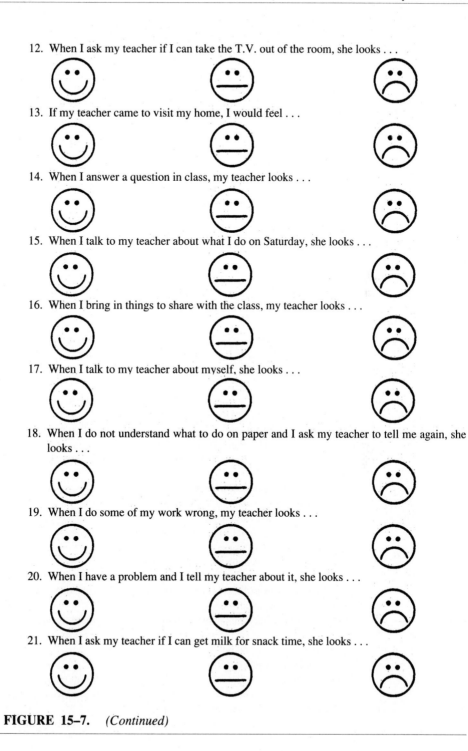

12. When I ask my teacher if I can take the T.V. out of the room, she looks . . .

13. If my teacher came to visit my home, I would feel . . .

14. When I answer a question in class, my teacher looks . . .

15. When I talk to my teacher about what I do on Saturday, she looks . . .

16. When I bring in things to share with the class, my teacher looks . . .

17. When I talk to my teacher about myself, she looks . . .

18. When I do not understand what to do on paper and I ask my teacher to tell me again, she looks . . .

19. When I do some of my work wrong, my teacher looks . . .

20. When I have a problem and I tell my teacher about it, she looks . . .

21. When I ask my teacher if I can get milk for snack time, she looks . . .

FIGURE 15–7. *(Continued)*

22. When I do good work, my teacher looks . . .

23. When I ask my teacher if I can take the lunch report to the office, she looks . . .

24. When I look at the walls and bulletin board in my classroom, I feel . . .

25. If I had my teacher next year, I would feel . . .

FIGURE 15–7. *(Continued)*

CALENDAR FOR APPRAISAL CYCLE

By June or end of September for new staff (principal and teachers):
Plan goals, targets, and activities (Step 1)
This can be an extension of the Annual Evaluation Conference for returning staff.)
By end of November (teachers and evaluators):
Achieve at least one job target using a preobservation, observation, and postobservation conference (Steps 2–5).
By end of January (teachers and evaluators):
Achievement of additional job targets (Steps 2–5)
By March 1 (teachers and evaluators):
Achievement of additional job targets and submission of all evaluative data to principal (Steps 2–5 for Step 6)
By March 15 (principal and nontenured teachers):
Completion of all annual evaluation conferences with nontenured teachers. All appropriate evaluation forms and recommendations forwarded to personnel office (Steps 6 and 7)
By April 1 (principal and teachers):
Completion of all other annual evaluation conferences where transfer or termination is to be recommended. All appropriate evaluation forms and recommendations forwarded to personnel office (Steps 6 and 7)
April 15 (principal and teachers):
Completion of all other annual evaluation conferences for all tenured staff. All appropriate forms and recommendations forwarded to the personnel office (Steps 6 and 7)
End of the school year (principal and teachers):
Planning conferences to set goals, targets, and activities for returning staff (Step 1)

FIGURE 15–8.

A Cyclical Process (Steps 2–5)

Steps 2 through 5 of the evaluation cycle may be repeated numerous times during the year for different job targets or for repeated evaluations of a particular job target. The relationship of the steps to each other over time is illustrated in Figure 15–4. Steps 1–6, and 7 are usually done only once each year.

Preparation of the Annual Individual Development Report (Step 6)

At the end of each annual evaluation cycle, and in time to meet the legal deadlines for contract renewal or termination, the evaluative data gathered during the year should be summarized. Each teacher should be sure that all the necessary data collection has been done for each target established. The actual task of analyzing and summarizing the evaluative data belongs to the principal.

Each set of goals and targets should be evaluated for the degree of achievement. The principal should not expect teachers to meet all targets, however. Teachers should work toward goals through the completion of set targets, but if they must achieve all targets each year, teachers will very quickly learn to set only achievable targets and will never reach out to challenging ones. Therefore, some targets may not have been reached. Each case, of course, must be judged on its individual merits.

Comments should be written about each job target and its degree of achievement. Recommendations should be considered as proposals for job targets for the following year. This evaluative summation can be recorded on a form similar to the one on which job goals, targets, and activities were entered earlier (See Figure 15–5).

Annual Evaluation Conference (Step 7)

The annual evaluation conference, held usually in March or April with each teacher, includes four distinct tasks:

1. A review of the year's IDP and the determination of the degree to which they have been achieved, using a form such as the one shown in Figure 15–5.

2. A summary evaluation by the principal of each teacher's overall performance, preferably in a narrative form but using a summary checklist if required.

3. The final personnel recommendation, using a form like the one in Figure 15–9.

4. Recommendations for next year's IDP. This should be the beginning of the new evaluation cycle. Plans made in the spring have the advantage of a full twelve months, including the summer, for fulfillment. Plans made in the fall allow for only six or seven months for completion.

Recommendations for staff development should take two forms. The first is the identification of a proposed set of individual targets or goals as recommended improvement points for the next cycle of staff evaluation. These recommendations become the basis for generating new goals.

The second major thrust focuses on staff development on a school-wide basis. Gathering the criticisms and target recommendations for teachers in a school portrays a particular pattern of staff training needs. This is a most useful planning tool for outlining group staff development activities (Figure 15–10). If, for example, a staff needs profile in-

Person Evaluated _____

                Last   First   Middle

School/Department _____

Grade, Subject, or Position _____

Period of Evaluation _____ to _____

Total years teaching experience _____

Total years teaching in present school _____

Total years teaching in this school system _____

Overall Rating

_____Teacher performance is outstanding and exceeds district expectations

_____Teacher performance is satisfactory and meets district expectations

_____Teacher performance is unsatisfactory and fails to meet district expectations

Recommendation

(Check as many as are applicable. Comment when appropriate.)

_____Reemploy

_____Do not reemploy

_____Recommend dismissal

_____Transfer

_____Reevaluate next year

_____Conditional reemploy

_____Recommend for Tenure

_____DO NOT recommend for tenure

As signature below indicates, this conference has been held and the person has been evaluated. The person evaluated does not necessarily agree with the evaluation.

_____   _____   _____

Signature of Person Evaluated   Evaluator's Signature, Title   Date

FIGURE 15–9.   Personnel Recommendation Form. This instrument is completed by the evaluator at the end of the evaluation cycle, is reviewed in a conference with the evaluatee, and becomes a part of the cumulative personnel file.

Source: Gerald C. Ubben and Larry W. Hughes, *The Principal: Creative Leadership for Effective Schools* (Boston: Allyn and Bacon, 1992), p. 325.

dicates a need for learning-center development or improvement, it would be helpful to organize a collective improvement program in that specific target area.

A collective staff development program can also be used on a school-district level if similar evaluation programs are used in each individual building. The more teachers available for the various parts of a planned, personalized inservice program, the greater will be its efficiency and effectiveness.

Mentoring

Our HRD focus to this point has been the relationship between the principal as supervisor and individual staff members. Mentoring proposes a relationship between peers: however, generally not peers of equal stature and experience. Mentoring is often used to assist in the orientation of new employees.

The term *mentor* comes from Greek mythology. Mentor was the friend and counselor to whom Ulysses entrusted his son when Ulysses set off on a ten-year odyssey. It was a complex role: Mentor was protector, advisor, teacher, and father-figure to the inexperienced boy. The relationship was one of trust and affection.

In today's organizational setting, a formalized mentor program typically involves a relationship between a veteran employee of some stature and a younger inexperienced colleague. When it is an aspect of a human resource development effort, the focus of the

Teachers	Group Interaction	Learning Centers	Small Group Instruction	Discipline	Record Keeping	Reading Skills Instruction	Team Skills	Other
Abbot, C.		X	X	X		X	X	X
Carson, B.			X	X	X			X
Dole, J.	X	X		X			X	X
Goff, R.	X	X			X			X
Harris, S.		X	X	X		X	X	X
Henderson, F.	X	X		X		X		X
Jones, B.	X	X		X			X	X
Nance, D.		X	X	X	X			X
Poriera, A.	X		X				X	X
Smith, L.		X			X	X		X
Wall, S.		X	X				X	X

FIGURE 15–10.   Staff Development Needs Survey

relationship is on career counseling, advanced skills development, and learning the culture of the organization from a broadened perspective. Less formal relationships, which are conceptually similar, are typified by labels such as *sponsor*, *coach*, or *senior advisor*.

Mentoring has come to take on a more precise role than that suggested by the other labels. Often, the practice is reserved to those who have been identified early as "fast trackers" or potential leaders. However, the concept is easily applied at the building level, albeit perhaps not quite as formally, but nevertheless to good effect. It can substantially improve the clinical approach to supervision and become a very sophisticated *peer* supervision program. It does require a cadre of excellent experienced staff, however.

As in any relationship, both parties in the mentoring process have important responsibilities. It is critical that the relationship be managed so that maximum benefit is achieved.

The responsibilities of the mentor include:

IDP Counseling. Specific guidance and suggestions are given for developmental experiences to be included in the protégé's IDP to strengthen competencies.

Monitoring and Feedback. An active role must be taken by the mentor in monitoring the progress and performance of the protégé. Regular feedback sessions need to be held at which time the IDP is reviewed, clinical observations made, and formative evaluation considerations discussed.

Career Strategy Advisement. The mentor provides general guidance and insight regarding the kinds of opportunities available in the organization and the career background and path necessary to qualify for such positions. In this capacity the mentor brings to bear an extensive knowledge of the history and culture of the system, as well as of projected trends. Many school systems, for example, have differentiated staffing patterns, extended-year contract opportunities, special assignments for staff with special qualifications, different salary arrangements depending on certification, interesting opportunities for those whose teaching areas are in high demand/short supply, as well as the usual administrative positions with opportunities for broadened leadership responsibilities. The mentor advises about these.

Sponsoring and Mediating. This aspect of the mentor's responsibility is to provide direction and assistance in arranging particular developmental assignments and promotion opportunities. The second dimension is to serve as a mediator in any conflicts that may arise that involve the advisee and others in the organization, including the "boss."

The developing person has responsibilities as well. Any productive relationship is mutually supportive and requires the active attention of both parties. The advisee needs to take the lead in several ways: by initiating meetings and actively seeking advice, by remaining open to the advice and suggestions of the mentor, and by a willingness to share personal and professional problems and aspirations.

Developing a Productive Relationship
Productive relationships are not automatically obtained. There is always the issue of the "interpersonal chemistry" of the involved individuals, for example. This notwithstanding

to the contrary, there are several other factors that can greatly facilitate the relationship. Administrators interested in developing productive mentoring arrangements need to consider such aspects as careful matching, good initial orientation, and a feedback and monitoring system.

Careful matching of individuals is essential. The administrator should develop an initial list of potential mentors before considering the process further. Important factors that result in a good mentor include willingness to act as a mentor, personal commitment to helping others develop, commitment to the school, extensive knowledge and insight about how things get done in the organization, solid experience, good professional relationships beyond the immediate building or system, and a proven record of success.

For example, when using a mentoring system as part of the orientation of new teachers, it is often best to select as mentors relatively young but experienced teachers. As mentors they will generally relate well to entering members of the profession having enough experience to share good advice, including a good memory for the problems of a first-year teacher.

Fundamental to a long-term relationship is an early orientation to the program at which the involved parties can, within a school system and school building policy, work through role definitions and expectations of each other. This process will clarify initial commitments to help foster the climate of trust and openness important to success.

The establishment of a regular feedback and monitoring system is essential. This must be encouraged and supported by organizational mechanisms. One approach is to schedule regular monthly luncheons, in addition to other spontaneous sessions, at which lengthier discussion can take place in a more relaxed atmosphere away from the usual interruptions.

Organizational Development

Organizational development (OD) is a process designed to improve the interaction and productivity of work groups. The work group may be a team of teachers, the staff of a particular school, or some other configuration of employees. OD methods work well as initial activities for newly formed teams or with established groups that are refocusing their efforts. Quality Circles as part of a Total Quality Management (TQM) program can use OD methodology to facilitate their interaction.

While HRD and organizational development (OD) are different and are employed for different outcomes, they are related. An OD intervention frequently results in the development of, or improvement of, the human resource development program. Frequently, as well, a well-functioning HRD program will bring about conditions which result in a better-functioning work group; an intended outcome of organizational development. Some theorists may argue otherwise, but for the practitioner and the student of management it is most useful to view the two approaches as parts of a whole.[8]

Healthy organizations systematically and regularly engage in introspective analyses of organizational activities, the purpose of such introspection is to maintain viability—to continue to effectively respond to client needs. Three questions must be asked:

- *Why are we doing what we are doing?* This is a goals question. Healthy organizations have well-developed and well-understood goals and objectives. From time to time there is need to reexamine these in the light of changing conditions—to reaffirm them, add to them, or modify them.

- *What are we doing?* This is a question about the nature and kind of processes that are being implemented to achieve the goals and objectives. This has to do with such things as the nature of the curriculum; scoping and sequencing of subject matter; and policy and procedures; among a host of other things that comprise the formal organizational structure and delivery systems.
- *Can it be done a better way?* This is an evaluation question. Once the goals have been clarified, and reaffirmed or modified, and once the processes have been identified and analyzed, it is necessary to decide what, if anything, could be done differently to achieve the goal more efficiently. Such issues as decision-making practices; communication practices; allocation of resources, additional resources needed (personnel and material); changes in organizational structure and curricular delivery systems; staffing arrangements; and any individual developmental activities are among the processes that must be examined.

As with any complex process issuing from the behavioral sciences, there is not complete agreement about just what organizational development is. Nevertheless, there are some common characteristics about which most in the field would agree.

Organizational development is systematic and involves a total organizational system *or* subsystems. The entire organization need not be involved. Any unified subsystem—a school building or a decentralized school system unit, for example—could engage in such a process *provided* the unit was relatively autonomous (i.e., free within wide bounds to determine its own long-range plans), and *top* management was aware and committed to the effort.

It has as its main focus that of changing the attitudes, behaviors, and performance patterns of work groups rather than individuals. The emphasis is on realistic group goal setting, systematic planning, and problem solving. Such aspects of effective work groups as how best to work together; how to capitalize on the skills of members; how to communicate effectively; and managing and resolving intra- and intergroup conflict are among problem areas addressed.

OD is an ongoing and long-term process. People learn to work effectively together only as they face real problems and develop effective problem-solving skills. This cannot be accomplished quickly; behavior change and the skills needed are acquired only after much practice. Frequently it is best to have a process consultant facilitate the work of the group. This person can be from within the parent organization but should be external to the target work group.

An OD process relies on action-research and experiential learning. The data that are of most use are data about the ongoing system—its characteristics, issues, problems, and resources. This information is collected, analyzed, and returned in summary form to the work group. It forms the basis for problem identification, goal setting, and systematic problem resolution. The survey-feedback method of data collection/data analysis action planning is most frequently employed to facilitate this process.

Survey-feedback methods have a rich history. The method is essentially a systematic way of collection information about the entire organization across several organizational dimensions. The process involves the development of an organizational questionnaire that is administered anonymously to organizational members.

The usual approach is to include questions about worker demographics and work group characteristics, as well as items that provide insight about such organizational dimensions as the nature of communication practices, organizational goal setting, decision-making practices; motivation and reward systems; and control practices, among other possible dimensions. In the often used survey of organizations, there is space for the organization to add its own questions about purely local issues and concerns.[9]

Once the data are collected, a computer analysis is performed and the information, appropriately categorized, is returned to the organization for the feedback/problem-solving effort to begin. Usually a consultant will feed the information back to the top administrative team first and then move through the organizational hierarchy. The process involves discussing the data, what the information means, and what might be done about it. Each administrator then meets with his or her own work group to interpret the data further and to develop corrective action plans.

Thus, just as HRD is far more than a cafeteria list of in-house seminars and on-the-job training, so is OD more than a few problem-solving groups working with a process consultant. Understanding and providing for the complexities of these two approaches brings sophistication and productivity to the staff and organizational development effort.

Implications for Leaders

The role of the principal in human resource and organizational development is a crucial one. Even if the school district is not operating on an enlightened development model, there is much that can occur at the school building level to address staff development systematically and provide for a responsive organization. Our earlier discussion of the way one principal began a school year with a new staff is one such illustration. Many other options are open, however.

The Needs Assessment

What does the staff need? What does the staff want? Where is this expertise available? It is appropriate to survey the staff formally and such surveys should be more than a once-in-a-while activity.

A formal survey is not the only source of information about staff needs. If principals have been regularly and routinely engaging in clinical supervision, then they clearly will be in good position to know what some of the important needs are on the faculty. Moreover, reviewing data in a systematic way about such things as pupil progress, demographic aspects of the community, changes in state law, federal programming, and impending curricular changes, among any number of other impinging forces, will be suggestive of current or impending development needs. The point here is that a principal must not feel bound to a survey when it is clear that there are pressing needs other than those recognized immediately by the staff.[10]

Making staff aware of changes on the horizon is one way to elevate a sense of need. Moreover, if the principal has been engaging in the postobservation feedback sessions essential to a clinical supervision process, this too is an awareness-raising activity. Urick and his colleagues prescribe the ARC model. The acronym stands for Awareness, Readiness, and Commitment, and the point of their manuscript is that these are the sequential building blocks to the success of any inservice development activity.[11]

Structuring and Monitoring the Development System

Whether the aspect of the human resource development program that is being addressed is individual in nature or is workgroup focused, there is a need for administrative support, an appropriate structure, and a monitoring system. Administrative support begins with needs assessment, of course. It continues when the expectations are established. It is buttressed by a willingness to engage others in the planning of the development efforts, and a willingness to secure time and dollar resources to support the effort.

The nature of the need, who is to be involved, and whether or not the development is to be workgroup focused or individually oriented will, for the most part, determine the structure of the programs. If the program is an individually oriented one, then the IDP is probably the best approach.

If it is workgroup development (schoolwide, department, grade-level, teaching team, or whatever), then the structuring of the experiences becomes somewhat more complex. Once it is clear what it is that the group needs to know, and assuming that the group is at the stage of commitment, it is probably best to turn the planning of the development events over to the group itself. The principal's role then becomes one of facilitation rather than direction.[12]

Monitoring progress at regular intervals is important. In the instance of the IDP, regular conferences with the individual and/or the mentor, if there is one, is essential. This keeps the process a formative one and allows for appropriate adjustments. In the instance of group development programs, it is equally essential that formative evaluation practices be present. All human resource development programs need regular assessment.

Positive Reinforcement

Learning and development, whether adult, adolescent, or child, are facilitated by positive reinforcement. Among a number of findings reported in a research synthesis about effective school practices was the following characteristic of leaders in these schools:

> Leaders set up systems of incentives and rewards to encourage excellence in student and teacher performance; they act as figureheads in delivering awards and highlighting the importance of excellence.[13]

These findings highly correlate with those about successful management in the private sector:

> The excellent companies have a deeply ingrained philosophy that says, in effect, "respect the individual," "make people winners," "let them stand out," "treat people as adults."[14]

In sum, then, there are four implications to the principal who wants a well-developed, highly motivated staff:

- Development needs of the staff must be accurately assessed. Self-assessment is a starting point, but the principal must also conduct an investigation, using clinical observations in classrooms, student data, and current and foreseeable school and community concerns among other data sources.
- High standards of performance must be established and advertised. Setting performance standards in cooperation with staff members has been revealed to be the most effective practice.
- Human resource development systems require careful planning and a variety of approaches. IDPs as well as group development events must focus on recognized needs and be regularly monitored.
- Positive reinforcement techniques need to be consistently and continually employed. Public pats on the back, award ceremonies, a private thank you, bonuses for jobs well done—what Peters and Waterman call "hoopla"[15]—all serve to keep people congruent with the needs of the organization, and productively motivated.

Summary

Negative responses to organized efforts in the name of staff development are the result of a history of bad experiences with activities that have gone on in the name of inservice training. However well-intended such activities may have been, too frequently they have not addressed either the needs of the individual staff members or the needs of the organization.

Better approaches exist, and these approaches issue from a model of human resource development that recognizes the varied needs of individual organization members; the needs of the organization; the nature of adult learners; time and effort required depending on the nature of the knowledge, skill, or attitude to be acquired; and the impact that individuals have on the very nature and culture of the workplace.

Endnotes

1. S. K. Miller, S. R. Cohn, and R. H. Sayre, "Significant Achievement Gains Using Effective Schools Model." *Educational Leadership, 42* (March 1985): 38–43.

2. Nevertheless, it is the responsibility of the principal to monitor these programs. Routine observations of staff members who exhibit less than adequate pedagogical skills or poor human relations skills or apparent deficiencies in knowledge of subject matter or bad communication skills, any or all, should be the basis for a conference, counseling, and prescribed remediation.

3. See Robert Goldhammer, *Clinical Supervision.* New York: Holt, Rinehart and Winston, 1969; and Morris Cogen, *Clinical Supervision.* New York: Houghton Mifflin, 1973.

4. Ronald Brandt, "On Teacher Evaluation: A Conversation with Tom McGreal." *Educational Leadership, 4,* 7 (July 1987): 20–24.

5. A. A. Glatthorn, *Differentiated Supervision*, Alexandria, VA: Association for Supervision and Curriculum Development, 1984; and Carl D. Glickman, *Developmental Supervision*. Alexandria, VA: Association for Supervision and Curriculum Development, 1981.

6. K. Blanchard, D. Zigarmi, and P. Zagarmi, "Situational Leadership: 'Different Strokes for Different Folks'." *Principal, 66*, 4 (March 1987): 12–16. EJ 349 202.

7. An excellent reference for client-centered evaluations is the publication of the Educational Research Service, *The Evaluatee Evaluates the Evaluator*. Washington, DC: American Association of School Administrators and Research Division, NEA, No. 5, 1970.

8. A good treatment of the relationship of individual development organizational development can be found in Edgar H. Schein, *Career Dynamics: Matching Individual and Organizational Needs*. Reading, MA: Addison-Wesley, 1978.

9. The Institute for Social Research at the University of Michigan has a "Survey of Organizations" designed specifically for schools. A good source to learn more about survey-feedback methodol-ogy is David G. Bowers and Jerome L. Franklin, *Data-Based Organizational Change*. La Jolla, CA: University Associates, 1977.

10. The survey should not be discounted, however. Commitment to improve is always more easily obtained when the individual to be improved personally recognize the need.

11. Ronald Urick, David Pendergast, and Larry W. Hillman, "Pre-Conditions for Staff Development." *Educational Leadership, 38*, 7 (April 1981): 546–549.

12. As always, it is important to establish the ground rules when delegating such tasks. The principal will want to work with the group at the beginning to set the essential conditions that any development process must meet. Such things as budget, impinging system-wide policies, and so on that must be lived with in order for the plan to be implemented should be discussed and understood.

13. Northwest Regional Educational Laboratory, *Effective Schooling Practices: A Research Synthesis*. Portland, OR: The Laboratory, 1984, p. 8.

14. Peters and Waterman, *In Search of Excellence*, p. 240.

15. *Ibid.*

Selected Readings

Acheson, Keith A. and Gall, Meredith, *Techniques in the Clinical Supervision of Teachers*, 2nd ed. New York: Longman, 1987.

Bernstein, H.T., Darling-Hammond, L., McLaughlin, M. W., and Wise, A. E., *Teacher Evaluation: A Study of Effective Practices*. Santa Monica, CA: Rand, 1984.

Costa, A. L. and Garmston, R., "Supervision for Intelligent Teaching." *Educational Leadership*, 42, 5 (1985): 75–80.

Cuccia, Nick J., "Systematic Observation Formats: Key to Improving Communications in Evaluation." *NASSP Bulletin, 68*, 469 (February 1984): 31–38.

DePasquale, Daniel, Jr., "Evaluating Tenured Teachers: A Practical Approach." *NASSP Bulletin, 74* (September 1990): 19–23.

Educational Research Service, *Teacher Evaluation: Practices and Procedures*. Arlington, VA: Educational Research Service, 1988.

Educational Resources Information Center, *The Best of ERIC on Educational Management: Teacher Evaluation*. NASSP Edition. Eugene, OR: Clearinghouse on Educational Management, College of Education, University of Oregon, October 1989.

Fitzpatrick, Kathleen, "A Building-Level Program for First-Year Teachers." *Educational Leadership, 40*, 1 (October 1982): 56.

Goldstein, Irwin L., *Training in Organizations: Needs Assessment, Development and Evaluation*, 2nd ed. Monterey, CA: Brooks/Cole Publishing Co., 1986.

Glatthorn, Allan, *Supervisory Leadership*. Glenview, IL: Scott, Foresman, 1990.

Glickman, Carl D., *Supervision of Instruction*. Boston: Allyn and Bacon, 1989.

Gordon, Bruce G., "Making Clinical Supervision a Reality: Steps Toward Implementation." *NASSP Bulletin, 76*, 542 (March 1992): 46–51.

Harris, Ben M., *Supervisory Behavior in Education*. Englewood Cliffs, NJ: Prentice-Hall, 1985.

Huddle, Gene, "Teacher Evaluation—How Important for Effective Schools: Eight Messages from Research." *NASSP Bulletin, 69* (March 1985): 58–63.

Hughes, Larry W.; Murphy, Mary; and Wong, Martha, "Quality Assurance: Positive Approaches to Teacher Improvement." *Record in Educational Administration and Supervision, 5,* 2 (Spring 1985): 11–13.

Hunter, M., "Knowing, Teaching, and Supervising." In Hosford, P. L. (ed.), *Using What We Know About Teaching*. Alexandria, VA: Association for Supervision and Curriculum Development, 1984, pp. 169–192.

Joyce, B., and Showers, B., *Student Achievement Through Self Development*. New York: Longman, 1988.

Katims, David S., and Henderson, Richard L., "Teacher Evaluation in Special Education." *NASSP Bulletin, 74* (September 1990): 46–52.

Lane, Bruce A., "Personnel Evaluation: From Problems to School Improvement." *Journal of Research and Development in Education, 23,* 4 (Summer 1990): 243–9.

McLaughlin, M. W., "Teacher Evaluation and School Improvement." *Teachers College Record, 86,* 1 (1984): 193–207.

Millman, Jason, *Handbook of Teacher Evaluation*. Beverly Hills, CA: Sage Publications, 1981.

Murphy, J. and Hallinger, P., "The Characteristics of Instructionally Effective School Districts." *Journal of Educational Research, 81,* 3 (1987): 175–81.

National Association of Elementary School Principals, *Effective Teachers: Effective Evaluation in America's Elementary and Middle Schools*. NAESP, 1988.

Olthoff, Richard J., "The Principal as Instructional Coach-Providing Quality Education." *NASSP Bulletin, 76,* 542 (March 1992): 6–12.

Pope, Carol A., "Indirect Teaching and Assessment: Are They Mutually Exclusive?" *NASSP Bulletin, 74* (September 1990): 1–5.

Scriven, M., "Validity in Personnel Evaluation." *Journal of Personnel Evaluation in Education, 1,* 1 (1987): 9–23.

Shelton, Maria M., Lane, Kenneth, and Yuhasz, Patt, "Great Beginnings." *The Executive Educator* (January 1992): 27–29.

Soar, R. S.; Medley, D. M.; and Coker, H. "Teacher Evaluation: A Critique of Currently Used Methods." *Phi Delta Kappan, 65,* 4 (1983): 239–246.

Stufflebeam, Daniel L., Chair, *The Personnel Evaluation Standards: How to Assess Systems for Evaluating Educators*. The Joint Committee on Standards for Educational Evaluation. Beverly Hill, CA: Sage Publications, 1988.

Thorson, J.R., *et al.*, "Instructional Improvement Through Personnel Evaluation." *Educational Leadership, 44* (April 1987): 52–54.

Wood, Carolyn J., "Toward More Effective Teacher Evaluation: Lessons from Naturalistic Inquiry." *NASSP Bulletin, 76,* 542 (March 1992): 52–59.

Zumwalt, K., *Improving Teaching* (1986 ASCD Yearbook). Arlington, VA: Association for Supervision and Curriculum Development, 1986.

Chapter 16

The Principal's Role in Collective Bargaining Agreements

Introduction

Written contracts between teacher organizations and school districts create a bilaterally developed uniform set of personnel policies for use across a school district. While the contracts vary from state to state and school district to district, they control and often restrict the discretionary powers of school administrators, including the principal.[1] The recent popularity of site-based management, which has at its heart the creation of diversity and local control of decisions in the school, runs directly counter to district uniformity demanded by district-wide teacher contracts.

Site-based management is less encumbered if no formal district teacher contract exists. If a contract is in place, then each school will need to work within the framework of that agreement and seek modifications in the agreement during renegotiation of the contract to provide the necessary freedom desired for good site-based management. Under any arrangement, the grievance procedures, which generally assume a highly centralized personnel process, will need to be followed until that process can be brought in line with a philosophy of decentralization congruent with site-based management.

Most teacher-board agreements include a procedure to guarantee employees a clear channel of communication to air complaints or grievances within the school system and to seek a just solution to problems. Most contracts state that employees may file a grievance if they believe they have been treated unfairly or if they disagree with their supervisors as to the application of a policy. The word *policy* refers primarily to written agreements negotiated by the teacher organization. However, it may also include written policies, procedures, and standards established by the school administration unilaterally.

When differences arise between a negotiated policy and an administrative policy, the negotiated policy controls.

The expression "treated unfairly" relates to matters not covered by policy. It might relate to a substantial deviation from customary practice or might challenge a practice. It might also relate to an action that discriminates against an employee as a person. The concept of unfair treatment does not apply to a disagreement with negotiated policy; an employee who attempts to file a grievance on the basis of such a disagreement would be better advised to present these views to his or her union or association representatives.

Occasionally the term *supervisor* will be used interchangeably in contracts with *principal*, but more often the term *supervisor* refers to any administrator with direct responsibility for the actions of a certain group of employees, teachers, and other personnel. The negotiated agreement will probably provide different ways to handle grievances within the district depending on the subject of the grievance, and different administrators will handle different problems.

Some contracts require the person with whom the grievance is being filed to inform the local representative of the teacher organization if the employee is not represented by a union or association, so that the union may take part as provided in the agreement. If the person bringing the grievance to a supervisor is not satisfied with the supervisor's determination, the agreement usually has a carefully defined set of appeal procedures.

While grievance procedures will vary in terminology and the number of appeal levels from contract to contract, they all seem to follow the same basic format. Figure 16–1 presents the grievance-and-complaint section of a recently negotiated contract. This four-level grievance procedure presents an elaborate plan for "communication within the organization."

How to Handle Grievances

What is a principal's role during a grievance procedure? When a grievance is filed, a principal has the opportunity to reestablish the effective relationship with the employee.

A. A grievance is defined as an alleged violation, misinterpretation, or misapplication of a provision(s) of this contract.

B. Informal Action

If a member of the bargaining unit feels he or she has a grievance, that member shall first discuss the matter in good faith with the immediate supervisor in an effort to resolve the problem informally. This informal action shall take place within twenty (20) teaching days after the grievant knew, or should have known, of the incident which is the basis of the grievance. In this informal action, the grievant shall verbally advise his or her supervisor of the particular section of the Agreement alleged to have been violated. The immediate supervisor will respond verbally to the grievance within six (6) teaching days after the informal meeting.

FIGURE 16–1.   Grievance Procedure

C. Formal Procedure

Step 1

If the informal action does not resolve the grievance satisfactorily, the grievant shall have the right to lodge a written grievance with his or her immediate supervisor within six (6) teaching days following the verbal response of the supervisor. If such grievance is not lodged within six (6) teaching days following conclusion of the informal action above, the right to proceed with the grievance procedure for this incident is waived. The written grievance shall be on a standard form as contained in the appendices to this contract and shall contain a concise statement of the facts upon which the grievance is based and a reference to the specific section of the negotiated agreement which is allegedly violated. A copy of such grievance shall be filed by the grievant with the superintendent and the association. A response shall be made by the immediate supervisor in writing within six (6) teaching days after the receipt of said grievance by the immediate supervisor. Copies shall be sent by the immediate supervisor to the superintendent and the association.

Step 2

If the grievant is not satisfied with the disposition of the grievance in Step 1, such grievant may appeal, by filing a form, as contained in the appendices to this contract, within six (6) teaching days after receipt of the decision of the immediate supervisor in Step 1, to the assistant to the superintendent for employee relations. At the request of either party to the grievance, within six (6) teaching days, the assistant to the superintendent for employee relations shall meet with the grievant and his or her representative and shall indicate the disposition of the grievance in writing within six (6) teaching days of such a meeting and shall furnish a copy thereof to the grievant, the immediate supervisor, the superintendent, and the association. At this step either party may introduce or present evidence to substantiate his, her, or its position in the matter.

Step 3

If the grievant is not satisfied with the disposition of the grievance at Step 2, he or she may appeal, by filing a form as contained in the appendices of this contract, within six (6) teaching days after receipt of the decision of the assistant to the superintendent for employee relations in Step 2 to the superintendent and request that the grievant be allowed to review the record in Steps 1 and 2 in connection with said grievance. Copies of such notice of the appeal shall be sent to the grievant's immediate supervisor, to the assistant to the superintendent for employee relations, and to the association. The superintendent shall render a decision in writing within ten (10) teaching days after receipt of the appeal. Copies of the decision shall be sent to the grievant, the grievant's immediate supervisor, the assistant to the superintendent for employee relations, and the association.

Step 4

If the association is not satisfied with the decision rendered after the review in Step 3 by the superintendent, the grievance may be submitted for arbitration. The association shall, within fifteen (15) teaching days after receipt of the decision of the superintendent, notify the superintendent of its intent to submit the grievance to arbitration.

FIGURE 16–1.   Grievance Procedure *(Continued)*

and to improve the relationship. The most can be made of this opportunity by observing the following principles:

Be Approachable

Principals should not place obstacles in the way of employees or their representatives that will suggest that the principal is not interested in discussing their problems with them. An appointment should be made for a definite time at a specific place to discuss the grievance in private.

Listen

Many times the grievance results from an action the principal has taken. The great temptation is for the principal to defend the action without further thought. However, if a principal adopts a defensive attitude the employee may feel even more grieved. When teachers or other employees have a complaint, they should have the opportunity to talk it out. If the employee is excited, or if the basis of the complaint is not clear, the complaint should be clarified. Calm, interested listening is required. Sometimes in the process of putting the complaint into words, the grievance will disappear.

Get the Facts

The principal should repeat the story after the employee has told it to clarify that both parties are discussing the same issue. Those facts agreed upon or accepted as true by both parties should be confirmed. Those aspects not perceived in the same way should be discussed further, and, if an agreement is not reached, more information should be secured before a decision is rendered.

Take Notes

During the discussion the principal should take notes about the facts presented. The notes will be helpful in reviewing the facts with the employee and when the matter is discussed later with the superintendent or personnel director. Notes are also helpful for a written report of a grievance discussion.

Make Decisions with Care

An immediate decision is not usually required, and the principal should carefully weigh all the facts. Employees must be reassured that they will receive a fair hearing based on the facts of an issue.

In all cases it is prudent, even necessary, to discuss the matter with the superintendent or personnel director before making a decision. This is especially important if the issue involves interpretation of a policy or a negotiated agreement. However, avoid undue delay in acting on the grievance.

Since action taken may result in the employee exercising the right of appeal, the principal's responsibility is to render the initial decision and inform the employee of his or her appeal rights.

It's the Principal's Decision

When the principal makes the decision, it should be clear that it is not that of the board, superintendent, or personnel director. Even though the action that is the subject of the complaint may be based upon some policy of the school district the principal did not help make, it it still the principal who applied that policy and who must accept first-line responsibility.

If grievances at this level are handled properly, most problems covered under the teacher's contract can be solved. If administrators follow reasonable procedures for the rapid but fair handling of grievances, relatively few grievances will need to be appealed to the next level in the established grievance procedure.

Appealed Grievances

When an employee is dissatisfied with the initial responses of the first-level supervisor or principal, a formal hearing may be requested to move the grievance procedure to Level Two. This appeal is usually made by written statements, affidavits, or hearings, or a combination thereof. A hearing is usually held at the request of the employee or the appeal administrator. As grievance procedures become more formal, standard forms may be desirable in processing and recording the grievance decision. Figure 15–2 depicts a suggested format to be used at the building level by the aggrieved employee. The administrator also needs documentation and Figure 15–3 depicts a suggested format.

The Principal's Role in Negotiation

The school principal has two major responsibilities in the collective negotiation process. The first responsibility is as a member of the administrative team. Every school district should have an administrative team consisting of building-level principals, supervisory staff, and central superintendent staff representing management in negotiation. Occasionally questions arise regarding the principal's role. Formal negotiations recognize that a principal must be part of the management team.

Each principal in small school districts with few principals should be an active member of the administrative team and participate in an advisory capacity during negotiations. In larger communities principals may find it both necessary and effective to have representation on the negotiating team to express their viewpoint. Principals should be represented, because to a great extent negotiation topics represent areas of direct concern to the building principal. In many cases the ensuing negotiations result in the erosion of the power or responsibility of the principal, often reducing administrative effectiveness.[2]

Contract Administration

The principal must be part of the management team because of the basic responsibility of administering the employee contract once it has been negotiated. The grievance procedure outlined above is part of that contract administration.

Name _____ Home Phone _____
      Last   First   Initial

Immediate Supervisor_____ Work Location _____

Contract Section Allegedly Violated _____

Date of Alleged Violation _____

Description:

Redress Sought:

Signature _____ Date _____

STEP I   Date Rec'd _____ Init. _____ Date Reply Rec'd _____ Init. _____

Disposition:

Denied   Granted   Reason:

Signature _____ Date _____

STEP II   Date Rec'd _____ Init. _____ Date Reply Rec'd _____ Init. _____

Disposition:

Denied   Granted   Reason:

Signature _____ Date _____

STEP III   Date Rec'd _____ Init. _____ Date Reply Rec'd _____ Init. _____

Disposition:

Denied   Granted   Reason:

Signature _____ Date _____

STEP IV   Date Rec'd _____ Init. _____ Date Reply Rec'd _____ Init. _____

ASSOCIATION RESPONSE:

( )   We hereby accept the review and decision of the Superintendent in Step III.

( )   We hereby appeal for arbitration of this grievance.

Signature of
Association President _____ Date _____

FIGURE 16–2. **Form for Contract Grievances (Members of Bargaining Unit Only)**

DECISION OF ADMINISTRATOR

(To be completed by principal, or other appropriate administrator, within 3 days of formal grievance presentation.)

AGGRIEVED PERSON(S) _____

DATE OF FORMAL PRESENTATION _____

SCHOOL _____

PRINCIPAL _____

DECISION OF PRINCIPAL (OR OTHER ADMINISTRATOR) AND
REASONS THEREFORE:

DATE OF DECISION _____   _____
                                              (signature of principal)

AGGRIEVED PERSON'S RESPONSE: (To be completed by aggrieved within 3 days of decision.)

( ) I accept the above decision of principal (or other administrator).
( ) I hereby refer the above decision to the Association's Professional Rights and Responsibilities Committee for appeal to the superintendent of schools.

DATE OF RESPONSE _____

                                    _____
                                              (signature of aggrieved)

FIGURE 16–3.

   The principal must be able to interpret the agreement reached with the teachers and to apply it in an acceptable manner. Each year principals should request a briefing about the new contract from the school district negotiator and an interpretation of agreements and information regarding implementation of that contract. Great care must be exercised to stick to the contract. Teachers will readily inform the principal if they are not granted all of the privileges called for in the contract but also will most willingly accept privileges that extend beyond the contract. This is where the danger lies. Principals can inadvertently grant permanent privileges to teachers by on occasion simply giving them certain extra privileges.

   Administrators should be aware of a key concept called *past practice*. It is the acceptance of duties or privileges that teachers have carried out or been granted over an extended period of time. Arbitrators will invoke the term past practice in dispute cases when the teacher organization claims that a principal has for an extended period of time allowed a certain privilege or action to take place. Past practices can become a part of the contract and thus a privilege to be exercised by the teachers.

Summary

Collective bargaining by teachers has changed the role of the principal. Grievance procedures provide formal guarantees of communication between teachers and administrators; principals now must abide by a specific set of rules, as spelled out by the contract, in dealing with teachers.

Site-based management may change the structure of the grievance procedure.

Endnotes

1. Gerald C. Ubben and Barbara Fulmer, "The Relationship of Collective Bargaining to the Decision-Making Power of the Public School Principal." *Journal of Collective Negotiations, 14*, 2 (1985). Baywood Publishing Co., Inc.

2. An increasing number of school districts provide for the direct negotiation of principals or negotiation in cooperation with other administrators or supervisors. Several states already have legislation requiring boards of education to recognize and negotiate with administrator units.

Selected Readings

Beer, Louis, D., "Unit Status of Supervisors in Public Education: A Management Perspective." *Journal of Law and Education, 11*, 2 (April 1982): 229–239.

Castetter, William B., *The Personnel Function in Educational Administration*, rev. ed. New York: Macmillan, 1986.

Coffinberger, Richard L., "A Primer on Unionization Motives." *Journal of Collective Negotiations in the Public Sector, 10*, 2 (1981): 123–132.

Conlon, E. J. and Gallagher, O. H., "Commitment to Employer and Union: Effects of Membership Status." *Academy of Management Journal, 30* (1987): 151–162.

Cresswell, Anthony M. and Murphy, Michael J., *Teachers, Unions, and Collective Bargaining in Public Education*. Berkeley, CA: McCutchan Publishing Company, 1980.

Harris, Ben M. *et al.*, *Personnel Administration in Education*. Boston: Allyn and Bacon, 1985.

Jascourt, Hugh D., "Collective Bargaining Issues in Public School Employment." (1983). ERIC ED 245 376.

Jascourt, Hugh D., "Looming Legal Issues in Labor Relations in Education." *Journal of Law and Education, 12*, 3 (July 1983): 443–449.

Mitchell, D. J. B., "Concession Bargaining in the Public Sector: A Lesser Force." 1987.

Mullins, Charles E., "Unit Status of Supervisors in Public Education: A Union Perspective." *Journal of Law and Education, 11*, 2 (April 1982): 213–227.

Neal, Richard, *School and Government Labor Relations: A Guidebook for School and Government Managers*. Manassas: Richard Neal Assoc., 1982.

Ostrander, Kenneth H., *A Grievance Arbitration Guide for Educators*. Boston: Allyn and Bacon, Inc., 1981.

Paterson, Lee T. and Murphy, Reginald T., *The Public Administrator's Grievance Arbitration Handbook*. New York: Longman, 1983.

Rebore, Ronald W., *Personnel Administration in Education: A Management Approach*, 2nd ed. Englewood Cliffs, NJ: Prentice-Hall, 1987.

Retsinas, Joan, "Teachers: Bargaining for Control." *American Educational Research Journal, 19*, 3 (Fall 1982): 353–372.

Scott, Clyde and Bain, Trevor, "How Arbitrators Interpret Ambiguous Contract Language." *Personnel* (August 1987): 10–14.

Stimson, Terry D. and Appelbaum, Richard P., "Empowering Teachers: Do Principals have the Power?" *Phi Delta Kappan, 70*, 4 (December 1988): 313–316.

Ubben, Gerald C. and Fulmer, Barbara, "The Relationship of Collective Bargaining to the Decision-Making Power of the Public School Principal." *Journal of Collective Negotiations in the Public Sector, 14*, 2 (1985): 141–150.

Wagner, Robert F. Jr., "The Case for Local Education Policy Boards." *Phi Delta Kappan, 74*, 3 (November 1992): 228–229.

Webster, William G., Sr., *Effective Collective Bargaining in Public Education*. Ames: Iowa State University Press, 1985.

Wentz, Charles Alvin, "Preserving a Union-Free Workplace." *Personnel* (October 1987): 68–72.

Wolfberg, Calvin J., "The Biggest Mistakes Boards Make in Collective Bargaining." (March 1983) ERIC ED 242 004.

Chapter *17*

Creative Budgeting and Sound Fiscal Accounting

... giving people who do the work the power to do it results in better quality and lower costs.[1]

Introduction

The quotation above says it all and, in these days of greater fiscal autonomy and control at the school site, is not only profound but also pregnant with implications for the principal. A concomitant of greater decentralization of school districts is greater budgetary and fiscal autonomy at the schoolhouse.

In some school districts, principals have for many years had much latitude in budget development and budget implementation, but in many others fiscal control for the most part has been limited to managing the "activity" accounts. These "local" monies are those generated at the site from donations, sales of merchandise or services from such things as school carnivals, booster club activities, business partnerships, soft drink and candy machines, and in-building school supply stores. The good use of such funds is important, of course. But, with increasing responsibility for funds that come from state foundation programs and local taxes, the pecuniary responsibilities of the principal become even more complex and precise.

Decentralized fiscal authority at the building level will extend as well to departments, or grade level units, and to other distinct units that have to do with delivering services to the student body. For example: libraries and instructional materials centers, athletic departments, guidance departments, school improvement committees, among other units that may exist in any particular school.

Nevertheless, while there will be increased staff involvement in budget development and expenditure plans, the responsibility for managing school funds in a systematic manner—a manner that will sustain audit—rests with the principal.

This chapter has two foci: budget development and fiscal management. The first focus has to do with how one might develop a budget that will provide the best in educational programming. This is a leadership function.

The second focus is how funds can be administered in a sound way. This is a management function. Principals don't have to be graduate accountants, but they do have to apply the principles of good fiscal accounting and oversee those who are charged specifically with bookkeeping.

The School Budget

A sound budget enhances the ability of the school to deliver on its promises to young people and the ability of the principal to advocate the school's needs persuasively before district-wide budget committees. Knowledge about good accounting procedures ensures that the principal will stay out of court and the school out of bankruptcy.

Managing a school budget requires great skill. Poor record-keeping procedures and other unsound fiscal practices result in mismanaged dollars—indefensible in today's economy of scarce resources.

Schools are big business. In many communities the school system is the single largest employer of personnel and the largest industry in terms of capital flow. School districts receive and disburse huge amounts of money for a variety of services and materials. Similarly, principals in individual school buildings administer sizable financial resources that come from the central district office as a result of local, state, and federal programs, as well as smaller sums from such sources as PTOs, school clubs, and plays.

The fiscal responsibility of the elementary principal is both active and supervisory. It is active in the sense that, within the guidelines set by the central office, the principal establishes the regular procedures governing the fiscal operation of each building. It is supervisory in that the principal regularly monitors the activities of those staff members charged with properly recording and reporting financial transactions involving the school.

The degree of autonomy that an elementary school principal has with respect to the fiscal operation of the school will vary. In some school systems virtually all financial decisions are made in the central office by the superintendent or the superintendent's designate. In other systems the principal has wide latitude in constructing a budget and in the expenditure of funds for personnel, operations, and capital outlay. Principals must know what expectations superordinates have with respect to financial decision making at the building level.

Managing the business side of an elementary school extends from simple record-keeping of modest amounts of activity-account money to the complexities of program-planning budget procedures, depending upon the size of the school and the school system and the degree of budgetary and financial-decision autonomy accorded individual principals. It is a changing world and the movement toward more decentralization in large school systems has increased fiscal decision-making autonomy and responsibility for many principals.

Budget Building

Good budgeting contains four distinct steps: planning and allocation of all costs, adoption, administration and coordination, and review and appraisal. The budget process itself is cyclical and continuous. The review and appraisal step, for example, immediately precedes the following fiscal year's planning and preparation step (Figure 17–1).

Good budgeting is much more than simply categorically allocating anticipated revenues and subsequently recording the expenditures made in these categories. Being able to cost-out the various activities of an educational program specifically is a meager accomplishment unless such costing out is the first step in evaluating the effectiveness of those activities in terms of the attainment of the goals of the institution. Thus, budget development should begin with an examination of the goals and objectives of the various aspects of the educational program. Total staff participation is desirable in the formative stages.

Setting Priorities

Foremost in budget building is education planning. The relationship between the educational goals and objectives of the school and the budget that supports these goals must be made obvious. Good budgeting is the result of careful educational planning; it is not a catalog of "outgoes" that lists retrospectively where the money went.

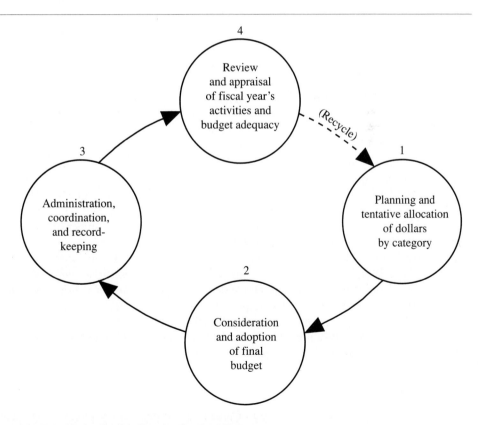

FIGURE 17–1. Budgeting: A Cyclical Process

Many school staffs get caught in an incremental budgeting game and, because they do, perform a great disservice to their clients. Incremental budgeting requires simple acceptance of the status quo. Any increases or losses in student population are projected for the next year, and, on the basis of what was required for the current year, dollar needs are established. Such a budget development process is simple, requires very little thought, and can be accomplished in a short period of time with a calculator and a census tract. It is also dysfunctional.

A budget development procedure that uses the basic elements of Program Planning Budgeting Systems (PPBS) is better.

Program Planning Budgeting System (PPBS)

At its simplest, PPBS involves five steps:

1. Establish the general goals to be achieved, keeping in mind the overall philosophy and beliefs of the organization.

2. Identify the specific objectives that define this goal.

3. Develop the program and processes that it is expected will achieve the objectives and goals.

4. Establish the formative and summative evaluation practices.

5. Establish a review and recycle procedure that indicates whether or not, or the degree to which, the program and processes resulted in the achievement of the objectives and goals. This helps determine other procedures, processes, and programs.

In other words, PPBS is designed to help a school staff decide specifically what they want to accomplish and how to go about it. PPBS focuses on goal accomplishment and, if sensitively and sensibly applied, will provide for efficient expenditures of monies.

Education planning is often concerned primarily with the inputs of education. Typically the school budget has been concerned with numbers: the number of staff, books, equipment, and buildings that must be secured, purchased, and assembled in order to educate a determined number of children. In this regard PPBS differs substantively from other budget-building procedures because it focuses first on desired outputs of the effort (goals and objectives) and afterward considers the number of staff, books, equipment, and buildings needed to obtain the desired end.

As the PPBS is implemented, data are being collected about the productivity of the several elements of the educational program. This is useful not only for budget building but also to meet increasing public demands for evidence of return on the investment of tax dollars. As the school enterprise has become more complex and diversified and more demanding on public funds and personnel, there has been a resultant anxiety about results. The PPBS process helps provide this important information and can form a solid basis for public and staff support.

Implementing PPBS

A budget should be the result of planning and educational program. The answer to the question of how one builds an educationally sound budget starts at the base—the educational program—and develops outward. One discovers the program needs by asking the people in the best position to provide the answer—the instructional staff. However, only careful organization provides an effective mechanism to translate the needs of the program efficiently into dollar amounts in the budget. If budget building is to be anything more than a means of classifying outgo, it must consider the future.

Challenging the Staff

Frequently staff members think solely in terms of additional materials for the department or the school, rather than in terms of the direction the educational program ought to be taking. "What do you need now?" is too often the question, when the question really should be "Where do you see this school, or your department, heading in the next few years, and what is it going to take to get there?" Since staff involvement in decision making is the most effective means for bringing about real change, the effort to involve staff in curricular study and change must extend to budget development.

Step One: Developing the Five-Year-Plan

The planning process begins with the development of a five-year plan well in advance of any specific budget proposals for the next fiscal year. This plan is not easily developed, and the process provides a good basis for inservice workshops with staff. It lends a substantive focus to faculty meetings and workshops held throughout the school year. The process begins by organizing the preschool workshop to focus on planning for the future and to develop several schoolwide, department, or grade-level brainstorming sessions to consider such topics as "what a child at the end of grade three should know," or "what this school needs is," or "outcomes of the K–6 social studies program should be," or any other topics generative of ideas that focus on curricular or student outcomes. Staff members should be encouraged not to be encumbered by any real-world constraints nor to think solely in terms of the current year, but rather to project their thinking as much as five or ten years in the future. Staff members convert the product of these sessions into a series of goals and objectives by a process of synthesizing, summarizing, and combining.[2]

Once the staff has refined the statements of objectives and goals, they should identify, often through another brainstorming session, the processes, materials, and personnel that will be necessary to implement these goals and objectives. Participants should take care not to get bogged down at this point. The statements are not written on stone and are subject to future modification and change. Less than perfection is acceptable lest the staff and the principal be victimized by the paralysis of analysis. The tentative five-year plan will have four major components:

1. A brief description of the current state of the art or discipline that simply describes where the grade level, or subject matter, or curricular field is at the present time in relation to what the literature and research reveal is the ideal state.

2. A statement of goals, objectives, and reasonable indicators of achievement of objectives for the department or grade level. It is important to establish objective indicators of achievement, but detailed lists do not have to be created at this time. It is important to move the staff as rapidly as possible through the initial five-year plan development into the actual budget development process so that they may achieve a reward for their hard work reasonably quickly. The five-year plan is subject to modification through the formative evaluation which will occur as it unfolds. Slavishly following the procedures suggested here would be unwise indeed; one must not let the principles of systematic budget development be subverted by unthinking observance of procedures. The sophistication of staff and local conditions must be taken into consideration.

3. A list of processes that will implement the objectives.

4. A list of equipment, materials, personnel, and other resources needed to support the process established in the previous section. (Figure 17–2 provides an outline for a statement of a five-year plan.)

This is the culmination point for the development of the five-year plan. It is subject to refinement and modification and will ultimately be submitted for executive review and discussion. It does not yet contain any dollar figures. The process needs adequate time for

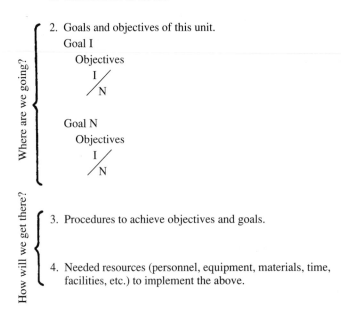

FIGURE 17–2.   The Five-Year Plan

creative and careful thinking, but definite timelines should be established for the completion of this process. Otherwise, it can become a rather cumbersome, never-ending intellectual exercise.

Step Two: Developing the One-Year Plan

The general direction for the department or grade level will have been plotted in the five-year plan. The one-year plan, in effect, asks the staff to spell out what should happen in the next year if the five-year plan is to be ultimately realized. Figure 17–3 provides the suggested format for the one-year plan.

Unit _____

Fiscal Year _____

Prepared by _____

Amount Requested _____

Amount Allocated _____

Request (Indicate after each item which long-term objective it supports.)	Estimated Cost	Suggested Source of Supply	Suggested Source of $ (Federal funds; local funds; donation; state experimental funds, etc.)
1. Needed Personnel			
2. Needed equipment and materials			
3. Needed other resources e.g., travel monies, consultants, etc.) *N.B.* List above in descending order of priority.			

Total Requested _____

_____

4. Attach a brief statement describing how this proposed budget is consistent with and supportive of the five-year plan

FIGURE 17–3. **The One-Year Plan**

This form translates the one-year plan into needed equipment, supplies, supplementary materials, immediate changes or addition of personnel, remodeling, and other resources such as travel monies and consultants. Justification for each specific item should be available in the one-year-plan document. This need not be elaborate but requires a brief statement about how the budget proposal is consistent with the five-year plan. An additional feature is that the departments or grade levels are asked to list their needs in order of priority. If cutting becomes necessary because of insufficient total dollars, it can begin with the lowest-priority items in each proposal.

Step Three: Setting a Timeline

Ample time must be provided in the initial effort for a five-year plan which can be ultimately translated into one-year budget proposals. This is an initial timeline only. Obviously, a five-year plan must be addressed totally only every five years, even though adjustments are necessary throughout the period. During the first year of developing a five-year plan, a school should also continue its former budget development procedure because startup and five-year-plan development will require most of the first year and new one-year budget proposals will not be available until the next fiscal year.

Subsequent Steps

These steps involve submitting budget and curriculum proposals to the principal and the administrative staff, their subsequent approval or return for clarification or modification, the preparation of a total school budget in summary form by the principal and staff for submission to the central office, negotiations, and approval of the school budget in some form by the ultimate fiscal authority in the school district.

Eventually an approved budget is returned by the principal to each department or grade level that will determine requisitions throughout the year. Each month a recapitulation of purchases to date is returned to the department. Figure 17–4 is an example of a monthly budget sheet for an elementary department. This is an excellent application for a computer spreadsheet or data base.

These procedures may sound quite involved and rather formalized, but in actual operation they need not be. Moreover, the process certainly gives staff much insight into the procedures of school finance as well as a great deal of control over the instructional budget.

Expectations and Product

Involvement of instructional staff in budget building does not make the administrator's job any easier. However, it does supply a principal with much of the data needed to justify increases in the budget to the superintendent or the board of education. Moreover, never will the central office and the board be as well informed about expenditures and the reasons behind them as they will be under this system.

The system must remain flexible. If the middle-school social studies department decides it has made a mistake or realizes that certain needs have changed, adjustments in the budget and in the plan must be possible.

DEPARTMENT BUDGET, CURRENT YEAR

Mathematics Department   Month _____
Hughes Elementary

Budget Area & Item	Allowable	Exp. this Month	Exp. to Date	Remainder
TEXTS (B–4)				
5th Modern Math	$ 1000.00			
Programmed Texts				
and Temac Binders				
21 @ $15.00	315.00			
Supplementary Texts	450.00			
EQUIPMENT (D–4)				
Volume Demonstration				
Set (1)	60.00			
Graph Board (multi-				
purpose) (1)	35.00			
Tightgrip Chalk-				
holder (6)	1.00			
Rack of Compasses	12.00			
Rack of Protractors	15.00			
SUPPLEMENTARY (B–6)				
Universal Encyclopedia				
of Math (2)	40.00			
Other References	100.00			
AUDIO VISUAL (D–7)				
Overhead Projector	275.00			
DISCRETIONARY				
SUPPLIES	200.00			
SUBTOTAL	$ 2504.00			
PERSONNEL (A–3)				
2 Consultants 2 days				
each for in-service plus				
expenses	1800.00			
SUBTOTAL	$ 1800.00			
TOTAL	$ 4,304.00			

FIGURE 17–4. Sample Departmental Budget

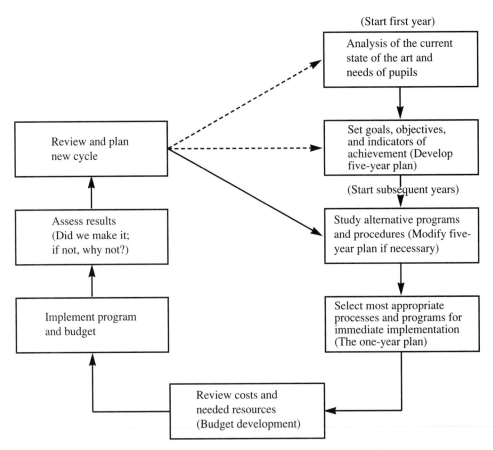

FIGURE 17–5. Systematic Program and Budget Development: Developing and Implementing the Five-Year Plan

The budget-building process just described attempts to accomplish three things. It gives the appropriate personnel a large measure of responsibility for initial budget preparation in their areas of instructional expertise. Second, it forces positive, foresighted curriculum planning. Third, it provides substantiation to the board and the community that tax dollars are being spent in an efficient and effective manner. Figure 17–5 depicts the entire process.

Once the budget is developed and approved, it becomes the responsibility of the principal to see that it is managed properly. Skillful budget management is the subject of the next section of this chapter.

Fiscal Management

All school systems have accounting procedures with which the principal must be familiar because most school principals at least oversee bookkeeping functions.

In general, school principals must keep and properly monitor a journal of receipts and disbursements (Figure 17–6). The principal may also have to maintain appropriate records for specially funded federal projects in the school. The government has established specific procedures that must be followed. In addition, the principal will secure supplies and materials, either through a requisition from central warehousing perhaps using a system of transfer vouchers or directly from a supplier. Much of the principal's accounting responsibilities will occur in the operations—e.g., supplies and equipment—part of the budget. Increasingly, however, principals have broadened authority in staffing the school and there may be a personnel budget that must be managed as well.

In most elementary schools a clerk or secretary will be responsible for keeping the books. Under the principal's supervision, this person will generally make the journal entries and keep the records in order. This *does not* relieve the principal of any executive responsibility, however. Regular review as well as an independent annual audit is essential. During the first few months on the job the principal should be involved very directly in the accounting procedures to learn the business side of the enterprise intimately. Proper accounting and budget procedures are essential to a well-managed school.

Faculty often misunderstand the need for accounting procedures and view requisitions, invoices, purchase orders, and receipts as unnecessarily cumbersome and designed to get in the way of their securing needed equipment and materials. Nevertheless, any good accounting system requires supporting or original documents such as bank deposit information, requisitions, and purchase orders. The accounting system exists in order for funds to be expended efficiently and in accordance with the plan incorporated in the budget document. In a sense, it also provides a history of spending and may be used to evaluate how the plan developed in the budget document is proceeding.

Financial resources are always in short supply and it is not likely that all the budgetary requests in support of the instructional objectives and school goals can be met in any one year. The principal interested in educational equity and the most efficient use of available dollars must keep in close touch with outgo, making sure that it is consistent with the budget plan and that sufficient funds remain for the purchase of high-priority items throughout the school year. Often improper accounting procedures result in an inadequate amount of money in April for the purchase of routine supplies necessary to complete the school year.

Most school districts use an accrual accounting system. This means that as soon as a purchase order is initiated or a requisition is approved, it is entered in the account book. Through such a process the principal knows immediately how much money remains to be expended in any particular account. This system prevents spending beyond the amount of money available.

The faculty and nonacademic personnel will not necessarily understand the intricacies of the accounting system and from time to time individuals on the faculty may view the entire process as a hindrance to the instructional program. Thus, the wise principal will spend some time in faculty and staff meetings—perhaps at a preschool workshop—informing the staff why good record keeping and accounting procedures are important to an instructional program. Beyond this, it is the principal's responsibility to make sure that the practices being followed are, in fact, efficient, that they do provide for quick delivery of materials and other services to the classroom, and that decision making with

MONTHLY STATEMENT OF RECEIPTS AND DISBURSEMENTS

Report for _____ 19 ____   Prepared by _____
                                                   Central
                                                   Treasurer

Account	Cash on Hand 1st of Month	Receipts This Month	Total	Disbursements	Balance End of Month
TOTAL	$_____	$_____	$_____	$_____	$_____

Reconciliation of Bank Statement

Bank balance as of _____ $_____
  Plus deposits not shown on statement _____ $_____
  Plus others _____ $_____
  Minus outstanding checks_____   TOTAL $_____
  _____ $_____
Book balance as of _____ $_____
_____ $_____

FIGURE 17–6.   A Monthly Report Form

respect to expenditures is consistent with the established instructional budget. Figure 17–7 depicts a flow of purchase requisitions.

Yet, a principal must make sure that emergency requests, unplanned expenses, unanticipated instructional opportunities, and similar last minute sorts of things that are important to a good teaching and learning climate do not get lost in a bureaucratic maze. A filmstrip that arrives a month after the completion of a unit is evidence of an unresponsive or inefficient administrative procedure. If this occurs often, it should not be surprising when teachers or staff attempt to circumvent established procedures. In other words, the principal should ensure that the procedures actually do facilitate rather than inhibit.

Regular Review

Once systematized, the accounting procedures require only regular monitoring by the principal. Receipt of materials ordered should be noted and materials must be properly inventoried. These are tasks easily performed by the school clerk with a little training. Keeping a separate set of books for district funds will provide the principal with a good

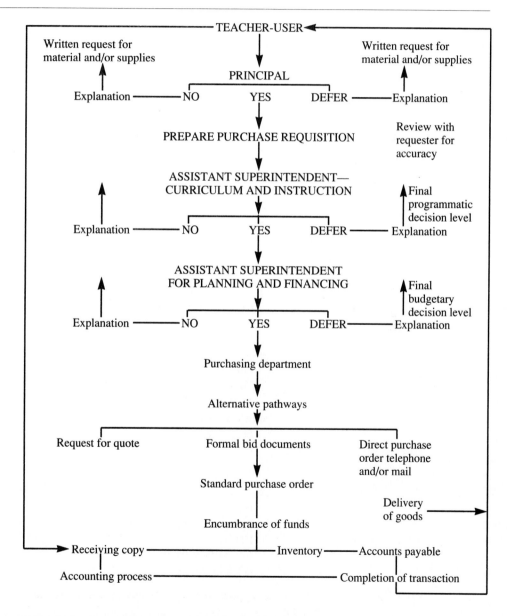

FIGURE 17–7.   Flow of a Purchase Requisition

check on expenditures against the accounts kept in the central business office. Mistakes are made from time to time and need to be rectified. In many school systems the central business office will supply the principal with periodic financial reports in the form of ledger sheet printouts. These are easily checked against the school's set of books for accuracy. Careful examination of these ledger sheets and a reconciliation with the school's books will provide sufficient financial records, especially if supplemented with additional notations by the principal.

Activity and Other Funds

Many elementary schools receive and distribute monies other than those disbursed by the district office. Such sources and accounts commonly include PTO funds, classroom accounts, insurance monies, candy sales, athletic funds, club treasuries, petty cash, funds from charity drives, and gifts. Individually the accounts are often quite small but collectively often amount to a considerable sum.

A separate set of books should be maintained for these funds, which are generally unaudited by the district. The unwary principal may get into trouble regarding these funds. No less precise bookkeeping procedures are required for these than for the district funds. Many states have passed special legislative acts requiring the establishment of orderly procedures for the administration of school activity funds. Some states as well as local school districts have developed careful policies and procedures to guide individual schools in such financial accounting. Figure 17–8 illustrates internal accounts typical of an elementary school.

MERCHANDISING SERVICE
    Bus Tickets
    Insurance
    Workbooks
PROFIT EARNING
    Coke Machine
    Pictures
    School Store
SPECIAL PURPOSE
    Field Trips
    Assemblies
    Hospitality
    Instructional Supplies
ORGANIZATIONS
    Faculty Club
    Student Council
    PTO
    Intramural Program
    All-School Chorus

FIGURE 17–8.   Outline of Typical Internal Ledger Accounts for an Elementary School

In general, specific procedures must be established to control the collection and disbursement of the activity funds. The following procedures provide a good guide:

1. Official receipts should be issued for all money received.

2. All money expended should be by check, except for small cash purchases made from the petty cash fund.

3. Supporting documents should be kept for all expenditures made.

4. Bank reconciliation statements should be made each month.

5. Monthly and yearly financial statements should be prepared.

6. An audit should be made each year and copies of the audit should be filed with persons having administrative authority for the school.

Figure 17–9 depicts a process for appropriate accounting of activity funds.

Consistent with good financial practice is requiring each group with an account administered by the school to file a simplified budget indicating anticipated income, anticipated expenditures, and persons designated to approve monies to be expended from the account. Further, all school employees who are responsible for the fund should be bonded, with the amount of the bond determined by the estimate of the amount of money the school will handle. Most school districts provide a bond covering all employees in the school system who are responsible for such funds. The principal should check whether or not this is so in a particular district.

Some school districts require the school principal to make a monthly report about the state of the internal funds in the school. Such a report commonly contains specific and general conditions of the accounts and expenditures. Whether or not this is specifically required by district policy, it is an important procedure for the principal, who should file the report in an appropriate place. It provides substantiation of the expenditure of funds and will assist in the annual audit. Figures 17–10 and 17–11 illustrate a monthly reporting procedure for activity accounts.

The Audit

Every elementary principal should have the internal account books audited annually by an outside accountant. The audit should be filed with the district office. An audit has two primary purposes: providing good professional suggestions for improving accounting procedures in the individual school and protecting all of those who have been responsible for handling school funds.

Before beginning a position as principal of an elementary school the incoming principal should insist on an audit of all funds as a means of being informed about current practices and improving these as necessary, as well as initially establishing the state of the accounts before assuming responsibility for them. The audit, in effect, red-lines the accounts, and the new principal can start with clear fiscal air.

Computers, Budgeting, and Accounting

Managing budgets has been greatly facilitated with the use of computers in the school office. Any number of spreadsheet and data base software programs are available to assist

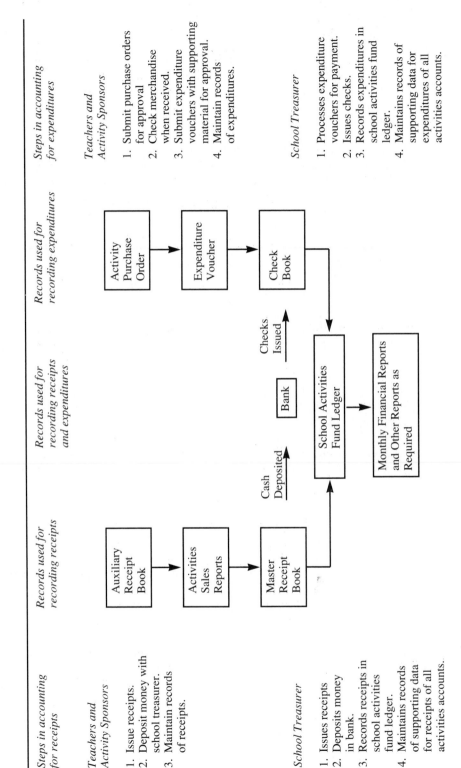

FIGURE 17–9. Procedures and Records Used in Accounting for School Activity

FINANCIAL REPORT

School: _____ Report for month of: _____

ASSETS

Cash on hand, petty cash $ _____

Cash in bank, checking   _____

Cash in bank, savings   _____

Other, accounts receivable, etc. (specify)   _____

TOTAL $ _____

FUND BALANCE

Activity	Beginning balance	Receipts Month	Month	Expenditures Month	Year to date	Ending balance
TOTALS						

We certify to the best of our knowledge and belief that this financial report reflects the true condition of the school activity fund.

_____   _____   _____
Principal   School Treasurer   Date

FIGURE 17–10.   Monthly Fiscal Report of the School Activity Fund

BANK RECONCILIATION

School ———————————————— Report for month of ——————————————

Bank ———————————————————————————————————————

Balance per bank statement ———————————————— $ ——————————
                              Date

Add   ——————————

  Deposits in transit   ——————————

  Other (specify)   ——————————

Total $ ——————————

Deduct

  Outstanding checks

Check Number	Date	Payee	Amount

$ ——————————

$ ——————————

Balance per general ledger ————————————————
                             Date

———————————— ———————————— ————————————
  Principal   School Treasurer   Date

FIGURE 17–11. Monthly Financial Report of the School Activity Fund

the principal in the collection, codification, and "if/then" analysis of appropriate data on which to base reasonable predictions and good arguments for budgets increases, reallocations, and staffing patterns. Excellent fund accounting software is also available.

Summary

The fiscal and record-keeping responsibilities of the principal are both active and supervisory. These responsibilities are active in the sense that, within the guidelines set by the district and the law, the principal establishes the procedures under which the record-keeping and budgeting processes are carried out. It is supervisory in that it is not usually the principal who actually performs the detailed functions of the school business office, but it is the principal who must monitor those staff members who are assigned these duties.

The degree of autonomy that a principal has with regard to the fiscal operation will vary depending on the policies of the particular school district. In some school systems virtually all financial decisions are made in the central administrative office. In other systems the principal has wide latitude—and heightened responsibility—in the construction of budget and in the allocation and expenditure of funds for personnel, operations, and even capital outlay. There is a decided move in the direction of greater decentralization of decision making in school systems and an increase in "site-based management." This has resulted in more fiscal decision-making authority for principals.

Financial resources are always in short supply and hard decisions must be made in allocating those monies that are available. Good financial planning—the kind of planning that delivers resources on a systematic basis to the point of greatest need—requires procedures for the involvement of the staff and the challenge to look beyond the current year. Incremental budgeting procedures, by definition, stress the status quo and assume that, except for different numbers of students, what was done last year should be done this year.

Once developed, the budget requires careful management. Sound accounting procedures are essential. The principal's role in this is primarily supervisory, but regular monitoring is necessary as is a firm understanding of district-wide fiscal policies.

Endnotes

1. Jim Barlow, financial columnist for the *Houston Chronicle* in a column describing the benefits of "expenditure control budgeting" and decentralized budget control in private and public organizations.

2. A *goal* is defined as a direction-setting statement of general worth that is timeless and not specifically measurable. An *objective* explicates the goal statement, is more specific, has a time dimension, and concludes with a series of indicators—subjective and objective—that will be accepted as evidence that the objective has been achieved.

Selected Readings

Bowman, Michael L., "Allocating Money for Priority Items—Easier with Participative Budgeting." *NASSP Bulletin, 70* (November, 1986), 5–9.

Brown, Daniel J., *Decentralization: The Administrators Guidebook to School District Change.* Newbury Park, CA: Corwin Press, 1991. (Chapters 6; 7; and 8 focus on fiscal planning and budget development.)

Candoli, Carl *et al., School Business Administration: A Planning Approach.* Boston: Allyn and Bacon, 1988.

Honeyman, David and Jenson, Rich, "School-Site Budgeting," *School Business Affairs,* 54, 2 (February, 1988), 14–18.

Ubben, Gerald C. and Hughes, Larry W., *The Principal: Creative Leadership for Effective Schools,* second edition. Boston: Allyn and Bacon, 1992. (See especially Chapters 15 and 16.)

Chapter *18*

Building and Facilities Management

*We keep this building clean and everyone pitches in. You can
see it's not a new building but that's no reason for disorder,
dull paint, and unpleasantness. Schools ought to be inviting
places. Takes some work to keep it that way, though.*[1]

Introduction

Properly housing the educational program and equipping the school are important
responsibilities that all of the staff shares. As indicated in the quotation that opens this
chapter, a poorly kept building, a building with unpleasant, colorless rooms, or a poorly
maintained site inhibit the development of a good educational program. These have a
most negative impact on staff and student morale and result, as well, in a loss of community pride. While all who live and work in the school and the community it serves share a
responsibility for the care of the building, the principal must assume ultimate responsibility and control. It's an important responsibility.

This chapter begins with a discussion of the instructional use of the school building.
Effective practices in both new and old facilities are discussed. How to care for the
school plant and school site and working well with custodians and maintenance personnel is the subject of the second part of the chapter. Supplies and equipment management
is yet another responsibility and the chapter concludes with a discussion of this subject.

Making the Most of the Facility

Whether the school building and site represents the latest in school design or reflects
architectural thinking in the 1950s, the principal's responsibility is the same: to ensure

the maximum efficient use of the structure to enhance the school program. Flexibility is an important consideration.

New Schools

Open-bay construction and the use of demountable walls are construction techniques that best meet the need for flexibility. Permanent construction provides large, carpeted, air-conditioned rooms equivalent in size to four or more regular classrooms. Demountable wall panels that press against the ceiling and floor, usually in four- or five-foot widths, can be used to create interior walls and doors where desired. These walls can be installed, moved, or removed by a custodian in a few hours. The walls are sound treated and can be purchased with chalkboard or bulletin board surfaces to make them extremely functional. The major advantage of demountable walls is the flexibility to create instructional areas of various sizes and shapes with low-cost, easy transition.

Folding walls are popular in many schools as a way to create flexible spaces. These are less desirable, however, because of high cost, permanency of location, and the tendency of most teachers to leave them either open or closed most of the time.

Open Space

The optimal flexible space is an open space large enough for three or more teachers and their children, with partial dividers such as bookcases and storage carts. Teachers can move these dividers at will and reorganize space several times each day if necessary. Open space is most functional with team teaching and flexible grouping.

There are many examples of schools designed with open spaces in which a traditional program was implemented. As a result, there was much dissatisfaction with the open areas. Space must follow function, and if traditional teaching is what one has in mind, the more traditional buildings are more appropriate. On the other hand, open areas enhance team teaching, individualized instruction, and flexible grouping. The major advantages of the open area are:

- The entire curriculum for a group of children can be housed in one area.
- The open area allows for the easy movement of children from one activity to another.
- It allows for great variation in group size from one child to the entire group.
- It allows one teacher to have visual supervision of the entire open area, freeing other teachers for small group work.
- It allows teachers to coordinate their instructional activities easily with one another because they maintain visual contact.

There are some disadvantages as well:

- There are often higher noise levels in the instructional area, because of teaching styles and greater student movement and activity.
- Some teachers do not like the disturbance caused by other teachers teaching in the same area. Most often the problem is one of inappropriate teacher style for the

open area or a lack of team coordination. Good individualized instruction and team coordination will solve this problem.

Space Utilization

Space utilization within the open area is important. An example of good space utilization coordinated with team planning, individualized instruction, flexible grouping, and a varied curriculum is shown in Figure 18–1. Each teacher is responsible for setting up and maintaining one-fourth of the room. Each area includes individual learning centers as well as an area for small groups to meet. Teacher desks are located near the center of the room so teachers can provide supervision of most of the room from their desks. Learning centers are built around the perimeter of the room, adjacent to the wall area for display purposes. Children have access to the entire instructional area, and a broadly based curriculum with a great variety and abundance of learning centers is available. Each learning center has space for student seating and study.

Teachers use the small-group seating area in their portion of the room for skill groups. Supervisory duties for learning centers have teachers moving throughout the entire area; it is possible to schedule large group lessons anywhere in the area. Teachers have instructional and supervisory responsibilities throughout the room.

The Use of Traditional Buildings for Flexible Programming

With a little planning, traditional buildings with separate classroom areas can be used for flexible programs. The most important factor in developing a flexible program in a traditional building is giving teaching teams and students adjacent rooms. Preferably, classrooms should be immediately across the hall. As shown in Figure 18–2, teachers may then set up corridor boundaries for the students and operate the classrooms and the adjacent corridor space as if they were one large open area.

Teachers as well as students should share assigned spaces with each other, moving about as needed. Specific assignment of space will vary from program to program. Greatest flexibility can be maintained if teachers do not look upon any particular room as their room. One way to do this is to organize classrooms by function, using one classroom as a quiet independent-study activity area, another for noisy independent-study activity, and a third for small-group activities. A fourth area may also serve for small-group activities and as the location for teachers' desks (Figure 18–2). Learning centers or small-group activities can also be set up in corridors if fire regulations permit.

Renovating Existing Facilities

A conventional school building can often be renovated to provide some larger instructional spaces. Removing walls between classrooms or corridors can create a series of two or more classrooms. Occasionally spaces as large as four or more classrooms can be developed. With the addition of carpeting, the improvement of lighting, and the addition of air conditioners, attractive open areas can be made available for flexible programs. New flexible furniture such as trapezoidal tables and movable bookcases also add to the attractiveness and function of a renovated building.

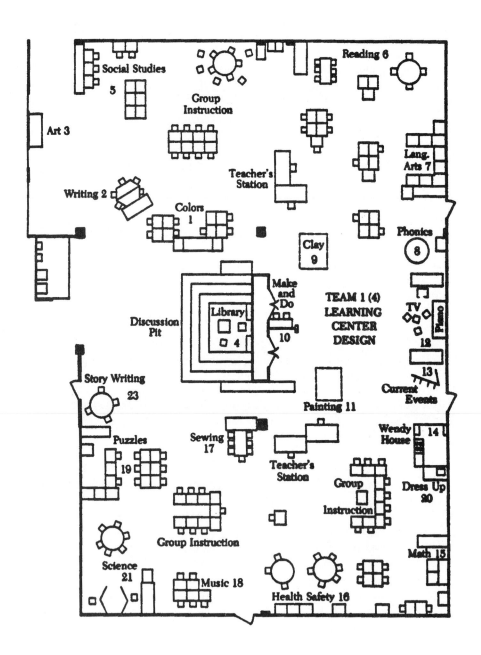

FIGURE 18–1.   Space Utilization in an Open-Space Classroom

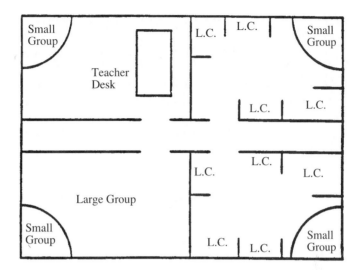

FIGURE 18–2.   Open-Space Classrooms Arranged by Function

Almost any school building, if utilized properly, can be made functional for the instructional program, but the program must be developed first. The building is a tool to enhance the curriculum and facilitate the implementation of the instructional program. Care must be taken not to allow the building to become a stumbling block because of a fixation on previous usage.

Care of the School Plant

The principal is not going to spend the day with hammer in hand and a shovel under an arm, but the principal must assume the ultimate responsibility for operating the building at maximum efficiency. There are two important reference groups: classified employees such as custodians, cleaning personnel, cooks, and kitchen personnel who are assigned to the building; and the school-district maintenance department.[2] Working effectively with nonacademic personnel to help them do their job requires the same kinds of human relations skills as working with academic staff. Further, as in any decision-making process, the counsel and advice of these persons should be sought and their expertise and insights utilized.

A recent survey of fifty-three "showcase" schools in the Houston Independent School District revealed thirteen practices which have resulted in well-kept buildings and grounds:

- The principal walks around the building frequently.
- Litter abatement or housekeeping is discussed at teachers' meetings.
- Principal sees that each member of the custodial staff has a specific work schedule.

- Custodial staff sweeps halls regularly during school day.
- Custodial staff inspects and cleans restrooms regularly during school day.
- Custodial staff is specifically instructed to pick up litter in and around the school on a daily basis.
- Overall appearance of school is a criterion for evaluating custodial staff members.
- Student organizations assist in responsibility for keeping school clean.
- Parents are involved in effort to maintain or beautify the campus.
- School newspapers print reminders of neatness, cleanliness, trash pickup, and litter control.
- Students are reprimanded for littering.
- Rules restrict the removal of food and beverages from the cafeteria area.
- Teachers stress maintaining the environment as part of their regular curriculum.

Keeping the school site and the building clean and litter-free is everyone's job, but it is up to the principal to set the tone and institute a system so that this occurs. Figure 18–3 depicts a checklist to identify potential trouble spots and provide corrective action.

The School Site

The high cost of land is often reflected in small school sites and inadequate play areas. This is especially true in urban areas where the children are often most in need of wide open spaces in which to play and experience nature. Nevertheless, there are maintenance and development responsibilities that accrue to the principal regardless of the size of the site. Frequent discussions with the custodial staff can result in maximum effective use of the site.

As a minimum, the site should be kept free of debris and safe, tasks that require daily attention by the custodial staff and regular inspection by an administrator. Playground equipment must be kept in good repair or taken out of service. Preventive maintenance of equipment and the playground surface is the most economical and sensible practice. No principal should tolerate less than this minimum; daily attention to the site will result in attractiveness, if not beauty.

It is essential that any debris be removed daily—more often if at all possible. Mobilizing student service organizations to help with this is a practical approach. A modest investment in additional rubbish removal may also pay dividends. At least weekly there should be a preventive maintenance check made by the principal or designee and any necessary follow-up made.

If the principal is fortunate to be the executive of a building located on a site that is not entirely composed of macadam, some creative opportunities may exist to enhance the attractiveness of the site while providing some excellent educational possibilities.

Help in developing or redeveloping a site may come from such diverse sources as the public library, the United States Department of Agriculture District Office, agricultural extension agents, appropriate university departments, or private landscape architectural firms with some commitment to public service. Such development need not be expensive, and free labor may be available from the PTO or similar organizations, including a local garden club. Perhaps a "partnership" with a local business or civic club could be arranged that would include beautification of school grounds.

Appearance   Yes   No
- Building is well kept in overall appearance.   _____   _____
- No litter is on the grounds.   _____   _____
- Grass is mown; shrubs are trimmed.   _____   _____
- Doormats are in use.   _____   _____
- Walls are void of graffiti.   _____   _____
- Hallways are swept.   _____   _____
- Trash cans are placed in accessible locations.   _____   _____
- Restrooms are clean and stocked with appropriate paper
  products.   _____   _____
- Classrooms are clean and orderly.   _____   _____
- Cafeteria/auditorium is free of food waste and
  wrappings   _____   _____
- Service area is without rubbish and debris.   _____   _____

Items sensed, but not observed
- The clean environment is the result of concerted effort,
  not happenstance.   _____   _____
- Custodial staff is efficient.   _____   _____
- Principal spends time out of office working with staff
  and making constructive suggestions.   _____   _____
- Good student habits related to building and grounds
  upkeep are reinforced.   _____   _____

Documentation
- School needs are assessed with regard to achieving the
  goal of a clean campus.   _____   _____
- There are specific work schedules for custodial staff.   _____   _____
- Custodial evaluation includes appearances of building.   _____   _____
- Budget shows allocation for cleaning supplies.   _____   _____
- Housekeeping responsibilities are outlined in school
  handbook.   _____   _____
- There is an agenda item for staff meetings re litter
  abatement or housekeeping procedures.   _____   _____
- There is a specific program directed at litter abatement.   _____   _____
- Student groups are assigned specific duties for keeping
  the school clean.   _____   _____
- Parent groups have donated plants, equipment, paint, or
  manpower to beautification project.   _____   _____

FIGURE 18–3. School Site and Building Maintenance Checklist

In all but the most macadamized of school sites, the development of a land laboratory to enhance the science programs as well as provide other kinds of educational experiences for children is a good possibility. The size of the site will only determine the nature and kind of flora to be cultivated. Help and inexpensive plantings are readily available, especially from the Department of Agriculture, specifically the Soil Conservation Office. It is possible for schools to become members of a Soil Conservation District by simple application by the school board. Trees and bushes may be purchased inexpensively with Soil Conservation District help. That office also will assist in the proper placement of plants and give instruction on care and nourishment. Other help in the development of a land laboratory is also available from some of the same agencies mentioned previously in the discussion of appropriate landscaping of the school site.

Maintenance of the Building

The inside of the building requires the same sort of attention to create an attractive and safe learning-living-working environment for pupils and staff. Even old buildings can be attractively maintained. Many districts have a director of maintenance and operations and employ skilled persons to respond to refurbishment and major maintenance needs of all buildings in the district. However, the principal, working with the custodial staff, must identify those major needs ahead of emergency conditions to ensure that they are systematically attended to. Even in large districts the day-to-day repairs and light maintenance functions may fall to the building custodial staff.

Be careful about these requests, though. A district-level director of maintenance advises, "[Our] custodians are not trained to perform maintenance or 'grounds-type' tasks. There is the possibility of causing personal harm as well as property damage when individuals attempt to perform tasks for which they are not trained." Moreover, he went on, "There could be a problem if a custodian earning one wage performs a task for which another person has been hired at a higher wage to perform. The custodian could then demand the higher wage."[3] The best advice is to check district policy.

Working with Custodial and Maintenance Personnel

The custodial and maintenance staff should be recognized as a part of the education team. Custodians, maintenance personnel, cooks, aides, and secretaries all have important parts to play in the development of the productive learning climate. Frequently, the contributions of this portion of the staff are not fully recognized. Unless attention is directed to the motivation, needs, and contributions of support personnel, probably at best a wary truce will exist between those personnel and the professional staff.

Evidence of such a condition will be found in the not-so-sly digs each will direct at the other in private meetings and in less than adequate services being rendered. Paper towel dispensers may always seem to be out of towels, corners of the cafeteria left unswept, inordinately long waits may occur for equipment to be delivered or repaired, among any number of other examples that any reader of this book could supply, are all indicators that all is not well. In some instances, of course, this may be because of a lack of skill or a lack of clear understanding about organizational expectations. If so, that should be quickly remedied—either with on-the-job training or replacement. More often than not, however, it is a failure of the administrator and professional staff to recognize the contributions possible from a well-informed support staff.

Engaging support personnel in the same kind of goal-setting and problem-solving activities that have been suggested for the professional staff is equally appropriate for the support staff. Administration by edict works no better with custodians and maintenance personnel than it does with the certificated staff. At the beginning of each school year the principal needs to meet with the custodial staff to chart the long-range objectives for building maintenance for the year and to work out a systematic plan for addressing these. Much of the custodial schedule will be routine and daily or weekly in nature, of course. Some will not be. Also, the performance of even the routine custodial functions will be impacted by such things as special events and even the time of day. Cooperative development of the work schedule is desirable and will result in the important things getting done, getting done well, and in a timely manner.

Scheduling the Work

As noted above, routine work schedules and well-understood expectations are important to the maintenance of the school plant. Time lines and systematic planning for the completion of the major maintenance and repair projects of the year need to be supplemented with a daily and weekly time schedule to ensure that the routine custodial and maintenance tasks are taken care of.

An example of a work schedule for a head custodian in an elementary school can be seen in Figure 18–4. Times are only approximations, of course. These schedules are best developed in concert with the staff so that the estimates are reasonable and appropriate to any unique features of the building.

Particular attention should be given to common internal building flaws such as inadequate lighting fixtures, roof or wall leaks, dirt in the corners, broken windows, or torn sashes. The entire staff, including instructional staff, should be asked to assist in identifying maintenance needs and reporting them immediately to the office for attention. Some defects, such as a torn sash or graffiti on a restroom wall, for example, breed others at an almost exponential rate until a major effort and expense is required. Overnight one torn sash becomes sixteen torn sashes, some torn to the point where no repair is possible. Similarly, one clever but obscene statement on a restroom wall provokes others at a geometric rate, to the point where the entire wall has to be repainted.

To keep regular and routine tabs on the condition of the building and equipment requires a commitment to do so, a simple survey checklist, and everyone's cooperation. Figure 18–5 depicts one district's inspection checklist. Many times annoying maintenance defects or disabled equipment go unrepaired because a teacher or other staff member has not reported the problem and it has gone unnoticed by the custodial staff. There needs to be some direct and simple way to get this information into the system and to alleviate the problem. The "It Needs Fixing" notice shown in Figure 18–6 works in many schools. It requires only a drop-box at the custodian's desk.

Supplies and Equipment Management

A major responsibility of the elementary school principal will be securing, inventorying, and allocating supplies and equipment to facilitate the educational program. It is essential

FREQUENCY OF SERVICE

SCHOOL: _____

NAME: _____

DESCRIPTION OF SERVICE	7 – 8:45	8:45 – 9:00	9 – 9:15	9:15 – 10	10 – 10:15	10:15 – 10:30	10:30 – 11	11 – 1:30	1:30 – 2	2 – 2:15	2:15 – 3:30
Unlock bldg. and turn off alarm	■										
Sweep all entrances & put out mats	■										
Police entire bldg.	■										
Police all restrooms & flush out commodes	■										
Drop cafeteria tables down		■									
Dust mop cafeteria, front & back hall			■								
Break											
Clean glass				■							
Set up for lunch					■						
Repolice restrooms before lunch						■					
Lunch							■				
Cafeteria Duty								■			
Dust mop back & front halls									■		
Recheck restrooms & clean wash areas										■	
Break											
Clean downstairs lounge											■
Clean upstairs lounge											■
Recheck restrooms & clean wash areas											■
Clean drinking fountain in cafeteria											■

FIGURE 18–4. Day Schedule for Head Custodian: Elementary School

Source: Gerald C. Ubben and Larry W. Hughes, *The Principal: Creative Leadership for Effective Schools* (Boston: Allyn and Bacon, 1992), p. 375.

Principal:	School:	Custodian:	Date:

Entrances:	S	G	A	P			Windows:	S	G	A	P
Walks:						Furniture:				
Floor Mats:						Fixtures:				
Door Facings:						Teachers Station:				
Glass:						Cafetorium:				
Transoms:						Floors:				
Door tracks:						Windows:				
Offices:						Fixtures:				
Doors:						Lights:				
Facings:						Fountains:				
Walls:						Machines:				
Floors:						Doors:				
Furniture:						Fixtures:				
Windows:						Storerooms:				
Fixtures:						Walls:				
Trash:						Tool racks:				
Hallways:						Supplies:				
Floors:						Equipment:				
Walls:						Restrooms:				
Lights:						Floors:				
Water Fountains:						Walls:				
Learning Center:						Partitions:				
Shelves:						Windows:				
Floor:						Commodes:				
Furniture:						Urinals:				
Glass:						Wash basins:				
Door:						Mirrors:				
Classrooms:						Floor Drains:				
Door facings:						Ventilation:				
Walls:						Lights:				
Lights:						Furniture:				
Floors:						GARBAGE AREA:				
Boards:						INCINERATOR:				
COMMENTS:										

S - SUPERIOR
G - GOOD
A - AVERAGE
P - POOR

FIGURE 18–5.   Custodian-Maintenance Survey: Building Inspection Checklist

Source: Gerald C. Ubben and Larry W. Hughes, *The Principal: Creative Leadership for Effective Schools* (Boston: Allyn and Bacon, 1992), p. 377.

to provide quantities of soft goods (supplies) and the appropriate number of hard goods (equipment) so that they are available ahead of educational needs and secured in the most economical manner possible. It is equally important to provide a management system that won't require the principal to spend an inordinate amount of time on this function. If the school operates under a budget system such as described in Chapter 17, the selection and purchase of needed supplies and equipment in support of educational goals can become routinized. At most it will require a regular review to see that (1) anticipated needs are met on schedule; (2) estimated coasts remain within budget; (3) appropriate discounts allowed by suppliers are taken; (4) inventories are adequate; and (5) equipment is appropriately tagged, recorded, conveniently stored, and used.

Flexible educational programming requires a great variety of educational materials and equipment, making the task of management somewhat complex. Nevertheless, even though managing supplies and equipment has become more complex, the expanding use of minicomputers in the school office has greatly improved the quality of the planning and monitoring effort.

Computerized Data-Based Management Systems

School records are easily stored and manipulated by using microcomputers and any of a number of data base software programs. Employing a microcomputer is especially effective for inventories of school equipment and supplies. With the proper program, projecting needs and costs becomes a simple matter of a pressed key or two. Equally easy to maintain are records of special projects and programs, including such building management issues as energy usage, food service, and sports program schedules.

Using an office microcomputer for building management has value well beyond being an efficient filing system. To ensure good building management it is desirable—even necessary—to be able to conduct an analysis of practices, procedures, and costs. This can be accomplished with those software programs that combine record keeping with data analysis.

Storage and Inventory Control

The day-to-day needs of instructional staff are such that amounts of common educational supplies such as copier paper, art paper, crayons, or chalk can be relatively easily predicted and kept in sufficient reserve to handle needs over a period of a few months. One should avoid taking up valuable storage space with an inordinate oversupply, but a quick comparison of projected needs and past experiences should be sufficient to avoid this. The school secretary or other designated person can have responsibility for ensuring that the appropriate amount of day-to-day supplies is available. This task need not and should not require much attention by the principal. An inventory control procedure will permit routine replenishment of supplies. Adequate inventories of educational materials and supplies that are unique to special aspects of the program can be maintained by the person responsible for that special aspect of the program. Replenishment of these supplies should also be simply a matter of routine.

For convenience, most educational equipment should be housed centrally in the building. Supplies used daily or frequently in the classroom or learning spaces should be located throughout the building. For example, equipment such as overheads and tape recorders should be located in almost all of the teaching and learning spaces or classrooms. Similarly, equipment and material supportive of the science program, social studies program, or the arts should be located in that part of the building designated for those programs.

All equipment, regardless of where it is housed, should be tagged or identified in some manner and inventoried. Further, equipment must be kept in good repair and staff should be aware of their responsibility to report immediately any malfunction of equipment. The principal can give each teacher a supply of notices for needed repairs or equipment malfunctions. The notice can identify the particular piece of equipment and describe the nature of the malfunction. These slips should be turned in immediately to the office for action. Figure 18–6 is a sample of such a form.

HI!
CLAMOR HERE,
YOUR MAINTENANCE MOLLUSK

It's my task to hammer away at any jobs that need fixing in your room. Is there anything that requires attention?

Don't clam up now.
We want a smooth sailing ship.

Please fill out this form and leave at the custodial desk for quick service.

Room: _____

Service Required: _____

_____

_____

_____

_____

For immediate needs, please call the office.

White: office
Pink: staff

FIGURE 18–6.   "It Needs Fixing" Notice

Source: Gerald C. Ubben and Larry W. Hughes, *The Principal: Creative Leadership for Effective Schools* (Boston: Allyn and Bacon, 1992), p. 373.

Staff Work Areas

Every school needs an instructional staff workroom for the preparation of transparencies, overlays, displays, and so forth. Large school systems may have educational technicians to handle the preparation of elaborate audiovisual aids, but often the school staff itself will want to be able to prepare simple kinds of visuals for immediate use. Supplies and equipment must be provided to make this possible. The production of less elaborate audiovisual aids can be the responsibility of paraprofessionals or parent volunteers.

Using Equipment

A school will often have very expensive equipment that is not used or is underused by staff. Many times the reason for this is that the staff has not been trained in the use of the equipment or does not understand its instructional possibilities. Thus, instructional and staff support services personnel must receive training in the use and function of the equipment available in the school. Many principals take extensive advantage of the expertise of sales personnel and technicians of the various suppliers and have these individuals available at inservice workshops to work with staff to put the equipment to best use.

Central Warehousing

Supply management in school systems is frequently handled at the central-office level. Even when the principal has a considerable amount of responsibility with respect to supply management, large systems will have a central warehouse from which most supplies and equipment are obtained. There is great advantage to this because systems can develop standardized lists of materials, with precise specifications. These can be periodically reviewed to provide maximum use of school system dollar resources.

Certain kinds of educational materials can be more efficiently housed centrally in the school district. Films, filmstrips, or audio- and videotapes that are used throughout the system but are not required in any individual unit of study except on an infrequent basis are best catalogued, inventoried, and housed centrally in the school district. Where this is the case, teachers most understand the need for more lead time in requisitioning and securing these for classroom use. This is not to say that last-minute requests should not be acted upon to the degree possible—only an unhealthy school system characterized by abundant bureaucratization cannot respond to unplanned "teaching moments."

Summary

Research on practices in effective schools done by the Northwest Regional Educational Laboratory included a finding about facilities management. Schools that were effective were invariably clean and attractive. Any damages were repaired immediately. There was obvious attention to the influence that the physical environment has on learner outcomes. The age or design of the building was not important; what was important was that much effort was expanded to make the environment safe and pleasant.[4]

The physical environment of the school contributes mightily to the learning environment. An attractive, well-kept, clean school building is essential. It is the principal's responsibility to see to it that custodians and other service personnel know what their jobs are and to arrange work conditions so that they can conduct their work with dispatch. Similarly, it is important that the principal provide the appropriate response mechanisms so that teachers can go about their work with the right equipment at the right time.

Endnotes

1. Dr. Sylvia Valverde, Principal, Shearn Elementary School, Houston Independent School District.

2. Different school districts are organized differently, however. In many districts, custodians and cafeteria personnel are within the jurisdiction of the principal. Some districts have a more centralized operation with these classified employees and others such as maintenance workers, craftspeople, and clerical staff selected and assigned by a central office personnel division. No matter what the structure and delivery system for custodial, maintenance, and other support services, if it happens in the school or on the school site, it is the principal's responsibility to see that it is done right.

3. Gary Butler, Klein Independent School District, Spring, Texas.

4. *Effective Schooling Practices: A Research Synthesis*. Portland, OR: Northwest Regional Educational Laboratory, 1984.

Selected Readings

Castadi, Basil, *Educational Facilities: Planning, Modernization, and Management*. Boston: Allyn and Bacon, 1987.

Foley, Dorothy M., "Restructuring with Technology." *Principal*, 72, 3 (January, 1993), 30–33.

Futral, Karen K., "The Principal's Role in School Renovation." *Principal, 72*, 3 (January, 1993), 30–33.

Kantlehner, Jerry, "Computerizing Custodial Services." *School Business Affairs, 49*, 2 (February 1983): 38+.

Natale, Joseph L., "A Design for Administering School Maintenance Programs." *Planning and Changing, 14*, 2 (Summer 1983): 83–90.

Shimanoff, Perry S., "Custodial Management Training for School Principals." *American School and University, 52*, 5 (January 1980): 9–10.

Ubben, Gerald C. and Hughes, Larry W., *The Principal: Creative Leadership for Effective Schools*. Boston: Allyn and Bacon, 1992, Chapter 16.

Wheeler, Louanne M., "New Designs for American Schools." *Principal, 72*, 3 (January 1993): 17–21.

Chapter *19*

Public Relations Processes and Techniques

> *Principals need to be trained in how to deal with the media.*
> *Too often they fear us and avoid us. We're not ogres. All we want is*
> *accurate information. . . . And, school district central offices do everyone a*
> *disservice when they discourage principals from talking with us. I lose*
> *patience when the response I get for an interview or for information is for me*
> *to check with the central office. That's just a runaround. . . . Talk to us.*[1]

Introduction

The reporter's lament cited above is only part of the story, of course, but it is worth heeding. "Talk to us"—that's what public relations—not just media relations—is all about. And "listen to us" finishes the equation. The focus of this chapter is on how to develop effective public relations programs, programs that contain both one-way information dissemination processes and two-way communication processes. Both are essential to improving the relationship of schools and the communities these schools serve.

Those who are at the beginning of their career as principals are often astonished at the amount of time and energy that must be devoted to interactions with school parents and patrons, to representatives of various community agencies, to any of a myriad of groups and individuals representing this or that "good cause" or point of view. Beyond this are the planned and unplanned interactions with the electronic and print media. Effective school building administrators have learned—sometimes not without pain— that cordial relations with a knowledgeable community are essential for the materiel and financial resources and the broadly based support conducive to effective schooling.

The "Public" is Plural

There is no such thing as a "public opinion." There are various "publics" and these publics have opinions about everything and, most pertinent to the concepts to be expressed in this chapter, especially about things that have to do with schooling. Attitudes and orientations of the citizenry are influenced by such things as previous experiences with schools and school administrators, membership in various reference groups; economic status, political philosophy; whether they have school age children or not; physical, emotional, and intellectual needs of children they care the most about; religious beliefs and ethnicity; among other factors.

The point is that the school public relations program must take into account the various publics. This will require different strategies and mechanisms depending on the nature of the public relations issue and a targeted public.

There is evidence of a gradual decline in the confidence Americans express in their schools. A salient finding in a relatively recent study was that schools that retained the confidence of their publics went beyond a standard public relations "get the word out" mode and moved into a "marketing" mode. The marketing mode is designed to sell schooling as a good product.[2] Such an effort is directed toward raised levels of involvement in an effort to get people closer to their schools.

Public relations and marketing endeavors may take several forms. Successful programs will employ a variety of media and methods, and an alert principal will suit the message to be conveyed to the most appropriate medium. Both one-way and two-way information dissemination processes need to be employed.

One-Way Public Relations Efforts

There are several one-way methods to publicize some aspect or activity in the school. The hope is that the message will reach the intended receivers, be read or listened to, and acted upon in some kind of positive way. The one-way nature of the medium used, however, does not permit much opportunity for the broadcaster to find out whether the message was received.

Newspapers and Other Mass Media

Few communities are not served by at least a weekly newspaper, and no community is outside the reach of radio and television. The following discussion will focus on newspapers, primarily because of their more localized nature and because the activities of the school principal are more likely to involve working with newspapers. Regardless of which mass medium is utilized, however, the same principles are appropriate.

Newspapers vary from weekly or biweekly advertisers with perhaps a few columns reporting highly localized activities, to urban dailies with several editions. Similarly, depending on the community, a principal's role may vary from writing news releases, published mostly word for word, to meeting with news reporters who will recast the stories in their own words.

In any case, the development of good relations with the working press is essential. Reporters or editors will ask principals for information about developing stories or news items more often than for stories containing general information about what's going on in the schools.

The news media have their problems, too. Newspapers and television stations are businesses, with advertising to sell, bills to pay, and subscribers to satisfy. Further, news editors deal with many pressure groups, championing various causes. School administrators are often surprised to learn that only 30 percent of newspaper space is devoted to stories and 70 percent to advertising. This percentage affects the amount of school news that will get printed.

Reporters have different assignments. On large city newspapers with large circulations, most frequently one or more persons may have the "education beat." These special assignment reporters can be expected to have a greater understanding of schools, school problems, and educational jargon. Smaller dailies use general assignment reports, i.e., reporters who have a variety of responsibilities only one of which includes school news. Or, these reporters may be assigned news beats on an as-needed basis. Thus, the principal may be faced with a person who has only a casual understanding of what schools are all about. In any case, the principal should not assume he or she is talking with someone who readily understands the "in-house" vocabulary or even understands very well the issue the reporter was sent to investigate.

Backgrounding

It is important to have available any printed material that will give reporters useful background information so that they can properly "frame" the story. Note-taking is an uncertain art even among reporters for whom it is a tool of the trade. Written material will help clarify points the principal wants to make. And, it is important to remember, *nothing is really off the record.* If the principal doesn't want his or her conjectures and opinions reported, then these should not be stated. "Just the facts, Ma'am," is the sensible approach.

Reporters complain that public agencies tend to engage only in "gold-star" story writing. Many school administrators are only too eager to publicize praiseworthy news items but back away from legitimate adverse criticism. An adverse story is legitimate news and when such a story breaks, the school official and the news media both have a job to do. Covering up a weakness or refusing to respond to a legitimate inquiry about a potentially embarrassing situation can only lead to bad press relations and a widening credibility gap.

The latitude a principal has with the press will depend in great part on the particular school district's press policy. News media personnel, however, are most sensitive to what they perceive to be censorship and normally respond negatively to the suggestion that every story or every interview must be cleared with the central office. A policy that requires all school personnel to refer reporters and editors to the central office rather than answer questions or that sends the news media to the central office for all information, if employed rigidly, will damage press relations. Obviously, fast-breaking news items of a potentially explosive nature will require discretion on the part of the school principal, but to attempt to close off news from the individual school building to members of the press will do little more than create antagonism.

Routine Story Development

There are many things going on in and about the school that would be of interest to the publics and perhaps to the mass media. To capitalize on the media's problems with "slow news days" and get the school's story out, it is important to have a bank of potentially good stories. The use of a School News Item File such as that depicted in Figure 19–1 is a convenient way to develop the news bank.

Each staff member should have a supply of the news items forms to jot down those projects that could be especially interesting and regularly send these to the principal's office. The principal can then file these reports in a folder labeled according to the kind of project, and a news reporter can simply review the files, selecting any particular items to follow up. This helps both the reporter, whose responsibility it is to find news, and the principal whose responsibility it is to supply news but not necessarily to write it.

SCHOOL NEWS ITEM FILE

Type of News Item:

_____ Curriculum Project

_____ Activities of Staff

_____ School Awards

_____ Pupil Activities (field trips, special recognition, etc.)

_____ New or Interesting Instructional Techniques

_____ Continuing Difficult Problems

_____ Other

Title of Project or Item:

Description of Project or Item:

Persons Involved: (how many, and who—names, addresses, titles, etc.)

Dollars Involved and Sources of These Dollars:

Who to Contact for Further Information:

FIGURE 19–1.

Media personnel have their jobs to perform. Understanding the nature of those jobs and the demands that these place on reporters will help the principal be better able to work effectively with representatives of the various media. The following list describes important issues for the principal to consider.

Working Effectively with the Media[3]

- Give reporters story ideas and information but remember that editors often decide what to cover.
- Be aware of when the reporters' deadlines fall and balance the time of releases so that morning and afternoon papers get an equal share and similar balance exists with regard to print and electronic media.
- Articles about scheduled events need to be prepared well in advance, with photographs of speakers or others involved in the event provided.
- News releases should be written to conform to the requirements of the different media. Releases for radio or television usually must be shorter, more repetitious, and in a more conversational style than those for newspapers.
- Don't provoke reporters with a "no comment" type of statement. Help the reporter write potentially adverse stories by giving all of the relevant facts.
- Have any appropriate background information available to reporters ahead of the story.
- Invite newspersons—reporters and editors—to the school for lunch and periodic tours without trying to sell them on a story at that time. Get them acquainted with the school scene.

Newsletters, Bulletins, and Report Cards

Frequently the principal and the school staff will attempt to communicate with the home and other agencies through newsletters and bulletins. These can be useful. If newsletters and bulletins are to be employed, the format should be simple, the information conveyed should be concisely written and to the point, free of educational jargon, and the method of getting them home should be via the mails. Newsletters sent home with children often do little but contribute to the neighborhood litter problem. If the newsletter is not produced with appropriate care and printed in an attractive manner, it is simply not worth the bother. The News Item File is a good way to keep information fresh and timely.

The Fog Index

Good writing skill is an important tool for the school principal. Newsletters, memos, and letters to patrons require clear written expression. Writing well requires careful consideration of who it is that will receive the message.[4]

Straightforward sentences, unencumbered nouns and verbs, and common language are what is required. Being conscious of the bi- and multi-linguality of many communities brings even another requirement. Simplicity, lack of clutter, and avoidance of jargon and pedagogical phraseology are necessary to good communication.

This can be done without "talking down" to people. Newspapers accomplish it daily. Principals can test their messages for clarity and ease of understanding by analyzing these with the "Fog Index" depicted in Figure 19–2. Messages should not rely on the recipient having a high school, much less a college education. The nearer messages come to a sixth or seventh grade reading level the more likelihood that it will be understood by all.[5]

THE FOG INDEX

1. Average the number of words per sentence in your message.

2. Count the number of words having three or more syllables.

3. Add the two factors above and multiply by 0.4. This will give you the fog index and corresponds roughly to the number of years of schooling a person would require to read the message with ease and understanding.

FIGURE 19–2. The Fog Index

Report Cards

Report cards are often overlooked as public relations mechanisms, but they are the single most regular way in which schools communicate with the home. Typically, both teachers and parents like them to be uncomplicated to simplify reporting and understanding. Yet consideration of all of the ways in which a child is growing, developing, and learning defies summing up with a single letter grade. Thus, the development of an appropriate reporting procedure will require careful study by the staff and include the use of a faculty-layperson committee to develop a report form that is easy to understand but also contains important kinds of information relative to the child's progress.

The Message Was Sent—What Happened?

The *co* in communication means a closed loop. That is, communication means that the message was not only sent but that it was received and responded to in a way that indicates it was understood. Following are important questions to ask when examining the quality of one-way informational devices:

1. If the message was received, was it read?
2. If it was read, was it understood?
3. If it was understood, was it understood in the right spirit?
4. If it was understood in the right spirit, will it be acted upon in a positive way?
5. How do you know? (The effort must be regularly evaluated.)

Care should also be taken to recognize the multilingual nature of many school communities.

Two-Way Public Relations Efforts

Many formal mechanisms provide two-way information sharing. However, nothing about these mechanisms makes them automatically effective. Careful organization is required. In this section several mechanisms to provide interactive public relations are described.

Working with Parents

The most important referent group in the school community will probably be parents. Too often formal relationships with parents are left to the one-way devices described in the previous section, with a PTA or PTO serving as the sole two-way network.

Parent-Teacher Organizations

Parent-teacher organizations can provide a useful avenue for interaction between school and community if the meetings are organized to provide an opportunity for both formal and informal interaction and if the organization is given important tasks to perform. The key would seem to be *active involvement in significant tasks*. Parent organizations, just like other community organizations, are competing for the time of their members. Whether or not a parent elects to spend time Thursday evening at a PTO meeting will depend upon whether or not that time is viewed as productively occupied. No one wants to give time to an activity that is dull, nonproductive, and not even entertaining.

A working PTO will spend less time meeting formally and more time in subgroups considering important tasks to be performed around the school and the community. Organizing business-industry-education days for the career development program in the school, developing after-school programs for the children and adults in the community, training paraprofessionals, and working on curriculum review teams are the kinds of activities developed by an effective parent-school organization.

Another problem is the nature of the membership itself. Many principals have suddenly realized that even though their school may serve a heterogeneous population, the active membership of the parent group is composed almost entirely of those who reflect only a single social, economic, or ethnic group. Thus, the principal should examine the membership rolls of the parent organization carefully. If these organizations are to be used as effective school-community relations devices, a membership that reflects the community at large becomes most important. If those who come to the meetings are the same kinds of people and reflect a consistent ideological unity, then the chances are that important opinions are not being secured nor is there an information exchange with the broader community.

One way to find out the degree to which the parent group reflects the population of the school is to conduct a modified survey about the PTA/PTO memberships. Such a survey might be conducted as described in Figure 19–3.

Such a study can determine whether or not the parent-teacher association serving the particular school is truly representative of the student population. If it is not, then it is not an adequate way to communicate with the community. Further, even if it is representative but is not active, or has a very small active membership, it will not serve as an adequate communication medium.

A microcomputer using a databased management system could be used for the entry and classification of these data. Multiple comparisons of the different classifications by dwelling area could then be made with relative ease.

Parent Training Programs

Most parents are interested in helping with their children's formal education. School personnel need to capitalize on this resource. To engage the home in collaborative efforts will pay rich educational dividends and enhance public relations as well. It takes organization, coordination, and hard work.

Getting started with a parent training program may be facilitated by surveying parents. Once survey results are in, it becomes a matter of arranging the appropriate "curriculum," securing expert presenters, and scheduling the training events. Depicted in Figure 19–4 is an example of a survey form employed successfully in a middle school.

Community Advisory Councils

The trend to greater autonomy at the school building level—the "operational site"—has brought with it increasing use by principals of community advisory councils. In some states (Texas, for example) legislation establishing greater school unit autonomy and the concomitant, greater principal accountability has also mandated that there be citizen advisory councils. Usually teachers, and sometimes students, are included in such councils.

AN INQUIRY TO DETERMINE THE REPRESENTATIVE NATURE OF THE LOCAL PTA/PTO

The initial effort would be to collect representative demographic information about the makeup of the student population of the respective school. Such information as general income levels or the nature and kinds of housing from which children come is what is sought. The kind of classifications that comprise Warner's Social Class Index will prove helpful. Those classifications are "occupation," "source of income," "house type," "dwelling area." These factors can be checked for a random sample of the students in the school if the school size is large.

Once the relevant demographic data about the student population has been collected, a questionnaire may be developed requesting the same general kinds of information and sent to the active membership of the PTO. It is important in this instance to be straightforward and simply explain to the recipients of the questionnaire what you are attempting to find out, that is, the representative nature of the PTO members.

A map of the attendance area served by the school should be developed and by using a color code of some sort, locate active members of the PTO according to where their home is on the map. Are some parts of the attendance area seemingly underrepresented? If it is available, secure a "pupil locater" map and compare the location of students with the location of PTO members. Is there a discrepancy? Using the same parent PTO locator map you can now, by applying the indices of quality of housing, sources of income, occupation, etc., determine whether or not the membership of the PTO is confined to certain social strata.

FIGURE 19–3

Issues often arise about what is "policy-making." Clearly, the reason for having advisory councils is so that there is a formally established way for community and faculty representatives to share information with the principal and suggest alternative approaches to the solution of problems of schools.

In the best of worlds this provides the principal with additional expertise and useful insights that will result in maximum feasible decisions. Such councils should not supplant local boards of education, although depending on the particulars of state or local policy, some arguments may occur on this point. Our point is that "advising" is not the same as "decisioning," although it would seem to be a foolish principal who found him- or herself always operating contrary to the best advice of the council.

PARENT SURVEY

We need your help to plan our inservice programs for parents. We would appreciate your taking a few minutes to answer the following questions.

Would you attend parent inservice meetings? _____Yes   _____No
If yes, please choose four of the following topics and rank them 1, 2, 3, and 4 with 1 being your first choice.

_____Stress Management/Reduction
_____Don't Be "Scared Off" by Those Kids
_____Working and Parenting
_____Parent/Teacher Disciplining the Child/Student
_____Stepfamily Adjustment
_____Handling Losses
_____Launching a Job Search
_____Sex Education for Adolescents
_____Behavior Problems and Hyperactivity in Childhood
_____Coping Skills in the 1990's
_____Help Your Kid Become a Winner
_____Structured Discipline Communication "A Discipline Approach to Enhance Self-Esteem"

Would you prefer afternoon or evening meeting times?_____

What day of the week would be best for you?_____

Do you have friends or neighbors that might attend? _____Yes _____No

Please return to your child's advisory teacher by Wednesday, October 8, or leave with your teacher tonight.

FIGURE 19–4. Involving Parents; Providing Services: A Survey

Membership on the Advisory Council

State law or local district policy may prescribe the nature of membership of the council and/or how members are to be selected. Lacking this, it would seem fundamental that members, whether elected or appointed by the principal, should represent a cross-section of the local community.

Achieving Maximum Output from an Advisory Council

Lack of clarity and understanding about the role of council members and about the difference between helping to make policy and policy implementation can become a source of conflict. People work best when they know what the expectations and limitations are. To establish a framework to guide advisory council activities the school principal should:

- Establish the essential conditions that any solution, action plan, or policy must meet if it is to be acceptable. That is, are there financial, legal, or district policy considerations that must be taken into account? Or, are there things that are known to not be in the best interests of learners? Or, are there things that in good conscience, the principal would not carry out?
- Help the group establish a specific time line and a set date for task completion.
- Indicate what resources are available for the group to work with.
- Detail what specific outcomes are desired.
- Establish the limits of the group's authority in the issue at hand. That is, is the principal asking for a final decision or for some alternative decisions or simply for some advice?

Community Volunteer Programs

All successful volunteer programs include a good initial orientation and training program. The orientation sessions are to explain the purposes of the program and clarify the roles of volunteers. The purpose of the training is to provide skills so that volunteers will be able to assist teachers and pupils maximally. It is wise to include teachers in the orientation and training sessions both as participants and presenters. Effective use of volunteers requires an understanding of program and the cooperation of the professional staff.

An especially noteworthy program is the Volunteers in Public Schools Program-Seniors of the Houston Independent Schools (VIPS-Seniors) which taps the rich source of human potential in the senior citizenry of the community. VIPS-Seniors serve in programs such as:

Regularly scheduled service in an elementary or secondary school. Here, volunteers are asked to serve two hours a week for eight weeks or more. With guidance from a teacher, volunteers tutor one or two children in reading, ESL, or math. Or they may share special skills in gardening, woodshop, computers, or journalism. Or they may serve in the clinic, lunchroom, office, or library. An effort is made to match special skills and interests with needs of the school.

Kindergarten screening. In the fall, seniors are used to help screen entering kindergarten children for potential learning problems. Volunteers spend two or more days screening children on such things as visual discrimination and impairment, language development, and other potential problems.

Living historians and resource speakers. Senior professionals and hobbyists share their expertise in such areas as nature study, economics, art, drama, and law. Living historians share unique experiences in their lives. In a recent month in Houston, topics included such subjects as Early Black Houston, The Holocaust, Big Bands and Jazz, and Life in the Theatre.

Capitalizing on the skills and interests of persons in the community not only enriches school life, it provides the basis for a community support system.

Interaction Sessions

Principals concerned about establishing and maintaining good relationships with students and their parents have initiated two kinds of sessions. One is a student-principal program conducted regularly in the principal's office. Attendance is limited to about ten students who sign up for the session in advance. An open-forum discussion is the mode, and in these sessions students express interests and discuss grievances they have, making suggestions about the general improvement of the school.

The same thing can be done for parents and other community members. Patrons may be notified by mail or through the newspaper of the meeting dates, and a secretary can take reservations for a dozen or so patrons. The rules for the meeting are that anything goes, except personal complaints about individual teachers. Two or three hours usually provide an adequate amount of time, creating an important opportunity for an informal exchange of ideas in a nonthreatening setting. For the principals it's an excellent sensing mechanism to find out the inside story of the operation of the school.

One of the problems in engendering community support for the schools is the inadequacy of the information exchange between school and home. Organized informal parent-principal forums address this problem. Complex ideas are difficult to express in the usual one-way bulletins or news stories that serve as major sources of information for parents and other community members. Complex ideas are best tested in a face-to-face setting.

Key Communicators

Many principals capitalize on the knowledge of the influence structure present in the local school community and develop a list of "key communicators" to be used when there is a need to disseminate good information quickly about important developments—positive or negative—in the school. Key communicators are influential people in the immediate community who have a well-known interest in education.

These persons are influential because they interact with large numbers of other people and are trusted and believed. Such persons may be contacted to form a loose organization that meets from time to time with the principal or other professionals in the building to discuss what is going on at the school that would be of general community interest. After an initial meeting, the key communicators are kept informed about such things as school budgets, new curricula, teacher turnover, and new construction. The group, as individuals and in collective feedback sessions, keeps the principal informed about "rumblings and rumors" in the community.

As always, care should be taken that the various dimensions of the school community are tapped. The notion of key communicators capitalizes on much research and communications theory which continues to indicate that other community members get most of their information and form their attitudes and beliefs in a word-of-mouth fashion, even in this mass media age.

Neighborhood Seminars

Neighborhood seminars have been successful in both large and small school districts. There are two important ingredients: an informed staff and careful initial organization. Neighborhood seminars will not be effective if they simply become a way of providing a forum for someone from the school to lecture to a collected group of individuals from the community. A deft discussion leader, careful planning, and an attitude not of propagandizing but rather of providing the opportunity for interchange of ideas and facts are required. Many of the characteristics of a good neighborhood seminar are the same as those of successful principal gripe sessions. The principal doesn't have to do it all; a cadre of well-informed staff who are especially adroit in leading discussions and who have been provided with a sufficient amount of general information about the school can assist the principal.

Properly organized seminars attended by people who represent a cross-section of attitudes and orientations in the community provide a most effective way to begin a new relationship with the community. Once underway, the neighborhood seminar approach creates a basis for sophisticated community involvement programs. Issues and problems discussed often lead to joint task force teams that engage in problem-solving efforts.

Program Analysis by Special Groups

Principals may invite identified groups in the community with an interest in certain parts of the school program to examine, in conjunction with appropriate school personnel, some of the special curricula of the school. A variation may be simply to involve a neighborhood school group in an analysis of the total school program.

Citizens Committees

Committees can be formed to study and make recommendations about discipline, budget, construction of the new schools, or vandalism. When such committees are employed, it is important that good techniques be used in the formulation; the committees should be representative and have a clear purpose. Forming one more committee simply to occupy people who might become critical of the school is a move transparent to most community members. The purpose of committees is to secure good, creative problem resolution. Better school-community relations will result because intelligent resources are being tapped.

The committee must know what the anticipated product is, and it must know the limits of its decision-making powers. If the principal is seeking advice and counsel but not final decision making, this should be stated at the outset.

Parent-Teacher Conferences

Planned parent-teacher conferences three times or more a year often are an important element in a school-community relations program. They provide excellent opportunities for direct relationships between the teacher and the home, but they require careful planning. Thought must be given to such factors as working parents, one parent in the home with responsibilities for other children, a parent's occupation that would preclude attendance at parent-teacher conferences scheduled during the normal school day, or transportation difficulties. These and other constraints, however, can be overcome with diligent work on the part of teachers and other school personnel. If the master contract under which the teachers perform precludes night meetings or restricts in other ways the orderly development of parent-teacher conferences, then this might be an item for negotiation at the next contract review.

Organizing for parent-teacher conferences can be a task of a joint community-teacher group although, of course, the group assigned the task of organizing the effort should be generally representative of the neighborhood or the community.

Surveys: Questionnaires and Opinionnaires

Surveys to determine the concerns and attitudes of the various publics can become an effective "sensing" mechanism if done routinely and regularly. There are a number of ways to conduct surveys.

Mailed questionnaires to a random sample of the population living in a particular school attendance area is the most common. The return rate is sometimes disappointing, and care must also be taken that what return there is is representative of the population surveyed. Sometimes house-to-house personal structured interviewing, even though the sample has a smaller number of people, will yield more useful results. There is an opportunity for followup questions for clarification and better information obtains. Surveys by telephone offer yet another alternative.

Finding out what community members think is very important. As we discussed in Chapter 4, the demographic makeup of a school community often changes rapidly; the "publics" opinions are fluid; attitudes, orientations, and expectations shift. Surveying the community can provide a useful information base for the school principal.

Focus Groups

Research organizations, professional associations, and advertising agencies, among other organizations have used focus groups for years to define issues, anticipate problems, explore reactions to potential problems, develop alternative scenarios, and plan leaps into the future. A focus group is an example of a *non-probability sampling* technique. The technique employs directional rather than quantitative data and can be used to great effectiveness as both a school public relations technique and a creative problem-solving technique.

But, focus groups are not decision-making bodies, nor are they even advisory bodies. They are groups of community members whose opinions about an issue the principal (or the superintendent) wants to learn. The purpose is both problem sensing and problem solving but the problem "sensor" and the problem "solver" are not the focus group. The focus group is to provide feeling, attitudes, and information.

Focus groups are composed of a small number of persons—eight to ten is the recommended number—each group representing a segment of the school-community population. The purpose of meeting with focus groups is to gain an assessment of how people feel about a school related issue or problem—or anticipated problem. Typically, the meetings last no more than an hour and no more than four questions are asked of the group. A moderator takes notes on the discussion, noting the key concepts, levels of intensity, and new information. To the extent possible, verbatim comments are recorded and are not edited when reported later.

It is not important that a focus group meets at the school. In any given instance it might be better if it did not. Union halls, church basements, apartment complex hospitality rooms might be more convenient and comfortable choices for meetings.

Business and Other Community Partnerships

There are many public relations benefits to be gained from well organized business-industry-education partnerships. There are also many educational benefits to be gained as well. Such benefits include:

- Getting important people—leaders, even—engaged in the important work of educating children. For examples, in one of the author's cities, the executives one of leading business have developed a training program in ethics and give their top staff released time to work with children in this program; a local psychiatric hospital offers free counseling services to its adopted school; a leading manufacturer of computers releases its personnel to work with teachers and students in more effective use of computer technology—and not just in the use of the manufacturer's own computers, either; another business sends school principals to its executive training program; still another employs science teachers in its research and development department summers and at other times; still others offer inservice programs as well as tutorial services; another has work opportunities for students who need financial help to stay in school; and the list could go on.
- Helping community leaders better understand the complexities of educating a child and helping them develop an appreciation for the problems and pleasures of teaching.
- Capitalizing on the technical expertise that is available in the community and using that expertise for staff updating as well as for program analysis and student tutoring.

GUIDELINES FOR PRODUCTIVE SCHOOL-BUSINESS PARTNERSHIPS

1. Be certain that the program that is implemented is objective, balanced, and that the goals of the business and the school are compatible. Just because it's "free" doesn't mean it is in the best interests of the students and staff of the school.

2. Focus on only that part of the curriculum about which the business partner has an interest or understands. The key word is "focus." Businesses can't solve all of the problems a school may have and may have difficulty staying interested in problems that are too broadly based.

3. Don't overlook staff development as a school need. Materials and equipment for the school are good. Instructional assistance is good. Dollars for special projects are good. But, so is expertise, materials, and money earmarked for projects that expand the abilities of teachers and administrators. These have a multiplier effect.

4. There must be a school-based coordinator. More good ideas have been bungled by poor management and bad communication than for any other reason. If it is worth doing, it is worth appointing a person with good management and public relations skills to oversee.

5. Businesses want some credit for their efforts. (Doesn't everyone?) Be gracious and give praise to your partner at every opportunity and do this publicly and often.

FIGURE 19–5.

To be maximally effective and to avoid costly misunderstandings, cooperative programs must be well coordinated. Although the principal doesn't need to be the one who manages the program, the principal is responsible for making sure that the program is well coordinated. Figure 19–5 provides guidance for the development of productive school-business partnerships.

Summary

Schools are a part of the greater social system of the community. People in the community have a right to not only be informed about school happenings but also to be engaged in these happenings. If school principals do not use available means to interact with members of the community, the school will become static and unresponsive to changing community and societal needs.

Principals need to analyze their existing public relations activities in light of the community being served. Are there both one- and two-way programs? Is membership and attendance at parent-teacher organizations, "booster groups" or room mother organizations representative of the school population? Are there focus groups and advisory committees in place? Are there partnerships with other agencies?

The skilled principal will analyze the existing public relations program and the community that is to be served. Modifications in the public relations program as well as, perhaps, school programming will be based on the analysis.

Endnotes

1. Melanie Markely, education reporter for the *Houston Chronicle*. Interview on November 20, 1992.

2. The word *sell* is used with caution. To "sell schooling as a good product" requires that the product indeed be good. There are no marketing practices that will be successful for very long with bad products.

3. See also, James T. Akers, "The Press Can Be Your Pal, But You Have to Treat It Right." *American School Board Journal* (October 1986): 27–29.

4. An excellent guide to the kind of writing a school administrator must do is Audrey B. Joyce, *Written Communications and the School Administrator*. Boston: Allyn and Bacon, 1991.

5. The previous two paragraphs in the text, when analyzed by using the "Fog Index," reveal a 13th or so grade level. What caused this mostly was the length of the sentences. Are we troubled by this? Not much. This is, after all, a graduate school textbook. This footnote rates a 5.6, however. Do you think it "talks down" to you?

Selected Readings

Davis, Don, "Schools Reaching Out." *Phi Delta Kappan, 72*, 5 (January, 1991), 376–380.

Helen, Owen, "Is Your School Family-Friendly?" *Principal, 72*, 2 (November 1992), 5–8.

Kindred, Leslie; Bagin, Donald; and Gallagher, Donald, *The School and Community Relations*, 4th edition. Englewood Cliffs, NJ: Prentice-Hall, 1990.

Joyce, Audrey B., *Written Communications and the School Administrator*. Boston: Allyn and Bacon, 1991.

Lewis, Anne, *The Schools and the Press*. Washington: National School Public Relations Association, not dated. This booklet includes instructions about how to organize school news, how to write good copy, what to do when there is unfavorable news, and how to develop good media relations.

Levine, Marsha and Trachtman, Roberta (eds.), *American Business and the Public School: Case Studies of Corporate Involvement in Public Education*. New York: Teachers College Press, 1988.

MacDowell, Michael A., "Partnerships: Getting a Return on the Investment." *Educational Leadership, 47*, 2 (October 1989), 8–11.

Parish, Jack and Prager, Dianne, "Communication: The Key to Effective Leadership." *Principal, 72*, 1 (September 1992), 37–39.

Reep, Beverly B., "Principals: Master These Skills to Survive in the P. R. Jungle." *The Executive Educator, 10*, 4 (April 1988), 20–21.

Seeley, David S., "A New Paradigm for Parent Involvement." *Educational Leadership, 47*, 2 (October 1989), 46–48.

Shaw, Robert C., "Do's and Don'ts for Dealing with the Press." *NASSP Bulletin, 71* (December 1987), 99–102.

Wilson, C. D. and Bailey, D., "Organizational Correlates of Citizen Participation Effectiveness." *Urban Education, 25*, 2 (January 1990), 175–194.

P a r t *3*

Leadership Processes

Succeeding as an elementary school principal requires more than understanding the various dimensions of the role and being knowledgeable about the functional aspects of the job. There is a pervasive need for skill in decision making and the ability to engage in systematic problem identification and problem resolution. When is it only sensible to make a unilateral decision? When is it only sensible to engage in agonizing consensus building?

Part 3 is composed of one chapter: "Decision Making at the School Site." Three important theoretical models are presented and applications to practice are made. Strategies to involve "stakeholders" in the decision-making process are described. The Vroom-Jago leadership model is presented and applied.

$C\ h\ a\ p\ t\ e\ r$ *20*

Decision Making at the School Site

Teacher leadership has become a key element of recent initiatives to . . . restructure schools . . . [These initiatives] have come from the formation of school improvement teams of teachers and administrators, teacher instructional support groups, and teacher-led principal advisory councils. They have also come from efforts of administrators to share and decentralize decision making related to teacher staff development, curriculum development, and program and personnel evaluation.[1]

Introduction

If decentralized decisioning means providing ample opportunities for teachers and other non-administrators to help make decisions that have to do with learning outcomes of children and youth, scoping and sequencing organized learning experiences, selecting and applying the technology of schooling, then that is simply consistent with research and good historical prescription and practice. And, if such so-labeled "empowerment" also means structured avenues for parent and community engagement to help solve local school problems—within a framework of advise and consent—then that too seems consistent with research and the ethos within which public institutions operate in the democratic world.

But, if "empowerment" conjures notions of schools or any other operating unit being managed by committees of persons who at best only mean well and at worst do not, then the practice should be denounced, for it does not bode well for good schooling in general and learners specifically.

Managing, leading, and policy analysis; educational change and productive innovation—these require more than good intentions. These require skill and professional insight.

But, decision-processing skills and decision-making skills can be learned. The effective principal will need to learn how to capitalize on the richness of competence that characterizes a school community to reach decisions that serve at once to improve schooling.

The subject of this chapter is problem solving and executive decision making. Both the staff and the community are "stakeholders" in decision processing and decision making. But stakeholders in what sorts of decisions? Who should be involved and when and what should be the nature of that involvement? These questions are addressed in the chapter.

Rational and non-rational (creative) decision processes are examined. Three important and useful models are presented, including the Vroom-Jago decision tree. Lancto's five levels of decision are used to provide guidance. The chapter concludes with ways to engage the school staff and community in the decision-making process.

Executive Decision Making: A Perspective

Decision making as discussed in this chapter is thought of as a problem-solving process rather than simply as a final visible act. The perspective is that to achieve good decisions it is necessary to engage in problem analysis and to select the best decision *process*.

The executive is always trying to achieve the *maximum feasible decision*; the perfect decision is seldom realized. The maximum feasible decision is the decision that works—the decision that will cause things to be much better off than they were and that staff at the operational level will work hard to achieve.

Throughout the chapter it is important to keep in mind those concepts that are central to effective decision making:

- *Decision making* is the essential executive act. It involves getting things done to help achieve the objectives of the organization.
- *Decision processing* is the manner one chooses to go about reaching a judgment.
- Decision making is not synonymous with decision implementation.
- The manner in which a decision is processed will affect implementation.
- The "maximum feasible decision" is the decision people will work hard to implement.
- One should be better off after taking action, not worse off.

Hasty Decisions: Big Mistakes

Any executive's day is characterized by almost constant involvement in problem solving, usually with other people. A single hurried trip from the office to "put out a fire" in the cafeteria may result in a half dozen or more encounters on the way with other organization members—teachers, children, custodians, counselors—many of whom want help with a problem. Frequently, these chance encounters result in decisions, hastily thrown over the shoulder as the principal progresses on the mission that required an absence from the office in the first place.

In such haste, mistakes are made. However, few things that happen in and about the school are of such an emergency nature that time cannot be taken for the reflection before a decisive act is required.

Decision making is the essential management act for it involves getting done those things that will help achieve the goals of the school. Good decision making requires qualitative judgments and is distinguished from seemingly involuntary or random responses to a stimulus. It is necessary to consider the difference between rational decision making and unilateral "kneejerks;" the former implies a systematic thought process, the latter is a mechanistic or visceral pattern of responses.

A Case in Point

Ralph Randall, a veteran bus driver, came into my office one morning about 10:00 a.m. I had been on the job as superintendent of the 2,300-pupil school district for just over two months and it was now the end of September.

"Chief," he said, "We've got a problem on the Bus 5 route that I drive." I told Ralph to sit down and asked him what *our* problem was. [Mistake number 1]

"As you know [I didn't know], when Bus 5 begins its route it approaches a grade level railroad crossing at North Thoman Street. Every morning at the time I'm beginning to pick up the children there is a regularly scheduled freight train that blocks the crossing. This causes me to be late to Southeast Elementary School which is the end of my route. The principal and teachers are complaining about the children arriving after the last bell.

"What I want to do is start my route by going in the other direction—the direction I would normally be coming from at the end of the route. This would avoid the problem of the freight train delay because the tracks are clear later. Can do?"

My response was: "Makes sense to me Ralph, go ahead. Just tell your riders so they know what's happening." A simple problem solved, and I went on to the other work of the day.

It was not a simple problem and things were not as they seemed. The immediate result was a lot of unnecessary pain, confusion, and embarrassment, internally and externally. The pain involved me, the transportation supervisor, some parents, and ultimately Ralph Randall. (But it was I who inflicted the pain on Ralph.) None of this was necessary; all of it was the result of a poor decision process and resulted in an absolutely terrible decision.

The facts were:

1. There was no regular freight on the North Thoman Street crossing. Ralph lied about this.

2. Small as it was, the system did have a transportation supervisor, one of whose responsibilities was bus schedules.

3. Changing the route in the morning (Ralph did not reverse the afternoon run) meant that those pupils who were picked up earliest were also the last to get off in the afternoon.

4. Changing the route also meant that the children first on the route, as revised, had to cross an arterial highway in front of their homes in order to be picked up. (This was the only arterial highway on the route and the route had been structured originally to provide for a pickup on the home side at the busiest time of the day, which was the morning hour.)

5. Ralph was having a feud with three of the parents of children served by his bus. Their homes were located on the highway and now were at the beginning of the route.

All of these facts were easily obtainable with only a modest information search.

H. L. Mencken once said, "For every complex problem there is a solution that is quick, simple and . . . wrong!" He might have said the same for seemingly simple problems as well. And I should have remembered Mencken.

First of all, the decision was not mine to make. The first step in any rational decision process is that, once the problem has been defined, to decide whose problem it is. This was not my problem; it fell well within the realm of another person—the transportation supervisor. That person was very troubled by my action, not so much because it was a bad decision but because he wondered what it was that he was supposed to be doing if not working on transportation problems. (It took a lot of time and reassurance to repair that relationship.)

Second, the decision was made without any information search. Few problems are of such an urgent and crisis-directed nature that time cannot be spent collecting additional relevant information. The results of the decision just described were angry parents, children placed in an unnecessarily hazardous position, a puzzled transportation supervisor, and a lot of time that had to be taken dealing with an insubordinate employee. That's a high price to pay for quick action.

It is fundamental that one should be better off—not worse off—after a decision. Failure to anticipate the consequences of an act often results in ineffective decision making.

Decision Making as Problem Solving

A problem can be said to exist when there is a state of uncertainty caused by either an unwelcome event or by the need to choose a course of action to achieve certain predetermined goals. Thus, something is a problem when there is a difference between what is currently occurring (the real situation) and what would desirably be happening (ideal situation).

Viewing decision making as problem solving has the decided advantage of delaying an act or judgment until there is a reasonable basis for that act or judgment. And, not all problems are worthy of any response at all. Some problems, on even a little reflection, will be solved only at the price of creating a larger problem; other problems are not important and are best ignored; still others are problems that belong to someone else and should be redirected to the appropriate person. The first decision that needs to be made is about the nature and severity of the problem.

Figure 20–1 depicts a rational problem-solving/decision-making model. Whether the problem is complex, such as one that has to do with responding to a school pressure group, or relatively simple, such as what to do with a sick student, the process should be the same if poor decisions are to be avoided.

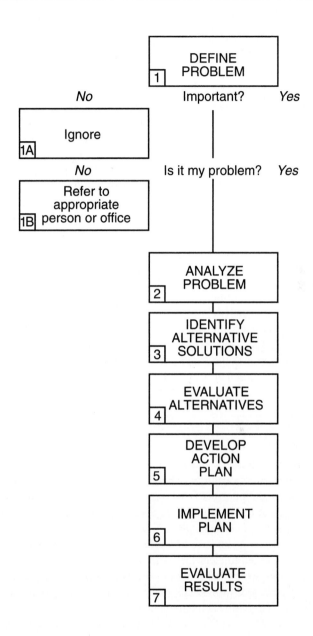

FIGURE 20–1.   Rational Decision Making: Steps in Systematic Problem Solving

How to deal with a sick student may not take very much time but assuming that the student is really ill and that it is the principal's problem, clearly the rest of the process makes sense. In the analysis of the problem, one considers the legal ramifications and school district policy. This provides a framework. Alternative solutions might include sending the student back to class but requiring no participation in class activities, sending the student to the health room until school is over, sending the student home, calling an ambulance and removing the student to a hospital, or various other possible alternatives.

Each of these alternatives can be quickly evaluated in the light of the severity of the problem, the feasibility of the solution, the age of the person, the time of day, and the anticipated consequences of any particular action. It will also make a difference whether or not there is a responsible adult present in the home.

Once a judgment is made about the best alternative and this is implemented, the results should be evaluated. Did it work? Was the principal or the school and especially the student better off or worse off? If not, why not? This, a basis for nonrepetitive error is established.

How long should such a process take? In the instance of the sick student, probably no more than five minutes—less for an experienced principal who knows the policies and the students. A relatively quick diagnosis and a phone call or two will do it.

In the instance of a citizens' group upset about a curricular issue or upset about grade placement policy, the process may require more elaboration but the steps are the same and the purpose is the same—to reach a sound judgment in a timely manner that will result in a solution that is in the best interests of all concerned.

Decision Settings

Problems occur in a variety of forms, differing in content, in the process by which the problem is addressed, and in the kind of impact it makes on the organization and the people in the organization. There is always the difficulty of matching the appropriate problem-resolution process with the decision setting. When should one make a straightforward, from-the-hip, unilateral decision? When should one involve groups in the agonizing process of consensus?

The answer is not hard to see in the extreme. If the situation is a fire in the basement, an order is issued to clear the building; one does not call a committee together to achieve consensus on which fire exits to use. (However, it would not be inappropriate to involve affected groups or individuals in advance in the development of policies and procedures for how to cope with such emergencies.)

It is more useful to think about decision settings than it is specific decisions. Problems may fall into two general decision settings: structured settings (routine, recurring issues) and multialternative and unstructured or innovative settings. Each setting presents unique problems.

Structured Decision Settings

Many things that happen in the school organization are recurring in nature. The basis for an orderly goal-oriented school is an array of proven, reliable, productive activities that are instituted, monitored, and terminated by an appropriate set of habituated routine acts. The range of responses to any given issue may be clearly limited by law, policy, and/or custom, as well as by time constraints and the maturity of the group affected by the decisions. The principal can expect certain kinds of problems to recur frequently and regularly, given a particular environment or set of circumstances. Routine response mechanisms to these are expected by members of the staff so that they can go about their work with a minimum of disruption. To the maximum degree possible, the decisions and decision processes that respond to recurring activities should be routinized.

Need for Written Policies

Arranging conditions in the school so that recurring problems are resolved with a minimum of disruption and false starts can be readily achieved. A school building policy and a rules and regulations manual carefully developed with the assistance of staff and students will provide much assistance. Such a manual should contain statements of basic responsibilities of teachers, counselors, administrators, and classified personnel, in each of five functional aspects of the school: pupil personnel services, staffing and staff relations, building management and financial operations, public relations, and curriculum and instructional development. In such a manual, the roles and responsibilities of various personnel with respect to matters pertaining to the functional aspects are carefully delineated, lines of communication are spelled out, and common procedural questions are answered. Importantly, too, such a document should also spell out student responsibilities—the rules and regulations every student is expected to live by.

In such a document, the delegation of specific management tasks to designated people will ensure a degree of stability because it clarifies the "who is to do what" question and also because it permits the principal to manage by exception rather than by direct participation in all decisions.

The Importance of Routine Decision Processes

In a properly managed school routine, day-to-day activities are carried on without the constant involvement of the principal. The primary responsibility of the principal is not the routine operation of the building but rather to create organizational conditions whereby school operations may be easily modified to meet changing demands and opportunities.

Structured or routine decision making, while encompassing problem situations running from the highly important to the mundane, is best formalized to the extent that relatively little stress on individuals or the organizations occurs as decisions are promulgated and implemented. Such is not the case in those settings wherein a variety of responses are available ("multi-alternative") or in those settings where no acceptable alternatives are apparent ("unstructured or innovative settings").

Multialternative and Unstructured or Innovative Settings

Even though many of the decisions that need to be made in and about the school are structured and only a limited number of options are available, there are issues for which many alternative actions are available and the principal may be confronted with a seemingly endless array of possibilities. Some of these may appear nearly equal in value *or* there may be an inadequate information base from which to determine the efficacy of the alternatives.

Unanticipated problems, unique situations, and fast-changing conditions are characteristics of organizational life. Decisions in such situations often require "leaps into the unknown"—creative problem resolution that produces both individual and organizational stress. In these decision settings a change is made from rational decision making to creative decision making.

It is not a once-for-all-times change, however. Generating creative responses to unstructured problems requires some structuring and a return to rational processes when the alternatives are ultimately weighed and an action plan developed.

The generation of alternatives and creative responses requires the combination of rational processes, frequent abrupt changes to creative processes, then a return to the rational. Problem definition, for example, is a rational process and goal setting or mission statements require rational processes. On the other hand, the development of alternative solutions to a complex problem is an intensely creative process.

It is not an either/or proposition. Groups or individuals do not have to be either creative or rational. Problem-solving groups, or individuals, make use of both orientations and must do so to be effective. Creative processes in the work organization need a structure or framework.

Three Techniques for Unstructured/Innovative Decision Processing

There are several managerial techniques that can be used to address problems of an unstructured nature. Three of these, *brainstorming*, *structured creativity*, and *nominal group*, are generally descriptive of the possibilities.

Brainstorming.   Brainstorming has as its only purpose the generation of ideas, no matter how impractical the ideas may seem at first consideration. Where the usual kinds of meetings or conferences tend to be noncreative, a brainstorming group devotes itself solely to creative thinking. During the period of the "storm," the group remains completely divorced from the mundane world.

Rules for Creative Group Problem Solving

1. The problem to be addressed must be stated clearly.
2. Criticism during the session is not permitted. Any idea is a good idea.
3. "Free wheeling" is encouraged. *Quantity* of ideas is what the group is after.
4. Combination and embellishment of ideas are sought.
5. Group size should be kept small to encourage maximum participation of members.
6. The role of the group leader is facilitator and co-participant.

A criticism of the brainstorming technique is that the results may be too easily affected by peer pressure (or hierarchical pressure if the "boss" participates). Unless the facilitator has good skills, a few outspoken members may dominate and thus reduce the number of contributions from other members. If either of the preceding conditions is likely to occur, it is best to turn to either the nominal group or to the structured absent-group technique.

Nominal Group Technique.   As in brainstorming, a small group is convened to focus on organizational issues or problems. The difference is that even though members of the group work on solutions to the problem in the presence of each other, they do so without immediate interaction.

Once the problem is defined and explained by the convenor, group members are given several minutes to write individually as many alternative solution possibilities as they can think of. After the time allotted for this has elapsed, a presentation of these alternatives is made.

Participants, in turn, give one alternative solution at a time and each is posted on flip chart paper as in the brainstorming process. This continues in round-robin fashion until all alternatives are posted.

The value of this process is that divergence is encouraged because the alternatives are privately developed and generation is thus not affected by other persons in the group. A disadvantage is that, unlike brainstorming, there is no way for one individual's idea to spark another individual. Nevertheless, a "creative tension" usually happens because participants are aware that others are working on the same problem and that everyone's product ultimately will be displayed.

Structured "Absent-Group" Technique.   Sometimes distances and individual schedules preclude convening a group. The absent-group technique does not require members to convene but can also result in creative idea generation and problem resolution.

Individuals are asked to participate in a simulation activity in which each is presented a case study describing an organizational problem or issue. Included are relevant descriptive data. Individuals are asked to respond to three questions:

1. Given the issue, what do you think is the problem? What might be some subproblems?

2. What might be two or three actions of a short-term nature that could be expected to reduce the negative aspects of the issue?

3. Suggest two or three other actions or processes that *ultimately* might resolve the problem.

Respondents submit their suggestions to whomever is charged with managing the solution to the problem.

Decision Processing

An array of decision-making processes are at the disposal of the school administrator, ranging from a unilateral "this is what must be done" process to engaging work groups in consensus decision making. The effective executive uses a range of techniques to arrive at the maximum feasible decision and no one process is always appropriate. The Maier model provides a basis for deciding how to decide. The Vroom-Yetton decision-processing technique extends and applies the conceptual approach of Maier.

The Maier Model

Maier[2] discusses the need for decision makers to consider two discrete elements: the requirement that a decision be one that is of high quality and the requirement that the decision be one that carries with it the likelihood that subordinates will accept and implement it.

Decision quality refers to objective aspects in the problem-solving process. This element refers to aspects of the decision that have to do with achieving organization goals and maintaining control, aside from any consideration of subordinate motivation. Is the decision technically sound? Is it based on the best information available? A high-quality decision occurs when the best available alternative is selected.

Decision acceptance refers to the degree of commitment required of subordinates in order for the decision to be effectively implemented. Acceptance is crucial when the administrator is dependent on subordinates to implement a decision. Although it is not possible to know unerringly when to involve others in a decision-making process, who those others should be, or what the nature of their involvement should be, there is always a need to consider the feelings, attitudes, and skills of those who will be charged with implementing the decision. Any decision that will require behavioral change will probably require work group commitment. The nature of work group involvement will depend in great part on the complexity of the problem to be solved, the degree to which those affected by the decision will be required to behave differently in order for the decision to be properly implemented, and the degree to which subordinates will accept a unilateral decision.

The Q/A Interaction

Using the two factors of technical expertise (quality of decision required) and need for group acceptance (hearty compliance and/or behavior change required) as prime determinants, a quadrant model can be developed to help determine the answer to the involvement question. Figure 20–2 displays such a model.[3]

That quadrant in which both the quality of the decision and the need for work group commitment is high (Q*A in the upper right quadrant) presents the greatest challenge to the leader. Into this quadrant fall those decisions that require much in the way of technical expertise and knowledge in order for a good decision to be reached. But it also describes a situation wherein no matter how technically superior the solution may be, in order for that solution to be put into effect, much work group acceptance will be necessary. That is, the decision must fall within the work group's "zone of hearty compliance." Without consideration of the needs and opinions of the group, compliance may be questionable.

This may be so for several reasons: because an apparent solution is contrary to present practice or present attitudes; because it requires work group members to perform in ways that are initially more difficult, or for which they have not been trained; because of a simple lack of agreement about the efficacy of the decision; or for any number of other reasons including threat, fear, distrust of administrators, or anger. If any of the previous conditions can be assumed, then something beyond a simple unilateral decision process will probably be required.

What kinds of issues might fall within this quadrant? Any curricular change certainly would, as would budget development. Changes in school policies affecting large numbers of students, and school constitutional questions would also seem to fit here. Operating in this quadrant will require good human relations skills as well as technical competence in the subject under review.

The upper left quadrant (A*q) depicts those situations where group feelings may be intense, but great technical expertise is not required because the subject is not a complex one. Any number of resolution schemes are available; the appropriate one must be that which is fair and sensitive to the needs and desires of the work group. Assignment of unpaid extracurricular duties, balanced work schedules for routine duties, school calendar development, among a myriad of other decision situations, might fall in this cate-

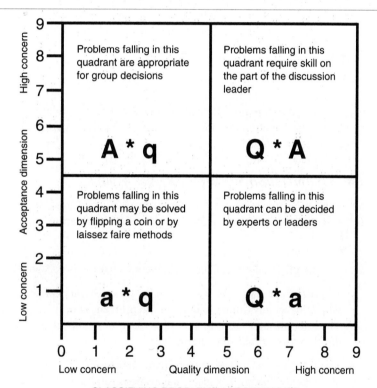

CLASSIFYING PROBLEMS ACCORDING TO
THE ACCEPTANCE AND QUALITY DIMENSIONS:
Problems may be rated in terms of the two dimensions essential for effective decisions. Each problem then becomes a point on the chart and falls in one of the four quarters. The method to be followed in solving the problem depends on the quarter in which it falls.

FIGURE 20–2. The Maier Model

Source: Norman R. F. Maier and Gertrude C. Verser: *Psychology in Industrial Organizations,* fifth edition. Copyright © 1982 by Houghton Mifflin Co. Used by permission.

gory. Among appropriate ways to handle problems in this quadrant would be the formation of advisory committees, delegation of decision making to standing or ad hoc bodies,
or informal consultation with leaders of the groups affected.

The Q*a quadrant contains those kinds of decisions that affect the quality of the
organization in a technical sense, but do not greatly impact the human side of the enterprise. Equipment selection, design of conflict-free schedules, and the design of a management information system, among other examples, might fall in this quadrant.

In the remaining quadrant (a*q) neither great technical competence nor sensitive
human relations is a critical consideration. What is needed is a concrete act to resolve a
simple problem. Time is the only critical element. A decision has to be made in a timely
manner so that people in the organization can go about their work in an orderly, efficient,
and knowledgeable manner. Any sensible convenient process that is timely will do.

The Maier model is a good analytical tool. It emphasizes that selection of the best
decision process will result from an analysis of the nature of the problem and the nature
of the work group.

Vroom and Yetton, and more recently Vroom and Jago,[4] extend these concepts and
provide a basis for choosing the decision process most likely to result in the maximum
feasible decision. Effective leadership, as that is manifest in good decision making,
depends on understanding the conditions of a problem situation and assessing correctly
how much participation or "power sharing" is required to be successful *and* the form that
this participation should take.[5]

The Vroom-Yetton Decision-Process Model

Vroom and Yetton explicate five available decision processes on a continuum from no
subordinate participation to maximum subordinate influence:*

> *The AI Procedure.* The leader solves the problem alone using whatever information
> is available at the time. (The available information is considered to be sufficient.)
>
> *The AII Procedure.* The leader obtains the necessary information from subordinates
> who may or may not be told about the problem or why the information is requested.
> The subordinates' role in this procedure is simply that of providing data, not in
> developing or evaluating alternatives.
>
> *The CI Procedure.* The leader shares the problem with one or more subordinates
> *individually*, asking for ideas, suggestions, and alternatives, but does *not* bring the
> relevant subordinates together to do this. The leader then makes the decision which
> may or may not take into account the ideas of the subordinates.
>
> *The CII Procedure.* The leader calls the appropriate subordinates together and shares
> the problem with the group, soliciting ideas, suggestions, and alternatives. Then the
> leader makes the decision which may or may not take into account the ideas of the
> subordinates.

*From *Leadership and Decision-Making*, by Victor H. Vroom and Philip Yetton, by permission of the
University of Pittsburgh Press. © 1973 by University of Pittsburgh Press.

The GII Procedure. The leader shares the problem with subordinates as a group. The group as a whole generates and evaluates alternatives, with the ascribed leader's role that of peer. The process is consensus decision making. The leader serves as chair or convenor of the meeting but does not attempt to exert "official" influence in the direction of any specific decision. The leader is willing to agree to and implement any solution which has the support of the group.

The Vroom-Yetton process offers much more guidance to the leader in selecting an appropriate decision procedure than Maier's model. Both AI and GII may appear at once to be the "riskiest" of the procedures. On the one extreme, the leader moves in a visibly assertive and clearly unilateral manner; on the other extreme, the leader reduces ascribed authority to *egalité*, but even so is still ultimately responsible for what happens.

In fact, none of the five is any more or less risky than the others, and when used appropriately each will provide the best route to the maximum feasible decision. But how does one choose among the processes?

The relative utility of the five procedures depends on several aspects of the situation within which the problem exists. It depends as well on leader judgments about the nature of these aspects. The aspects are:

1. A clear definition of the problem (i.e., what is it that is not what is desired?).

2. The amount of information possessed by the leader and subordinates or, if the information is not currently possessed, whether or not it is known where to find the needed information.

3. The degree to which the problem is "structured." An unstructured problem would be one for which inadequate information is available, it is uncertain where to find the information or what kind of information is required, and multiple objectives are to be obtained. The less familiar a problem, the more unstructured it is. A structured problem is one in which the objectives to be obtained are clear or singular, needed information is readily available, the alternatives are limited, and the available mechanisms for getting to the desired state are well known.

4. Whether or not it is likely that subordinates will accept a unilateral decision from the leader.

5. Whether or not it is likely that subordinates will cooperate—with the leader or with each other—in collectively trying to reach a good decision (i.e., one that would be in the best interests of the organization).

6. The amount and intensity of disagreement the leader perceives to exist among subordinates about preferred alternatives.

Vroom and Jago: An Expanded Model

The continuing research of Vroom and Jago[6] has led to refinements in the original Vroom-Yetton model. The conceptual frame and the basic assumptions remain unchanged, however.

An important enhancement is that the model has been extended to include considerations about the extent to which a given problem solution is either "time driven" or one in which good opportunity for work group development exists; that is, it is "development" driven.

Time-Driven Considerations

The available time to resolve an issue may impinge greatly on the degree to which members of a work group can be involved in problem solving and the form that this involvement takes. CII and GII decisional forms require an investment of time considerably greater than the other forms. Is the problem important enough; that is, is group commitment necessary, and is a high-quality decision required to justify the expenditure of the person-hours that will be required?

Even if the quality of the decision is not crucial (i.e., there are a number of alternatives, any one of which would adequately resolve the issue), but acceptance is critical and not likely to result from a unilateral decision, then an investment of time will be worth the trouble.

Judicious use of time is an important consideration, however. CII and GII decision processes do use up both the time and the energy of subordinates and peers. A four-hour group meeting between the principal and an advisory group of eight others consumes 36 person-hours of work time. What other important activities had to be delayed or not done because of the meeting?

Development-Driven Considerations

There is much to be gained from broad participation in decision making by a school staff and school community. Such involvement encourages idea sharing, trust, high performance standards, and work group effectiveness. It also capitalizes on the abilities of the informal leaders on the staff.

However, skills in decision making need to be nurtured and work groups need to be helped to improve these skills. Consider a school or a department with many new personnel or a school suddenly functioning under a district or state mandate for site-based management and similarly a mandated teacher and/or community advisory council. If group members have heretofore been relatively involved and unfamiliar with decision making in an organizational context, there is work to be done by the principal.

Thus, the principal might employ a CII or a GII process on less intense problems with a new group as a way to provide a basis for group members to learn to work together. Later on in this chapter there is a discussion about how to set an appropriate framework for participative decision making.

The principal is taken in the direction of a CII or GII decisional process when the problem possesses a quality requirement. Similarly, this direction would be selected when subordinates share the organizational goals and there is potential conflict among subordinates about preferred solutions.

The Decision Tree

Help in selecting the most likely process to lead to the maximum feasible decision is available in the form of a decision tree.[7] Eight questions to be answered yes or no comprise the branches of the tree. These questions are addressed *only* after the problem to be solved has been satisfactorily defined.

The eight questions are:

1. How important is the technical quality of this decision?
2. How important is subordinate commitment to the decision?
3. Does the leader have sufficient information to make a high-quality decision?
4. Is the problem well structured?[8]
5. If the leader were to make the decision alone, is it reasonably certain that subordinates would be committed to the decision?
6. Do subordinates share the organizational goals to be attained in solving this problem?
7. Is conflict among subordinates over preferred solutions likely?
8. Do subordinates have sufficient information to make a high-quality decision?

Figures 20–3 and 20–4 depict the "tree." Figure 20–3 would be used in instances where the principal considered group development the driving factor; Figure 20–4 would be used where time was the primary concern.

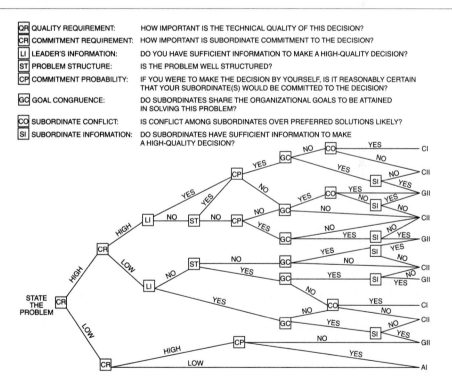

QR	QUALITY REQUIREMENT:	HOW IMPORTANT IS THE TECHNICAL QUALITY OF THIS DECISION?
CR	COMMITMENT REQUIREMENT:	HOW IMPORTANT IS SUBORDINATE COMMITMENT TO THE DECISION?
LI	LEADER'S INFORMATION:	DO YOU HAVE SUFFICIENT INFORMATION TO MAKE A HIGH-QUALITY DECISION?
ST	PROBLEM STRUCTURE:	IS THE PROBLEM WELL STRUCTURED?
CP	COMMITMENT PROBABILITY:	IF YOU WERE TO MAKE THE DECISION BY YOURSELF, IS IT REASONABLY CERTAIN THAT YOUR SUBORDINATE(S) WOULD BE COMMITTED TO THE DECISION?
GC	GOAL CONGRUENCE:	DO SUBORDINATES SHARE THE ORGANIZATIONAL GOALS TO BE ATTAINED IN SOLVING THIS PROBLEM?
CO	SUBORDINATE CONFLICT:	IS CONFLICT AMONG SUBORDINATES OVER PREFERRED SOLUTIONS LIKELY?
SI	SUBORDINATE INFORMATION:	DO SUBORDINATES HAVE SUFFICIENT INFORMATION TO MAKE A HIGH-QUALITY DECISION?

FIGURE 20–3. **Vroom-Jago Development-Driven Decision Tree: Group Problems**

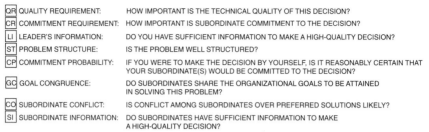

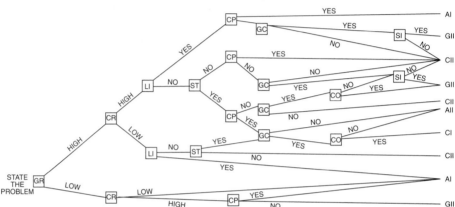

FIGURE 20–4.   Vroom-Jago Time-Driven Decision Tree: Group Problems

Reprinted from *The New Leadership: Managing Participation in Organizations* by Victor H. Vroom and Arthur G. Jago, 1988, Englewood Cliffs, NJ: Prentice-Hall. Copyright 1987 by V.H. Vroom and A.G. Jago. Used with permission of the authors.

Implications of Decision-Processing Models

Using such tools as the Maier model or the Vroom-Jago decision tree for problem analysis does not remove the need for sensitive judgment. Indeed, the effective use of these models requires the highest order of judgment. The administrator is after the maximum feasible decision—the decision that offers promise of long-term problem resolution or problem mitigation *and* the one which those most affected will work to carry out. The processes described herein are designed to take the administrator to this sort of decision.

What one has, with the rational decision processes just presented, is a basis for reducing the risks and analyzing the strengths and weaknesses of relative positions. The decision tree, the Maier model, and any of a number of other rational processes are tools for the manager to use to arrive at a maximum feasible decision. The models are not a substitute for thinking; they are to stimulate thinking to provide the basis for sound judgments.

Your Turn

You are the principal of a 1,200-pupil middle school and are confronted with the situation stated below. Analyze the situation. At the conclusion of the case you will apply the Vroom-Jago tree.

Case Study

The school houses grades 5–8. There is need to review the social studies series currently in use. Because your own teaching field is social studies you have more than a casual interest in and knowledge about the situation. You also have a strong opinion that the current series does not adequately depict the contributions made by minorities.

The social studies department seems split on the issue, containing two teachers who do not want to use any text at all; several teachers who are very satisfied with the current text; and three or four others who favor at least two other series. (Board of education policy requires one adopted text series but does permit supplemental works when it can be shown that there is good reason to do so.)

The chairperson of the department is undecided on the matter and requests that you "do something." A review of staff evaluations reveals that one of the teachers who wants no text at all is among the top rated in the school. She is unhappy with the more conservative posture of many of her colleagues and has indicated that unless a more positive stand on the multicultural nature of society is taken by the department she will go elsewhere. A *cause célèbre* looms.

Your task is to decide what decision process will lead you to the maximum feasible decision by applying the Vroom-Jago model.

Using the Decision Tree

To use the Vroom-Jago tree, first clearly state what you believe to be the problem. Then, assume you are development driven and, using Figure 20–3, begin at the left side of the model with question "QR." If your response to this question is "high," then you proceed to question "CR," and so on.

For each answer, take a moment to justify your response. Proceed through the decision tree until a terminal is reached. The terminal will indicate the feasible decision procedure.

Authors' Analysis of the Case

We consider this to be a "development-driven" problem. There is adequate time and clearly the department needs some help in learning how to make decisions, as well as how to work together more effectively.

Using the tree, the maximum feasible process appears to us to be CII. At issue is the selection of the social science series, and this is what we see as the problem to be solved. So stating, the tree is entered and question QR receives a "high." (There is clearly a quality requirement; the issue is a high priority and there are "unequal" solutions.)

The next question asks about the importance of subordinate commitment to the decision. We believe there is a need for "high" commitment. Little commitment would seem to mean the text would not be used or would be misused. We are at the leader information question and our answer to that is that the leader (us) does not have enough information. Nor do we believe the problem is "structured"—the answer to this particular issue would not seem to be "programmable." We are now at "CP." Do we think that subordinates will commit to a unilateral decision made by us? Perhaps, you'd really have to be there to know, but given the nature of the problem and the presumed intensity of feelings, our answer is "no." And, how about "goal congruence?" It wouldn't seem that you could count on this given the information about the range of beliefs on the staff, so we said "no" and the terminal we are taken to is CII. Had the response to the goal congruence question been "yes," we would have had to address the conflict question. Depending on the answer to that—and a "yes" there would seem the likely response—we could have ended up at GII.

In either instance—and good judgment must be present for good decision processing—you are taken to the process that will most likely achieve the best result.

Try Another One

Take the following case through the tree twice. First operate on time-driven assumptions, then on development-driven assumptions.

Case Study

You are principal of an elementary school with an enrollment of 525. Your school district has always searched for ways to increase student learning and has frequently been on the "cutting edge" statewide in its efforts to do this. Recently the district has adopted the Whole Language approach as a curricular and instructional thrust. To the surprise of everyone, including yourself, the expected increase in student learning as evidenced by the results on state and national standardized tests has not been realized in your school. In fact, scores have dropped significantly in English, reading, and social studies. Moreover, your staff turnover rate has increased greatly over what it was just two years ago.

You suspect that there must be at least some parts of the new curriculum that are responsible for the lack of success of your students. And, you are not all that satisfied that some of your teachers are really working hard to implement the program fully.

This view is not widely shared among your immediate subordinates—department and grade level chairs, the assistant principal, and your dean of instruction. Most of them attribute the problem to poor in-service training of the teachers, to a lack of additional resources to provide for the extra time teachers say the program requires, and to generally low morale on your staff. There is a considerable depth of feeling on the part of your staff and much potential disagreement among subordinates about the issue. Some are angry with the students for the poor test scores; others are becoming openly hostile about the "extra" time they say the program is taking; still others resent the implication that they are not doing a good job.

This morning you receive a phone call from your district superintendent. The superintendent has just reviewed the test scores for the district, school by school and was calling to express concern. The superintendent indicated that the problem was yours to solve in any way you think best, but wants to know within the week what steps you plan to take.

The Work Group as a Problem-Solving Unit

The school executive is looking for the best solutions to problems—routine and nonroutine. Such solutions will not occur in an organization of interacting humans unless processes are employed that make appropriate use of the collective intelligence of these humans. Thus, effective principals deliberately and frequently engage their staff in problem-solving activities.

Four assumptions guide such an executive:

1. Initiative and creativity are widely distributed in the population.
2. People will work hard to achieve objectives they have helped develop.
3. People at the working level tend to know the problems best.
4. The face-to-face work group is most often the best unit for diagnosis and change.

Productive relationships develop as a result of engaging in important activities together. These activities reveal the strengths and weaknesses of fellow group members, showing who can be counted on for which kind of expertise. Knowing where certain kinds of expertise exist permits the principal to create effective teams to focus on troubling schoolwide issues, existent or anticipated.

Setting Realistic Decision-Making Limits

Regardless of the maturity of the staff, few problem-solving groups can be permitted to operate completely unfettered. Real-world constraints must always be contended with. Any group charged with helping to resolve an issue needs to know the "rules of the game" if the expectation is a decision that can be implemented. The following considerations provide a solid basis for maximum effective use of problem-solving groups:

1. Decide if the task force is to be advisory in nature. That is, is it a "CII" or is it a "GII?" Are decisions to be suggestions only, or is the group to be charged with coming up with final decisions?
2. Cooperatively set a realistic time line. This would include further data collection periods, preparation of final reports, generation of new program alternatives, and the anticipated implementation date, among other milestones.
3. Establish a tentative budget for the project phases. Possible line items include released time costs, materials costs, transportation, and meals.
4. Review any district-wide policies or state laws that might impinge on the nature of any resolution scheme. For example, is there a system-wide or statewide adopted basal reading series that must be "lived with" no matter what? Does the state provide for experimental programs?
5. Establish the "essential conditions" that any decision must fit in order to be acceptable.
6. Set up regular interaction sessions about progress and findings.

Participative Decision Making

Engaging a staff in participative decision making may not be easy. Vogt and Hunt[9] concluded that about half of all organized participative groups will dissolve before changes are implemented or problems solved. This results in part because most such groups are not well integrated into the organization's hierarchy. These researchers also found that organization members typically are not accustomed to consensus decision-making processes and thus are uncertain about how to proceed. To this we would add as well that in any particular group there may be skepticism about the value of the process and perhaps suspicion about the degree to which decisions reached by such groups will actually be implemented by administrators.

Two things seem apparent if broad-based decision-making participation is to achieve good results. First, great attention must be given to the kinds of decisions that are assigned to various groups and individuals. Lancto's work is helpful here.[10]

Second, a formal structure that facilitates the involvement of others in decision-making must be present. If this is in place, it then becomes a matter of "testing" the process by participating in it. After the testing will come "trusting." Establishing school improvement committees is one place to start.

Levels of Decision Making and Participation

Lancto proposes five levels of decisional authority, the levels determined by the nature of the problem to be solved and decision to be made. Figure 20–5 illustrates the decision levels and provides examples of the kinds of decisions to be made at the several levels.

The model is useful because it clearly sets forth varying degrees of participation in school-based decision making. It helps avoid misunderstandings about roles, responsibilities, and authority to act. And, it clearly establishes the leadership expected of principals in all of this.

Who should be involved in decision processing? Who makes the final decision? Does participatory management mean committees for everything? How will anything get done? Good decisions require good information and a willingness on the part of those affected to implement the decision. But, that does not translate to mean the same approach to every problem-solving activity, nor does it mean the executive never takes action without some kind of agonizing consensus session.

The persons to be involved in decision processing *and the nature of that involvement* of necessity will differ depending on the issue to be resolved if the product is to be the maximum feasible decision. Sometimes the participation is at the advisory level; sometimes it will result in final decisions. In shared decision making the staff works with the principal in two ways: (1) giving advice before the principal makes certain decisions and (2) making decisions in predetermined domains.

School Improvement Committees

Some problems are better addressed and solved at the basic operational level, without interference from a superordinate structure. In such instances the superordinate structure serves as a support unit providing such resources that might be needed and performing in an oversight role only.

The argument in favor of such committees is that autonomy is placed appropriately, permitting maximum latitude in decision making at the operating level. The school improvement committee is an action group. It resolves problems rather than simply identifying them.

LEVELS OF PARTICIPATION

1. Decisions made by individual teachers.

2. Decisions made collectively by teachers (may also involve students and parents in an advisory role).

3. Decisions made collectively by teachers, principals, and other auxiliary administrators (parent and student participation where appropriate).

4. Decisions made by administrators, department heads, and building supervisors after consultation with staff (schoolwide advisory councils are often a good mechanism for this).

5. Decisions made solely by the principal or other designated administrator.

TYPICAL KINDS OF DECISIONS TO BE MADE AT EACH LEVEL

Level 1:　Classroom teaching strategies; enrichment; remediation.

Level 2:　Selection of instructional materials and texts; use of time and allocation of resources within a grade level or department—including staffing patterns.

Level 3:　Curriculum decisions involving more than one group or instructional unit; scheduling; scoping and sequencing across subjects and grade levels; sequential texts, materials, and other instructional protocols involving two or more instructional, support, or administrative units; any other decisional matters affecting more than one unit.

Level 4:　Schoolwide scheduling; budget recommendations to the central office; balancing resources/resolving conflicts; appraisal and evaluation strategies; development of school effectiveness reports to district offices and state agencies.

Level 5:　Legal issues such as student and teacher discipline; official recommendations to superintendent on the reemployment of staff and tenure; final decisions on the general use of the building and other physical facilities; allocation of resources for the school plant in general; selection and assignment of support staff.

FIGURE 20–5.　School-Based Decision-Making Levels

Distinguishing Features of a School Improvement Committee

- It consists primarily of a regular work group (department, grade level, or cross-level group of teachers, librarians, counselors, for example.) Community members may or may not be members.
- It is voluntary.
- It meets regularly.
- It solves problems instead of simply identifying problems for the principal or others to solve.

The principal may or may not be a member of the committee but someone who is a member of the school's administrative team is. The role of the administrator is that of convenor and facilitator. Having an administrative representative who may also serve as group leader is helpful because it ensures upward communication.

Types of Solvable Problems.   Not all problems confronting a school or school system are appropriate for committee action. Consider the following simple typology of organizational problems:

1. Those organizational problems over which members have control.
2. Those organizational problems over which members have influence but the solutions will require the actions of outside parties.
3. Those organizational problems over which members have neither control nor influence.

A school improvement committee can be effective if it focuses on the analysis and solution of the numerous Type 1 problems. As the group matures, it may take on the more complex Type 2 problems, over which it has only partial control. (Type 2 problems frequently affect more than one organizational unit and usually require the assistance of others in the organization.)

Ways to get started with a community improvement committee are discussed in Chapter 6. Advisory councils are discussed in Chapter 19.

Summary

The focus of this chapter has been organizational problem solving. Arriving at decisions that resolve, or at least mitigate, school problems requires finely honed conceptual skills and a repertoire of possible response patterns. The key to good decision making is good decision processing.

Much research about decision processing has been conducted over the years. One of the most useful applications of this research has been the Vroom-Jago Model. In this approach, various conditions existing in a problem situation are subjected to analysis, and the decision maker is led to a decision process that is most likely to result in a maximum feasible decision.

Increasing freedom to take action and solve problems at the school site has resulted in greater involvement of all of the stakeholders—the school staff and community members—in problem identification, problem analysis, and problem solution. The principal is the executive who makes it happen, however. Mobilizing a staff to take greater responsibility for what goes on in the school will require much skill and the selection of the appropriate processes. In this chapter we have identified the important issues in school-based decision making and discussed the skills required.

Endnotes

1. Mark A. Smylie and Jean Brownlee-Conyers, "Teacher Leaders and Their Principals: Exploring the Development of New Working Relationships." *Educational Administration Quarterly, 28,* 2 (May 1992), 150.

2. Norman R. F. Maier and Gertrude Verser. *Psychology in Industrial Organizations*, 5th ed. New York: Houghton Mifflin Company, 1982.

3. *Ibid.*, p. 173.

4. Victor H. Vroom and Arthur G. Jago, *The New Leadership: Managing Participation in Organizations.* Englewood Cliffs: Prentice-Hall, 1988. See also the earlier work by Vroom and Philip W. Yetton, *Leadership and Decision-Making.* Pittsburgh: The University of Pittsburgh Press, 1973.

5. Vroom and Jago's, Vroom and Yetton's and Maier's works appear directly related to earlier concepts advanced by Simon. Simon's "Zone of Acceptance" was based on two questions: "Is the problem relevant to others in the organization?" and "Do others in the organization have expertise to solve the particular problem?" Simon wrote that if the answer to both of these questions was "no" then whatever decision was made was likely to fall with the sub-ordinates' zone of acceptance. If the answer to either of the questions was "yes" then there was a need to engage subordinates in some way to examine alternatives or at least to collect additional information.

6. Victor H. Vroom and Arthur G. Jago, *The New Leadership: Managing Participation in Organizations.* Englewood Cliffs: Prentice-Hall, 1988.

7. There is a computer program to assist in this. "Managing Participation in Organizations" (MPO) developed by Vroom and Jago is an "expert system" that explicates the process with a series of questions based on the decision tree. "MPO: Managing Participation in Organizations," Leadership Software, Inc., Houston, Texas, 1987.

8. A "structured" problem is one where the executive is familiar with the current state, the desired state, and the best way(s) to get to the desired state.

9. J.F. Vogt and B.D. Hunt, "What Really Goes Wrong with Participative Groups?" *Training and Development Journal, 42,* 5 (May 1988), 96–100.

10. Robert M. Lancto, "An Inquiry: Shared Decision-Making." *The Journal of SAANYS, 18,* 3 (Winter 1987-88), 13–17.

Selected Readings

Chapman, Judith (ed.), *School-Based Decision-Making and Management.* London: Falmer, 1990.

Greer, John T. and Short, Paula M., "Restructuring Schools," Chapter 6, in Larry W. Hughes, *The Principal as Leader.* Columbus: Merrill, 1994.

Keith, Sherry and Girling, Robert H., *Education Management and Participation.* Boston: Allyn and Bacon, 1991.

Lancto, Robert M., "An Inquiry: Shared Decision-Making." *The Journal of SAANYS, 18,* 3 (Winter, 1987-88), 13–17.

Maier, Norman R.F. and Verser, Gertrude C., *Psychology in Industrial Organizations.* New York: Houghton Mifflin, 1982.

Rosen, Maggie, "Sharing Power: A Blueprint for Collaboration." *Principal, 72,* 3 (January 1993), 37–39.

Simon, Herbert A., *Administrative Behavior.* New York: Macmillan, 1947.

Smylie, Mark A. and Brownlee-Conyers, Jean, "Teacher Leaders and Their Principals: Exploring the Development of New Working Relationships." *Educational Administration Quarterly, 28,* 2 (May 1992), 150–184.

Vogt, J.F. and Hunt, B.D., "What Really Goes Wrong with Participative Groups?" *Training and Development Journal, 42,* 5 (May 1988), 96–100.

Vroom, Victor H. and Jago, Arthur G., *The New Leadership: Managing Participation in Organizations.* Englewood Cliffs, NJ: Prentice-Hall, 1988.

Index

Index

A

Ability grouping, 124
Absent group technique, 353
Academic learning time, 182, 198, 223
Achilles, Charles M., 5
Activity accounts, 291, 304-305
Advisor-Advisee systems, 143-144
Americans with Disabilities Act, 42-43
Audits, 305

B

Belief statement, 90
Beliefs, 83
Benedictine Rule, 3
Bennis, Warren, 12
Bill of Rights, 31-32
Blake, Robert (and Mouton), 8
Bloom, B.S., 172
    Taxonomy of Cognitive Objectives, 172
Blut und bod, 72-73
Brainstorming, 352

Budget cycle, 292-294
Buildings
    new schools, 312
    open space, 312-313
    renovation, 313
    space utilization, 313, 314
    traditional, 313, 315

C

Campus planning, 101-102
    self study and, 102
Child abuse, 59-60, 166
Citizen committees, 338-339
Class size, 123
Clinical supervision, 257
Collaborative professional development, 259
Collective bargaining
    contract administration, 285
    grievance form, 286
    principal's role, 281, 285
Community
    advisory councils, 334-336
    agencies, working with, 77-78, 151

Community, cont.

   influence systems, 68

   pluralism in, 65-66, 71

   power structure, 69-71

   sacred, 66

   secular, 66-67

   volunteer programs, 336-337

Communicators, Key, 337-338

Contingency theory, 11

Cook, Walter W., 127

Corporal punishment, 55-56

Counseling programs, 142-144

Creative insubordination, 12

Curriculum

   Annehurst Curriculum System, 175

   alignment, 175, 178

   basic skills, 182

   breadth, 185

   children with disabilities, 186

   classification system, 175

   common learnings, 182

   congruence, 122

   continuity, 181

   density, 179

   departmentalized, 174

   development, 171

   exploratory, 182

    labs, 186

   flexibility, 180

   individual differences, 180

   individual specialization, 184

   interdisciplinary, 175

    unit, 176

   interrelationships, 183

   learning centers, 185

   model, 181

   organization, 86, 172

   outlines, 173

   redesign, 179

   restructuring, 179

   special students, 176

   specialization, 182

   structure, 172

   student maturity, 179

   test item bank, 178

   time spent, 184

   tradition, 181

Curriculum development

   site-based management, 171

   teacher empowerment, 172

   total quality management, 187

Curriculum structure

   horizontal, 174

   vertical, 173

Custodians

   schedules, 319, 320-321

   working with, 318

D

Decisions

   levels of, 364-365

   participative, 363-364

   processing, 353

   settings, 350

structured, 350-351

unstructured, 351-353

why involve others, 27-28

Deming, W. Edwards, 12, 252

Demont, Roger (and Hughes), 6

Dewey, John, 119

Dimensions of the principalship, 5

Dress codes, 46-47

Drug Abuse Resistance Education (DARE), 77

Due process

procedural, 49-50

substantive, 48-49

E

Effective schools, 87

Empowerment staff, 207

Evaluation

activities, 196

formative, 197

summative, 197

Expulsions and suspensions, 56-57

F

Facility utilization, 86

Faculty advisory council, 206

Fiedler, Fred, 8-9

Financial reports, 307-308

Fiscal

authority, 291, 292

management, 300-304

Focus groups, 339-340

Force-field analysis, 103-105

Fourteenth Amendment applied, 32-33

Functions of the principalship, 4, 5

G

Gantt charts, 107, 108

Getzels, Jacob (and Guba), 21

Gifted students, 185

Glass, Gene V., 123

Goal setting, 27-28

Goals, 83

developing, 88

learner, 85

program, 85

selecting, 91

staff, 85

Goldhammer, Keith, 4

Grades, assigning, 197

Grievance procedure, 282

how to handle, 282

Group

composition, 124

flexibility, 129

size, 123

Grouping

achievement, 129

age, 128

alternate solutions, 127

computer-based, 131

Grouping, cont.

   empowering teachers, 130

    guidelines, 130

    heterogeneous, 126, 128

    homogeneous, 125

    interest, 128

    multiage, 128

    problems of regrouping, 130

    skill, 129

    students, 123

Guidance counselors, 148, 151

H

Halpin, Andrew (and Croft), 4

Hersey, Paul (and Blanchard), 9-10

Hoopla, 28-29, 140-141

House, R.J., 10-11

Hughes, Larry W. (and Demont), 6

Hughes, Larry W., 23, 66-67

Human resource development, 251

   building level, 255

   model, 253

Human service agencies, 166

Hunter, M., 194

I

Individual differences, 117, 120

Individuals with disabilities, 155

Instruction, 191

   computer-assisted, 201

   cooperative learning, 199

   group, 192

   individual, 192

   individualized, 198

   lecture, 192

   mastery learning, 200

   planning skills, 193

   processes, 86

   research, 193

   types, 192

Instructional

   model, 194

   tools, 199

Inventory control, 322-323

J

Job interviews, 243

Juvenile court, 167

   child abuse, 167

   status offenders, 167

L

Lancto, Robert M., 364-365

Law enforcement agencies, 167

Leadership, four perspectives, 6
  theories, 7-11
Learning
  centers scheduling, 230
  interests, 119
  mastery, 193
  restructuring, 191
  styles, 118
Legal bases for schools, 33-35
Lesson implementation, 194
Lewin, Kurt, 103
Lezotte, Larry W., 5
Loose coupling, 25
Likert, Rensis, 7-8

M

Maier Model, 354-356
Management
  loosely coupled, 84
  tightly coupled, 84
Managers
  characteristics of effective, 6
  distinguished from leadership, 5, 7-11
  site-based, 11
Maslow, Abraham, 121
Mastery learning, 201
Math skills outline, 174
Matrix management, 206
Maximal feasible decision, 346, 357
Mencken, H.L., 348

Mentoring, 271
Michigan Leadership Studies, 7-8
Middle school schedule, 234
Mitchell, Douglas, 5
Motivation
  student, 195
  theory, 121
Multi-unit school staffing, 207

N

National Association of Secondary
School Principals, 6
Needs assessment, 89, 92, 99-101
Neighborhood
  influence systems, 71-72
  seminars, 338
Nip it in the bud, 138
Nominal group technique, 353
Norris, Cynthia, 12
Nurses, 169

O

Objectives, 83
Ohio State Leadership Studies, 7
Open space, 312-313
Organizational
  climate, 205

Organizational, cont.
    development, 273
    iceberg, 23
Organizations
    culture of, 26-27, 135-136, 140-141
    individuals in, 22, 25

P

Paraprofessionals
    recruitment, 218
    selection, 218
    training, 218
Parent-teacher conferences, 339
Parent Teacher Organizations, 333-334
Path-Goal Theory, 10-11
Partnerships, 340-341
Peterfreund, Stanley, 5
Philosophy, 84
Police, 167
Political acumen, 12
Pressure groups
    defined, 73-74
    negotiating with, 74-75
    review boards, 77
Principal's role, 85
Professional staff interest/needs
        questionnaire, 256
Program improvement objectives, 95
Program Planning Budget System (PPBS),
    294-300

Project planning document, 105-107
Public Health Departments, 168
Public Law 94-142, 37-39
Public relations
    one-way, 328-332
    two-way, 333-340
Public welfare agencies, 166
Publications, student, 44-45
Purkey, W.W., 135

R

Rational decision-making model, 349
Reeves, Jennifer (and Reitzug), 5
Reitzug, Ulrich C. (and Reeves), 5
Restructuring
    learning, 191
    staff, 205
    time, 223
Retention of students, 126
Rules and regulations, 43-44

S

Scheduling, 86
    block, 226
    complexity, 224
    decisions, 225
    efficiency, 224

elementary schools, 227

flexibility, 224

four-teacher team, 234

learning centers, 230

middle schools, 234

parallel, 230

rotating, 226

sample, 227

simplicity, 224

skill groups, 228

staff, 223

students, 223

team planning time, 230

techniques, 225

School Excellence Inventory, 92

School, site, care of, 316-317

Search and seizure, 47-48

Self-esteem, 121

Sergiovanni, Thomas J., 26

Site-based management, 11, 281

   curriculum development, 171

   faculty council, 206

   staffing, 208

Situational models of supervision, 260

Social systems theory, 19-23

Space utilization, 313

Special Education, 155

   due process, 156

   Individual Education Program, 158

   multidisciplinary team, 156

   parent rights, 161

   parents, 162

placement recommendations, 159

prereferral actions, 157

principal's role, 158

regular classroom teachers, 164

related services, 156

screening, 156

student discipline, 161

support team, 157

Staff

   empowerment, 207

   matrix management, 206

   needs assessment, 275

   needs, interests, skills, 255

   organization, 86

   positive reinforcement, 276

   team, 207

   termination, 245

   utilization, 205

Staff development

   needs survey, 271

   program, 254

Staff dismissal

   equal rights, 247

   evidence, 246

   procedures, 248

Staff evaluation

   annual evaluation conference, 269

   appraisal calendar, 268

   appraisal schedules, 264

   classroom observation, 263

   cycle, 259

   individual development plans, 260

Staff evaluation, cont.

   personnel recommendation form, 270

   postobservation conference, 264

   preobservation conference, 262

   student evaluation form, 265

Staff selection

   interviews, 243

   reference checks, 243

   screening, 242

Staff termination, voluntary, 247

Staffing

   Americans with Disabilities, 242

   EEOC regulations, 241

   grade level teams, 211

   job descriptions, 238

   job interviews, 243

   learning communities, 214

   multi-unit school, 207, 212

   paraprofessionals, 211, 217

   patterns, 208

   recruitment, 237

   resource teachers, 212

   selection, 242

   self-contained classrooms, 209

   teacher specialists, 209

   team

     integration, 213

     models, 213

     organization, 212

     planning, 214

     teaching, 209

Student achievement, 118

Student

   ability, 118

   feedback, 196

   grouping, 86

   growth, 120

   maturity, 120

   motivation, 196

   placement, 117

   ranking, 126

   retention, 126

Surveys (questionnaires and opinionnaires), 339

Suspensions and expulsions, 56-57

T

Taylor, Calvin, 120

Teacher appraisal, 258

Teacher dismissal, 246

   due process, 246

Teacher's probationary, 245

Teacher's tenure, 245

Team meetings

   agendas, 216

   design, 215

   evaluation, 215

   goal setting, 215

   scheduling, 215

Team planning, 214

   consensus, 88

   staffing, 207

   teaching, 207

Test item bank, 178

Tightly coupled management, 84

Time on task, 198

Title IX, 36-37

Total Quality Management (TQM), 12-14, 84,
      146-148, 252
   curriculum development, 187
   staffing, 208

Truancy, 167

Trump, J. Lloyd, 4

V

Vision, 11-12

Volunteers, 219

Vroom-Jago Model, 357-360

Vroom-Yetton Model, 356-357

W

Weick, Karl E., 25

Welfare agencies, student records, 168

Work groups
   characteristics of, 25-26
   informal, 23-24
   maturity, 9-10